Modern Military Weapons

Modern Military Weapons

Editors: Chris Bishop and David Donald

Viscount Books

This edition published by Viscount Books 1986

Prepared for them by Temple Press
an imprint of The Hamlyn Publishing Group Limited
Bridge House, 69 London Road, Twickenham,
Middlesex, England, TW1 3SB

Produced by Aerospace Publishing Ltd
179 Dalling Road, Hammersmith, London W6 0ES

Copyright © Aerospace Publishing Ltd 1986

ISBN 0 600 55108 3

Printed in Italy by Poligrafici Calderara S.p.A. Bologna

Picture acknowledgements

The publishers would like to thank the following people and organisations for their help in supplying
photographs for this book.

Cover: US Navy/US Army/Mod. **Page 6:** US Navy. **8:** US Air Force/US Air Force. **10:** US Air Force/US Army/US Air Force. **11:** US Department of Defense (four)/US Air Force/ECP Armées. **12:** General Dynamics. **13:** US Department of Defense/US Navy/General Dynamics/US Navy. **14:** US Air Force/US Air Force. **15:** US Air Force/Dassault-Breguet/US Department of Defense. **16:** US Air Force/US Air Force/US Air Force. **17:** National Atomic Museum, Albuquerque/US Air Force. **18:** US Army/US Air Force. **19:** Royal Ordnance/US Department of Defense/US Department of Defense. **20:** US Air Force. **21:** US Department of Defense/US Department of Defense/US Air Force. **22:** MoD. **24:** US Air Force/US Department of Defense/US Navy. **25:** US Air Force. **26:** Swedish Air Force/US Air Force/US Air Force. **27:** Swedish Air Force/Dassault-Breguet. **28:** Dassault-Breguet/Lindsay Peacock/Dassault-Breguet. **29:** Lindsay Peacock. **30:** Saab/McDonnell Douglas/Norwegian Air Force/Saab/US Air Force. **31:** US Air Force. **32:** Bob Munro/British Aerospace/US Department of Defense/US Air Force. **33:** US Air Force/US Department of Defense/Associated Press/No. 92 Squadron RAF. **34:** MoD/FMA/Vaclav Jukl/US Air Force. **35:** Cessna/US Air Force/US Air Force. **36:** US Air Force/Saab/Dassault-Breguet. **37:** Peter Foster/McDonnell Douglas. **38:** British Aerospace/US Air Force. **39:** British Aerospace/Flight Lieutenant Steve Wilson/British Aerospace. **40:** Aérospatiale/Herman Potgieter/British Aerospace. **41:** Austin J. Brown/British Aerospace. **42:** Peter Foster. **43:** MoD/Peter Foster. **44:** US Air Force/Bob Munro. **45:** US Air Force. **46:** Peter Foster/US Navy/US Air Force/Lockheed/Jon Lake/Peter Foster. **47:** US Department of Defense. **48:** Westland/US Navy/US Navy. **49:** British Aerospace/Grumman. **50:** US Air Force/Boeing/Bob Munro/Lindsay Peacock. **51:** US Air Force/Lindsay Peacock/Lindsay Peacock/Boeing/Boeing/US Navy. **52:** US Navy/Stan Morse/MoD/Bob Munro. **53:** US Navy/Lockheed/Bob Munro. **54:** US Navy/Malcolm English. **55:** US Navy. **56:** Fokker/EMBRAER/Dassault-Breguet/Shin Meiwa/Peter Foster/Dassault-Breguet. **57:** Boeing. **58:** McDonnell Douglas/Lockheed/Robert L. Lawson. **59:** British Aerospace. **60:** MoD/Dassault-Breguet/Robet L. Lawson/US Navy. **61:** McDonnell Douglas. **62:** Dassault-Breguet/US Navy/McDonnell Douglas/Robert L. Lawson. **63:** US Navy/Grumman (three)/David Donald. **64:** Agusta/US Navy/Westland/Westland/US Navy. **65:** Sikorsky/US Navy/Aérospatiale/Peter Foster. **66:** Sikorsky. **67:** US Navy/MoD/MoD. **68:** Gamma/Hughes/US Air Force. **69:** Hughes/Bell. **70:** US Air Force/Bell/Westland. **71:** Aérospatiale/Hughes. **72:** Westland/Gamma/Bell. **73:** Bell/MBB. **74:** US Air Force/US Air Force/Aérospatiale. **75:** Herman Potgieter. **76:** Lindsay Peacock. **77:** Lieutenant K.P. White. **78:** US Department of Defense/US Air Force/Sikorsky. **79:** Westland/US Navy/Peter Foster/US Air Force/Westland. **80:** US Air Force/US Air Force/Malcolm English/Robbie Shaw. **81:** US Air Force. **82:** Lockheed/Herman Potgieter/Aeritalia/US Air Force. **83:** Austin J. Brown. **84:** MoD/US Air Force. **85:** US Air Force/Gamma. **86:** GAF/Peter Foster/Austin J. Brown/IAI. **87:** Gates/Shorts/Herman Potgieter. **88:** Lockheed/Malcolm English/Lockheed/US Air Force. **89:** Lockheed/US Navy/McDonnell Douglas. **90:** Boeing/Beech/David Donald/MoD/Bob Archer. **92:** Fairchild/McDonnell Douglas/US Navy. **93:** McDonnell Douglas/David Donald/MoD. **94:** McDonnell Douglas/US Air Force/Fairchild/Herman Potgieter. **95:** Panavia/US Air Force/British Aerospace/MoD. **96:** US Air Force/US Navy. **97:** US Navy/US Navy (four). **98:** Aérospatiale/Bell/Aérospatiale. **99:** Grumman/US Air Force/Boeing/Boeing/British Aerospace/Texas Instruments. **100:** US Navy. **102:** US Navy (three)/British Aerospace. **103:** US Navy. **104:** US Navy (four). **105:** US Navy. **106:** US Department of Defense. **108:** US Navy (three). **109:** US Navy/US Navy. **110:** Royal Navy/US Department of Defense/US Navy. **112:** Lieutenant K.P. White/US Navy/US Navy. **113:** US Navy/Australian Defence Department/US Department of Defense. **114:** HDW/HDW. **116:** US Navy/Royal Navy/US Navy. **117:** US Navy. **118:** US Navy/US Navy. **119:** Lieutenant K.P. White. **120:** Brazilian Navy/ECP Armées/US Navy/US Navy/Royal Air Force. **121:** **US Navy.** **122:** Royal Navy/US Navy. **123:** US Navy. **24:** US Navy (four). **125:** US Navy (four). **126:** US Navy/Italian Navy. **127:** ECP Armées. **128:** US Navy/Royal Navy/US Navy/ECP Armées. **129:** Royal Navy. **130:** Italian Navy/US Navy/US Navy. **131:** US Navy/Royal Air Force/Royal Navy. **132:** ECP Armées. **133:** Press Association/US Navy/Royal Navy/Royal Navy. **134:** Royal Navy/Royal Navy. **136:** Royal Netherlands Navy/US Navy. **137:** US Navy. **138:** ECP Armées/MARS, Lincs/Italian Navy/Brazilian Navy. **139:** TASS. **140:** Associated Press/MARS, Lincs. **142:** US Department of Defense/Saab-Bofors. **143:** British Hovercraft Corporation/Vosper Thornycroft/Italian Navy/US Navy. **144:** Lieutenant K.P. White/COI/COI. **145:** Lieutenant K.P. White. **146:** US Navy. **147:** US Navy/US Navy. **148:** US Navy (four). **149:** US Navy. **150:** Royal Netherlands Navy. **151:** US Navy. **152:** MARS, Lincs (three)/Royal Navy. **153:** US Navy. **154:** US Navy (three). **156:** COI/Royal Navy/Royal Navy/US Navy. **157:** US Navy/COI/COI/US Navy/US Navy. **158:** MBB/IAI/Novosti/Aérospatiale. **159:** Saab-Bofors/McDonnell Douglas/Kongsberg. **160:** MARS, Lincs/ECP Armées. **161:** US Navy/US Navy. **162:** US Navy/Royal Navy. **163:** US Navy/Royal Navy/US Navy (three)/Ed Rasen. **164:** US Navy/US Navy/Hollandse-Signaal/General Dynamics/US Navy. **165:** US Navy. **166:** Marconi/US Navy/Italian Navy. **167:** US Navy/Boeing/US Department of Defense/Marconi. **168:** US Army. **170:** Militar Teknic/Pakistan Army/US Department of Defense. **171:** Finnish Army/Xian-Hua Press Agency. **172:** US Army/US Army. **174:** MARS, Lincs/Royal Norwegian Army. **175:** ECP Armées/Japan Self Defence Force/GIAT/ENGESA. **177:** Royal Ordnance/Royal Norwegian Army/Royal Ordnance/Swedish Army/Vickers. **178:** Eshel Dramit/IDI/General Dynamics. **181:** MoD/MoD. **182:** General Motors Canada/Panhard. **183:** ENGESA/General Motors Canada/ENGESA. **184:** Arrowpointe Corp/Royal Ordnance. **185:** Royal Ordnance/US Army. **186:** SIBMAS/ACMAT/US Army. **187:** Herman Potgieter. **189:** Royal Ordnance/R.F./Chrysler Corp. **190:** Royal Ordnance/Dramit. **191:** Finnish Army/R.F./R.F. **192:** Portuguese Army/US Army. **193:** US Department of Defense. **194:** GIAT/US Navy/US Army/R.F. **195:** MoD/R.F./Militar Technik/US Army. **196:** US Marine Corps/Iraqi Army/Pegaso. **198:** Imperial War Museum/Associated Press/US Army. **199:** US Army. **200:** Armscor/US Army. **201:** Bofors/R.F./COI/Iraqi Army. **202:** Iraqi Army/ENGESA. **204:** Xiang-Hua Press Agency/Armscor/Xiang-Hua Press Agency (three)/R.F. **205:** Vought (three). **206:** US Army/British Aerospace/US Navy. **207:** US Army. **208:** US Army/R.F./US Army. **209:** Avco/Euromissile. **210:** Oerlikon. **211:** R.F./Bofors. **212:** British Aerospace/R.F./US Army/Panhard. **213:** R.F./Rheinmetall. **214:** British Aerospce/US Department of Defense. **215:** COI/US Army/US Air Force/US Air Force. **216:** US Army. **217:** Oerlikon. **218:** Oerlikon/IDI. **210:** Rheinmetall/Bofors/US Army/Breda. **220:** Associated Press/US Army/Contraves. **221:** IDI/US Air Force (three). **222:** Fabrique Nationale. **225:** Associated Press. **226:** Press Association/Herman Potgieter/Carl Gustav/Beretta. **230:** Associated Press/US Army/MARS, Lincs. **231:** MoD/US Army. **232:** Duncan Mil. **233:** Pakistan Army. **234:** MoD/Federal Directorate of Supply and Procurment, Beograd, Yugoslavia. **236:** Iraqi Army/Bell. **237:** Herman Potgieter/Royal Ordnance/Australian War Memorial. **238:** Ed Rasen/US Army. **239:** US Army. **240:** US Army/Belgian Army/MoD. **241:** Associated Press/US Army. **242:** Ed Rasen/US Army. **243:** Associated Press/US Army/US Army. **244:** US Army. **245:** ECP Armées/Finnish Army/R.F. **246:** T.J./US Army/Brandt. **247:** US Army. **248:** Royal Ordnance/R.F. **249:** Royal Ordnance/Avco. **250:** Bofors/Cincinnati Electronics. **251:** Cincinnati Electronics.

CONTENTS

Strategic Power

Air Power

Sea Power

Land Power

Index

Glossary

Strategic Power

The atom bomb explosions over Hiroshima and Nagasaki in August 1945
heralded a new and more frightening age. Since that time, man's destructive ingenuity has reached new
heights, and now there are weapons capable of obliterating cities across
intercontinental distances with unprecedented accuracy. The fact remains, however, that the weapons
have not been used, and in spite of periods of great tension general war
between East and West has not broken out.

Contents

Intercontinental Ballistic Missiles

In understanding the technology of nuclear weapon systems, it is worth from the beginning distinguishing between the weapon system itself and the means by which it reaches its target, which is the 'delivery system'. For the past two decades the most important strategic nuclear delivery system in the world, and that on which depends the whole doctrine of deterrence, has been the ballistic missile in its various forms, intermediate- and long-range, land- and sea-based. This analysis is concerned with land-based ballistic missiles and in particular those configured to carry multiple nuclear warheads over very long ranges, the so-called intercontinental ballistic missiles (ICBMs).

Germany's A-4 (V-2 'revenge weapon') developed during World War II was a ballistic missile. In its day it certainly could be considered as a strategic delivery system, but it could carry no more than 975 kg (2,150 lb) of high explosive and bombard, at comparatively close range, only area targets such as the sprawling city of London or the port of Antwerp with woeful inaccuracy. Over 1,000 V-2s fell in London, but killed less than one individual per missile. Two atom bombs dropped by aircraft on Japan killed over a quarter of a million people.

But what made the V-2 so terrifying and potentially so dangerous was the very fact that it was a ballistic missile. Once launched it was quite unstoppable and travelling at several times the speed of sound it arrived with terrifying suddenness. A ballistic missile uses chemical energy in its opening 'boost' phase to propel it at great velocity into a trajectory which gravity thereafter makes predictable. It is very much like a shell being fired from a gun, but a ballistic missile can fly over very much longer ranges because it carries its chemical propellant with it in the boost phase rather than burning it in a controlled explosion inside the gun barrel. A ballistic missile, unlike a cruise system, does not use wings to fly through the atmosphere, nor does its motor powerplant need to 'breathe' air in flight, because fuel and oxidant is carried with it in a closed system.

The parallel technological development in the 1950s and 1960s of single, very large rockets with multiple stages capable of escaping the earth's gravity and the

Below: Minuteman ICBM silos are very strongly built to withstand nuclear attack, but are wide enough to allow the rocket exhaust to escape safely.

Right: An MGM-118 Peacekeeper is test launched at Vandenberg AFB in California. The missile has 10 re-entry vehicles, each assigned its own target.

SS-18
Length: 35 m
Diameter: 3 m
Launch weight: 225000 kg
Range: 10000 km or 16000 km (depending on warhead)
Warhead type: 1×20 megaton or 27 megaton, or 8×900 kiloton or 10×500 kiloton MIRV
CEP: 260/425 m depending on warhead

Below: The SS-18 has caused deep concern in the West, since this terrifying missile is the largest and most powerful ballistic system ever to be deployed.

ICBMs capable of carrying nuclear weapons thousands of miles over oceans and continents into the heartland of any enemy was intimately related. An ICBM is in fact a small space rocket but instead of being designed to place its payload in orbit, it carries it on a trajectory which departs from the atmosphere only briefly, so that the payload will 're-enter' close to the target area.

In the first generation of ICBMs that payload was a single, large and comparatively inaccurate nuclear warhead, contained in a casing capable of standing the heat of re-entry called simply a re-entry vehicle (RV). In the late 1960s, with the development of powerful but lightweight computers, it became possible to refine the 'front end' of an ICBM from a single simple warhead into a miniature spacecraft in its own right, with thruster motors to make course corrections and on-board guidance to tell them to do so. This is the Post Boost Vehicle (PBV) or 'bus' on a MIRVed ICBM (MIRV stands for Multiple Independently-targetable Re-entry

Vehicles) which can be configured to carry a number of individual RVs and dispense them in flight to fall in the required pattern or 'footprint'. The PBV has a very accurate inertial guidance system which can be further refined to take a starshot of the heavens to update its position (stellar-inertial guidance). Given such accuracy and the ability of the PBV to make powered adjustments to the flightpath, targets can be reached with great precision over very long ranges. The accuracy of a ballistic missile is expressed as the Circular Error Probable (CEP), the radius of a circle within which half the missiles aimed at it will land. The smaller the radius, the more accurate the missile.

Land-based MIRVed ICBMs are the most powerful nuclear weapon delivery systems in the world today, and also the most contentious. Because they are land-based, fired from fixed-site silos, they can be considered tempting targets for a pre-emptive first strike. Again because they are land based, in the past they

have been more accurate than submarine-based missiles, and thus are the ideal instruments for such a first strike. They are said to have greater 'counterforce' potential, in that they are so accurate that they can be used for pinpoint attacks on rival weapon systems thousands of miles away in their silos rather than on sprawling cities, which is all the first generation of submarine-based missiles could be guaranteed to bring under threat. And because ICBMs are so big and powerful they can each carry many of the warheads with which to do it: in the jargon they have a large 'throw-weight'.

Hence land-based ICBMs are held to be particularly destabilizing and are amongst the most contentious issues in arms control negotiations. To make things more difficult, the USSR with its large land mass has concentrated on deploying large numbers of massively powerful ICBMs in preference to submarine-based SLBMs.

Current strategic ballistic missiles

SS-17
Length: 24 m
Diameter: 2.5 m
Weight: 65 tonnes
Range: (mods 1 & 3) 10000 km; (mod 2) 11000 km
Warhead: (mod 1) 4×750 kiloton MIRVs; (mod 2) 1×6 megaton RV
CEP: 350/440 m

First deployed in 1975, SS-17 is an accurate missile which replaces some older SS-11 weapons.

SS-19
Length: 22.5 m
Diameter: 2.75 m
Weight: 78000 kg
Range: (mod 1) 9600 km; (mod 3) 10000 km
Warhead: 6×550 kiloton MIRVs or 1×10 megaton RV (mod 2 only)
CEP: 260/390 m

The SS-19 is one of the most accurate of Soviet ICBMs and provides powerful counterforce capability to the Strategic Rocket Forces.

SS-20
Length: 16 m
Diameter: 1.7 m
Weight: 25000 kg
Range: (mods 1 & 2) 5000 km; (mod 3) 7000 km
Warheads: (mod 1) 1×650 kiloton RV; (mod 2) 3×150 kiloton RVs; (mod 3) 1×50 kiloton RV
CEP: 425 m

SS-20 is one of the smallest of Soviet missiles with any strategic capacity, but its mobility in deployment makes it a highly significant system.

CSS-4
Length: 32.5 m
Diameter: 3.35 m
Weight: 200000 kg
Range: 10000 km or 13000 km
Warhead: 4 or 5 megaton
CEP: 930 m

Under the Chinese designation DF-5 or DF-6, the CSS-4 was first tested in 1980. It has also formed the basis for China's satellite launch programme.

CSS-3 (DF-4)
Length: 26.8 m
Diameter: 2.46 m
Weight: 50000 kg
Range: 6960 km
Warhead: 1×3 megaton or 3/4×200 kiloton MRV or MIRVs
CEP: 930 m

The DF-4 missile was the first operational Chinese ICBM, and was deployed in the mid 1970s.

MGM-118 Peacekeeper
Length: 21.6 m
Diameter: 2.3 m
Weight: 88500 kg
Range: 14000 km
Warhead: 10×335 kiloton MIRVs
CEP: 60/90 m
Solid propellant

Peacekeeper promises levels of accuracy undreamed-of in the previous generation of ICBMs.

LGM-30 Minuteman III
Length: 18.2 m
Diameter: 1.83 m
Weight: 31750 kg (model F) or 34500 kg (model G)
Range: 12500 km (F) or 14000 km (G)
Warhead: 1×1.2 megaton SRV(F) or 3×165 or 335 kiloton MIRVs (G)
CEP: 2200 m
Solid propellant

Backbone of the US land-based deterrent for two decades, Minuteman has been subject to continuous improvement programmes.

SSBS S-3
Length: 13.8 m
Diameter: 1.5 m
Weight: 25800 kg
Range: 3150 km
Warhead: 1×1.2 megaton SRV
CEP: 830 m
Solid propellant

France has deployed 18 SSBS S-3 IRBMs in hardened silos on the Plateau d'Albion, east of Avignon in Haute Provence.

Intercontinental Ballistic Missiles

It was the build up of the Soviet ICBM force in the 1970s and the deployment of such large and apparently accurate weapons as the 10-warhead SS-18 Mod 4 that chipped away at the original deterrent idea of Mutual Assured Destruction (MAD) and eventually buried it. The existence of a very powerful and accurate Soviet land-based missile force with multiple warheads, it was argued in the USA, opened a 'window of vulnerability' which gravely imperilled the United States. A proportion of these ICBMs could be used to eliminate the land-based leg of the US strategic triad, the Minuteman ICBMs, by attacking with MIRVs. The hydra-headed ICBMs could target more silos with multiple warheads than missiles actually launched, leaving a proportion in reserve to threaten an equally devastating second strike. The US supreme commander would only have a single option: that of attacking Soviet cities with the surviving submarine-based missiles and thus inviting the destruction of US cities by the remainder of the enemy force in return. That option was closed and thus the US would 'lose' a nuclear war with the destruction of the strategic 'warfighting' element, the counterforce-capable ICBMs.

That was why the development of the Missile Experimental (MX, now renamed Peacekeeper) was for so long such a politically important issue in the USA. While it could carry 10 MIRVs in comparison with the Minuteman's three, it was the missile's mode of basing which was so important: the MX was originally designed to be land mobile with an advanced inertial guidance system that kept its own launch position updated in its computer memory as it was moved around (on railway cars, by transport aircraft or through vast underground tunnels) to be out of the enemy's counterforce reach. After many different and bizarre basing modes had been considered, it was eventually decided to deploy 100 Peacekeepers in modified Minuteman fixed-site silos.

While the Peacekeeper ended as just another although very powerful ICBM, its AIRS (Advanced Inertial Reference Sphere) inertial guidance system is to be used in a project called Midgetman to build a small single-warhead ICBM. Midgetman is to be land mobile, shuttling around on armoured launchers inside vast military reservations in the US south west, but because it will be so hard to hit and have only a single warhead, it will be a far less tempting target for a first strike, and thus add to rather than detract from strategic stability.

Meanwhile the Soviets have continued development of a formidable new generation of ICBMs including the 10000-km (6,215-mile) range MIRVed SS-19 first de-

Left: The first completely assembled Peacekeeper ICBM photographed on static test in 1982. Formerly known as MX, the Peacekeeper had already been planned for 12 years. It weighs over twice as much as Minuteman III.

Above: The cumbersome Pershing I missile was introduced to the US Army units in Europe in 1964, but its tracked vehicles were unsatisfactory. Pershing Ia, seen here, was mounted on a wheeled chassis.

ployed in 1974, and the still experimental SS-X-24 and SS-X-25. The big three-stage solid-propellant SS-X-24, thought to be a replacement for the SS-18, is the broad equivalent to the US Peacekeeper with 10 MIRVs and range up to 16000 km (9,940 miles). US intelligence predicts initial deployment in fixed-site silos, followed by rail-mobile basing; another mobile model carried on a tracked cross-country vehicle is said to be under development. The smaller single-warhead SS-X-25 has apparently been developed to be road mobile from its original deployment, and is possibly a

development of the intermediate range SS-20, capable of operating from roughly prepared bases.

Intermediate-range ballistic missiles

Two shorter-range ballistic missiles deployed in the late 1970s and early 1980s certainly did not add to strategic stability and fuelled fears of a nuclear war being fought in Europe. These were the Soviet SS-20, which first became operational in 1977, and the US Army's Pershing II, deployed from 1983 onwards along with the USAF's ground-launched cruise mis-

Missile deployment

Right: How the world's nuclear missiles are deployed and targeted. As China's nuclear power grows, so an increasing number of Soviet missiles have been installed in the east.

Below: A Minuteman III is launched from Vandenberg towards the US missile range at Kwajalein in the central Pacific. The higher accuracy of American missiles means that warheads can be of lower yield than those of the Soviets.

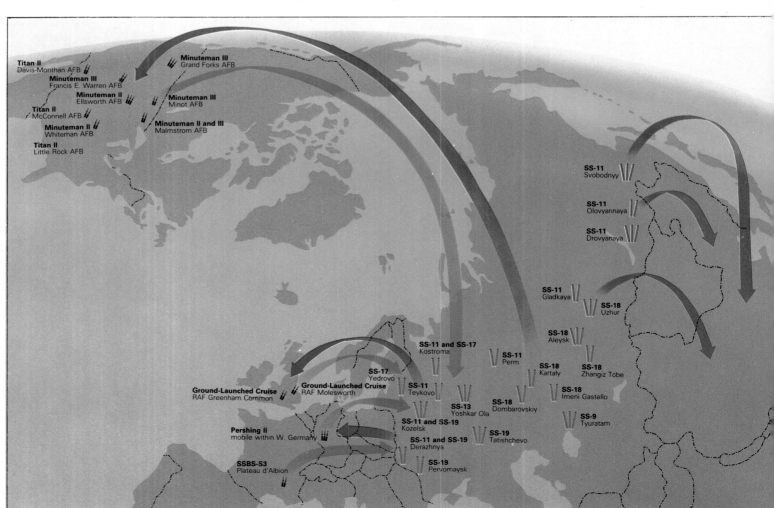

sile, which is examined in detail elsewhere.

The SS-20 is a triple-warhead, land-mobile missile with a range that allows it to cover the whole of Western Europe from bases in the western USSR. US sources quote the system as carrying three independently-targetable RVs each with a yield of 150 kilotons. They attribute a range of 5000 km (3,105 miles), while the Soviets admit to 4000 km (2,485 miles). Inertial guidance is employed, and a CEP figure of 400 m (437 yards) is generally accepted. As a counterweight to the SS-20 deployment, after a long period of political debate in 1979 the western NATO alliance began the process known as Theatre Nuclear Force (TNF) modernization which brought the Pershing IIs and GLCMs to Europe.

At the end of 1983 there were 108 Pershing IA missiles deployed in West Germany. The 1960s-vintage Pershing IA, which the Pershing II is set to replace on a one-for-one basis, is the only US Army nuclear system aimed at present targets deep in Warsaw Pact territory, and forms part of the Supreme Allied Commander Europe's QRA (Quick Reaction Alert) forces kept at permanent readiness according to a three-stage 'Force Generation' level.

The Pershing IA (which superseded the Pershing I in the early 1970s, the upgrades being confined to the mobility of the fire-support units and the ability to operate from unsurveyed firing positions) has a range of up to 740 km (460 miles) and uses an inertial guidance system to achieve accuracies of 400-m (437-yard) CEP at maximum range. The warhead is the W50 with selectable yields of 60, 200 and 400 kilotons.

The Pershing II in fact has a warhead (the W85 based on a new-generation free-fall bomb) with a much smaller yield than the weapon which it is replacing, reportedly selectable from 1- to 20-kiloton yield. It has, however, a far longer reach, variously quoted as between 1300 and 1800 km (810 and 1,120 miles), flies extremely fast (Mach 8 in the boost phase) and is far more accurate than the system it replaces. The Pershing II is a ballistic missile, but has a radar guidance system in its nose. The guidance system developed by Goodyear Aerospace and Norden Systems is called Radar Area Guidance (RADAG). In the terminal descent phase, the radar starts scanning (at 120 rpm) an initial reference area, and then compares the return with a pre-stored reference map. Guidance commands are generated and transmitted as course corrections to the re-entry vehicle's control vanes.

The result is a reduction of CEP to under 50 m (55 yards) over ranges which, from launch in West Germany, bring targets deep within the western USSR under the Pershing's thrall. This, allied to the weapons' very short flight time, is why the Pershings in particular were seen by the Soviets as especially menacing and such stumbling blocks in the Geneva intermediate-range nuclear weapons talks which collapsed at the end of 1983.

The Pershing II is particularly effective against hardened point and underground targets because of its high accuracy and the unique earth penetrator warhead capability. Its accuracy and range, in spite of the smaller-yield warhead, considerably raised the temperature of arms control diplomacy. The fact that it was seen by NATO as a counterdeployment to the Soviet SS-20 did little to soothe Europe's nuclear jitters during the approach to and aftermath of the initial deployment.

Left: The joker in the nuclear pack – the French Force de Frappe consists of land-based SSBS S-3 IRBMs as well as submarine-launched ICBMs.

Right: Multiple Re-Entry Vehicles have greatly increased the destructive power of ICBMs and created horrendous difficulties for would-be negotiators of arms limitation treaties. Re-entry vehicles from an MGM-118 Peacekeeper are seen here at Kwajalein Island at the successful conclusion of a test launch.

Above: The SS-X-15 mobile missile on parade. Missile silos are vulnerable to a first strike, making mobility an important factor.

Below: An SS-9 is loaded into its silo. These sites were rebuilt for extra survivability in the 1970s and were then fitted with SS-18 ICBMs.

Above: The SS-X-14 mobile IRBM was mounted in a container called the 'Iron Maiden' on a modified IS-III tank chassis.

Below: SS-8 'Sasin' was a second-generation ICBM introduced in 1963, and carried a two-megaton warhead to a maximum range of 11000 km.

Cruise Missiles

In contrast with a ballistic missile, which uses all its energy in its boost phase to set it on the right course and trajectory, a cruise missile flies through the atmosphere using wings for lift and under continuous power, drawing oxygen from the air to mix with its own fuel. In essence it is an unmanned aircraft with a computer for a pilot.

The idea of the cruise missile goes back a long way. The German navy experimented with unmanned but explosive-packed aircraft to be carried beneath Zeppelins and launched against London during World War I. Far more menacingly, in World War II the Germans developed the Fi 103 (V-1) flying bomb, a small winged aircraft with an autopilot and a simple pulse-jet motor which cut out when at a predetermined range, the missile then plunging earthwards with its 850-kg (1,870-lb) high explosive warhead. The V-1 was stoppable however, for it could be shot down by anti-aircraft gunfire or intercepted by high-performance piston-engined aircraft. In contrast, the V-2 ballistic rocket was terrifyingly unstoppable.

That is why the cruise missile largely fell from favour in the post-war years. The US Air Force developed the ground-launched intercontinental-range Snark and the intermediate-range Mace and Matador cruise missiles which were based in Europe during the late 1950s, but these were clumsy weapons, their bases were vulnerable and they were in any event liable to interception in flight by the increasingly sophisticated Soviet air defences. The same strictures applied to the US Navy's warship-launched Regulus I and submarine-launched Regulus II strategic cruise missiles, quietly abandoned once the Polaris-submarine launched ballistic missile became operational. The Boeing B-52s of USAF Strategic Air Command operated air-launched Hound Dog cruise missiles, each with a 1-megaton warhead, in the period 1961-76.

The USSR kept cruise missiles under development as nuclear delivery systems from the mid-1950s onwards, but only for launch by warship or aircraft at short ranges, while concentrating on ballistic missiles as strategic delivery systems. Nevertheless the Soviets are now reported to be developing a long-range advanced cruise missile similar to the US Tomahawk examined in detail below.

In the early 1970s a range of new technologies being developed in the USA seemed to revive the potential of the cruise missile as a long-range strategic delivery system. These factors were much smaller (and thus lighter) nuclear warheads, modern guidance technology combined with satellite mapping, and small fuel-efficient turbofan engines which sipped fuel and thus made possible very long ranges. Moreover, cruise missiles were outside the scope of the SALT negotiations which began in 1972. Here was an elegant new system typifying American technological superiority, and the more the Soviets tried to include cruise systems in SALT 2, the more such weapons' reputation as wonder weapons grew.

Both the USAF and US Navy sponsored development programmes in the 1970s, and the result is a plethora of systems in all sorts of permutations, but nonetheless all developments of either Boeing's AGM-86 Air-Launched Cruise Missile (ALCM) developed for the air force or General Dynamics' BGM-109 Tomahawk, developed originally for the US Navy but also adopted by the USAF as its Ground-Launched Cruise Missile (GLCM). The operational ALCM is considered in more detail in the section on air-launched missiles.

The General Dynamics Tomahawk is one of the most significant weapons of the 1980s. Its ground-launched BGM-109G variant was adopted along with the Pershing II ballistic missile as part of the NATO Intermediate Nuclear Force (INF) modernization programme: 464 GLCMs are to be forward-deployed at six main operating bases in Europe. In addition to this, the Tomahawk provides the airframe for a range of sea-launched cruise missiles (SLCMs) which are set to increase by a huge degree the strike power aboard American surface warships and attack submarines, and to give quite humble vessels the capability of making long-range strategic attacks. The interlocking development programmes are summarized below.

Cruise missiles are relatively small, cheap and flexible. In their palletized launch tubes they can be fired from a wide range of launch platforms. In the GLCM, for example, the missile rests in an aluminium canister with its wings, control fins and engine air inlet folded. On firing, a solid-propellant rocket booster punches the missile out, whereupon the fins deploy, the wings fold out and the engine inlet pops down. The turbofan

engine then starts up while after 13 seconds the booster motor burns out and is jettisoned. The Tomahawk flies slowly, in fact at about the speed of a jet airliner, far slower than the Pershing's Mach 8. But what it loses in speed it gains in accuracy, again showing the results of the targeting revolution (made possible by satellite mapping and onboard computer power) in being able to 'snipe' at critical point targets over long ranges delivering a nuclear weapon with devastating accuracy. US cruise missiles in their ground-, sea- and air-launched varieties use a guidance technique called TERCOM (TERrain COntour Matching). Like the Pershing's RADAG system, this uses a hybrid of inertial navigation and computer analysis of geographical information, but TERCOM sustains the process over far greater distances, taking multiple readings along the approach route to its target.

The system uses a down-looking radar altimeter to measure height above ground allied to an altimeter reading atmospheric pressure and thus height above an absolute datum such as sea level. The difference between these two readings provides a measure of the height of the ground surveyed below. The reading obtained is the average for 1500 m^2 (1,795 sq yards) of land. By taking repeated readings, the digital results can be compared by the guidance computer with a preset matrix of the approach route prepared from information obtained by satellite reconnaissance and stored inside the guidance computer. By comparing

Ground-launched cruise missiles are popped from their tubes by a short-burn rocket, coasting the missile while control surfaces unfurl and firing up the small turbojet cruise engine.

the measured track with all possible similar tracks in the matrix, any along-track or cross-track deviations can be detected and thus corrected.

The disadvantages of cruise missiles are the same as those which might affect the penetrating bomber which cruise technology goes some way to supersede. Both types are vulnerable to counter-air defences such as surface-to-air missiles and interceptor aircraft armed with look-down/shoot-down air-to-air missiles, and while in themselves comparatively 'cheap', cruise missiles need reconnaissance satellites to provide the appropriate guidance data. The USA is therefore working on a new generation of cruise missiles which will fly supersonically, employ new forms of guidance technique and have radar-baffling 'stealth' technology engineered into them.

US cruise missile programme summary
Sea-launched

TASM: Tactical anti-ship missile (BGM-109B/E Tomahawk, non-strategic)
TLAM-C: Conventional land-attack missile (BGM-109C Tomahawk, non-strategic)
TLAM-N: Nuclear land attack missile (BGM-109A

Above: A US DoD impression of a sub-launched SS-NX-21 being fired from a cruising submarine. According to the Pentagon, the missile is a rough equivalent to Tomahawk.

Left: A ship-launched BGM-109A Tomahawk is seen cruising over the California coast during early trials. Tomahawk is made in several versions, and is capable of conventional land attack and anti-ship missions in addition to the strategic nuclear attack role.

Tomahawk). This missile, combined with the VLS (Vertical Launch System), will arm US Navy attack submarines and warships of destroyer size and upwards giving them a strategic nuclear attack capability over a 2500-km (1,550-mile) range.

Air-launched
The Boeing-developed AGM-86B ALCM is a key component of the US strategic arms modernization programme keeping the B-52 force in the front line until the late 1990s. Current plans call for 170 B-52Gs and B-52Hs to be re-engineered with 20 ALCMs each while development of an advanced air-launched cruise missile with longer range is also under way.

Ground-launched
The BGM-109G Tomahawk is the missile operated by USAF Tactical Air Command forward-based in Europe with operational sites in England, Belgium, Italy, the Netherlands and West Germany. The warhead is the 150-kiloton W84, and can be carried over a range of 2500 km (1,550 miles). Operationally, the GLCM is deployed in 'flights' of 22 vehicles (two launch-control centres, four Transporter Erector Launchers, carrying a total of 16 missiles, and support vehicles) manned by 69 men. The flights are contained in secure main operating bases, emerging periodically to travel to remote dispersed launch sites.

Soviet strategic cruise missile development
Recent US reports have consistently pointed to the development of a Soviet equivalent to the Tomahawk cruise missile, also expected to appear in sea-launched (codenamed SS-NX-21), air-launched (AS-X-15) and ground-launched (SSC-X-4) variants. An air-breathing turbojet, a single nuclear warhead and a range of up to

3000 km (1,865 miles) have been confidently assigned by Western analysts, but the guidance system remains a matter for conjecture. A larger weapon up to 13 m (42.65 ft) long (codenamed SS-NX-25) is also reported to be under development, with a sea-launched model expected to begin testing in 'Yankee' class submarines by the late 1980s.

Above: A BGM-109G ground launched Tomahawk is seen in flight over the Mojave desert, at the relatively high level it would be at during the early stage of a mission. During the final phase the missile would be much nearer the ground.

Below: The rejuvenated battleships of the US Navy have been fitted to fire BGM-109 Tomahawks, giving the class a strategic capability, as well as facilitating long-range land attack and anti-ship missions.

Air-Launched Missiles

The original nuclear-delivery system was the manned bomber, the Boeing B-29 Superfortresses that dropped the free-fall 'Little Boy' and 'Fat Man' atomic bombs on Hiroshima and Nagasaki. The long-range bomber remained the most important instrument of strategic nuclear delivery until the late 1950s, when missile research opened up the potential of the ICBM and then the SLBM (Submarine-Launched Ballistic Missile), and at the same time made possible the high-altitude guided surface-to-air missile like the Soviet SA-2 which knocked Gary Powers' Lockheed U-2 spy-plane out of the sky above Sverdlovsk in 1960. After that it seemed that the days of the penetrating bomber cruising invulnerably at high altitude were over.

Meanwhile through the 1950s, USAF Strategic Air Command had built up an enormous fleet of turbojet powered Boeing B-47 and Boeing B-52 strategic bombers. The RAF similarly deployed the 'V-Force' of Vickers Valiant, Handley Page Victor and Avro Vulcan bombers, the French Force Aérienne Stratégique became operational with Dassault Mirage IVAs, and the Soviet Long-Range Aviation put small numbers of long-range bombers, the jet-powered Myasishchev M-4 'Bison' and turboprop-powered Tupolev Tu-95 'Bear', into service. While the development of ICBMs seemed to make irrelevant the development of a second generation of supersonic bombers such as the US Convair B-58 and North American XB-70, the Soviet Myasishchev M-50 'Bounder' and the British BAC TSR-2, remarkably, numerous representatives of that first generation of strategic subsonic jet bombers soldiered on (and continue to do so) in front-line service. This results from the capacity of their big airframes to soak up re-engineering and avionic retrofits, and from the development of new weapon systems (in particular air-launched strategic missiles), which put a modern combat capability in an old airframe. The most important recent example of this process is the reworking of the USAF's B-52 fleet to carry nuclear-armed Air-Launched Cruise Missiles (ALCMs).

It was realized at an early stage that in the era of the guided surface-to-air missile it was the weapon rather than the manned bomber that should ideally undertake the final penetration to a defended target. In terms of the strategy of deterrence the manned bomber became merely a mobile platform that, because it could be kept on airborne alert, was relatively invulnerable to a first strike but would make its attack with 'stand-off' weapons outside the range of air defences. The Douglas Skybolt, for example, was developed in the early 1960s as an 'air-launched ballistic missile', an otherwise unique configuration. It was planned that four 1600-km (1,000-mile) range Skybolts would be carried aloft by each available B-52, but that the missile rather than the aircraft would thereafter do the job of taking a thermonuclear weapon to its target like a silo-launched ICBM. The Skybolt was cancelled for 'technical

Air-launched cruise missiles have added yet another strand to the distinguished career of the USAF's old warhorse, the Boeing B-52. The 'G' model of this old design can carry 12 missiles on wing pylons.

reasons' on 11 December 1962, the same day that it completed a perfect test flight. The missile which B-52 crews did, however, carry operationally in 1961-76 was the North American AGM-28 Hound Dog, a turbojet-powered winged cruise missile with a preprogrammable inertial guidance system, a range of 1125 km (700 miles) and a speed as high as Mach 2.1, carrying a 1-megaton warhead.

The Victor and Vulcan bombers of the British V-Force were similarly equipped with the Avro Blue Steel 'stand-off' bomb from 1962 to 1975. Blue Steel was an inertially-guided, rocket-propelled winged missile launched at high altitude from a 160-km (100-mile) range. Once released the missile could fly any preprogrammed trajectory at speeds up to Mach 2, delivering a 1-megaton warhead.

The French Force Aérienne Stratégique originally armed its Mirage IVA strategic bombers with free-fall weapons, but in 1978 started development of a ramjet-powered stand-off missile called ASMP (Air-Sol Moyenne Portée) originally for tactical nuclear weapon delivery, but initial deployment in 1985 was on 18 upgraded Mirage IVs. The 100-kiloton yield ASMP has a reported range of 100 km (62 miles) and several flight profiles are possible, including flight at Mach 3 at high altitude. It is also expected to arm Dassault-Bre-

guet Mirage 2000Ns and carrier-based Dassault-Breguet Super Etendards.

Short-range attack missiles

An important rationale for the retention of manned bombers, however, was their very ability to cover targets (such as mobile systems) by direct penetration, and to carry big free-fall weapons with very large yields up to 20 megatons. That is indeed why the USAF is spending so much in getting a force of 100 Rockwell B-1Bs into service by 1990 as penetration bombers.

It was apparent by the early 1960s that, no matter how smart the electronic countermeasures and no matter what altitude was flown, penetrating B-52s would have to blast their way into defended Soviet airspace, 'rolling up' radars and SAM sites as they went. What was needed was lots of low-yield weapons per bomber, hence the development of the SRAM (Short-Range

The ALCM is an entirely different design to the land- and sea-launched Tomahawk, although the engine and guidance system of this Boeing design are the same as that of the GLCM and SLCM.

Attack Missile) which arms B-52Gs, and B-52Hs and General Dynamics FB-111As of SAC.

The SRAM's W69 nuclear warhead has the same yield as a Minuteman III warhead, while later SRAM-B models have a W80 warhead like that carried by Air-Launched Cruise Missiles (ALCMs). The inertial guidance system is highly accurate and, once launched on a preprogrammed trajectory and flying at Mach 3, the missile is virtually invulnerable to electronic jamming or interception on its three-minute flight from bomber to target. The B-52 can carry up to 20 SRAMs, six on each wing pylon and eight in a rotary launcher in the bomb bay. FB-111As carry two SRAMs under each wing and two more in the internal weapons bay. SRAMs first became operational in 1972 and production formally ceased in 1984 after 1,500 had been delivered.

SRAM is just that: a system with a maximum range of 160 km (100 miles) if launched at high altitude and 60 km (37 miles) if launched at low level. A very different strategic weapon is also being deployed on the venerable B-52 force but with a range of up to 2500 km (1550 miles). This is the AGM-86 ALCM designed to carry a nuclear warhead and deliver it with great accuracy over long ranges, its ability to follow the terrain at very low altitude, its small size and its minimal radar cross section all improving its chances of penetration.

Air-launched cruise missiles

The ALCM was developed by Boeing in a separate programme to the General Dynamics Tomahawk, which emerged as the ground- and sea-launched cruise missiles, but it shares the TERCOM terrain-matching navigation system and the tiny Williams F107 turbofan with the SLCM and GLCM. The first squadron of reworked ALCM-carrying B-52Gs became operational at the end of 1982 and by early 1985 five operational squadrons, 90 B-52Gs each carrying 12 missiles, had been equipped with ALCMs. Production meanwhile was switched from the AGM-86A, which was designed originally to be compatible with the SRAM rotary launcher, to the larger and longer-ranged AGM-86B. Wing sweep was also altered from 35° to 25°. Starting in 1986, as the first B-1Bs become available, the 90-strong B-52H force at present armed with SRAMs and gravity bombs for the penetration role will themselves undergo conversion to carry 20 ALCMs, serving into the 1990s.

By then the B-1B itself will become an ALCM carrier, armed with 20 Advanced Cruise Missiles (ACMs), for which development contracts were awarded to General Dynamics in 1983. The US Department of Defense's 1986 report stated that the development of the ACM would incorporate radar-baffling 'stealth' technology and that the missile would have a longer stand-off range than the existing ALCM.

Soviet strategic ALMs

The USSR began developing air-launched stand-off missiles in the late 1940s. The AS-3 'Kangaroo' appeared in 1961 and is associated with the Tupolev Tu-95 'Bear' bomber. The AS-3, which is carried under the big turboprop-powered bomber's belly, looks like and is as big as a swept-wing fighter aircraft. It is powered by an air-breathing turbojet and speed is thought to be subsonic. Guidance is considered to be by autopilot with command override, although the AS-3 is thought to be not very accurate, with area targets such as coastal cities the objective for its 800-kiloton warhead.

The smaller AS-4 'Kitchen' carried by Tu-95s and Tupolev Tu-26 'Backfire' variable-geometry bombers is thought to be a more advanced weapon with supersonic speed, a range perhaps as great as 800 km (500 miles) and a warhead of 200 kilotons. Propulsion is by liquid-fuel rocket motor, and mid-course inertial guidance is complemented by terminal-homing active radar. The AS-6 'Kingfish' missile associated with Tu-16s and Tu-26s of the Soviet naval air force is also thought to come in nuclear- as well as conventionally-armed versions, the former having a yield of 350 kilotons. Range is estimated at 200 km (125 miles) and speed as Mach 3.

The US Department of Defense has also postulated that the Soviets have developed and deployed an equivalent to the USAF's Air-Launched Cruise Missile with a range of up to 3000 km (1,865 miles). Coded AS-15, the weapon is thought to be turbojet-powered, nuclear-armed and associated with the Tu-95 'Bear-H', reworked as an ALCM carrier just as the B-52 has been. There has been no overt speculation about the AS-15's method of guidance.

An FB-111A of the USAF Strategic Air Command displays a Short Range Attack Missile (SRAM) in its internal weapons bay. This supersonic missile is designed to give strategic attack aircraft some stand-off capability, allowing B-52s and FB-111s to make their attacks from a range of 60 km at low level.

France has developed a stand-off missile called ASMP (Air-Sol Moyen-Portée, or medium-range air-to-ground missile) for use with the Mirage IV bombers of the Force de Frappe. It will also equip the Mirage 2000N strike aircraft, as seen here.

The Soviet Union has recommenced production of the Tu-95 'Bear' as a carrier for the new generation of air-launched cruise missiles. 'Bear-H' will be armed with the AS-15 cruise missile, thought to be equivalent to the USAF's ALCM.

Free-Fall Nuclear Bombs

The only nuclear weapons ever used in anger were free-fall (or more correctly parachute-retarded) atomic bombs, the weapons codenamed 'Little Boy' and 'Fat Man' which were used to destroy Hiroshima and Nagasaki in August 1945. For 15 years after this the strategic bomber armed with free-fall 'gravity' bombs remained the most important method of nuclear delivery until the development of high-altitude SAMs and long-range strategic missiles ended the bomber's predominance. But meanwhile strategic and so called tactical nuclear bombs had entered the arsenals of the USA and USSR in comparatively large numbers, and their air forces and navies proved reluctant to give them up or to stop development of new-generation weapons. The British, French and Chinese air forces also acquired small stockpiles of free-fall nuclear weapons.

Development of nuclear weapons from the comparatively clumsy fission devices of 1945 to thermonuclear gravity bombs of huge destructive power weighing less than 450 kg (1,000 lb) and capable of mass production was remarkably rapid, taking less than 10 years. In the USA the long-range bomber force grew dramatically in size through the 1950s while at the same time the first small lightweight bombs for tactical use (Mk 5, Mk 7 and Mk 21) made their appearance, as did the first anti-submarine depth bombs. The Mk 12 is typical of its generation: it became operational in 1954, weighed less than 454 kg (1,000 lb) and could be delivered by a supersonic jet. At the same time strategic bombs appeared with very high yields in the form of the Mks 6, 13 and 18.) The Mk 18 was the first high-yield fusion (thermonuclear) bomb, deployed in 1953 for interim use pending deployment of the 'deliverable' Mk 15 and 17 thermonuclear bombs which entered the stockpile in 1954-5, the latter a massive weapon weighing some 21 tons. On 1 May 1956 a Mk 17 with a yield of 25 megatons was detonated over Bikini Atoll in Operation 'Redwing'.

The first US warheads were all gravity bombs, and it was not until 1952 that the first land tactical artillery fired warhead was deployed. In the following three years the versatile Mk 7 bomb was adapted as the

warhead of the Corporal and Sergeant SSMs and as the first atomic demolition munition or nuclear landmine.

By the 1980s the first-generation bombs had been retired but older weapons still make up a large part of the US stockpile. US bomber and strike aircraft carry five nuclear bomb types (B28, B43, B53, B57 and B61) depending on mission, these bombs varying in yield from approximately 5 kilotons to 9 megatons. A new free-fall nuclear weapon, the 1.1-megaton yield B83, began to enter service in 1984, and it is believed that over 20 types of US or NATO aircraft can carry nuclear weapons.

Amid all the talk of deterrents and megatonnage, it is salutary to consider the effects of two small (by current standards) fission weapons on a pair of Japanese towns in August 1945. This is what Hiroshima looked like after the explosion of the first atomic bomb 'Little Boy', on 6 August.

A nuclear-capable aircraft is simply one with the proper wiring to carry and release a nuclear bomb, just as it would a conventional one. The AMAC (Aircraft Monitoring and Control) system in US nuclear strike aircraft monitors and controls fusing, arming and safing of the actual bombs themselves while there is a so called PAL (Permissive Action Link) or nuclear 'voting' device in the cockpit. Great attention is given to incorporation of failsafe devices to prevent accidental detonation should the aircraft crash (there have been many such incidents since 1950) to a point where 'one-point safety' is achieved. This means that the probability of a nuclear detonation is reduced to one in a million should there be an unwarranted detonation initiated at a single point in the high explosive trigger mechanism. A table of US and NATO nuclear-capable aircraft is given at the end of this chapter.

Gravity bombs must usually be dropped directly over their targets to assure accuracy and high enough to avoid airburst detonation too close to the ground, but this is where the aircraft itself is most vulnerable. The newer bombs such as the B61 and B83 allow the bomb to be released at low level with a rapidly deployed drogue parachute and a time delay fuse. When used at low altitude this delayed low-level 'laydown' technique is highly accurate. The accuracy of the B61 and B83 is on average 185 m (600 ft) circular error probable (CEP the radius of a circle into which half the missiles aimed at a target in its centre will land), while the older bombs have a minimum delivery altitude of 90 to 180 m (300 to 600 ft).

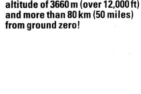

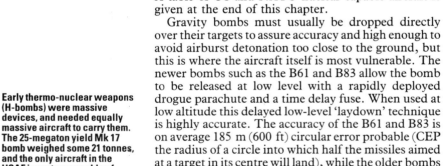

The moment of detonation of a 25-megaton weapon at Bikini atoll in May 1956. The photograph was taken from a Strategic Air Command RB-57 reconnaissance aircraft at an altitude of 3660 m (over 12,000 ft) and more than 80 km (50 miles) from ground zero!

Early thermo-nuclear weapons (H-bombs) were massive devices, and needed equally massive aircraft to carry them. The 25-megaton yield Mk 17 bomb weighed some 21 tonnes, and the only aircraft in the USAF inventory capable of carrying it was the giant Convair B-36.

Operational US gravity nuclear bombs

The B28 (first stockpile entry 1958) is a strategic and tactical thermonuclear bomb built in various modifications with yields from 70 kilotons to 1.45 megatons. Fusing must be selected on the ground. Approximately 1,220 were deployed by 1984 and the weapon is compatible with a wide variety of nuclear-capable aircraft.

The B43 (first stockpile entry 1959) is a high-yield thermonuclear bomb again compatible with US and NATO strike aircraft such as the F-111, FB-111, F-16, A-4, A-6, A-7, B-52 etc. It is estimated that 2,000 were deployed in 1983. The B53 is the highest-yield gravity bomb in the US stockpile, at 9 megatons the same as the Titan II ICBM warhead with which it is very similar. Formerly carried by Convair B-58s and Boeing B-47s, all 150 of these large weapons are carried by B-52s and will be retired as the B-52s are reworked as ALCM carriers.

The B57 (first stockpile entry 1980) is a lightweight nuclear depth bomb also usable in tactical land roles. Approximately 1,000 are estimated to be deployed with the US fleet, at shore bases and with NATO fleet air arms including the Royal Navy. The weapon can be carried by maritime patrol aircraft such as the Lockheed P-3 Orion and BAe Nimrod and by helicopters. Yield is estimated at between 1 and 10 (perhaps 20) kilotons.

The B61 (first stockpile entry 1968 for Mods 0 and 1, and about 1975 for Mods 2, 3, 4 and 5) is a new-generation tactical bomb manufactured through the 1970s so that some 3,000 are deployed in a series of modifications with various yield options from 100 kiloton (Mods 0, 2, 3, 4 and 5) to over 1 megaton (Mod 1). Later models have highly sophisticated inbuilt PAL failsafe devices. Fusing can be selected in flight, and delivery can be made at very low level at supersonic speed. The B61 is compatible with all US Air Force, Navy and Marine Corps nuclear-capable aircraft, and is also held under dual-key control by the air forces of Belgium, Italy, the Netherlands, West Germany, Greece and Turkey.

The B83 (first stockpiled entry 1984) is a new strategic bomb designed specifically for ground-burst retarded or laydown delivery against hard targets such as missile silos and underground command centres. With a 1.1-megaton yield, the B83 is replacing the B28, B53 and B43, and is planned as the major gravity weapon for the Rockwell B-1B, which can carry perhaps 38 such weapons.

Soviet weapons

Soviet strategic and tactical nuclear bombs are reported to be of consistently higher yields than their US counterparts. The standard tactical bomb has a yield of 350 kilotons and weighs about 1000 kg (1,543 lb) is now being succeeded by a bomb of 700 kg (1,543 lb) with a lower yield. Strategic bombs have been developed with yields of 5, 20 and even 50 megatons. Nuclear-capable aircraft include the Su-7, Su-17 and Su-24, the MiG-21, MiG-23 and MiG-27, and the Tu-16, Tu-95, Tu-22 and Tu-26. Nuclear depth bombs are carried by the Tu-142, Il-38 and Be-12 aircraft, and Ka-25 and Mi-14 ASW helicopters.

NATO nuclear-capable non-strategic strike aircraft

A-4 Skyhawk: USMC light attack aircraft; being replaced by AV-8B; can carry one B43, B57 or B61

A-6 Intruder: US Navy carrier-based medium attack aircraft; can carry three B28, B43, B57 or B61

A-7 Corsair II: US Navy carrier and USAF Air National Guard strike aircraft; being replaced in USN by F/A-18; can carry four B28, B43, B57 or B61

AV-8B: USMC V/STOL strike fighter; can carry one (?) B43, B57 or B61

B-52: USAF 'big stick' bomber; can carry four or eight (depending upon what other weapons are carried) B28, B43, B57, B61 or B83

F-4 Phantom: USAF, Navy, Marine and NATO-wide strike aircraft; NATO nuclear-capable F-4s only in Greek, Turkish and West German air forces; can carry one B28, B43, B57 or B61

F-15 Eagle: USAF interceptor/strike fighter; can carry four B28, B43, B57 or B61

F-16 Fighting Falcon: USAF and NATO-wide strike fighter; can carry up to five nuclear bombs but general configuration is single B61

F/A-18 Hornet: US Navy and USMC carrierborne strike fighter; can carry two B57 or B61

F-104G Starfighter: can carry one B28, B57 or B61 in strike role, but phasing out of NATO air forces

F-111E/F: on constant quick reaction alert at two UK bases; generally carries three B43, B57, B61 or B83, but can carry up to six

FB-111A: USAF medium-range bomber; can carry six (normally two) B43, B61 or B83

P-3 Orion: land-based US Navy maritime patrol aircraft; can carry two B57

S-3A Viking: US Navy carrier-based ASW aircraft; can carry one B57

SH-3 Sea King: shipborne ASW helicopter; can carry one B57

SH-60 Seahawk: new-generation shipborne ASW helicopter; can carry one B57

Tornado: British/German/Italian-developed interdictor and strike aircraft: can carry two B61s

Sea Harrier: Royal Navy V/STOL strike fighter; nuclear capable

Nimrod: RAF land-based maritime patrol aircraft; can carry nuclear depth bombs

Jaguar: Anglo-French light strike aircraft; nuclear-capable

Super Etendard: French carrierborne strike aircraft; nuclear-capable with one 15-kiloton AN-52 gravity bomb

Mirage 2000N: French interdictor and strike aircraft; nuclear-capable with one 15-kiloton AN-52 gravity bomb

Mirage IIIE: French strike aircraft; can carry two (?) 15-kiloton AN-52 gravity bombs

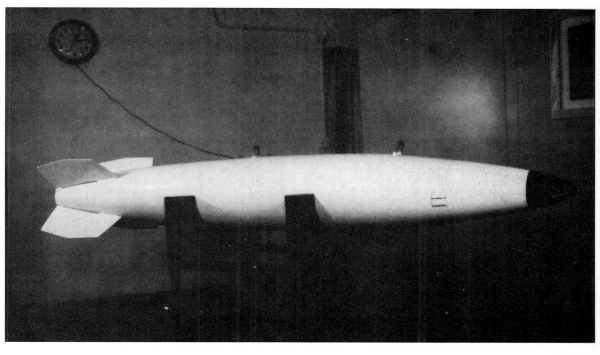

The Mk 57 nuclear weapon, displayed at the US National Atomic Museum in Albuquerque, is a dual-purpose weapon primarily used as an anti-submarine depth bomb, but with a low kiloton yield is also usable against tactical targets on land.

The awesome destructive power of nuclear weapons is graphically ilustrated by the classic mushroom cloud towering over the mountains of Nevada. Also visible is the cloud of dust around the base of the mushroom – heavy particles of radio-active soil kicked up by the explosion, and a prime component of nuclear fallout.

Chemical and Biological Weapons

'Chemical' agents are compounds which are intended for use in military operations to incapacitate, kill or seriously injure through their physiological effects. Their use in battle might be considered offensively to disrupt the defence, or defensively to create contaminated areas difficult for the enemy to cross or occupy. This is why chemical agents have been developed with such a range of effects, not just in degree of lethality but in persistence once dispensed, the latter being affected by factors such as climatic conditions, wind speed and direction, temperature and temperature gradient.

Any country with a chemical industry can manufacture chemical weapons, although their storage and maintenance presents problems. Chemical stockpiles deteriorate, unstable compounds break down, and the handling and security of such deadly materials is a grave problem. For these reasons the development of 'binary' weapons (in which two individually harmless compounds are combined into a deadly chemical agent only in the operational weapon, an artillery shell or aircraft bomb for example) was hastened in the 1960s.

Chemical agents were used in World War I from 1915 onwards, although the widespread use of such gases as Phosgene and Mustard, after their initial shock successes, signally failed to break the trench deadlock. Since then chemical agents have been used extensively by technically advanced troops against guerrillas or other insurgents, but never on European battlefields. During World War II the Germans developed the deadly new generation of 'nerve agents', but although these were manufactured and stockpiled, they were never used for fear of a 'deterrent' Allied stockpile which in fact did not exist.

Military equipment, electronics and weapons can still function even though contaminated: chemical agents have just one target, the human body. They enter by one of three routes: the skin, the lungs and the gastric tract. There are different sorts of chemicals grouped according to their effects on their human target and method of operation: incapacitating, vomiting, choking, blood, blister and nerve agents. Chemical herbicides, defoliants, smoke and flame agents are often included in consideration of chemical warfare, but as their principal targets are not the human body they are not covered here. A further category, irritants, are not covered by the definition of chemical agents

Chemical weapons are the easiest of all 'strategic' weaponry to manufacture, and could be faced in conflict throughout the world. A USAF security policeman is seen fully protected against chemical attack at Osan Air Base in the Republic of Korea during Exercise 'Team Spirit 85'.

used in the 1925 Geneva Protocol, but as they are the most frequently used of all chemical agents (in riot control, police and internal security operations) they are included in the following summary.

Choking agents
Chlorine, Phosgene and Diphosgene, the gases of World War I, are the main choking agents. They attack through the lungs and are fatal. They are susceptible to wind direction and disperse within hours.

Blood agents
Hydrogen Cyanide and Cyanogen Chloride are deadly if absorbed via the lungs. These agents are very volatile, dispersing rapidly after deployment. A rapid saturation of blood agents (delivered for example by a multiple rocket-launcher barrage) would force the defenders to take protective action but would not necessarily hinder the attacker.

Blister agents
These agents, such as Mustard gas and Lewisite, come in liquid or vapour form and attack protein enzymes in body tissue causing disabling skin blisters. The eyes and lungs are very susceptible, and mustard gas is deadly if inhaled. Blister agents can be odourless and persist for days.

Irritants
There are two groups of irritants, tear and sneezing agents. They are designed to act directly on the eyes and mucous membranes. Their effects are immediate, but recovery is rapid once the sufferer is clear of the saturated area. Distribution is usually by aerosol, rifle or hand-thrown grenades. CS gas is a typical irritant causing immediate copious tears, coughing, nausea and burning skin at very low dosages.

Incapacitating agents
These act on the victim's mind, causing disorientation and hallucination. Recovery is predictable, but effects may persist for hours or days after exposure.

Vomiting agents
These attack eyes and mucous membrane causing very severe cold symptoms, headache and vomiting. The effects persist from 30 minutes to three hours.

Smoke is used to simulate chemical attack at Sola Air Base in Norway during one of the regular 'Reforger' exercises undertaken by US forces. Interestingly, the Soviet Union regards smoke as a response to chemicals being used by NATO in the eyes of the Warsaw Pact, but a first use of chemical weapons as seen from the western side of the Iron Curtain.

Nerve agents

Tabun, Soman and Sarin (US codes GA, VX and GB) are the most deadly of chemical agents. They are highly toxic, odourless, colourless, and hard to detect. They are generally non-persistent but can be thickened to disperse more slowly. They can be absorbed into the body via the lungs or skin to react with an enzyme (cholinesterase) in the body and so disrupt the central nervous system. Convulsion, paralysis, bronchial restriction, asphyxia and death follow within 15 minutes of receiving a fatal dose, which can be as little as 0.7 milligrammes. Distribution of nerve gas can be via artillery shell, land mines, aircraft-delivered free-fall bomb or multiple rocket-launcher.

The USSR has a very large stockpile of chemical weapons, and the USA has announced its intention of rebuilding its offensive capacity with the facilitation of a binary munition plant at Pine Bluff, Arkansas to manufacture 155-mm (6.1-in) shells and 'Bigeye' free-fall bombs. The UK destroyed its stockpile in the mid-1950s, leaving in Europe only France with a reported offensive capability. Actual stock levels are hard to assess, although reports suggest that the largely obsolete US stockpile is about 42,000 tons and the Soviet stockpile 350,000 tons. The USA cites a total strength of 4,700 troops assigned to Chemical Warfare (CW), of which half are reservists. The Soviet and Warsaw Pact armies have specialist CW units from company level upwards, a total of up to 100,000 troops.

Chemical troops are an integrated part of the Soviet doctrine of combined-arms warfare, and these have a range of agents and delivery systems for different tactical requirements. Each tank and motor rifle division has a chemical defence battalion with 32 decontamination vehicles. Many tanks and infantry fighting vehicles are pressurized as an NBC (nuclear, biological and chemical) protection measure, as are NATO's armoured fighting vehicles, although individual War-Pac soldier's protective clothing is not as comprehensive as NATO equivalents.

NATO protective clothing is typically an all-over suit with a permeable skin and a charcoal interliner to protect the skin against blister and nerve agents, plus a respirator with chemical filter. Warsaw Pact clothing is a cape of impermeable rubber, but all NBC suits are uncomfortable and physically hamper the wearer. Special electro-chemical detectors can provide early warning of the presence of agents, but the current US M8 alarm can apparently detect only vapour and not liquid persistent agents, and can also be set off by vehicle exhaust fumes.

After exposure, men and equipment must be decontaminated with an oxidizing agent on the body (such as Fuller's earth) and vehicles must be washed down with soapy water or bleach. Nerve agents require immediate special treatment. An injection of a mixture of trimedoxine, atropine and benactyzine is an immediate therapy, and both NATO and the Warsaw Pact have standardized antidotes (BAT/TAB and Nemicol-5).

Biological weapons

While chemical warfare has a particular horror about it, biological warfare adds a further dimension. Biological weapons owe their effects to the multiplication of bacteriological organisms within the victim, while 'toxins' are poisonous chemicals initially isolated from organic sources which may include micro-organisms. There are over 30 known viruses, micro-organisms and toxins suitable for use as weapons. The UN Convention of 1972 that prohibits the manufacture and stockpiling of biological and toxin weapons was signed by 109 nations including those of NATO and the Warsaw Pact. A major provision of the convention entreats its signatories never in any circumstances to 'develop, stockpile, acquire or retain microbial or other biological agents or toxins of types other than quantities that have justification for prophylactic, protective or other peaceful purposes, as well as weapons, equipment and means of delivery designed to use such agents or toxins for hostile purposes or in armed conflict'.

This 'defensive' research into biological weapons is permitted, and continues at several major centres. In 1979 a reported explosion in a military compound at Sverdlovsk led to a release of anthrax spores into the atmosphere, reawakening fears that the USSR is mass producing biological agents. The Soviet authorities claimed the outbreak was the result of contaminated meat and accused the CIA of fabricating the whole thing. The anthrax bacillus has characteristics that make it a terrifyingly efficient agent of biological warfare. It is the hardiest, most easily produced and most easily disseminated disease-producing organism for

use against humans. In its pulmonary form, anthrax has almost a 100 per cent mortality rate. Anthrax spores can remain in the soil for decades: the Scottish island of Gruinard, used for dispersal experiments of Anthrax B in 1941, has been barred from the outside world ever since.

Above: The modern soldier must be trained to perform all his tasks encased in an NBC (Nuclear, Biological, Chemical) suit which hampers his every move. Wearing it is important nonetheless – it could save his life.

Below: According to US sources, the Soviets have maintained a massive stock of chemical weapons, and most artillery systems are chemical-capable. This is a US DoD impression of a Soviet chemical storage base.

Above: All Soviet troops are trained to operate on an NBC-contaminated battlefield, but in addition the USSR has large numbers of troops serving from company level upwards specifically trained in decontamination procedures.

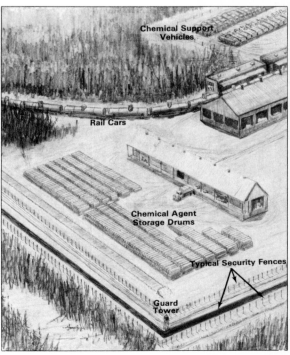

The Strategic Uses of Space

In the 1980s the issue of space as a potential battlefield came to the forefront as never before. Multiple technological and political strands have intertwined to make it so, but three in particular are of signal importance. These are the development by both superpowers of operational 'anti-satellite' capability; the initial success of the US reusable Earth orbiter programme, the Space Shuttle, and its increasing use for military purposes (although that has been severely set back by the *Challenger* disaster); and above all the initiative launched by President Reagan in 1983 calling for the development of a space-based defence against ballistic missiles, the Strategic Defense Initiative (SDI) popularly known as 'Star Wars'.

In spite of the Outer Space Treaty of 1967, which (in Article IV/1) forbids its signatories 'to place in orbit around the Earth any objects carrying nuclear weapons or any other kind of weapon of mass destruction, install such weapons on celestial bodies or station such weapons in outer space in any other manner', about three-quarters of all earth satellites launched have been for military purposes. Satellites are not themselves 'weapons' as such, but they are vital for providing early warning and C^3 (Command, Control and Communications) for the strategic weapons that wait on Earth and have been almost since the very beginning of the space age in the late 1950s. The treaty, which entered force in October 1967, left significant loopholes. While this high-minded agreement was meant to rule out the possibility of nuclear, chemical or biological weapons being placed in 'storage' orbits and called down on command, it did not necessarily proscribe the placing in orbit of 'tactical' space systems capable of attacking each other (rival satellites, for example) or weapons which would enter space en route to their targets, such as ICBMs or the Soviet FOBS (Fractional Orbit Bombardment System) 'wrong way round the globe' rockets.

By the early 1970s the Soviets had successfully tested low-altitude killer satellites able to close in on a target in orbit and explode close enough to destroy it. The USA began testing a low altitude ASAT (Anti-SATellite) missile in 1982. ASAT technology failed to be proscribed meanwhile by arms control diplomacy in the late 1970s, but by the mid-1980s the ASAT issue had been overshadowed by the far greater technological and political conundrum of a space based 'defence' against ballistic missiles using directed energy weapons, the so-called 'Star Wars' issue.

Satellites

'Tactical' space weapons such as an ASATs are of great significance because they are designed to attack the strategic space systems without which the nuclear world order of today would be impossible. The very concept of deterrence depends on the idea of 'warning': an inbound attack should be verified in enough time for an assured retaliatory attack to be made. Destroy C^3 networks and deterrence no longer works. Early warning and the C^3 net begin and end with space-based systems for their execution and for nuclear war planning.

Intelligence and reconnaissance satellites with their highly accurate mapping led strategic targeting doctrines away from the idea of MAD (Mutual Assured Destruction), which depended on targeting big targets such as cities, towards 'counterforce' strategies based on pinpoint precision targeting of rival control centres and missiles in their silos. Cruise missile navigation depends on satellite mapping and the same is true for the submarine-launched ballistic missiles of the Trident II generation which are as accurate as their land-based counterparts, a fact made possible by space-based navigation satellites. At the same time global superpowers like the USA and USSR simply cannot hold together their military machine without satellite communications.

Satellites are the principal protagonists in military space, broadly fulfilling the following functions: global communications, early warning of long-range missile attack, surveillance of events on the ground and at sea, electronic intelligence, weather reconnaissance, navigational reference and position fixing, and (on the Soviet side) anti-satellite warfare.

Earth satellites are not permanent features. According to the way they are put into orbit (angle in relation to the Earth, height and speed), the track of their orbit can be shaped for the maximum effectiveness. Some navigation, communication, surveillance and early warning satellites are designed for permanence and thus put into 'geostationary' orbits at an altitude above the equator and at a velocity where the period of orbit matches the Earth's rotation, so that the satellite is stationary relative to a point on the Earth below. Photo-reconnaissance satellites are, in contrast, generally placed into low Earth orbit (lasting a matter of days) to reach their perigee (the lowest point of the orbit) over the area of maximum interest for a close look.

A more detailed glance at one particular kind of military satellite, the photo-reconnaissance variety, shows how sophisticated and critically important these multi-billion dollar systems have become. The most significant reconnaissance satellite in the US line up is the so-called 'Big Bird' series developed by Lockheed's Space and Missile Division. As orbited it weighs over 13000 kg (28,660 lb) and consists of a modified Agena rocket upper stage over 15 m (49.2 ft) long and 3.05 m (10 ft) in diameter. The fact that it has a rocket engine, restartable on command, means it can stay in low Earth orbit for up to 190 days, much longer than the 10 days that would normally be possible with such a large vehicle encountering drag at such a low altitude.

'Big Bird' is a flying photolaboratory. It carries a very high resolution Perkin-Elmer camera capable of identifying objects as small as 0.3 m (1 ft) across from heights of up to 160 km (100 miles). Film is either processed on board, scanned and then transmitted digitally to a global network of seven receiving stations, or ejected in capsules which are caught in mid-air by specially modified aircraft. The operational technique is similar to that of Earth resource satellites. The chosen orbit is 'sun synchronous', so the 'Big Bird' passes over the same target every day at the same time, making easier before-and-after comparisons of events and objects on the ground in identical lighting conditions. In the same way passes can be timed when sun angles are greatest to give the extra definition of long shadows.

In 1976 the first of the next generation US spy satellites, codenamed 'Keyhole', was launched. The KH11 series satellites are placed in higher orbit than 'Big Birds' (up to 500 km/310 miles) after launch from Vandenberg AFB in California by Titan 34D boosters. They also have restartable manoeuvring motors able to restore the original orbit on command, so giving a two-year lifetime. KH11 does not use the capsule recovery technique, but transmits data in near real time based on digital interpretation of what its high-resolution cameras, IR sensors and side-looking radar pick up. Of the series, KH9 is a low-altitude film-return spacecraft used only to photograph the highest-priority targets: a KH9 was launched on 31 July 1983 to inspect a new Soviet missile radar in central Siberia. KH8 missions are classified. It was reported in early 1984 that production of the KH8 and KH9 had been terminated because of heavy cost overrun, while the Soviets had apparently learned how to camouflage certain activities effectively by keeping them hidden from prying eyes in the sky.

The Shuttle

While these close-look 'reconsats' are designed to fly specific missions, communications, ocean reconnaissance and navigation satellites are designed for much longer lifespans. These complex satellite networks require careful building and rebuilding as the orbits decay and systems malfunction or wear out. This is part of the military significance of the US Shuttle, which is able not only to place systems in orbit, but to tend them afterwards and conceivably to disable or capture rival systems. It is worth noting that the Soviets have all along tried to claim that the Shuttle is an ASAT system. The Shuttle can put nearly 30000 kg (66,138 lb) of useful load into a 1100-km (685-mile) orbit. A joint NASA/US DoD committee was set up in 1982 to investigate the means required such as strap-on rockets and 'space tugs' to boost Shuttle payloads into higher orbits.

Large boosters meanwhile continue to have an important role. The US Air Force, for example, has pressed for the big Titan 3 booster to be put back into production as an insurance against Shuttle failings, and there have been proposals that an emergency system for rebuilding nuclear war fighting networks in space should be part of the MX (Peacekeeper) ICBM programme. The USSR so far has used boosters based on early ICBM designs. The A-2 is derived from the early 1960s vintage SS-6 'Sapwood' ICBM with a 7000-kg (15,432-lb) payload, and the F-1 is based on the SS-9 which is able to put a 4000-kg (8,818-lb) payload into low orbit. Persistent reports of a gigantic Soviet booster began in the late 1960s and were revived by the DoD in 1983. Lift-off thrust was estimated at up to 4082500 kg (9,000,000 lb) and the system was reported as capable of putting a huge payload of 150000 kg (330,700 lb) into a 180-km (112-mile) orbit.

The launch pad area at Space Launch Complex Six (SLC-6) of Vandenberg AFB in California. Originally constructed for the Manned Orbiting Laboratory programme in the late 1960s, it was 'mothballed' throughout the 1970s until the advent of the Shuttle programme. It is to be the West Coast launch site for the system, and will be used for the more specialized missions with purely military payloads. The Challenger disaster has understandably set back launches, but the shuttle is too important to the Defense Department for the whole programme to be cancelled.

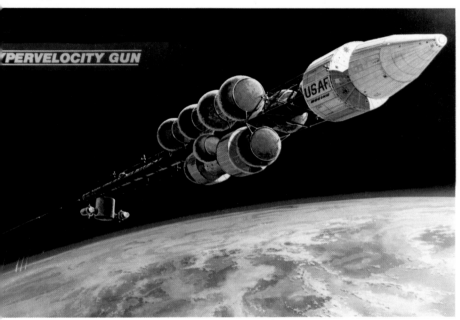

Above: The Soviet Union is believed to have had an operational ASAT (Anti-Satellite) capability for several years. Launched aboard a conventional missile, the system kills satellites by firing a cloud of small projectiles, like a giant shotgun, into the path of the target.

Below: The Strategic Defense Initiative (or 'Star Wars', as it is commonly known) has encouraged the development of a number of unusual weapon systems, such as the Hypervelocity Rail-Gun which accelerates projectiles electromagnetically at speeds of up to 20 km per second.

Right: The US Air Force maintained a supply of conventional rockets as a failsafe system should the Shuttle programme be delayed. The tragedy of the *Challenger* mission in January 1986 made launchers such as converted and boosted Titan ICBMs an invaluable asset.

'Star Wars'

In April 1983 President Reagan made the now famous speech containing, in his words, 'a vision of the future which offers hope'. The President called for the threat of retaliation to be abandoned in favour of a defensive strategy offering the notion of 'assured survival' based on great effort by the US and Western scientific communities to develop directed-energy systems based in space and capable of destroying or disabling intercontinental ballistic missiles early in their flight. There are, however, important shades of opinion as to just what a space-based defence force is designed to defend: the so-called 'Star Wars One' would try to erect a 'leak-proof umbrella' over the whole of the USA, while 'Star Wars Two' would be a defence of certain military and political targets only. As it stands in the short term, directed-energy weapons in space would be ASAT systems only. Next would be a space-based ABM (Anti-Ballistic Missile) system which might protect purely military targets such as missile silos from attack by rival ICBMs.

However all-embracing the goal, space-based ABM defence would require multiple layers which would begin with orbiting 'battlestars; and end with ground-based terminal defence. One study proposes 18 battle-stars, placed in 1750-km (1,087-mile) polar orbits in three rings, and armed with chemical lasers. The systtems would have a maximum of 300 seconds to destroy up to 3,000 attacking missiles, 300 seconds being the

time between the missile leaving the atmosphere and the burnout of the final stage before the multiple warheads separate. The study concludes that two or three shuttle payloads would be enough to place each battle-star in orbit, the first mission taking up the laser itself, its battle management computers and target-acquisition systems, and subsequent flights carrying up fuel tanks for up to 19 minutes of laser firings.

There are simple countermeasures which could be adopted, however, such as 'fast-burn' boosters which reach escape velocity before leaving the atmosphere and burn out before early warning satellites can pick them up. Furthermore, ICBMs theoretically could be 'hardened' to resist the effects of laser illumination by covering them in ablative heat-absorbing material, polishing their surfaces into highly reflective mirror coatings or spinning them so that the surface area is constantly sweeping round so laser energy cannot be concentrated on one spot.

Anti-satellite weapons

One aspect of war in space is already well established in the shape of ASATs. The Soviets began tests in 1967 of a co-orbital ASAT using a hunter-killer technique: it was designed to close in on its victim then self-destruct lethally. Tests continued through the 1970s, but were suspended during the abortive US-Soviet ASAT limitation talks of 1978-9. Soviet tests were resumed in 1980 using a new 'pop-up' technique enabling an in-

terception to be made half an hour from the ASAT's launch. But such weapons would take more than six hours to reach the critical systems which are placed in geosynchronous orbit and there is no evidence yet of an ability to close on manoeuvring targets. Nevertheless, using the measure that manoeuvring within 1 km (0.6 mile) of a target satellite is success, 13 out of 20 have fulfilled their mission in the orbital altitudes at which US transit, SSBN navigation, Elint, weather and some photo-reconnaissance satellites operate.

The USA has regained an ASAT capacity with the McDonnell Douglas F-15 Eagle aircraft and Vought ASAT missile combination, whose first test firing took place in January 1984. The system is a two-stage rocket launched at the fighter aircraft's extreme altitude either in a zoom climb or flying straight and level. The 'kill mechanism' is the Vought Miniature Vehicle which is intended to destroy its target by direct high-velocity impact. The seeker head contains a cryogenically-cooled IR sensor with eight telescopes revolving at high speed and able to pick up the target against the cold background of space. Some 46 radially-disposed miniature one-shot rocket motors obey the onboard guidance commands to steer the system towards the heat source. It is not yet effective against manoeuvring systems (including therefore rival Soviet ASATs) and only functions in comparatively low orbit.

Air Power

Nowhere are the developments of modern science manifested more quickly
or better than in military air power, complete with their advantages and disadvantages. Throughout the
aerial combat spectrum, designers and operators are torn between
high-powered radars and stealth considerations. In today's ultra high-tech environment, simple aircraft
with little equipment can still be surprisingly effective.

Contents

Bombers

Nothing emphasizes the potential of air power more forcefully than the spectacle of a bomber fleet bearing down upon its target. Immense, powerful and intimidating, the heavy bomber is a weapon almost entirely restricted in use to the world's two leading military nations, although its continued development in the USA at one time appeared less than certain.

The first aeroplanes to drop explosive devices in war may be seen as forerunners of the strike/attack aircraft. The heavy bomber's genesis is to be found in the German airships which raided as far afield as the UK from 1915 onwards, their role being to destroy property and morale even though targets were supposedly restricted to those of a military nature. The large aeroplane had become firmly established as an airship replacement by 1918, with Germany, the UK and France employing their Gothas, Handley Pages and Breguets in the strategic role.

In World War II it was the UK and USA which spearheaded development of the 'heavy' and its massed use over Germany and Japan, culminating in the destruction of Hiroshima and Nagasaki by long-range Boeing B-29s carrying the first nuclear weapons. The potential of such a combination was sufficient to interest the USSR in the build-up of its hitherto neglected heavy bomber arm, and thus directly influenced world events up to the present day. The ballistic missile has reduced the bomber's complete dominance of strategic warfare from the skies, but has not completely supplanted it.

Medium- and long-range bombers which now stand at readiness on their airfields have a task little different in many respects from the Kaiser's Zeppelins. Although the term 'theatre-nuclear' has been coined to describe power projection over medium distances, heavy bombers are a strategic weapon whose targets will often be cities and towns far removed from the front line troops. Since the early days of World War II, warring nations have abandoned the fiction that enemy civilian casualties are an unfortunate by-product of attacks upon war factories in built-up areas. The medium- and long-range bomber is, by threat or direct action, intended to crush a nation's will to resist.

The restricted latitude for diversity in strategic bomber design has been exploited to the full by the USSR. Most remarkable of all is that apparent anachronism, the propeller-driven bomber of which there is but one: the Tupolev Tu-95/142 'Bear'. Flown in 1954, at a time when turbojet power was viewed elsewhere as the only logical propulsion system for combat aircraft, the 'Bear' justified its designers' pioneering efforts and remains in production to this day. Heaviest of the serving Soviet bombers and with an immense radius of action (8285 km/5,150 miles), it is by no means as slow as at first predicted by Western sources.

The 'Bear' has been assigned to additional duties such as maritime reconnaissance and intelligence-

Above: The mighty Boeing B-52 is still a force to be reckoned with. It has taken on the low-level stand-off role, using advanced avionics to enter the war zone at tree-top height.

Right: Many Tupolev Tu-16 'Badgers' are still in use with the Soviet Union and China, and a handful fly on with Egypt (illustrated). The 'Badger' has had a long service life.

gathering, as has the USSR's first jet bomber, the Myasishchev M-4 'Bison' which, again, dates from 1954. Also born of the need to carry a nuclear weapon to the USA, the M-4 is a giant which is now in the twilight of its career as a bomber.

Theatre-nuclear forces are represented by a further pair of bombers also designed in the 1950s. These have a shorter radius of action than the strategic aircraft, at about 3000 km (1,865 miles), and consequently lighter loaded weight. The Tupolev Tu-16 'Badger' continues to serve in large numbers with the bomber force as well as diversifying into other areas, whilst the Tupolev Tu-22 'Blinder' was a more limited edition. 'Blinder' was also the Soviets' first supersonic heavy bomber and has been followed by the variable-geometry Tupolev Tu-22M 'Backfire' which can achieve Mach 2. In prospect is the Tupolev bomber codenamed 'Blackjack', which combines Mach 2 dash performance with a strategic range potential, allowing the type to fly a two-way mission against any part of the USA from bases in the Soviet Arctic.

The American answer is the Rockwell B-1B. Just entering service in late 1985 after a protracted and uncertain development period, the B-1 is another vari-

able-geometry strategic aircraft, although its maximum speed is restricted to Mach 1.25. The B-1 reflects the major changes in strategic air assault philosophy since the USAF's current heavy bomber, the Boeing B-52, was designed: notably these are low-level penetration of the defences and a cruise missile armament, in place of free-fall bombardment from high altitude. Remarkably, the gigantic B-52 has taken these modifications in its stride during a long (and still actively continuing) service history, so that it remains a potent weapon and the world's longest-range bomber. The next generation aircraft will feature 'stealth' technology for additional concealment, but the security curtain is almost complete around this Northrop ATB project.

Left: Tupolev's 'Bear' family has long carried the Soviet nuclear deterrent. These lumbering aircraft usually carry missiles, although large bombloads can also be uplifted. This aircraft is a 'Bear-C' dual-purpose bomber/reconnaissance platform. Among recently-produced versions is the 'Bear-H' cruise missile carrier.

Right: The mighty 'Buff' soldiers on in the front line. As well as its cruise missile carrying role, the B-52 is used for free-fall bombing in areas of little opposition. Other roles for the B-52 force include long-range maritime patrol armed with Harpoon anti-ship missiles and aerial minelaying.

Bombers

Boeing B-52G
Span: 56.39 m (185 ft 0 in)
Length: 49.05 m (160 ft 11 in)
Height: 12.40 m (40 ft 8 in)
Speed: 958 km/h (595 mph)
Range: 12070 km (7,500 miles)
Ceiling: 16765 m (55,000 ft)
Armament: up to 50,000 lb of weapons including 12 ALCMs, free-fall weapons, mines etc; four 12.7 mm (0.5 in) guns in tail

Only the B-52G and B-52H remain in the USAF's inventory, this aircraft being a TF33 turbofan-engined B-52H.

Rockwell B-1B
Span: 41.67 m (136 ft 8.5 in) (wings spread)
Length: 44.81 m (147 ft 0 in)
Height: 10.36 m (34 ft 0 in)
Speed: Mach 1.25 at high level
Range: 11998 km (7,455 miles)
Armament: up to eight ALCMs
internally and 14 externally; 24 SRAMs and free-fall weapons; conventional load can reach 34,500 kg (76,000 lbs)

Now entering service, the Rockwell B-1B will form the main strategic airborne element of the USAF. A total of 100 are on order.

Dassault-Breguet Mirage IVP
Span: 11.85 m (38 ft 10.5 in)
Length: 23.50 m (77 ft 1.2 in)
Height: 5.65 m (18 ft 6.4 in)
Speed: Mach 2.2 at high level
Range: 4000 km (2,485 miles)
Ceiling: 20000 m (65,615 ft)
Armament: one Aérospatiale ASMP supersonic cruise missile

France's Forces Aériennes Stratégiques employ the Mirage IVA for nuclear bomber duties. Several are being updated to IVP standard.

Tupolev Tu-26 'Backfire'
Span: 34.45 m (113 ft 0 in) wings spread
Length: 42.5 m (139 ft 5.2 in)
Height: 10.06 m (33 ft 0 in)
Speed: Mach 1.92 at high level
Range: 10940 km (6,800 miles)
Armament: twin 23-mm cannon in tail; up to three AS-4 or AS-6 cruise missiles or 12,000 kg (26,455 lb) of stores

Tupolev Tu-26 'Backfire-B' of the AV-MF (Soviet naval aviation), armed with an AS-4 'Kitchen' for anti-ship duties.

Tupolev Tu-95 'Bear-A'
Span: 48.50 m (159 ft 0 in)
Length: 47.50 m (155 ft 10 in)
Height: 12.12 m (39 ft 9 in)
Speed: 805 km/h (500 mph)
Range: 12550 km (7,800 miles)
Ceiling: 13700 m (45,000 ft)
Armament: three pairs of 23-mm cannon; nuclear and conventional bombload to 20400 kg (45,000 lb)

A limited number of 'Bear-A' free-fall bombers are still in use with the Soviet air force, perhaps for use in undefended areas.

Xian H-6 (Tupolev Tu-16 'Badger')
Span: 32.93 m (108 ft 0.5 in)
Length: 34.80 m (114 ft 2.1 in)
Height: 10.80 m (35 ft 5.2 in)
Speed: 992 km/h (616 mph)
Range: 6400 km (3,977 miles)
Ceiling: 14000 m (45,930 ft)
Armament: seven 23-mm cannon; two stand-off missiles under wings or up to 9000 kg (19,842 lb) of stores

China's primary bomber is the Xian H-6, which is a copy of the Tupolev Tu-16.

Now a veteran in the Soviet air force, the Tupolev Tu-22 'Blinder' can still pack a mighty punch as a bomber. Iraq and Libya have both used their aircraft in action recently.

There remains a limited place for free-fall nuclear weapons such as the US 70/150-kiloton B28 and 1-megaton B43, and their new replacement, the B83. The Soviet have their equivalents, and China has a 1-megaton bomb to arm the Xian H-6 (Tu-16 'Badger') it is still building locally in the absence of a more modern design. However, both superpowers rely to a great extent on air-launched cruise missiles to obviate the requirement for aircraft to overfly heavily-defended targets.

Principal American weapons are the AGM-69A SRAM and AGM-86B ALCM, the latter having a range of up to 2500 km (1,550 miles). The Soviet USSR uses some ageing AS-3 'Kangaroos', which are the size of a small fighter aircraft, as well as AS-4 'Kitchens' and AS-6 'Kingfishes'. The longest reach which can be achieved by one of these (the AS-3) is only 650 km (405 miles), but the strategic balance is maintained by the fact that the USA has far more cities within this distance from the coast than has the USSR. Preparing for deployment, however, is the AS-X-15 air-launched cruise missile which will give the 'Bear', 'Backfire' and 'Blackjack' a stand-off range of some 3000 km (1,865 miles) and, in later versions using TERCOM guidance, an accuracy of 50 m (55 yards). Tomorrow, the weapons carried by heavy bombers will eclipse the potential of today's aircraft. (For more detail on SRAM and ALCMs see p. 000.)

Above: The Rockwell B-1 has been designed from the outset for low-level, high-speed operations, incorporating a terrain-following radar into its avionics. The wings sweep back to allow a more comfortable ride at low level, and this is further aided by small vanes at the nose, which detect gusts and turbulence and direct the main control surfaces.

Left: Spearhead of the Soviet long-range strike forces is the mighty Tu-26 'Backfire', able to carry massive bombloads or the AS-4 or AS-6 nuclear missile. These monsters serve with both the air force and the navy, the latter's aircraft being employed mainly on anti-ship duties. The 'Backfire' is shortly to be supplemented by the even larger supersonic 'Blackjack', which is larger even than the Rockwell B-1.

Above: The 'Backfire' is a massive aircraft which can carry its missile over a long range. Three missiles can be carried over short distances, the other two being carried on wing pylons (inboard of the wing pivot). Racks on the fuselage can accommodate a large weight of conventional weapons.

Left: Full water-injection is needed to lift a fully-laden B-52G off the runway, and this produces clouds of thick smoke. Noticeable in this photograph are the bicycle-type landing gear and enormous 'barn door' flaps.

Right: The Dassault-Breguet Mirage IVP is an updated version of the Mirage IVA nuclear bomber, the modifications giving it low-level penetration avionics and the ability to carry the Aérospatiale ASMP stand-off missile. Eighteen of the fleet are being converted to this standard. This example demonstrates RATO (rocket-assisted take-off)

Fighters

Unquestionably, the fighter is king of the air. Streamlined, powerful and equipped with avionics which are in the forefront of technology, it is every inch a potent combat machine. Fighters, together with their pilots, have captured the public imagination in a way that no other aircraft has done, their exploits at times transcending the boundary between history and legend. For Britons, in particular, it was the fighter which saved the nation at a time of mortal danger, so changing the course of World War II and assuring freedom's ultimate victory. In the ensuing years, the fighter has seen action over Korea and Israel, as well as in several smaller conflicts, employing new tactics and new weaponry as science has progressed.

Development was no less rapid during the early days of the fighter, for the aircraft was not invented, but evolved when World War I reconnaissance machines (slow, steady platforms for visual or photographic observation) diversified into attacking each other with guns. It soon became apparent that a fast and man-oeuvrable aircraft was more successful in these combats than the stable reconnaissance aircraft, and thus the fighter was born. By definition, therefore, the fighter is an aeroplane optimized for the destruction of an opponent's aircraft and not charged with additional duties which might detract from this requirement.

At first, a moderate margin of superiority over bomber and reconnaissance aircraft was enough for success. The enemy then began escorting slow air fleets with a screen of his own defensive aircraft and so fighter versus fighter combat became an end in its own right. The requirement to meet and conquer the best available on the opponent's side has acted as the principal spur to development for nearly three-quarters of a century. Other needs have also left their mark, so that offshoots of the fighter line have evolved. Most often, these have concerned aircraft types eclipsed in air combat, yet still assessed to be useful in the ground-attack or photo-reconnaissance roles. Lately, modern design has enabled the production of aircraft which perform well as multi-role interceptor and strike/attack machines.

Three main streams of fighter sophistication may be immediately perceived in current service with the world's air forces. At the lowest level are the non-radar fighters, usually dating from the 1950s and typified by the Hawker Hunter and Mikoyan-Gurevich MiG-19 'Farmer' (built in China as the Shenyang J-6). Designed for gun armament, these aircraft may aspire to a simple ranging radar which lacks any search capability, and so must be classified as day and fair weather oper-

ators. Of course, their potential can be simply and rapidly upgraded by arming them with heat-seeking missiles such as the Sidewinder (even some jet trainers are so equipped), but they remain closely tied to ground control and of limited value in a modern war.

Next, comes the radar-equipped fighter and multi-role aircraft, which is by far the most common strain of interceptor. Airborne radar provides the means whereby a target can be located at considerable distances from the interceptor, more than sufficient to overcome small inaccuracies in the ground-based radar which places the fighter in the general area of its quarry. Such aircraft have either a full or limited all-weather capability, according to the sophistication of their avionics and weaponry.

Foremost in this field are the Dassault Mirage III, and its successors, the Mirage F1 and Mirage 2000. Exemplifying the French philosophy of multi-role capability which has done so much for Dassault's order book and French prestige, the Mirages were offered from the outset for interception and attack. The key to success has been the production of an airframe and avionics which require no modification for changes of

role, so that the Mirage can land after an air-defence sortie and take off soon afterwards as a fighter-bomber. The financial advantages are obvious to any air force which does not have almost unlimited funding.

National trends in fighter production are by no means restricted to France. The USSR relies on a process of incremental improvements to keep abreast of technological developments without being required to design a new airframe each time the electronics and weapon establishments make a breakthrough. No better example exists of such methods than the Mikoyan-Gurevich MiG-21 'Fishbed', which was little more than a day fighter when it entered production in 1957. Two decades and two major updates later, the MiG-21 was still foremost in its field, having been equipped (amongst other things) with new radar and a new engine. Now being replaced in its parent country and Warsaw Pact allies by a later design from the same stable, the MiG-21 has also served many other air forces, gaining the distinction of having been built in greater numbers than any other post-1945 combat aircraft.

The USA was once assumed to have sufficient funds

Left: The elderly MiG-19 and its Chinese licence-build, the Shenyang J-6, are still in widespread use as fighters because of their tough structure and hard-hitting guns.

Right: Used in massive numbers worldwide, the MiG-21 in its many forms is the most numerous of the world's fighters. The 'Fishbed' suffers from lack of range but can put up a brave fight.

Below: France's newest generation of fighters is the Mirage 2000, which will equip units involved in the air defence of France.

Mikoyan-Gurevich MiG-21bis 'Fishbed'

Span: 7.16 m (23 ft 6 in)
Length: 15.75 m (51 ft 9 in)
Height: 4.50 m (14 ft 9 in)
Speed: Mach 2.1 at high level

Range: 640 km (400 miles)
Ceiling: 18000 m (59050 ft)
Armament: one twin-barrel GSh-23 cannon; up to 1500 kg

(3,300 lb) of ordnance on wing pylons, including 'Atoll' or 'Aphid' missiles, rockets, bombs or drop tanks

Armed with IR and SARH versions of the AA-2 'Atoll' Sidewinder copy, this MiG-21 is typical of those employed by Iraq.

Dassault-Breguet Mirage IIIC

Span: 8.22 m (26 ft 11.6 in)
Length: 15.03 m (49 ft 3.7 in)
Height: 4.50 m (14 ft 9.2 in)

Speed: Mach 2.2 at high level
Range: 2400 km (1,490 miles)
Ceiling: 1800 m (59,050 ft)

Armament: two 30-mm DEFA cannon; usual load is two Magic AAMs and one Matra R530 AAM.

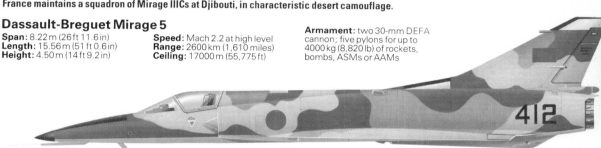

France maintains a squadron of Mirage IIICs at Djibouti, in characteristic desert camouflage.

Dassault-Breguet Mirage 5

Span: 8.22 m (26 ft 11.6 in)
Length: 15.56 m (51 ft 0.6 in)
Height: 4.50 m (14 ft 9.2 in)

Speed: Mach 2.2 at high level
Range: 2600 km (1,610 miles)
Ceiling: 17000 m (55,775 ft)

Armament: two 30-mm DEFA cannon; five pylons for up to 4000 kg (8,820 lb) of rockets, bombs, ASMs or AAMs

The Mirage 5 is a radarless version of the Mirage III; Libya is a major user.

Dassault-Breguet Mirage F1C

Span: 8.44 m (27 ft 8.3 in)
Length: 15.25 m (50 ft 0.4 in)
Height: 4.50 m (14 ft 9.2 in)

Speed: Mach 2.2 at high level
Range: 1500 km (932 miles)
Ceiling: 18500 m (60,695 ft)

Armament: two 30-mm DEFA cannon, two Magic or Sidewinder AAMs, and two Super 530 AAMs

Greece operates the Mirage F1 on fighter duties. These are being supplemented by Mirage 2000s and another as yet unnamed fighter.

Left: At present forming the bulk of France's interceptor force, as well as several other nations, the Mirage F1 is a nimble fighter with a fast reaction time.

Above: The venerable Mirage III is still one of the world's most important fighters, serving with many air arms. This is a French air force Mirage IIIE.

available to produce a specialized aircraft for every purpose, but it too is moving towards the dual-role fighter as a consequence of defence budget restrictions. More than any other jet aircraft, it was the McDonnell Douglas Phantom which proved that an air force which expected nothing short of the best could achieve it from a single airframe – and one designed initially for the navy, at that. Two other notable American fighters have been supplied in considerable numbers to allies: the Northrop F-5 and Lockheed F-104 Starfighter. The F-5 is primarily an export fighter and a close parallel to the MiG-21 in so far as three generations have been developed to keep abreast of improvements in Soviet light combat aircraft. The latest of these, designated F-20 because of major changes including replacement of two small engines by one larger power unit, has yet to find a buyer. The Starfighter has been widely used by NATO in its multi-role F-104G form, having evolved from the USAF's F-104A/C models when they proved disappointing in the specialist high-altitude interception and tactical strike roles.

Indeed, there are few aircraft types which have existed as in the third and final fighter category: pure

Fighters

Above: Differing little from its carrierborne cousin, the McDonnell Douglas F-18 Hornet is used by Canada, Spain and Australia. Illustrated is a Canadian two-seat trainer, complete with Sparrow and Sidewinder missiles.

Above left: Sweden, Finland and Denmark (illustrated) operate the Draken for interceptor duties. Despite its obsolescence, Austria has just ordered refurbished aircraft for its air force.

Left: The Northrop F-5 is cheap and extremely agile. Available in two main versions, there are also two-seat trainers. This is a Norwegian F-5A.

interceptors. In the West, only the Convair F-106 Delta Dart has remained faithful to the air-defence role, its successor, the McDonnell Douglas F-15 Eagle, having recently spawned a dual-use version. The USSR's Tupolev Tu-28 'Fiddler' (an aircraft so large that it was first thought to be a bomber) also serves solely as an interceptor. According to some analysts, it may be replaced by an even more fantastic 'fighter' based on the Tupolev Tu-144 'Concordski' supersonic transport.

Diversity of role

Neatly illustrating diversity in British defensive requirements, the BAe Lightning is an interceptor produced in a ground-attack version for export, whilst its follow-on, the Panavia Tornado ADV, began life as a strike/attack aircraft and developed a parallel strain to meet an RAF need for a long-range fighter. Sweden has followed the same path in adapting the attack-optimized AJ 37 Viggen into the JA 37 interceptor. However, among the latest products of the superpowers, the McDonnell Douglas F/A-18 Hornet and MiG-29 'Fulcrum' are claimed to be fully dual role and equipped with state-of-the-art radar and missiles.

Although only used by Sweden, the JA 37 Viggen combines a good load with excellent performance, agility and a powerful radar. Missiles are the ubiquitous Sidewinder and British Aerospace's Sky Flash.

McDonnell Douglas F-15 Eagle

This view of a trio of F-15 Eagles shows the enormous wing area of the type, which bestows upon it its remarkable agility for an aircraft of such size. The broad fuselage also gives a large amount of lift.

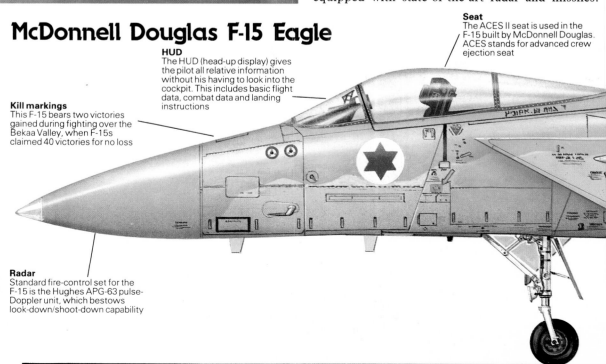

Seat
The ACES II seat is used in the F-15 built by McDonnell Douglas. ACES stands for advanced crew ejection seat

HUD
The HUD (head-up display) gives the pilot all relative information without his having to look into the cockpit. This includes basic flight data, combat data and landing instructions

Kill markings
This F-15 bears two victories gained during fighting over the Bekaa Valley, when F-15s claimed 40 victories for no loss

Radar
Standard fire-control set for the F-15 is the Hughes APG-63 pulse-Doppler unit, which bestows look-down/shoot-down capability

Largely replaced by the F-16, the Lockheed F-104 Starfighter continues in large numbers with the air forces of Greece, Turkey and Taiwan. Straight line speed is excellent, but weapon load, range and manoeuvrability leave a lot to be desired in today's environment.

Right: Soldiering on alongside the F-15 for the defence of the United States, the Convair F-106 Delta Dart is an out-and-out interceptor, possessing no internal gun and little agility. Weapons are the ancient AIM-4 Falcon and Genie missiles, carried internally in the forward fuselage.

Similar versatility is required for the new European combat aircraft being produced by France (the Dassault-Breguet Rafale) and a multi-national consortium which will use the BAe EAP as its basis.

Aircraft design being a business of constant trade-offs between conflicting requirements, there are numerous themes within the basic fighter frameworks described above. A classic case of compromise is in blending the proportions of speed and agility needed for interception. In the 1950s, the high-flying bombers was seen as the main threat, and so fast-climbing fighters were ordered into production. Typically, the F-104A Starfighter, ascended like a rocket, but required half a state in which to execute a 180° turn. A movement towards low-level interdiction, combined with the practical lessons of Arab-Israeli wars (particularly that of 1973), saw agility come back into fashion, with a vengeance in the case of the General Dynamics F-16 Fighting Falcon.

From the F-16 onwards, fighters have profited from advanced aerodynamic techniques which have allowed them to carry extensive weaponry and avionics, yet manoeuvre like aircraft of far lighter weight. The main breakthrough has been relaxed stability, or 'fly-by-wire' (FBW) control. Previously, all aircraft required a measure of built-in stability so that their pilots could maintain control. But stability is the enemy of agility, so by employing an airframe designed to be unstable, and assigning the task of keeping it under control to a fast-thinking computer, the fighter has been able to enter a new realm of unimagined manoeuvrability in which the computer acts as middle-man between pilot and control surfaces.

FBW is of advantage not only to the short-range, limited all-weather aircraft; it has also profited larger, long-range fighters like the Tornado, which must carry powerful radar and heavy armament far from base.

However, there seems little prospect on the horizon of combining in a single aircraft the very different needs of these two families of fighters. Middle East wars have shown that the dogfight is not passé, and there is a continuing need for a highly agile close-defence aircraft using heat-seeking missiles. The UK's needs are seen to be for long-range patrols to intercept low-flying intruders, in all probability destroying them with radar-guided missiles when they are too far away to be seen visually. The Tornado ADV is ideal for this role and, though endowed with a respectable manoeuvrability, does not pretend to be a first-rate dogfighter.

Contemporaneously with FBW, features such as leading edge root extensions (known as LERX) have given fighters the ability to fly at high angles of attack whilst at low airspeed. Advances in engine design produced aircraft with a thrust-to-weight ratio in excess of 1 (or, put another way, enough power to bore vertically into the heavens without running out of momentum). These aspects, allied to FBW, are the principal advances in fighter airframes during the past decade, and are to be found singly or in combination in the Tornado ADV, Mirage 2000, MiG-29, Sukhoi Su-27 'Flanker' and F/A-18 Hornet.

Northrop F-5E Tiger II

Span: 8.13 m (26 ft 8 in)
Length: 14.45 m (47 ft 5 in)
Height: 4.06 m (13 ft 4 in)

Speed: 1743 km/h (1,083 mph) at high level
Range: 2112 km (1,312 miles)

Ceiling: 15790 m (51,800 ft)
Armament: two M39A2 20-mm cannon and two AIM-9 Sidewinder missiles on wingtips

Northrop F-5E Tiger II of the Chilean air force. The F-5E is the major version of this popular fighter.

Lockheed (Aeritalia) F-104S Starfighter

Span: 6.68 m (21 ft 11 in)
Length: 16.69 m (54 ft 9 in)
Height: 4.15 m (13 ft 6 in)

Speed: 2092 km/h (1,300 mph) at high level
Range: 2220 km (1,380 miles)
Ceiling: 16764 m (55,000 ft)

Armament: one M61 20-mm six-barrelled cannon; two Sidewinder and two Selenia Aspide AAMs

Most capable of the Starfighters is the Aeritalia-built F-104S. These are flown by Italy and Turkey (illustrated).

McDonnell Douglas F-15 Eagle

Span: 13.05 m (42 ft 9.75 in)
Length: 19.43 m (63 ft 9 in)
Height: 5.63 m (18 ft 5.5 in)

Speed: Mach 2.5 at high level
Range: 4631 km (2,878 miles)
Ceiling: 18,300 m (60,000 ft)

Armament: one M61 20-mm six-barrelled cannon; four Sidewinder and four Sparrow AAMs

AIM-9P Sidewinder
Four of these short-range missiles are carried. In Israeli machines these are sometimes replaced by Shafrir or Python missiles

Arguably the world's best fighter, the McDonnell Douglas F-15 Eagle has been in business since 1974, rapidly becoming the standard by which other fighters are measured. Sparrows on the fuselage and Sidewinders on the wing pylons are the usual missile armament, although Israeli aircraft may carry Shafrir or Python weapons in place of the Sidewinder. This Israeli aircraft took part in the hectic fighting over the Bekaa Valley, when Israeli aircraft claimed 84 Syrian aircraft downed (40 by F-15s). Israeli aircraft have also shot down Syrian MiG-25 'Foxbats'.

Fin
The twin fins give extraordinary control at high angles of attack and low speed, a condition often encountered in dogfighting

AIM-7F Sparrow
This medium-range missile is carried by the F-15, fitting neatly around the corners of the fuselage

Serving with two RAF squadrons, the BAC Lightning is among the first generation of supersonic fighters. Updates in equipment, general defence budget restraints, and the type's phenomenal climb performance have kept it in the front-line inventory. This is a Firestreak-armed F.Mk 3 of No. 11 Sqn.

The hopes of Britain's air defence rest squarely on the shoulders of the Panavia Tornado F.Mk 2 and F.Mk 3. These thoroughbreds are optimized for long-range interceptions over the barren wastes of the Atlantic, fitted with the long-range Foxhunter radar and BAe Sky Flash missiles.

In the same time-frame, avionics have undergone a revolution with the coming of pulse-Doppler radars. Early all-weather fighters were limited by the fact that their radar could not pick out a target against the 'clutter' from ground-returns and so were forced to seek their prey from below. By identifying the Doppler shift of radar pulses reflected by a low-flying enemy, the latest fighters can overcome this restriction and achieve 'look-down/shoot-down' capability. Widely available in the West for over a decade, true LD/SD is now to be found in the latest generation of Soviet fighters.

In some respects, fighter development during recent years appears to have marked time or shown some uncertainty as to the way forward. Regarding the former, it will be noted that the interceptor speeds topped Mach 2 at high altitude as long ago as the mid-1950s and have generally progressed no further. There are sound reasons for this levelling off, not the least of which is the fact that air battles tend to be medium- and low-level subsonic affairs. A notable exception, the MiG-25 'Foxbat', was produced to combat the Mach 3 North American B-70 Valkyrie bomber. The MiG-25 entered production; the B-70 did not. Different designs of aircraft are needed when the requirement is for high speed close to the ground, and a star performer in this arena is the Tornado ADV, which has demons-

trated 1480 km/h (920 mph).

The controversy between one- and two-man fighter crews continues. When radar was first introduced, a second man was added. Radar operation was then simplified, and it was back to pilot only. Additional avionics such as ESM and ECM were brought in, and the navigator (the USAF's weapon systems operator) returned to vogue. These aids have now been given to a computer to operate, and 'pilot only' is seen by some

A pure interceptor, the MiG-25M 'Foxbat-E' is an uprated version of the basic 'Foxbat' incorporating an infra-red sensor under the nose. The missiles are the giant AA-6 'Acrid' in IR and SARH versions.

authorities as the way to go. Not all agree, hence two men in the Tornado ADV to handle the high workload of modern air combat.

Some uncertainty had also surrounded the airborne gun. The story is told by the Lightning, which was designed with a pair of internal 30-mm Aden cannon, opted for missiles only in the F.Mk 6 model modified in service to carry two Aden weapons externally in the belly pack. Now a 20-mm or 30-mm cannon is carried by most fighters, following the realization that missiles are not the ultimate weapon in air-to-air missions, and that lack of guns also detracts from secondary ground-attack capability. Indeed, it may be argued that fighter evolution as a whole proceeds in cycles, within which improvements on one side are neutralized by new features introduced by a potential adversary. When the advances of modern technology have cancelled each other, it can be seen that the basic tactics of air fighting have changed little since formulated by Mannock, von Richthofen and their kind in World War I: he who seizes the initiative is invariably the victor.

Left: The Mikoyan-Gurevich MiG-23 'Flogger' fighter is available with two radar fits. This East German 'Flogger-B' has the 'High Lark' unit fitted for Warsaw Pact air forces, while other export customers usually have the 'Flogger-E' with the less capable 'Jay Bird'.

Below left: The General Dynamics F-16 is the most nimble of the modern fighters. It has been supplied to many Western countries as well as being the standard tactical fighter of the USAF.

Below: Optimized for air defence, the 'Flogger-G' version features a reduced dorsal fin. It appears in the Soviet inventory only. The MiG-23's Tumansky R-29 engine is extremely powerful and produces great shock triangles.

Several air forces still rely on the remarkable F-4 Phantom for air defence, as well as using it for tactical attack duties. South Korea has a large force of Phantoms, including this F-4D. The D-model does not have an internal cannon but can carry a SUU-11 gun pod on the centreline pylon, as here.

Part of the F-16's excellent high-G capability comes from the leading edge extension and intake position, which allows the aircraft to pull phenomenal high positive G manoeuvres. Load-carrying ability is also excellent, illustrated by this 8th TFW machine loaded with five ferry tanks. Sidewinder missiles are fitted on the wingtip rails.

Currently the world's largest fighter, the Tupolev Tu-128 'Fiddler' is used to patrol the vast areas in the north of the Soviet Union, utilizing the type's good endurance. Missiles are usually AA-5 'Ash'.

'Foxhound' is the codename applied to the MiG-31. This MiG-25 derivative carries two crew and the new AA-9 missile. The radar is thought to possess true look-down/shoot-down capability.

The most fascinating of the new crop of Soviet fighters is the Sukhoi Su-27 'Flanker', which incorporates a blended wing leading edge. Some doubt exists as to whether the wingtips will be rounded or square.

Until the Tornado F.Mk 3 enters service, the Phantom shoulders the brunt of Britain's air defence. The RAF's Phantoms have the Spey engine and different systems from their cousins around the world.

General Dynamics F-16 Fighting Falcon

Span: 9.45 m (31 ft 0 in)
Length: 15.01 m (49 ft 3 in)
Height: 5.09 m (16 ft 8.5 in)
Speed: Mach 2 at high level
Range: 3890 km (2,415 miles)
Ceiling: 15240 m (50,000 ft)
Armament: one M61 20-mm six-barrelled cannon; two or four Sidewinders, two Sparrow or AMRAAM missiles

The Netherlands is one of the NATO countries that has adopted the F-16 as its standard tactical aircraft, asking it to perform both fighter and attack duties.

Panavia Tornado F.Mk 2

Span: 13.91 m (45 ft 7.5 in) wings spread
Length: 18.09 m (59 ft 4 in)
Height: 5.95 m (19 ft 6.25 in)
Speed: Mach 2.2 at high level
Range: 3800 km (2, 361 miles) approx.
Armament: one 27-mm IWKA Mauser cannon; two AIM-9L Sidewinder and four BAe Sky Flash missiles

The first Tornado F.Mk 2s have been delivered to No. 229 OCU to begin pilot training.

Strike/Attack Aircraft

One of the most common purposes to which military aircraft are assigned is the assault upon the enemy's surface forces and ground installations. Almost every one of the world's air forces possesses an aircraft capable of this task (even those lacking air-defence fighters), as a consequence of which the diversity of aircraft types employed is remarkable. Converted light transports and supersonic jets packed with sophisticated avionics each have a role to play in providing offensive capability in particular circumstances.

Before reviewing the broad field of strike/attack aircraft, it is as well to define the two categories of aeroplane which are under discussion. Roles of 'strike' and 'attack' are often confused, to the extent that the terms have become popularly interchangeable. This is far from the case, for there is a simple, yet clear division between the two. According to NATO definitions, when an attack is carried out with nuclear weapons it is termed 'strike'. With this in mind, it will be found that many types of aircraft are suited for both roles: as a general rule all strike aircraft are capable of attack, but by no means all attack aircraft have the ability to conduct a strike mission.

Attack is normally taken to imply a sortie against forces close to the front line of combatant ground troops, or in the immediate rear area of the battlefield. Strike missions are often concerned targets farther away, and in this respect the strike aeroplane has some overlap with the duties of the heavy bomber. Within these broad classifications there are subdivisions, most notably when attack aircraft are assigned to close support or counter-insurgency (COIN).

Counter-insurgency is perhaps the least demanding of the attack-type missions, although the use by some guerrilla forces of shoulder-launched SAMs such as the SA-7 'Grail' has recently made it a more hazardous operation. The insurgent normally lacks fighter and other forms of air support enjoyed by regular armies, and consequently a less sophisticated type of air attack can be employed to good effect against him. For that reason, numerous jet trainers have secondary COIN roles, as do a few propeller-driven transports and specialized COIN aircraft.

The Pilatus/Britten-Norman Defender (an armed Islander) and the new DHC-6-300M version of the de Havilland Twin Otter are turboprop twins used for COIN and security missions, and have even been adapted for maritime attack. In Argentina, the FMA Pucará is one of the few purpose-designed COIN aircraft to have turboprop power, but its employment during the 1982 Falklands war with the UK showed

Principal RAF close support aircraft is the remarkable Harrier. Its STOVL capability enable it to operate from quickly-prepared landing strips close to the front and away from the fixed airfields which would rapidly come under attack during wartime. It suffers from lack of load-carrying, but makes up for this by being able to make many more sorties than a conventional aircraft. Among weaponry available to the Harrier are laser-guided bombs, iron bombs, cluster bombs and unguided rockets, the latter being demonstrated by this No. 1 Sqn machine.

Employed during the Falklands war, Argentina's FMA Pucará was developed for counter-insurgency work. Due to its excellent agility and choice of weaponry, the Pucará was feared by the British troops. However, it proved to be wanting in the face of modern battlefield defences, and would be of far greater use in the COIN role.

some areas for possible improvement, notably heavier gun armament. An updated twin-prop which has achieved limited sales is an adaptation on the lines of the Cessna O-2A forward air controller by Summit Aviation, and known as the Sentry O2-337.

Armament for this range of attack aircraft includes light bombs up to 113 kg (250 lb) or 227 kg (500 lb) in weight, podded machine-guns of about 7.62-mm (0.3-in) calibre, and packs of rockets such as the Matra range of 68-mm (2.68-in) projectiles. An adapted transport may even launch a wire-guided anti-tank missile of the type carried by helicopters. When a type is optimized for COIN, machine-guns are carried internally, such as the Pucará's 7.62-mm and 20-mm weapons, some of which the Argentine air force wishes to exchange for twin 30-mm armament. Similarly equipped are light jets assigned to COIN, notably the Cessna A-37 Dragonfly adaptation of the T-37 basic trainer.

Before leaving propeller-power altogether, mention must be made of the gunships developed by the US for use in Vietnam. The Douglas AC-47 and Lockheed AC-130 are based on the widely-used Dakota/Skytrain and Hercules transports, and are used to pour withering fire upon ground positions. Their cabins contain one or more rapid-firing weapons whose barrels are so aligned that when the aircraft flies a banked circle the guns remain directed at a single spot. Starting with a 7.62-mm weapon, the aerial gunship has developed via 20-mm and 40-mm to the 105-mm (4.13-in) gun employed by the AC-130H Spectre. Indeed, the Spectre is a veritable 'gun ship', having one each of the two

Above: Resembling the Northrop A-9, and performing a similar role to the USAF's A-10, the Sukhoi Su-25 'Frogfoot' has seen action in Afghanistan, where it has been used against Mujahideen guerrillas.

Left: One of the most feared weapons of the Vietnam war was the Lockheed AC-130 Hercules gunship, and it is still in business today, its most recent action being in Grenada. Guns of 20-mm, 40-mm or 105-mm are mounted in the cabin, firing on a single point when the aircraft performs a circle. FLIR, LLLTV and other avionics make the AC-130 an immensely capable flying fortress.

Light attack and FAC duties are assigned to the Cessna O-2 in the USAF. Other countries use this, and other lightplane conversions, for such roles.

Close support aircraft

Sukhoi Su-25 'Frogfoot'
Span: 15.50 m (50 ft 10 in)
Length: 14.50 m (47 ft 6 in)
Height: 4.95 m (16 ft 3 in) approx
Speed: 880 km/h (546 mph)
Range: 1112 km (690 miles)
Armament: one GSh-23 twin-barrelled cannon; 10 pylons for up to 4,500 kg (9,920 lb) of stores, including rocket pods and cluster bombs

This Soviet air force Sukhoi Su-25 'Frogfoot' is typical of the aircraft that have seen service since 1980 in Afghanistan.

British Aerospace Harrier GR.Mk 3
Span: 7.70 m (25 ft 3 in)
Length: 14.27 m (46 ft 10 in)
Height: 3.63 m (11 ft 11 in)
Speed: 1176 km/h (730 mph)
Range: 3425 km (2,129 miles)
Ceiling: 15,600 m (51,200 ft)
Armament: two 30-mm Aden cannon; over 2,270 kg (5,000 lb) can be carried externally, including SNEB rocket pods, cluster bombs and LGBs

No. 1 Sqn RAF's Harriers went to the Falklands aboard carriers to augment the Sea Harrier force on air defence. For this they carried Sidewinders.

Fairchild A-10A Thunderbolt II
Span: 17.53 m (57 ft 6 in)
Length: 16.26 m (53 ft 4 in)
Height: 4.47 m (14 ft 8 in)
Speed: 706 km/h (439 mph)
Range: 3949 km (2,454 miles)
Armament: one GAU-8/A Avenger 30-mm seven-barrelled cannon; up to 7258 kg (16,000 lb) of stores carried externally; usual weapons are Maverick ASMs, Rockeye cluster units and LGBs

Fairchild A-10A of the 23rd TFW based at England AFB in Florida. The projection under the cockpit is the Pave Penny laser seeker.

FMA IA-58A Pucará
Span: 14.50 m (47 ft 7 in)
Length: 14.25 m (46 ft 9 in)
Height: 5.36 m (17 ft 7 in)
Speed: 500 km/h (310 mph)
Range: 3710 km (2,305 miles)
Ceiling: 10000 m (32,800 ft)
Armament: two 20-mm Hispano cannon and four FN-Browning 7.62 mm machine guns; 1000 kg (2,205 lb) can be carried externally with drop tanks, including most light stores

FMA IA-58A Pucará as used by the Argentine air force in the Falklands. An extra gun pod is carried under the fuselage, with rocket pods on the wings.

Several air arms operate the Cessna A-37 Dragonfly close support and COIN aircraft, including the United States and Ecuador (illustrated). This successful type relies on agility to defend itself, while being able to carry an extraordinary load for its size.

larger-calibre guns and two each of the smaller pair, for a total of six guns. Obviously vulnerable to SAM retaliation, the gunship remains highly effective in the right theatres, its recent employment including the 1983 invasion of Grenada by US troops.

When modern armies are in contact, their demands invariably include CAS (Close Air Support). Operating in a hostile air environment, CAS aircraft often rely upon speed and small size to evade the defences, and so large gunships are out of the question for employment. The battlefield targets which these aircraft attack can lie within a few hundred yards of friendly troops, and so precision release of weapons is essential, even though fitment of radar is a rarity.

Specific designs
Ageing fighters were once regularly found in the attack role; now, most aircraft are designed specifically for the mission, or at least intended to be fully dual-role. Ageing, but still regarded with respect by their pilots, are the McDonnell Douglas A-4 Skyhawk and the Sukhoi Su-7 'Fitter-A'. The Su-7 is deficient on range and lifting capability and has been supplanted by the Su-17/20/22 series of variable-geometry 'Fitters'. Extensive modifications (especially in Israel) also kept the Skyhawk abreast of technical developments, as did a far reaching redesign of Europe's Aeritalia G91R to produce the more capable G91Y.

In a class of its own is the BAe Harrier, whose STOVL (Short Take-off and Vertical Landing) attributes make it ideal for basing close to the battlefield to ensure a high sortie rate. Another aircraft which has been considerably updated for continued service, the Harrier is used by the RAF in Germany and is also viewed by the US Marine Corps as the most versatile and valuable accompaniment to a beach assault. Land-

Right: The A-10's ability to survive over the modern battlefield depends on ECM and the dramatic low-flying tactics used by its pilots.

Below: Although not as flexible as the Harrier, the A-10 can still operate away from its fixed bases, using stretches of road for its runway. At the heart of the aircraft is the seven-barrelled GAU-8/A Avenger cannon.

based air arms elsewhere in the world have been less certain of STOVL's worth and preferred to protect their strike/attack assets with concrete, rather than an ability to merge into the countryside.

The attack category may now be said to embrace elderly light bombers such as the BAC Canberra and Ilyushin Il-28 'Beagle', although their vulnerability would restrict them to night missions of limited effectiveness. International partnerships have produced some of the more recent additions to attack inventories (the Italian-Brazilian AMX and Romanian-Yugoslav IAR.93/Orao, for example), whilst the two superpowers have developed their own designs optimized for anti-armour and close support. When the USA's Fairchild-Republic A-10 Thunderbolt II flew in 1972 it simultaneously set new standards of battlefield survivability and ugliness. Built around a giant Avenger 30-mm cannon which fires lethal tank-busting shells at a very high rate, the manoeuvrable A-10 is intended to spend protracted periods over the battlefield, relying on armour, airframe redundancy and ultra-low flying

As well as its fighter role, the General Dynamics F.16 is an excellent attack platform, able to carry large bombloads over relatively long distances. This USAF machine carries a pair of 2,000-pounders.

Left: Sweden's main attack aircraft is the AJ 37 Viggen. These double-delta canard fighters have impressive load-carrying ability and a comprehensive defensive avionics fit, including ECM 'bullets' incorporated in the dog-tooth in the wing leading edge. Swedish Viggens regularly practise operations from motorways.

Above: The Dassault-Breguet Mirage 5 is widely used by small air arms for fighter-bomber duties. Some aircraft have the Atar 50 engine, giving exceptional performance.

Below: Israel's F-16s have been used on several attack sorties, including a daring raid on an Iraqi nuclear reactor.

Left: Developed as an unlicensed copy of the Mirage III with a J79 engine, the IAI Kfir has seen much action with the Israeli forces as a fighter-bomber.

Above: Illustrating the dual roles of many of today's fighters are the Canadian F/A-18 Hornets, which are employed for both attack and fighting.

to offset its low speed. The A-10 concept has been copied by the USSR in the form of the Su-25 'Frogfoot' which, though lacking the heavy cannon, has a similar large capacity for underwing stores. Whilst not doubting the heavy firepower of such aircraft, there are those who question their survivability in the face of modern defensive weapons and the apparent lack of wisdom of the US decision not to produce a two-seat sensor-assisted night and adverse weather A-10 for the European environment.

Weapon-carrying capability of the more widely employed attack aircraft ranges between the Su-7's 2500 kg (5,512 lb) and the Thunderbolt's 7258 kg (16,000 lb). Armament options normally include a cannon of 20-mm or 30-mm calibre and the full range of bombs, rocket-pods, cluster bombs and, occasionally, air-to-surface missiles. In the past two decades methods have been devised of considerably improving the effectiveness of attack aircraft by increasing the hit probability of ordnance, notably by the use of lasers. In close-support situations, troops can 'illuminate' a target for a laser-guided bomb or the marked target seeker fitted to an aircraft. Friendly aircraft with appropriate equipment can provide laser designation far behind the front. Aircraft laser equipment is also able to provide accurate target ranges so that weapons may be dropped automatically with remarkable precision after a computer has made allowances for even minute variables such as wind speed and direction.

Electronic capabilities

It is the abilities of modern electronics and the devastating nature of nuclear weapons which have together permitted the small strike aircraft to wield a destructive power rivalling that of the heavy bomber. Even though aircraft as basic as the Su-7 'Fitter-A' are nuclear-capable, true strike aircraft are today regarded as being those with the ability to find their targets in all weathers. They must thus have sophisticated navigation aids (almost invariably including ground-mapping radar) allied to the penetration aids (jamming equipment, chaff/flare dispensers, self-defence AAMs, etc.) necessary during the transit of enemy-held airspace to targets in the rear. The more advanced have two crew members, one of whom is a weapon systems operator responsible for managing the considerable amount of electronic equipment.

Where once the nuclear weapon's considerable force was used to offset the navigational inaccuracies of old avionics, today's strike aircraft are designed to achieve 'pickle barrel' accuracy. Primarily, this is to reduce the risk of escalation, through an ability to use conventional weapons to good effect or, if a conflict becomes nuclear, only those weapons with the lowest possible yield. Infra-red vision equipment and high-resolution radar are being added to modern aircraft as further methods of ensuring rapid and precise target acquisition.

The 'Scooter', as the McDonnell Douglas A-4 Skyhawk is affectionately known, is a remarkable attack platform which began life as a carrierborne aircraft. A fantastic load can be carried for its size, and it figures in the inventories of many countries.

Mikoyan-Gurevich MiG-23BN 'Flogger'

Span: 14.25 m (46 ft 9 in) wings spread
Length: 16.00 m (52 ft 6 in)
Height: 4.50 m (14 ft 9 in)
Speed: Mach 1.7 at high level
Range: 2600 km (1,610 miles)
Ceiling: 18600 m (61,000 ft)
Armament: one GSh-23 23-mm

twin-barrelled cannon; underwing and fuselage pylons for 4000 kg (8818 lb) of stores, usually bombs and cluster units

The MiG-23BN (illustrated) and MiG-27 are widely used by the Soviet Union and its allies for ground attack. The nose lacks radar but is redesigned for better downward visibility.

Sukhoi Su-7 'Fitter-A'

Span: 8.77 m (28 ft 9.25 in)
Length: 16.80 m (55 ft 1.5 in)
Height: 4.80 m (15 ft 9 in)
Speed: Mach 1.6 at high level
Range: 1,450 km (900 miles)
Ceiling: 18000 m (59,050 ft)

Armament: two 30-mm NR-30 cannon; weapon load is 1000 kg (2,205 lb) with fuel tanks fitted; most Soviet 'dumb' stores can be carried, including nuclear

Veteran of the Soviet armoury is the Sukhoi Su-7 'Fitter'. These tough old birds serve with several nations, such as Egypt.

Nanchang Q-5

Span: 9.70 m (31 ft 10 in)
Length: 16.73 m (54 ft 11 in)
Height: 4.51 m (14 ft 9.5 in)
Speed: Mach 1.12 at high level
Range: 2000 km (1,243 miles)
Ceiling: 16000 m (52,500 ft)

Armament: two 23-mm cannon; eight pylons for 2000 kg (4,410 lb) conventional or nuclear stores

Derived from the J-6 copy of the MiG-19, the Nanzhang Q-5 features a redesigned nose for attack duties.

Dassault-Mirage F1E

Span: 8.40 m (27 ft 7 in)
Length: 15.30 m (50 ft 2.5 in)
Height: 4.50 m (14 ft 9 in)
Speed: Mach 2.2 at high level
Range: 1500 km (932 miles)
Ceiling: 18500 m (60,695 ft)
Armament: two 30-mm DEFA

cannon; provision for Magic AAMs, bombs, Exocet missiles etc. to a total of 6300 kg (13,900 lb)

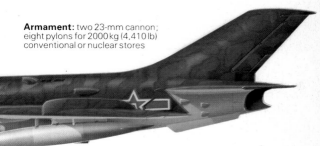

The Dassault-Breguet Mirage F1 has occasionally been used for attack duties, especially by Iraq, Morocco and South Africa (illustrated).

Saab AJ 37 Viggen

Span: 10.60 m (34 ft 9.25 in)
Length: 16.30 m (53 ft 6 in)
Height: 5.80 m (19 ft 0.25 in)
Speed: Mach 2 at high level
Range: 2500 km (1,550 miles)
Ceiling: 18500 m (60,695 ft)
Armament: seven hardpoints

can take all manner of air-to-ground stores such as RB04E and RB05A; Sidewinders can be carried for self-defence

Saab AJ 37 Viggen of F15, Swedish air force. The Viggen has one of the most complex camouflage schemes ever applied to a warplane.

SEPECAT Jaguar

Span: 8.69 m (28 ft 6 in)
Length: 16.83 m (55 ft 2.5 in)
Height: 4.89 m (16 ft 0.5 in)
Speed: Mach 1.6 at high level
Range: 3500 km (2175 miles)
Ceiling: 15240 m (50,000 ft)
Armament: two 30-mm Aden or DEFA cannon; maximum

external load is 4763 kg (10,500 lb), including virtually all British and French air-to-ground weapons; Magic and Sidewinder capable

SEPECAT Jaguars have been supplied to a handful of countries, including Ecuador. The fin-tip fairing houses a radar warning receiver.

Strike/Attack Aircraft

Left: Two Omani Jaguars streak across the desert. The aircraft excels at low-level flying, capable of riding the bumps and pulling wild manoeuvres to hug the terrain. An advanced weapons system ensures accurate delivery and a useful defensive avionics suite wards off potential attackers.

Above: Similar in concept to the Jaguar, though lacking the performance, avionics and all-round finesse, the JuRom IAR-93 Orao is a bold attempt by Romania and Yugoslavia to produce a viable but cheap attack aircraft. The aircraft is in service with both countries.

With few exceptions, strike aircraft are assigned to the tactical role. That is to say, their missions are restricted to the immediate confines of the war zone, leaving the heavy bombers and intercontinental missiles to execute the strategic tasks. Typical NATO targets for tactical strike/attack in the NATO areas would include Warsaw Pact airfields and supply lines in a move to starve the front of all forms of support. The UK and France rely on the non-radar SEPECAT Jaguar to provide part of their tactical nuclear strike potential, even though this aircraft is not truly all-weather. The Jaguar has an INS (Inertial Navigation System) allied to a pilot's moving map display, but can be more than 1.6 km (1 mile) off target after an average

penetration unless visual updates are available. Less capable, because it does not have access to the West's INS technology, the Chinese Nanchang Q-5 is nuclear-capable, but normally assigned to attack.

No such limitations afflict the Panavia Tornado IDS, whose attributes include an automatic terrain-following radar mode for 'hands-off' low-level (down to 61 m/200 ft) interdiction, day or night. The Tornado has ushered in a new era in strike aircraft capability, bettering the terrain-avoidance radar which provides only a warning of obstacles ahead for follow-up pilots in action in the earlier generation, typified by the General Dynamics F-111. A strategic F-111 variant, the FB-111, is in USAF service as an earlier parallel to the

assignment of the USSR's equivalent, the Sukhoi Su-24 'Fencer', to strategic tasks. Equally to be assigned to both forms of nuclear offensive operation is France's Dassault-Breguet Mirage 2000N, which is designed to carry the ASMP stand-off missile.

Many other aircraft are technically equipped for the strike role, but for several reasons would not normally be so assigned. Sweden's Saab AJ 37 Viggen is a capable aeroplane for conventional attack only, because its sole operator does not possess nuclear weapons. Other nations have been supplied with strike aircraft by their allies, but not the weaponry for the primary role. In yet a further category are interceptor fighters with strike/attack capability (such as the McDonnell Douglas F/A-18 Hornet) or purpose-built derivatives (e.g. the F-15E versions of the McDonnell Douglas F-15 Eagle). France's Dassault-Breguet Mirage F1 covers a broad range of customer options, from the non-radar Mirage F1A to the well-equipped multi-role Mirage F1E. The USSR has taken the process one stage further in the opposite direction and complemented the Mikoyan-Gurevich MiG-23 'Flogger' fighter-bomber with a MiG-27 variant which lacks (amongst other things) the nose radar, and so is more suited for attack.

The nuclear weapons available for tactical strike are of such a size and weight that they can be carried with ease by almost all combat aircraft. External carriage is almost universal, and even in the Q-5 the internal weapons bay has reportedly been discarded. Most is known about US weapons, the commonest of which is the B61 bomb which weighs only about 363 kg (800 lb) and has a yield variable between 100 and 500 kilotons. Also available for smaller targets (including submarines) is the B57, weighing some 318 kg (700 lb) and producing a blast equal to between 1 and 20 kilotons. For comparative purposes, the Hiroshima bomb was of the latter rating. The UK has equivalents to the B57 and B61, and France employs the 15-kiloton AN 52 free-fall device as well as planning to install a 150-kiloton warhead in its ASMP. There is a reasonable degree of certainty that China's Q-5 has a small-yield (5/20-kiloton) nuclear bomb available, and suspicions that Israel and South Africa each have (or could rapidly produce) similar weapons.

Above: With wings at minimum sweep, a F-111 climbs out with afterburners screaming. The F-111 is an excellent performer in terms of speed and load carrying.

Below: The Soviet Union's F-111/Tornado equivalent is the Sukhoi Su-24 'Fencer', which resembles both aircraft closely.

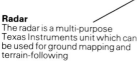

Radar
The radar is a multi-purpose Texas Instruments unit which can be used for ground mapping and terrain-following

Cannon
The Tornado GR.Mk 1 carries two IWKA-Mauser 27-mm weapons with 180 rounds per gun

General Dynamics F-111

Span: 19.20 m (63 ft 0 in) wings spread
Length: 22.40 m (73 ft 6 in)
Height: 5.22 m (17 ft 1.4 in)

Speed: Mach 2.5 at high level
Range: 4707 km (2,925 miles)
Ceiling: 18000 m (59,000 ft)
Armament: one M61 20-mm six-barrelled cannon; internal bomb bay and underwing pylons can carry a wide variety of conventional and nuclear stores

The Royal Australian Air Force employs the F-111C for strike duties, this being the only user apart from the US. A reconnaissance version is also used by Australia.

Sukhoi Su-24 'Fencer'

Span: 17.25 m (56 ft 7 in) wing spread
Length: 21.29 m (69 ft 10 in)

Height: 5.50 m (18 ft 0 in)
Speed: Mach 2.18 at high level
Range: 3600 km (2,230 miles)
Ceiling: 16500 m (54,135 ft)

Armament: unidentified cannon in fuselage; 11000 kg (24.250 lb) of stores can be carried including the AS-7 ASM; nuclear-capable

The rear cockpit of a Tornado shows the degree of complexity found in the modern strike aircraft. VDUs give target, ballistics and navigation information, while most of the weapon release actions are carried out automatically.

Sukhoi's mighty 'Fencer' carries an impressive bombload and is nuclear capable. Well-defended targets such as airfields and command posts would be its natural prey.

Due to their avionics, the Tornado and other strike aircraft, such as the F-111 and Su-24, are able to undertake missions in all weather and at night. Such missions can be flown almost totally 'hands off'.

Tornados, go! The twin Rolls-Royce RB.199 engines of the Tornado can push it at speeds well in excess of Mach 1 at sea level, making it the fastest strike aircraft in the world. This speed over target, allied to the terrain-following radar, makes the Tornado an extremely difficult target to hit.

Wings
The variable sweep wings allow the Tornado to lift a heavy load off the runway with wings swept forward, and to fly fast and stable at low level with wings swept back

Inlet
This prominent inlet feeds the heat exchanger for cooling the air system

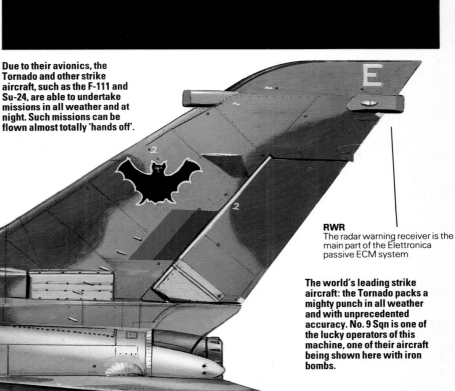

RWR
The radar warning receiver is the main part of the Elettronica passive ECM system

The world's leading strike aircraft: the Tornado packs a mighty punch in all weather and with unprecedented accuracy. No. 9 Sqn is one of the lucky operators of this machine, one of their aircraft being shown here with iron bombs.

Weapons
The majority of the Tornado's heavy weapon load is carried under the fuselage. Conventional bombs are shown

Powerplant
The two Turbo-Union RB.199 engines have thrust reversers fitted to reduce landing run

Panavia Tornado GR.Mk 1

Span: 13.91 m (45 ft 7.5 in) fully spread
Length: 16.72 m (54 ft 10 in)
Height: 5.95 m (19 ft 6.25 in)
Speed: Mach 2.2 at high level
Range: 3890 km (2,420 miles)
Armament: two 27-mm IWKA Mauser cannon; 9000 kg (19,840 lb) of stores, including JP 233 and MW-1 cratering stores, can be carried; nuclear capable

Attack Trainers

Although the proportion of training aircraft types equipped to perform attack missions has increased in recent years, the joint role is by no means a new one. In fact, it stems from the long-established requirement to provide student pilots with experience in weaponry before they graduate and take up positions in combat squadrons. In the days before the classifications of instructional aircraft became less distinct, courses on primary, then basic trainers, were followed by a programme involving an Advanced trainer. Those in the last stage.were, broadly, of two types: the purpose-designed machine, and the retired former front-line aircraft. The latter retained, but probably did not fully employ, its normal weapon-carrying capability.

A few of the world's smaller air forces still train their pilots on the combat aircraft of yesteryear, but the specialized advanced trainer has been the norm in others since before World War II. One of the longest-lived and most famous of these is the North American T-6 Texan (or Harvard in the British Commonwealth), which still serves in a few areas. Aircraft like the Texan were designed with provision for carriage of light practice bombs and perhaps a single machine-gun of the size needed for demonstration rather than devastation. It soon became apparent that the advanced trainer could serve in a combat role if strengthened to carry heavier loads, and thus began a trend which today has extended even to some elementary instructional aircraft.

In the face of unsophisticated opposition (or in a dire emergency) the Texan proved an ideal light attack and target-marking aircraft, participating with distinction and success in the Korean War and the French anti-guerrilla operations in Algeria during the second half of the 1950s. Its successor from the North American stable, the T-28 Trojan, was even modified specifically to French ground-attack requirements as the T-28S Fennec. Nowadays, however, there is little need for most trainers to be revamped for carriage of weapons, because designers have realized that their products are more likely to sell to smaller, less wealthy air forces if armament capability is built-in from the outset. Even the ultra-light Caproni Vizzola C22J from Italy can carry up to 250 kg (551 lb).

At the lowest end of the attack trainer range are the converted lightplanes exemplified by the SOCATA R 235 Guerrier version of the popular Rallye (or Gabier) four-seat tourer and trainer. One of the few concessions to the military role of such aircraft is a simple weapon sight for light ordanance, and such has been fitted to, for example, the Reims-Cessna FR172s

Converted lightplanes are in widespread use around the world on light attack and weapons training duties. This a SOCATA Rallye.

Right: The popular Aermacchi M.B.326 is a jet trainer that is often used to carry weapons, either for operations or training.

of the Irish Air Corps. The value of such equipment in limited conflicts should not be underestimated, for the power and accuracy of modern armament can transform the most innocuous-looking lightplane into a highly-destructive weapon against a broad spectrum of targets.

Compact machine-gun pods, typically of 7.62-mm (0.3-in) calibre, may be fitted quickly beneath wings for fire support missions. Bombs are available in a variety of sizes, those with a weight of 50 kg (110 lb) striking an acceptable compromise between quality (in the explosive sense) and quantity in cases where load is restricted. On higher-powered propeller-driven attack trainers, several bombs weighing 250 kg (551 lb)

Left: The Aermacchi M.B.326K is a single-seat version of the trainer optimized for close support and COIN. Atlas licence-build the type in South Africa as the Impala Mk II.

Below: The British Aerospace Hawk is among the most capable of attack trainers. It is used for weapons training by the RAF, as shown here by this No. 1 TWU aircraft.

might be carried. Rockets, too, are a potent weapon for their weight, with even the smallest armed trainers being able to carry at least two pods of 18 each at 68-mm (2.68-in) or similar 2-in (69.85-mm) calibre. An 18-round launcher weighs about 175 kg (386 lb), and it is possible to trade off larger size against smaller num-

European counterpart to the Hawk is the Dassault-Breguet/Dornier Alpha Jet, which can carry a wide variety of stores. It can also be equipped (as here) with an underfuselage gun.

bers and so progress to 81-mm (3.2-in) or even 100-mm (3.94-in) calibres in six- or four-round pods, or even on individual launch rails.

The options increase with the progression to higher-powered trainers employing a turboprop or light jet(s). Aircraft such as the Saab 105, BAe Strikemaster, Fouga Magister and Aermacchi M.B.326 are recognized as fully dual role, some air forces using them only for training whilst other have purchased the same type specifically for combat roles. At the upper end of this bracket are the advanced high-performance trainers, whose ability in the attack role rivals that of specialist machines.

The air arm whose finances just stretch to such aircraft might opt for the Aermacchi M.B.339K Veltro 2, early marks of the Spanish CASA C.101 Aviojet or Yugoslavia's SOKO Galeb 4. Like their less sophisticated equivalents, these are restricted to day operation, but they do have the edge in speed and manoeuvrability. Top line in the attack trainer bracket are the British BAe Hawk and Franco-German Dassault-Breguet/Dornier Alpha Jet, combining high subsonic speed with the ability to carry a typical weapon load of 2500 kg (5,511 lb) to a target 550 km (342 miles) distant. Reliability in marginal weather was first enhanced in the Alpha Jet by introduction of the NGEA model with advanced navigation aids and a laser rangefinder of the types to be found in the equipment of the world's most sophisticated combat aircraft.

The Hawk Srs 100 was the UK's counter, and this aircraft is now leapfrogging its competitor with the debut of the single-seat Hawk Srs 200 model which will include nose radar. German-operated Alpha Jets are already dedicated front-line attack aircraft with a secondary anti-helicopter 'fighter' commitment, whilst the new Hawk will have an all-weather capability with the latest generation of 'smart' weapons and missiles which technically promote it to the next bracket of warplane roles. The attack trainer classification does, indeed, embrace the widest range of aircraft to be found in military service.

In Commonwealth and Middle East countries, the Strikemaster has proved popular. The type is a stable weapons delivery platform, and can carry a good variety. This is a New Zealand machine.

British Aerospace Hawk

Span: 9.39 m (30 ft 9.75 in)
Length: 11.17 m (36 ft 7.75 in)
Height: 3.99 m (13 ft 1.25 in)
Speed: 1037 km/h (644 mph)

Range: 2433 km (1,510 miles)
Ceiling: 15250 m (50,000 ft)
Armament: optional 30-mm Aden cannon; two Sidewinder

AAMs for air defence; 3084 kg (6,800 lb) of light stores for ground attack

In time of war, some of the RAF's Hawks would take up air defence positions, armed with two AIM-9L Sidewinders and a 30-mm cannon.

British Aerospace Strikemaster

Span: 11.23 m (36 ft 10 in)
Length: 10.27 m (33 ft 8.5 in)
Height: 3.34 m (10 ft 11.5 in)

Speed: 774 km/h (481 mph)
Range: 2224 km (1,382 miles)
Ceiling: 12200 m (40,000 ft)

Armament: two 7.62 mm FN machine guns; 1200 kg (2,650 lb) of stores, mainly rockets and bombs

Renowned for its toughness, the British Aerospace Strikemaster flies as a weapons trainer with the Royal Saudi Air Force.

Aermacchi M.B.339A

Span: 10.86 m (35 ft 7.5 in)
Length: 10.97 m (36 ft 0 in)
Height: 3.99 m (13 ft 1 in)

Speed: 898 km/h (588 mph)
Range: 1760 km (1,094 miles)
Ceiling: 14630 m (48,000 ft)

Armament: 1815 kg (4,000 lb) of stores can include 30-mm gun pods, rocket pods, bombs or Magic AAMs

The Aermacchi M.B.339 is the follow-on to the successful M.B.326, and has succeeded in gaining many orders.

Dassault-Breguet/Dornier Alpha Jet A

Span: 9.11 m (29 ft 11 in)
Length: 13.23 m (43 ft 5 in)
Height: 4.19 m (13 ft 9 in)

Speed: 1038 km/h (645 mph)
Range: 2460 km (1,528 miles)
Ceiling: 14630 m (48,000 ft)

Armament: one 27-mm Mauser cannon; underwing stores for 2500 kg (5,510 lb) of rockets, bombs, Mavericks or AAMs

Germany's Alpha Jets have a front-line attack role, which includes anti-helicopter operations.

CASA C-101 Aviojet

Span: 10.60 m (34 ft 9.5 in)
Length: 12.50 m (41 ft 0 in)
Height: 4.25 m (13 ft 11.25 in)
Speed: 834 km/h (518 mph)

Range: 3706 km (2,303 miles)
Ceiling: 12800 m (42,000 ft)
Armament: quick change internal equipment pod holds one

30-mm cannon, twin 12.7-mm machine guns, recon pod or ECM package; 2250 kg (4,960 lb) of stores externally

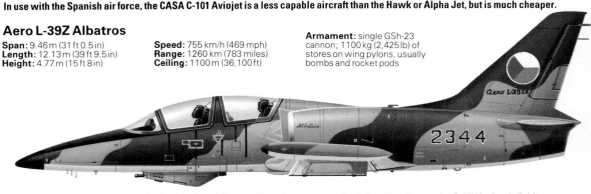

In use with the Spanish air force, the CASA C-101 Aviojet is a less capable aircraft than the Hawk or Alpha Jet, but is much cheaper.

Aero L-39Z Albatros

Span: 9.46 m (31 ft 0.5 in)
Length: 12.13 m (39 ft 9.5 in)
Height: 4.77 m (15 ft 8 in)

Speed: 755 km/h (469 mph)
Range: 1260 km (783 miles)
Ceiling: 1100 m (36,100 ft)

Armament: single GSh-23 cannon; 1100 kg (2,425 lb) of stores on wing pylons, usually bombs and rocket pods

The Warsaw Pact's armed trainer is the Aero L-39 Albatros. These have seen action in Iraqi hands over the Gulf War battlefields.

Tactical Reconnaissance

The aeroplane's first military use was that of spotting for the army, and to this day this role has played an important part of most air forces' duties. This tactical reconnaissance fills many requirements, the most important of which are pre-attack surveillance to identify targets for both attack aircraft and ground forces, and post-attack assessment, which follows up any attack to ensure the target has been destroyed and the threat negated.

Today's tactical reconnaissance platforms still carry the black and white camera as their main sensor, often in the combination of forward-looking oblique, sideways-looking oblique and vertical panoramic cameras. These cameras give high-resolution images which can be developed and interpreted quickly. Despite the high technological level that these cameras have reached, they still require a certain amount of light to work. Consequently, night and adverse weather prevent their use. To combat this, the more advanced reconnaissance aircraft carry IR linescan, which produces an image of heat emissions. Linescan is also helpful for detecting targets underneath either natural or artificial cover and camouflage, which the optical camera cannot pick up. For example, a group of trucks sheltering under a stand of trees will give off a heat image through the tree cover, but a camera will only see the trees. In aircraft such as the Mikoyan-Gurevich MiG-25R 'Foxbat-B' and the McDonnell Douglas RF-4 Phantom, a small SLAR (Side-Looking Airborne Radar) is carried, which builds up an image using radar returns. This further increases night/adverse weather capability. Other sensors which are carried are usually of a Sigint (Signals intelligence) nature, allowing aircraft to eavesdrop on battlefield communications or radar stations.

There are a plethora of types used for surveillance over the battlefield, from the Mach 3 'Foxbat-B' to the lightplane spotters. King of the tactical reconnaissance arena is the Lockheed TR-1, which carries a wide array of electronic sensors, including SLARs, at great altitude. From its perch high above friendly territory, the TR-1 can look deep across the front and give up-to-the-minute radar pictures (via a digital data link) to ground commanders. In this way, tank formations can be seen heading for the front long before they arrive, and the ground forces can be ready for them. So far, the TR-1 is in a class of its own, but the UK is developing the CASTOR radar to perform a similar job, and the USSR is test-flying a TR-1 type aircraft known to NATO as 'Ram-M'. This form of tactical reconnaissance is likely to gain ever greater importance as the low-level environment gets more dangerous.

The main category of tactical reconnaissance aircraft are the low- and medium-level high-performance jets. Without exception these are conversions of existing fighter aircraft, which have the necessary speed and agility to dodge the heavy groundfire they can expect during their sensor run. These fall into two basic types: the special conversions and the 'strap-on' reconnaissance aircraft. The former group are permanent conversions of fighters which incorporate the sensors in the aircraft itself. These usually have the fire-control radar in the nose replaced with a collection of cameras. The McDonnell Douglas RF-4 and RF-18, Dassault-Breguet Mirage IIIR and Mirage F1R, MiG-25R 'Foxbat-B' and Saab SF37 Viggen are prime examples of this trend. The 'strap-on' brigade are fighters which carry the sensors in a pod mounted under the fuselage or wing. This increases drag, but allows the aircraft to operate in a more active way if so desired. Examples of this are the SEPECAT Jaguar, MiG-21 and General Dynamics F-16. Some types employ both methods of carrying their sensors. While not performing reconnaissance as their major role, many fighters and ground-attack aircraft carry at least one camera to give them a secondary capability. The BAe Harrier is a good example of this, carrying one 70-mm oblique camera in the nose.

The human eyeball is still one of the most reliable and capable reconnaissance sensors available over the battlefield, and there are large numbers of spotting and observation types which rely on this. These lightplanes and scout helicopters are an important part of the ground action and serve in large numbers, often wearing army rather than air force colours. Most are purely

Grumman OV-1 Mohawk

Span: 14.63 m (48 ft 0 in)
Length: 12.50 m (41 ft 0 in)
Height: 3.86 m (12 ft 8 in)

Speed: 491 km/h (305 mph)
Range: 1738 km (1,080 miles)
Ceiling: 7620 m (25,000 ft)

Armament: usually none, although bombs and rockets can be carried; large side-looking radar under fuselage

Equipped with a SLAR under the forward fuselage, the Grumman OV-1 Mohawk is used for battlefield reconnaissance. Israel (illustrated) and the US Army are the operators.

Beech RC-12D

Span: 17.63 m (57 ft 10 in)
Length: 13.34 m (43 ft 9 in)
Height: 4.57 m (15 ft 0 in)

Speed: 545 km/h (339 mph)
Range: 2209 km (1,372 miles)
Ceiling: 10670 m (35,000 ft)

Armament: none – carries comprehensive Sigint suite

The Beech RC-12D Guardrail V is the latest in this family of battlefield Sigint aircraft, operated by the US Army. These aircraft carry a plethora of listening and direction-finding gear for detecting radars on the battlefield and eavesdropping on enemy communications. Much of the equipment is automated and linked to ground stations.

Left: The USAF's primary tactical reconnaissance platform is the McDonnell Douglas RF-4C Phantom. Packed into the nose and forward fuselage are four cameras, a small SLAR, infrared linescan and the TEREC kit (tactical electronic reconnaissance), which plots enemy radars, for possible follow-up strike by F-4G 'Wild Weasels'.

Left: A typical conversion of an existing fighter to tactical reconnaissance standard is the Dassault-Breguet Mirage IIIR, which is used by many of the countries that use the fighter version. In common with many such conversions, the fire control radar has been deleted in favour of a fan of cameras. Switzerland uses the Mirage IIIRS to provide its entire reconnaissance requirement.

Right: Prime tactical reconnaissance platform for the Soviet Union is the Mikoyan-Gurevich MiG-25R 'Foxbat-B'. This aircraft is equivalent in systems capability to the RF-4C, but lacks the TEREC system. Four or five cameras are carried, in addition to a small SLAR hidden behind a dielectric panel on the nose. A small 'Jay Bird' radar is carried for mapping and weather purposes. Although low-flying qualities are considerably inferior to the RF-4, top speed at high altitude can reach Mach 3.

means of getting a pair of eyes into a position to see what cannot be seen from ground level, but certain aircraft, such as the Grumman OV-1 Mohawk, employ a SLAR to help with surveillance. Others, such as the Beech RC-12 and certain helicopters, have complex listening gear aboard for battlefield Comint (Communications intelligence). These 'specials' are not widespread, but do greatly enhance the commander's knowledge of the enemy's intentions.

To get the images of a target requires, in most cases, flying close to that target, and it is obvious that if a target is worth attacking, then it must also be worth defending. Thus the tactical reconnaissance aircraft has to run the gauntlet of groundfire every time it goes into action. Speed, agility and countermeasures are employed to avoid the aircraft being hit, and the reconnaissance platforms are often escorted by fighters for protection from eager enemy pilots. Countermeasures consist of jamming, chaff, flares and jinking the aircraft to make life difficult for enemy gunners. For the spotting aircraft and scouts, who have none of this sophisticated capability, agility and terrain-masking are their only means of defence.

Becoming increasingly important as a means of performing reconnaissance in highly defended areas without endangering crews are RPVs (Remotely-Piloted Vehicles), which can carry most sensors into the target area. These are likely to be shot down at some point of the mission and so incorporate a datalink which allows the imagery to be returned. Israel and the USA have used these drones widely for reconnaissance, and there are likely to be many countries following suit following the success of this method in Vietnam and Lebanon.

Mikoyan-Gurevich MiG-21R 'Fishbed-H'

Span: 7.15 m (23 ft 5.5 in)
Length: 15.76 m (51 ft 8.5 in)
Height: 4.50 m (14 ft 9 in)
Speed: Mach 2.1 at high level
Range: 1100 km (683 miles)
Ceiling: 18000 m (59,050 ft)
Armament: self-defence missiles sometimes carried on wing pylons; camera pack in belly with others in centreline pod.

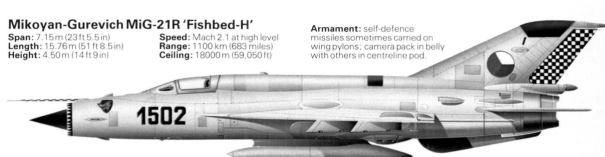

Present in the WarPac inventory in large numbers, the Mikoyan-Gurevich MiG-21R 'Fishbed-H' carries its sensors in the lower fuselage and in a centreline pod. This is a Czech air force machine.

Saab SF 37 Viggen

Span: 10.60 m (34 ft 9.25 in)
Length: 16.30 m (53 ft 6 in)
Height: 5.80 m (19 ft 0.25 in)
Speed: Mach 2 at high level
Range: 2500 km (1,550 miles)
Ceiling: 18500 m (60,695 ft)
Armament: two Sidewinders
can be carried for self-defence; cameras in nose and optional underfuselage pod

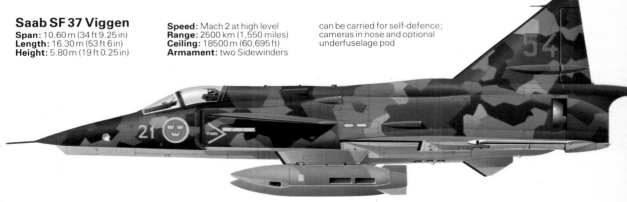

Saab's SF 37 Viggen has both a fuselage-mounted pod and a camera nose. These are particularly active photographing Soviet ships.

Above: Tac recon in the RAF is handled by two squadrons of SEPECAT Jaguar GR.Mk 1s carrying a centreline pod containing five cameras and a linescan unit. The nearest aircraft in this photograph is from No. 2 Squadron, and is shown with the pod.

Right: France's reconnaissance requirements are met by the Dassault-Breguet Mirage F1CR, which has a small camera installation in the nose as well as a centreline pod. Missiles can be carried for self-defence.

Strategic Reconnaissance

The art of keeping an eye on the enemy in peacetime has evolved rapidly since the end of World War II as aircraft and sensors have enabled this activity to become a safer and more plausible operation. Following the end of World War II, the USA realized that it could not keep check on military growth behind the Iron Curtain, so aircraft were brought in to perform this task. These were initially modified Boeing B-29 Superfortresses, which had the altitude and endurance performance necessary for long, undetected flights over the Soviet Arctic. The early successes of these aircraft introduced strategic reconnaissance as a major operation.

The rapid advances in jet interceptor and in radar design and capability meant that direct overflights could no longer be undertaken, and the strategic reconnaissance role split into two basic strands: direct overflight by either covert methods or by high-performance specialist aircraft for photographic reconnaissance, and signals intelligence (Sigint) gathering by aircraft flying around the periphery of the target nation. In the 1950s, two aircraft were developed for the first role, the Martin RB-57D and the Lockheed U-2. Both employed enormous wings to get to unprecedented altitudes and thus avoid interception, and both continued the overflights, bringing back many valuable photographs of Soviet installations. The U-2 was superlative in this role, until in 1960 an aircraft piloted by Francis Gary Powers was brought down by a surface-to-air missile near Sverdlovsk. This incident provoked an international outcry, and with one telling blow, the Soviet SAM designers had finished the U-2's career as a spy over the USSR. However, the U-2 has continued its role in other, less well-defended areas of the world to this day. The current version is the U-2R, which is larger and carries a greater payload than earlier versions. These have been used widely in Central America, keeping tabs on communist activity in the area. The U-2R has recently adopted a more tactical role as the TR-1, which is used to carry a side-looking airborne radar to look over the battlefront in the event of a European war. Increasingly the U-2/TR-1 family has changed from carrying sensors to electronic ones.

Following the Powers incident, Lockheed developed an even more unbelievable aircraft than the U-2 in the shape of the A-12 and its later incarnation, the SR-71. These black monsters flying at well over 25900 m (85,000 ft) and Mach 3, are the highest-flying and fastest aircraft in the world, a good pointer to the importance attached to the strategic reconnaissance. It has never been revealed if A-12/SR-71s made overflights of the USSR, but in today's defence climate even those phenomenal aircraft would not have the performance to escape SAMs, and are likely to perform their tasks from international or friendly airspace. The SR-71's main advantage is that, from its great operational altitude, its sensors can look much farther into dangerous territory than aircraft flying lower down. The SR-71 can carry many sensors, including a SLAR, and those carried today are more often than not electro-

The remarkable shape of the Lockheed SR-71A 'Blackbird' is more than anything the symbol of strategic reconnaissance. The 85-tonne monster is seen here turning on to the runway at RAF Mildenhall before beginning another mission.

nic. The USSR has tried to emulate those aircraft with the Yakovlev Yak-25RD 'Mandrake', which featured outsize wings, and the Mikoyan-Gurevich MiG-25R 'Foxbat'. Neither has matched its US counterpart in either performance or capability, but the 'Foxbat' has carried out many important strategic flights at high altitude, especially in the Middle East. The only other aircraft with this sort of capability is the UK's BAC Canberra PR.Mk9, which can attain an altitude of about 18290 m (60,000 ft).

Covert means of overflight often involve civil airliners, which have been known to stray 'accidentally' off course over an important military installation. Cuba-

na's Ilyushin Il-62s and Balkan's Tupolev Tu-134s have been notorious over the years for this. The dangers of an airliner operating accidentally or otherwise in the vicinity of secure areas was highlighted dramatically by the tragic shooting down of a Korean Airlines Boeing 747 in 1982 near Sakhalin Island by Soviet fighters.

Direct overflights of the opposition's territory are largely a thing of the past, the capabilities of modern

Lockheed TR-1A

Span: 31.39 m (103 ft 0 in)	**Speed:** 692 km/h (430 mph)	**Armament:** none; sensor
Length: 19.20 m (63 ft 0 in)	**Range:** 9655 km (6,000 miles) approx.	systems carried in bay behind cockpit, nose and wing pods
Height: 4.88 m (16 ft 0 in)	**Ceiling:** 24380 m (80,000 ft) approx.	

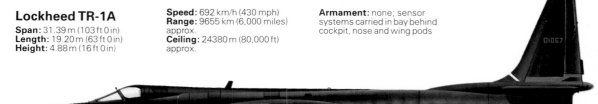

The Lockheed TR-1A is based at Alconbury in England in order to provide high-altitude reconnaissance coverage for USAF Europe.

Mikoyan-Gurevich MiG-25R 'Foxbat-D'

Span: 13.40 m (44 ft 0 in)	**Speed:** Mach 3.2 at high level	**Armament:** none; large side-looking radar in side of nose
Length: 23.82 m (78 ft 2 in)	**Range:** 1800 km (1,120 miles)	
Height: 19.40 m (63 ft 8 in)	**Ceiling:** 27000 m (88,580 ft)	

Above: The Soviet Union's SR-71 equivalent (although not as capable) is the Mikoyan-Gurevich MiG-25R 'Foxbat-D'. Differing from the tactical version by having no cameras and a much larger SLAR, the 'Foxbat-D' has carried out several important reconnaissance flights at speeds up to Mach 3.

Left: Based in Europe for battlefield surveillance duties, the TR-1A can also undertake all the strategic duties performed by the very similar U-2R. Pods on the wingtips contain comprehensive radar warning gear, and also have hardened skids fitted in case the aircraft tips onto its wingtips at the end of the landing run.

Right: Undisputed master of the air-breathing reconnaissance platforms is the Lockheed SR-71A. Flying at speeds in excess of Mach 3 and at heights approaching 100,000 ft, the SR-71 relies on an astro-inertial navigation system which tracks stars through a window behind the cockpit.

Above: This view of a Lockheed U-2R taxiing in at its home base at Beale in California shows the enormous wing span which gives the type its phenomenal altitude performance. The 'pogo' wheels on the wings are jettisoned on take-off, being replaced by hand after the landing run.

Left: The U-2R and TR-1A have been seen sporting an enlarged nose section with extraneous bumps. This is believed to house the ASARS radar.

Sigint covers a multitude of operations which include Comint (Communications intelligence) or listening to enemy communications, Elint (Electronic intelligence) or analysing non-communicative emissions such as radars, Rint (Radiation intelligence) or analysts of non-emitted signals such as a dormant radar station or powerlines, and Telint (Telemetry intelligence) such as rocket and missile guidance analysis. Increasingly, aircraft are configured to perform one of these specific tasks.

By its very nature, Sigint is a dangerous game. Precise navigation is necessary to avoid unintentional incursions into enemy airspace, as the result could well be fatal. The USSR is certainly not reticent about shooting down aircraft straying into its air. Over the years, many American and a few other Western aircraft have been attacked by both Soviet and Chinese defences while engaged in Sigint. Sometimes, these incursions are planned deliberately, to elicit a response to the incursion, much valuable information being gained about the interception procedures. These 'ferrets' play the most dangerous game of all. Other ploys involve active jamming, forcing the opposition to use alternative, and perhaps secret, frequencies to maintain their defence network, while foreign language specialists are used both to translate the communications which are being received for immediate analysis (such a specialist on board an RC-135 over the Mediterranean overheard Libyan controllers vectoring fighters towards the air-

SAMs having dictated that this role be taken over largely by satellites. The reconnaissance specialists indulge widely in operations around the borders, however. These are the Sigint gatherers, and in general these aircraft do not require high performance, preferring load-carrying capability to haul vast quantities of equipment and often large crews to man it. Consequently, most of the types are conversions of transports and bombers. Sigint is rapidly becoming the concern of many air forces, and in most areas of the world where tension is found the 'listeners' can be found too. The USA and UK were the pioneers of the art, soon realiz-

ing that as much could be learned by 'listening' to the other side as by photographing them. Early Sigint specialists were the Boeing RB-29 and the British Washington variant, these giving way to the Boeing RB-47 and de Havilland Comet. Conditions were primitive in these aircraft, operators ('Ravens' in the USAF) spending many hours staring at dials and twiddling knobs, with no windows to look out of, slung in the belly of a noisy old bomber. Knob-twiddling has gradually given way to automation and, as newer and roomier aircraft were converted, conditions have become more comfortable.

Left: Officially described as 'radar calibration' aircraft, the three British Aerospace Nimrod R.Mk 1s of No. 51 Sqn are used for Sigint gathering around the western borders of the Eastern Bloc. Little is known of the equipment carried, but the three radomes on the wingpods and tailcone presumably house spiral receiver antennas. Loral ESM pods are also fitted to the wingtips.

Above: Operating under codenames such as 'Combat Sent' and 'Combat Pink', the two Boeing RC-135Us of the 55th Strategic Reconnaissance Wing, based at Offutt AFB in Nebraska, have been in service for many years and have appeared in many parts of the world. They differ from the rest of the RC-135 fleet by having no 'thimble' nose, larger SLAR arrays, extra antennas on the wingtips, fin and rear fuselage, and characteristic 'rabbit's ear' antennas.

Derived from the civil Il-18 airliner, the Ilyushin Il-20 'Coot-A' is widely encountered by NATO fighters while it performs its Sigint tasks. Principal sensor is a large SLAR carried in a canoe fairing under the fuselage, while other excrescences house further Elint and Comint gear.

craft, allowing time to escape before the Libyan fighters attacked it), or to broadcast spurious commands on the defence frequency to try to gain further knowledge. All the intelligence gathered (from voices to radar signals) is recorded on tape for analysis back at base, while some aircraft may have a digital data-link which can transmit the data for real-time analysis. All goes to build up an overall picture of the opposition's military strategy, and allow countermeasures to be formulated.

Sigint aircraft come in a variety of shapes and sizes. Some of the smallest are the Beech 99s used by Chile to keep watch on Argentina, while that country in turn has used the Lockheed Electra, Hercules, Neptune and the Gates Learjet. In Europe, France has a single Douglas DC-8, Sweden two Aérospatiale Caravelles, West Germany, five Dassault-Breguet Atlantics and the UK three Nimrod R.Mk 1s, which are worthy successors to the Washingtons, Comets and Canberras which have been in use for many years. Israel has a fleet of Boeing 707s similar to the RC-135. The USSR was slow to begin Sigint development, but now has a large fleet of Tupolev Tu-95 and Tu-142 'Bears', Tu-16 'Badgers', Antonov An-12 'Cubs' and Ilyushin Il-20 'Coots' assigned to this task. Kings of the electronic-gatherers are the USAF's RC-135s. These carry giant SLARs to gain a radar image deep into WarPac territory, and all manner of listening and direction finding gear to suck up all electromagnetic emissions from their target areas: 'from DC to light' is how the RC crews put it. While the majority of the RC-135 force is committed to general global Sigint, two RC-135S aircraft fly from Alaska on Telint missions. As their operational areas are gradually closed down, the expensive high flyers such as the U-2 and SR-71 join their less glamorous cousins on Sigint duties, creating a large force of aircraft flying in most parts of the world listening to the 'other side'.

Strategic reconnaissance is a quiet operation, aircraft being prepared in anonymity on a remote piece of airfield or behind closed doors, often taking advantage of darkness to take-off and land, and usually operating in complete radio silence. On some missions, in some of the highly classified aircraft such as the Nimrod R.Mk 1 and RC-135s, the flight deck is cut off from the main cabin by means of a frangible partition. Thus the flight crew know where they are flying, yet not what the area of intelligence interest is, while the electronics operators, language specialists and 'government officials' can only listen to what is happening, not knowing which part of the world they are flying over, looking at blocked-in portholes. Thus complete security is maintained. Many of the aircraft either do not officially exist or have spurious roles to veil their true function. Favourites are radar calibration, weather reconnaissance and air sampling. So strategic reconnaissance goes about its business quietly; only when a 'ferret' strays fatally inside enemy airspace, or when an important discovery is made, does the world of the 'spyplane' enter the world of the man in the street.

'Bear-C' is a dual-purpose reconnaissance and missile-carrying version of this well-known Soviet snooper, but has been seen recently more in the first role. The fuselage drips with small radomes housing various electronic receivers and it carries Elint or ECM pods on the wing pylons. 'Bears' regularly probe at Western defence areas.

Sigint aircraft

Dassault-Breguet Atlantic
Span: 37.70 m (123 ft 8 in)
Length: 32.62 m (107 ft 0 in)
Height: 10.80 m (35 ft 5 in)
Speed: 657 km/h (408 mph)
Ceiling: 9145 m (30,000 ft)
Armament: none; large blister

under fuselage and tail fairing house Elint gear

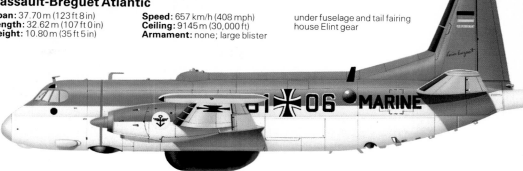

Five of the German navy's (Marineflieger) Atlantic fleet have been specially equipped under the 'Peace Peek' programme to carry out Sigint duties.

Boeing RC-135V
Span: 39.88 m (130 ft 10 in)
Length: 42.5 m (139 ft 5 in)
Height: 12.69 m (41 ft 8 in)
Speed: 853 km/h (530 mph)
Range: 16100 km (10,000 miles) approx.
Ceiling: 13700 m (45,000 ft)
Armament: none; comprehensive Sigint suite fills aircraft cabin; large SLARs on cheeks, many antennas for receiving signals

Nine Boeing RC-135V aircraft are used for general global Sigint duties by the 55th SRW. These regularly deploy to RAF Mildenhall.

British Aerospace Nimrod R.Mk 1
Span: 35.00 m (114 ft 10 in)
Length: 36.60 m (120 ft 1 in)
Height: 9.08 m (29 ft 8.5 in)
Speed: 926 km/h (575 mph)
Range: 8340 km (5,180 miles)
Ceiling: 12800 m (42,000 ft)
Armament: none; receivers housed in nose and ventral radomes with extra antennas

This single Nimrod R.Mk 1 received a refuelling probe for operations during the Falklands war. The other two may follow this lead.

Aérospatiale Caravelle
Span: 34.30 m (112 ft 6.4 in)
Length: 33 m (108 ft 3 in) approx.
Height: 8.72 m (28 ft 7.3 in)
Speed: 800 km/h (497 mph)
Range: 2300 km (1,429 miles)
Ceiling: 12800 m (42,000 ft)
Armament: none; receivers housed in nose and ventral radomes with extra antennas

Sweden operates two Sigint-configured Aérospatiale Caravelles over the Baltic Sea, using the cover of the National Defence Research Institute.

Antonov An-12 'Cub-B'
Span: 38.00 m (124 ft 8 in)
Length: 33.10 m (108 ft 7.25 in)
Height: 10.53 m (34 ft 6.5 in)
Speed: 777 km/h (482 mph)
Range: 5700 km (3,540 miles)
Ceiling: 10200 m (33,500 ft)
Armament: two NR-23 cannon in tail; several Elint fits noted

Commonly intercepted over the Baltic, the Antonov An-12 'Cub-B' is a Sigint gathering conversion of the well-known transport.

Tupolev Tu-142 'Bear-D'
Span: 51.10 m (167 ft 8 in)
Length: 49.50 m (162 ft 5 in)
Height: 12.12 m (39 ft 9 in)
Speed: 925 km/h (575 mph)
Range: 12550 km (7,800 miles)
Ceiling: 13700 m (45,000 ft)
Armament: usually four, sometimes six NR-23 cannon; differing Sigint fits

A large part of the Tu-142 'Bear-D's' role is electronic intelligence gathering. Some aircraft have an extended tailcone in place of the rear gun turret, presumably housing more electronic gear.

AEW and Control Aircraft

Neither fast nor agile, and not even possessing great destructive power, the AEW (Airborne Early Warning) aircraft has at least one case for an entry in the record books: cost. Those few air forces with sufficient funds to purchase it justify the phenomenal expense on the very firm grounds that one AWACS (Airborne Warning And Control System) is worth at least squadron of fighters and, even then, can perform tasks which any other aeroplane would find impossible. AEW is the central pillar of modern air-defence systems and the most effective means by which a nation can avert the catastrophe of a surprise air attack.

Radar is the prime sensor of detection systems (land, sea or air) and its development since the crude era immediately before World War II has made possible today's powerful airborne systems. What has made them necessary is the change in offensive tactics from high- to low-level penetration adopted by strike aircraft in response to early radars. Reliant on shorter wavelengths for its detection capability, surface-based radar is limited to line-of-sight observation and so oblivious to the aircraft beyond the horizon. Even with the careful positioning of radars on mountain tops, the time between a fast enemy being sighted and releasing its weapons is little enough for countermeasures to be taken, even on the generous assumption that correct identification is instantaneous.

Whilst carrying an air-defence radar aloft may have seemed the obvious solution, it was a far from ideal remedy. Physical limits on scanner size and electronic generating power reduce range, and in any case there is the problem of surface 'clutter', or unwanted returns. Viewed from the lofty AEW platform, low-level intruders are seen against a surface background and present a far more difficult target to locate and track. Nevertheless, the sea generates less problems for the simpler AEW aircraft and thus was the area of operations for specially equipped Grumman Avengers operating from US Navy carriers and the larger, land-based Lockheed EC-121 versions of the Constellation. The Royal Navy also employed Avengers before the service entry of the Fairey Gannet AEW.Mk 3.

Gannets, Avengers and EC-121s have now been retired, but the first-mentioned donated its APS-20 radar to the oldest AEW aircraft still flying, the HS (Avro) Shackleton. The Shackleton, whose long overdue de-

Above: Currently the only helicopter AEW platform, Westland's Sea King AEW.Mk 2 is a conversion of anti-submarine aircraft to carry the Thorn-EMI Searchwater in an inflatable radome. The radome swivels backwards.

Right: Around a dozen Tupolev Tu-126 'Moss' AWACS aircraft were converted from the Tu-114 airliner to provide AEW cover. These are believed to be ineffective over land.

Below: Carrierborne AEW coverage is provided for the US Navy by the Grumman E-2C Hawkeye. These aircraft fly out ahead of the carrier, warning fighter defences of impending aircraft or missile attack.

parture from the RAF's front line has been further delayed by development problems with its intended successor, can trace its ancestry back to a twin-engined bomber which first flew in 1939. It is thus a clear illustration of the fact that the capability of an AEW aircraft depends more on its internal equipment than on airframe design, at least up to a point. All of the current and planned land-based AEW aircraft are adaptations of aeroplanes originally designed for other duties. The Shackleton's piston engines are clearly passé and the speed and height of jets a clear advantage, yet new AEW models are even now being proposed of turboprop-powered aircraft.

What, then, are the items of equipment necessary to the modern AEW aircraft? Firstly, there is a radar scanner. Two types are employed, the most obvious of which is the apparatus carried above the fuselage of US and Soviet AEW aircraft. In the Boeing E-3 Sentry it is the aerial of the Westinghouse APY-1 equipment which rotates once every 10 seconds like a lazily twirled parasol above the rear fuselage. Mounted on the back of the aerial, within the same saucer-shaped envelope, is a complementary antenna for the IFF and secondary surveillance radar. The UK prefers separate scanners mounted in bulbous fairings at the carrier's nose and tail. Such an arrangement has the advantage that there is no blanking-off of the radar signal by the fuselage, but the two aerials must be synchronized and their findings combined accurately to provide a complete picture.

Multi-mode operation

Radars of AEW aircraft operate in more than one mode to maximize detection possibilities. Modern AEW radars are of the pulse-Doppler (PD) type, permitting them to locate targets flying close to the ground (in the face of unwanted 'clutter' from surface objects) by the Doppler shift induced in reflected signal pulses. By using a sharp beam and narrow Doppler filter, very low-level intruders can be tracked with accuracy in the PDNES (PD Non-Elevation Scan) model. If target elevation is required, the returning signal is electronically scanned in the vertical plane to elicit the data, this being known as PDES (PD Elevation Scan) mode. For targets beyond the horizon, there is BTH scan available, using pulse radar without the Doppler option because ground clutter is in the shadow of the horizon.

For maritime operations, a very short pulse is employed to reduce sea clutter and so reveal moving or stationary vessels. Maps of coastal areas stored in the aircraft's computer will even automatically remove shoreline returns from the screen. Finally, there is the passive mode in which the radar is silent and only the ESM (Electronic Support Measures) equipment is listening for signs of radar and radio transmissions from other aircraft and ships. It is usually possible in at least Western AEW aircraft to 'go passive' only in selected segments of the compass and interleave radar modes on each scan.

ESM equipment (prominently mounted on the Nim-

Tupolev Tu-126 'Moss'

Span: 51.20 m (168 ft 0 in)
Length: 55.20 m (181 ft 1 in)
Height: 16.05 m (52 ft 8 in)
Speed: 850 km/h (528 mph)
Range: 12550 km (7,800 miles)
Ceiling: 12200 m (40,000 ft)
Armament: none

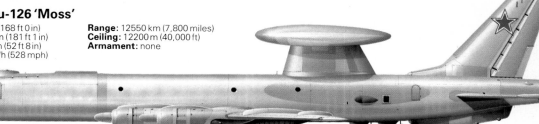

The Tu-126 'Moss' carries its large radar/IFF interrogator in a rotodome. The type is expected to be supplanted in service by the Ilyushin Il-76 'Mainstay'.

British Aerospace Nimrod AEW.Mk 3

Span: 35.08 m (115 ft 1 in)
Length: 41.97 m (137 ft 8.5 in)
Height: 10.67 m (35 ft 0 in)
Speed: 926 km/h (575)
Range: 8340 km (5,180 miles)
Ceiling: 12800 m (42,000 ft)
Armament: none

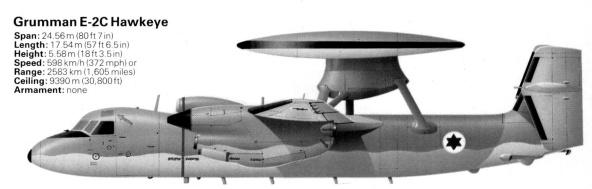

British Aerospace's trouble-ridden attempt at an AEW aircraft is the Nimrod AEW.Mk 3. This carries its radars in enormous bulges at each end of the aircraft.

Grumman E-2C Hawkeye

Span: 24.56 m (80 ft 7 in)
Length: 17.54 m (57 ft 6.5 in)
Height: 5.58 m (18 ft 3.5 in)
Speed: 598 km/h (372 mph) or
Range: 2583 km (1,605 miles)
Ceiling: 9390 m (30,800 ft)
Armament: none

Israel used its land-based Hawkeyes to great effect during the fighting over the Bekaa Valley. These maintained close watch over Syrian fighters.

Boeing E-3 Sentry

Span: 44.42 m (145 ft 9 in)
Length: 46.61 m (152 ft 11 in)
Height: 12.73 m (41 ft 9 in)
Speed: 853 km/h (530 mph)
Range: 7000 km (4350 miles) approx.
Ceiling: 8850 m (29,000 ft)
Armament: none

NATO countries have joined together to procure 18 E-3A aircraft. These are home-based at Geilenkirchen in Germany but deploy around Europe.

Above: Pending delivery of a replacement, the ancient Shackleton struggles on providing the UK with early warning of aircraft attack. The equipment for these veterans originally came from the Gannet carrierborne AEW aircraft and has none of the automation found on modern AEW aircraft. The main AN/APS-20 radar is carried in a large radome under the fuselage.

Right: Japan is one of the several countries that operate the Hawkeye from land bases, despite its carrierborne pedigree. These aircraft are flown by No. 601 Sqn at Misawa, on the northern part of Honshu island. The large Soviet threat to the north of Japan mean these aircraft are worth their weight in gold, giving advance warning of any attack, and then vectoring and controlling fighters.

AEW and Control Aircraft

Left: Thirty-four Boeing E-3 Sentries form the entire AWACS fleet for the USAF, and are seen on deployment to many parts of the world, including Saudi Arabia, Iceland, Turkey and Japan. Since their introduction into service, the fleet has undergone updating through E-3B and E-3C standard, most modifications concerning the avionics and computer capability. The engines are the Pratt and Whitney TF33 turbofan, as fitted to the B-52H bomber.

Below: Inflight-refuelling greatly increases the time on station and so increases coverage capability. The giant rotodome houses the AN/APY-1 radar on one side, and the TADIL C IFF interrogator on the other, and rotates at 6 rpm during surveillance operations. Other avionics take the form of an IBM CC-2 computer, accurate nav systems and secure communications.

The radar of the E-3 Sentry can operate in a number of modes: PDNES (pulse-Doppler non-elevation scan) when range of coverage is paramount, PDES which gives elevation details with a corresponding loss of range, BTH (beyond the horizon) which gives long-range information, Maritime, for surface objects, and Passive, where no transmissions are made but the aircraft listens to enemy transmissions.

The roomy cabin and good basic airframe of the Nimrod made it a natural choice for an AWACS platform. The radar scanners and their associated IFF interrogators are housed at each end of the aircraft, the two images meeting to produce an entire all-round coverage, with no airframe intrusions as found with rotodome aircraft. Comprehensive ESM, navigation and communications gear is fitted, with a weather and navigation radar in the starboard wing pod.

rod's wingtips) and IFF are important complements to radar. Data received by all sensors is processed by an onboard computer, filtered for extraneous signals and presented to the tactical crew in the body of the aircraft. The avionics automatically open a file on each new plot; track its progress; and correlate radar. ESM and IFF returns. When a member of the crew views his video screen he sees not a flickering display swamped by clutter, but a clear, computer-generated picture in which each target is annotated with its vital characteristics.

The tactical crew varies in number between the Nimrod's six and the E-3 Sentry's 13. Under the lead-ership of a tactical controller, the team monitors target tracks and handle communications with air and ground units, one of their number perhaps specializing in ESM operations. Here will be found the subtle difference between AEW and AWACS: the former is an observer and reporter; the latter is able to assume the additional task of directing fighter interception missions. In fact, both Nimrod and Sentry are AWACS-capable, although their prime role is as AEW transmitters of data for incorporation in NATO's overall air-defence picture.

As a counterpart to the two NATO aircraft, the USSR fields the Tupolev Tu-126 'Moss'. Virtually use-less over land and with only limited over-water capability, it is in urgent need of replacement, hence the current development of an AEW & C (AEW and Control) version of the Ilyushin Il-76 jet transport, known to NATO as 'Mainstay'. This aircraft may enable the USSR to reduce some of the lead established in the West and exemplified by the compression of AEW avionics to fit the carrier-operated Grumman E-2 Hawkeye. Based on land by countries such as Japan and Israel, the Hawkeye has been used to control offensive operations by the latter against its Arab neighbours. A variant of the E-2's current radar, designated APS-138, is being offered for fitment in converted

Lockheed P-3 Orions, and a variant of the Lockheed Hercules transport is available with the Nimrod's APY-920 avionics and twin scanners.

Closely related to the AEW/AWACS family is a further group of aircraft packed with electronics and communications equipment. These are the airborne command posts whose principal duties are intimately connected with maintenance of credible deterrent forces. Realizing the vulnerability of ground-based headquarters, no matter how deep below the surface, it was the USA which first adopted the practice of maintaining a second war room aloft, using Boeing EC-135s. These aircraft, codenamed 'Looking Glass', carried sealed orders from the President and the authority and means to launch the US nuclear missile deterrent. The 24 hours-per-day 'Looking Glass' commitment has now been scaled down and the EC-135s largely supplanted by variants of the Boeing 747 airliner, designated AABNCP (Advanced Airborne Command Post), but lacking ICBM launch capability. No doubt, there is a 'Flying Kremlin' manned by a Soviet battle staff with similar wartime responsibilities.

American nuclear missile submarines have their own communications system in peace as well as war, this being known as TACAMO (TAke Charge And Move Out). Currently fitted in Lockheed EC-130 Hercules, which are to give way to Boeing E-6 variants of the Model 707 airliner, the TACAMO system has also been adopted by a pair of Transall C.160s in connection with the French submarine deterrent. Because normal radio waves will not travel through water, and deterrence is compromised by surfacing, the only method of communicating with a submarine on patrol is by very low frequency (VLF) transmissions. VLF requires an inordinately long aerial, typcially some 8 km (5 miles) in length, and a special method of deploying it: before transmissions can begin, the aircraft enters a tight circular flight path, allowing the wire to fall to almost a vertical position. In this unusual manner, the TACAMO aircraft signals to the prowling submarines of the deep, fulfilling (like the AWACS) a little-appreciated, yet vital role.

Boeing EC-135H

Span: 39.98 m (130 ft 10 in)
Length: 42.5 m (139 ft 5 in)
Height: 12.69 m (41 ft 8 in)
Speed: 853 km/h (530 mph)

Range: 16100 km (10,000 miles) approx.
Ceiling: 13700 m (45,000 ft)
Armament: none

Boeing EC-135H of the 6th Airborne Command and Control Squadron based at Langley, Virginia.

The Lockheed EC-130Es of the 193rd Electronic Combat Squadron, Pennsylvania ANG, fly on battlefield control and surveillance duties, and recently saw combat over Grenada. Characterized by the large aerials under the wing and on the fin, these operate under the Coronet Solo II programme.

Four Boeing EC-135H aircraft are stationed at RAF Mildenhall to act as airborne command posts for USAF Europe. These aircraft retain their inflight-refuelling capability but this is seldom used. Principal aerial is a long wire which is trailed from underneath the centre-section.

Several EC-135C aircraft are on the strength of the 2nd ACCS, 55th Strategic Reconnaissance Wing at SAC headquarters to provide command posts for SAC's top brass. SAC handles two-thirds of the US nuclear deterrent, and so the EC-135C's job is more important than most. Equipment has been systematically updated.

Left: Aircraft position and identification information is displayed on several SDCs (situation display consoles) in the E-3 Sentry. Fourteen such SDCs are carried by the E-3C, the number in use at any given time depending on mission requirements.

Above: Based at Offutt with SAC, the Boeing E-4 fleet is far more capable than the EC-135. Operating as vast command posts, the nation's top brass (including the President) would take to the air in time of war and control developments from there.

Below: Lockheed EC-130Qs serve with the US Navy's VQ-3 and VQ-4 on submarine communications and control. The operation is dubbed 'Tacamo' (take charge and move out), and the Hercules are expected to be replaced by the E-6 derivative of the E-3.

Maritime Reconnaissance

Few nations with a shoreline are not interested in monitoring the activities of vessels in (and under) their local waters. Those with a maritime tradition or large defensive commitments range farther afield to plot the shipping movements over vast tracts of ocean and keep a wary eye on a potential adversary. MR (Maritime Reconnaissance) is most efficiently accomplished by aircraft, whether it to be to watch the activities of nuclear missile-armed submarines or catch a small boatload of smugglers. Naturally, the aviation industry has aeroplanes available for both tasks, and to suit every intermediate need and pocket.

Since the earliest days of military flying, MR has been assigned to aeroplanes. Some small seaplanes were used by battleships to pinpoint the enemy and spot the fall of shot, but the forebears of today's large patrollers were the flying-boats which flew from coastal bases on medium-range sorties. During World War I, the UK scanned the North Sea with flying-boats and small dirigibles ('blimps') as a means of countering the German submarine and surface raider, the former being hampered in its activities when aircraft were in the vicinity.

Unreliable engines made the flying-boat hull a most welcome aspect of the MR aircraft during the time of pioneering. However, even when patrols could be almost guaranteed trouble-free the flying-boat remained a useful complement to the growing number of land-based MR aircraft because of its ability to land almost anywhere. The UK's last MR 'boats were not withdrawn from service until 1959, whilst in the USA jet power was investigated for such 'boats before land-

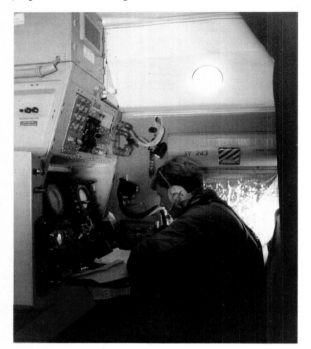

planes gained exclusivity. Now, there is only one large purpose-built MR flying boat in operation and a pair of amphibians (flying-boats with retractable landing gear, which allows them to land on runways) in limited employment.

This division between land and sea has resulted in the world's MR aircraft being assigned to either air forces or naval air arms, according to tradition (or even historical accident) in their owner countries. In the UK and many Commonwealth nations, the air force is responsible for land-based operations because the RAF retained the long-range surveillance task when it handed over the rest of the Fleet Air Arm to the Royal Navy in 1939. Elsewhere, notably the USA, navies have always controlled aeroplanes with maritime connections, although in Italy mixed-service crews fly aircraft officially belonging to the air force.

World War II confirmed the value to navies of the long-range patroller both for finding the enemy and for baulking submarine attacks on convoys. When Allied aircraft at last gained the ability to close the air cover

An important task of maritime aircraft is photographing enemy ships, especially in the melting pots of the Far East and Europe, where East and West clash regularly in the ocean wastes. Many aircraft, such aa this Nimrod, have special observation ports.

An important member of the modern MR crew is the ESM operator. Listening to enemy electronic activity, he is the key member during the radar silent approach to an enemy ship.

Right: This example of a Nimrod MR.Mk 2P is in the most up-to-date configuration, with inflight-refuelling probe and its associated ventral fin and wingtip Loral ESM pods.

Below: The RAF's Nimrod fleet is split between Kinloss in Scotland and St Mawgan in Cornwall. From opposite ends of the country, they are well placed to cover the Atlantic approaches and the vital North Sea oilfields. Fishery patrols and search and rescue missions are other duties for the force.

Left: The US Navy has 26 front-line P-3 Orion units, with several more in the reserve. They are divided between East and West coasts, and are seen regularly in other parts of the world, Japan, Diego Garcia and Iceland being notable.

Right: The US Navy's Orion fleet carry some of the brightest colours to be found on a warplane, but their cheerful schemes hide a deadly aircraft. Its submarine and ship detection systems are among the finest in the world, and it can carry a wide range of weapons including depth charges, torpedoes and the Harpoon anti-ship missile.

Silent approach

For anti-shipping duties, the Nimrod uses its ESM gear to home in on the ship's radar. Operating 'silently', the Nimrod does not employ its own radar as this would give its position away.

The ESM operator detects that the aircraft is entering the ship's radar lobe. Before the aircraft is spotted by the ship it dives out of the lobe. By repeating the procedure the aircraft can creep up on the ship undetected.

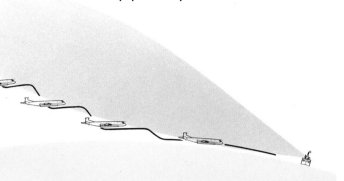

Above: Looking externally identical to the P-3 Orion, the Lockheed CP-140 Aurora is based on the same airframe but contains the anti-submarine detection gear of the S-3 Viking carrierborne ASW aircraft.

Maritime Reconnaissance

Above: Most common Soviet snooper intercepted by Western fighters is the Tu-142 'Bear-D'. This is a general-purpose maritime reconnaissance, strategic reconnaissance and mid-course missile targeting platform. The 'Big Bulge' radar under the fuselage is one of the largest fitted to an aircraft. This example receives a visit from a VF-142 'Ghostriders' F-14 during Atlantic operations.

Left: Primary Soviet anti-submarine patroller is the Tu-142 'Bear-F'. This version has a lengthened fuselage, a raised cockpit and usually has a magnetic anomaly detector (MAD) mounted on the top of the fin. Three fuselage bays hold a plethora of anti-sub weapons and sonobuoys and the aircraft can patrol for hours longer than any Western aircraft.

gap in mid-Atlantic, U-boat victories fell dramatically, the Allies being aided by the availability of increasingly efficient airborne sensors.

Today, peacetime appears to have little effect on the activities of NATO and Warsaw Pact MR aircraft. The US Navy attempts to monitor the movements of all Soviet naval vessels, surface and submarine, as a way of providing early warning of possible confrontation or conflict. Nuclear ballistic missile submarines generate the most interest, and some 60 per cent of these are based with the Northern Fleet around the Kola peninsula, and make their way into the Atlantic for patrols via the tip of Norway. Normally the level of deployment is around 15 per cent, and any increase in this proportion is a sure sign that East-West tensions are increasing.

In an example of co-ordinated action between allies,

Norway's Lockheed Orions locate submarines transiting the North Cape, then pass them to RAF BAe Nimrods or US and Netherlands navy Orions for continued surveillance. In association with other friendly nations, American forces watch the movements of the Baltic, Black Sea and Pacific Fleets of the USSR in a similar manner. Cuba provides a convenient base for reciprocal activities by Soviet MR aircraft watching the US eastern seaboard. Marxism's spread to other countries means that the South Atlantic can be observed from Angola, the Indian Ocean from South Yemeni territory, the Arabian Sea from Ethiopia, and the South China Sea from Vietnam.

Tupolev Tu-95 'Bear-B'

Smaller aircraft with less complex equipment suffice for those countries interested only in their immediate surroundings. With the development of offshore oilfields and concern for fish stocks, many countries are now declaring a 320-km (200-mile) exclusive economic zone which can be covered by appropriately converted light transports. Anti-smuggling operations are the forte of such aircraft, as are piracy patrols by the Thai naval air force using GAF Nomads for reconnaissance, backed by armed Summit/Cessna T-337SPs.

MRF and short-range MP (Maritime Patrol) aircraft have a valuable part to play in SAR (Search And Rescue) missions. Whilst only a few can now land on the

Complete with search radar in the nose and MAD sting in the tail, the Beriev Be-12 amphibian is a useful coastal ASW platform.

Refuelling probe
Most 'Bears' carry a probe to extend their time on patrol. A pipe takes the fuel back along the starboard fuselage into the central fuel system

Observation hatch
This is used for upwards observation and for astral navigation

Propellers
These are massive eight-blade contra-rotating units, with a diameter of 5.6 m (18.37 ft)

Nose radar
The giant 'Crown Drum' unit is used for surveillance and target acquisition

Soviet maritime patrol aircraft

Many versions of the Tupolev Tu-16 'Badger' exist, many of which are used for various maritime duties. This is a 'Badger-F', identified by the electronic intelligence pods carried on a pylon under each wing.

Myasishchev M-4 'Bison'

Span: 50.48 m (165 ft 7.5 in)
Length: 47.20 m (154 ft 10 in)
Height: 14.24 m (46 ft 0 in)
Speed: 998 km/h (620 mph)
Range: 10700 km (6,650 miles)
Ceiling: 13700 m (45,000 ft)
Armament: up to 10 NR.23 cannon; bomb bay can accommodate up to 15000 kg (33,068 lb)

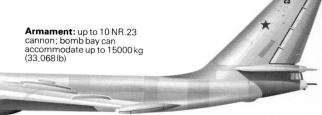

The venerable Myasishchev M-4 'Bison' is used for maritime reconnaissance duties in its 'Bison-B' and 'Bison-C' forms. Illustrated is the latter.

Tupolev Tu-16 'Badger-G'

Span: 32.93 m (108 ft 0.5 in)
Length: 34.80 m (114 ft 2 in)
Height: 10.80 m (35 ft 6 in)
Speed: 992 km/h (616 mph)
Range: 5800 m (3,600 miles)
Ceiling: 12300 m (40,350 ft)
Armament: seven NR-23 cannon, one fixed firing forward in nose; two 'Kelt' or 'Kitchen'

Nearly 90 'Badger-Gs' are employed by the Soviet navy for anti-ship and patrol duties. They carry the enormous AS-6 'Kingfish' missile.

Tupolev Tu-22 'Blinder-C'

Span: 23.75 m (78 ft 0 in)
Length: 40.53 m (132 ft 11.5 in)
Height: 10.67 m (35 ft 0 in)
Speed: 1480 km/h (920 mph) or Mach 1.4 at high level
Range: 6200 km (3,850 miles)
Ceiling: 18,300 m (60,000 ft)
Armament: single NR-23 in cannon; cameras and Elint gear in bomb bay

Serving mainly in the Black and Baltic Seas, the Tu-22 'Blinder-C' is a highly capable maritime reconnaissance platform.

Ilyushin Il-38 'May'

Span: 37.42 m (122 ft 9 in)
Length: 39.60 m (129 ft 10 in)
Height: 10.16 m (33 ft 4 in)
Speed: 645 km/h (400 mph)
Range: 7200 km (4,473 miles)
Ceiling: 10000 m (32,800 ft)
Armament: two weapons bays in fuselage for sonobuoys, torpedoes and depth charges

The Ilyushin Il-38 'May' ASW aircraft is a derivative of the Il-18 airliner. The massive radar installation has necessitated moving the wings forward.

Beriev Be-12 'Mail'

Span: 29.71 m (97 ft 6 in)
Length: 30.17 m (99 ft 0 in)
Height: 7.00 m (22 ft 11.5 in)
Speed: 608 km/h (378 mph)
Range: 7500 km (4,660 miles)
Ceiling: 11280 m (37,000 ft)
Armament: internal bay and external pylons for ASW weapons

Around 80 Be-12 'Mails' remain in service, but their ASW role has diminished, being employed for general coastal patrol and SAR duties.

Tupolev Tu-142 'Bear-C'

Span: 48.50 m (159 ft 0 in)
Length: 47.50 m (155 ft 0 in)
Height: 12.12 m (39 ft 9 in)
Speed: 925 km/h (575 mph)
Range: 12550 km (7,800 miles)
Ceiling: 13700 m (45,00 ft)
Armament: four or six NR-23 cannon; one 'Kangaroo' missile semi-recessed under fuselage; much Elint gear and maritime reconnaissance equipment

The mighty 'Bear' is the symbol of Soviet naval aviation, with slightly under a hundred aircraft in service. These are regularly intercepted by Western fighters as they attempt to observe NATO ships and snoop around territorial waters. All the navy's 'Bears' are employed for reconnaissance duties, but several can also carry large stand-off missiles. This is a 'Bear-C' multi-purpose patrol, Elint platform and missile carrier.

Dorsal turret
Twin 23-mm cannon are carried semi-recessed in the rear fuselage. These are remotely sighted

Rear turret
Twin 23-mm cannon are radar-controlled by the 'Box Tail' rear warning radar mounted above the turret

Antenna
This blister is believed to house a lateral-looking radar or other electronic gear

Air-to-surface missile
The giant AS-3 'Kangaroo' is carried semi-recessed under the centre fuselage

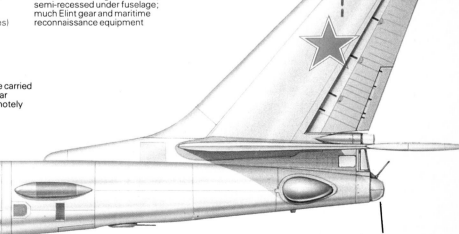

sea to rescue survivors (helicopters or ships must be used instead), they can respond quickly to an emergency call and find the exact site by radar with minimal delay. A small amount of survival equipment is carried on most MR and MP missions so that an aircraft can be diverted in mid-sortie to a humanitarian task. At base, a short-notice SAR stand-by is often maintained with more extensive gear such as large inflatable liferafts. Major rescue operations involving several ships and aircraft may be co-ordinated by an orbiting MR aircraft using its extensive communications links.

When surveying the ocean's vastness for a submarine which is trying its best not to be seen, the MR patroller needs all the assistance it can summon. The human eyeball still has a role to play in the age of modern electronics, but sophisticated equipment is able to augment it in quite remarkable ways. First to be taken into the air, during World War II, was radar. Useful for rapid surveillance of a large area from high altitude before a low-level visual check on selected targets, radar can also be used to catch submarines on the surface. Submarines are equipped with radar-warning devices, so the technique has been evolved of flying 'silently' for a time and then switching on the radar suddenly. Any plot on the screen which promptly disappears is likely to be an embarrassed submarine. The latest radars can measure the hull length of a target and are sufficiently precise to locate just a periscope at medium distance in rough seas.

Considerable stocks of sonobuoys are carried by the patroller to listen for the sound of submarines. Tubular devices some 124 mm (4.9 in) in diameter and up to 914 mm (36 in) long, sonobuoys are either passive (to listen silently for sounds without alerting the quarry) or active (to bounce sound waves off a silent object and so reveal its presence). Sonobuoys lower their microphones to the optimum depth for detection, bearing in mind that different oceanic conditions of temperature and salinity play curious tricks with sound. After laying a pattern of sonobuoys on a routine blind search or in response to an alert from other sensors, the aircraft receives signals transmitted from the surface for processing by its complex onboard computer equipment. After the noise of friendly vessels, whales and similar clutter has been discarded, it might be possible to identify even the class of a Soviet submarine by its 'sound signature'.

Other aids aboard the MR aircraft include Auto-

Keith Fretwell

Above: Spain is one of the countries that uses the Fokker F.27 as a maritime patrol aircraft. The type's good load-carrying ability and long endurance are admirably matched to the maritime job.

Below: Executive jets form a good basis for maritime patrol aircraft and such types as the Gulfstream III, Gates Learjet and Dassault-Breguet Falcon 20 have all been used. The latter has been ordered by the US Coast Guard.

Above: Brazil's indigenous maritime aircraft is the EMB-111 (air force designation P-95) conversion of the Bandeirante airliner. Rails under the wings can accommodate rockets.

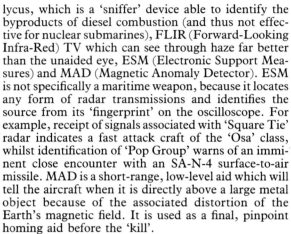

Left: Used for ASW and SAR duties, the Shin Meiwa PS-1 and US-1 flying boats are the last of their genre along with the Be-12. A wide variety of stores can be carried.

Below: The Dassault-Breguet Atlantic is in the service of MFG 3 for maritime patrol of the North Sea and Baltic.

Below right: The updated version of the Atlantic is called Atlantique, and will serve with the French navy. As well as updated reconnaissance equipment, the Atlantique can carry four Exocet anti-ship missiles.

lycus, which is a 'sniffer' device able to identify the byproducts of diesel combustion (and thus not effective for nuclear submarines), FLIR (Forward-Looking Infra-Red) TV which can see through haze far better than the unaided eye, ESM (Electronic Support Measures) and MAD (Magnetic Anomaly Detector). ESM is not specifically a maritime weapon, because it locates any form of radar transmissions and identifies the source from its 'fingerprint' on the oscilloscope. For example, receipt of signals associated with 'Square Tie' radar indicates a fast attack craft of the 'Osa' class, whilst identification of 'Pop Group' warns of an imminent close encounter with an SA-N-4 surface-to-air missile. MAD is a short-range, low-level aid which will tell the aircraft when it is directly above a large metal object because of the associated distortion of the Earth's magnetic field. It is used as a final, pinpoint homing aid before the 'kill'.

MR weaponry varies according to the attack strategy of the operating air arm. As a rule, the UK's Nimrods would attempt to destroy a submarine below the water but leave BAe Buccaneer attack aircraft to deal with a surface combat group which could shoot back. Since 1982, however, the RAF has joined other MR operators in making provision for carriage of an air-launched anti-ship weapon (McDonnell Douglas Harpoon) which can be released in excess of 92 km (57 miles) from the target, and thus from outside the engagement zone of its SAMs. Homing torpedoes are a prime MR weapon throughout the world, augmented sometimes by free-fall bombs, mines and depth-charges. The USN and RAF can use the B57 nuclear depth bomb of between 1 and 20 kilotons yield.

The USSR is likely to have comparable weapons, the most obvious of which is the AS-2 'Kipper' conventional warhead anti-ship cruise missile carried by the Tupolev Tu-16 'Badger-C'. Uniquely, the naval air force includes a heavy bomber arm with maritime strike responsibility, whose targets are located by both jet bombers converted for reconnaissance and the more usual type of patroller. Long-range MR is assigned to the Tupolev Tu-142 'Bear' and a few remaining Myasishchev M-4 'Bisons', augmented by the Ilyushin Il-38 'May' at medium distances and the Beriev M-12 'Mail' amphibian closer to land. The Mach 1.4 Tupolev Tu-22 'Blinder-C' is without doubt the world's fastest MR aircraft, although the even speedier Tu-22M 'Backfire' is part of the navy's strike force (and has no reconnaissance role).

Turboprop power is preferred for many MR aircraft as the most efficient means of cruising on patrol in the region of 390 km/h (242 mph). The disadvantage to jets (such as the UK's unique Nimrod MR.Mk 2) is that the turboprop has a slower transit speed from base to the operational area. Once on station, four-engined

Two Boeing 737 airliners have been supplied to Indonesia complete with SLAMMR (side-looking airborne multi-mission radar) pods mounted on the rear fuselage.

Dassault-Breguet Atlantic

Span: 37.70 m (123 ft 8 in)
Length: 32.62 m (107 ft 0 in)
Height: 10.80 m (35 ft 5 in)
Speed: 657 km/h (408 mph)
Ceiling: 9145 m (30,000 ft)
Armament: 3000 kg (6,600 lb) of

ASW stores carried internally and on wing pylons

Italy uses the Dassault-Breguet Atlantic for mounting patrols in the Mediterranean. They replaced S-2 Trackers.

Grumman S-2 Tracker

Span: 22.12 m (72 ft 7 in)
Length: 13.26 m (43 ft 6 in)
Height: 5.05 m (16 ft 7 in)
Speed: 426 km/h (265 mph)
Range: 2092 km (1,300 miles)
Armament: one depth charge

and sonobuoys carried internally; six wing pylons for torpedoes, bombs or rockets

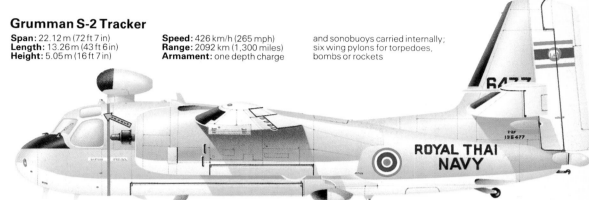

ROYAL THAI NAVY

One of the few remaining operators of the venerable Grumman S-2 Tracker is the Royal Thai Navy. This example is an S-2F.

aircraft can shut down up to two engines for fuel economy. Endurance is typically some 12 hours, limited by the onset of crew fatigue, so long-distance refuelled sorties of 19 hours by Nimrods in the Falklands war were highly unusual.

It should be borne in mind that the MR aircraft is merely a carrier for its sensor equipment and that updates can greatly improve its potential with few external clues. The Nimrod, Orion, Dassault-Breguet Atlantic and Lockheed (Kawasaki) P-2 Neptune have all been the subject of far-reaching internal changes, whilst the Lockheed CP-140 Aurora is an Orion airframe fitted with alternative avionics exclusively for Canada. Notably, the L-188 Electra airliner upon which the Orion is based is now being equipped for MR duties by the Argentine navy. Unique in another way, Japan's Shin Meiwa PS-1 is able to alight on the water and lower a sonar unit of the type normally seen dangling from a helicopter.

Lighter types

Bridging the gap between MP and MR is the Fokker Maritime Enforcer version of the F.27 Friendship transport. What is now a growing family of variants began with a coastal surveillance model equipped with search radar, and now embraces sub-hunting capability with sonobuoys and appropriate torpedoes and anti-ship missiles. Intended for shipboard operation, the Grumman S-2 Tracker is an older design still found in land-based service throughout the world, several of them recently refurbished. The ageing Grumman HU-16 Albatross is to find a fresh lease of life in Greek service after an update programme begun in 1986.

Search radar of various models is to be found beneath or prominently on the nose of many light twins, the former position having the advantage of constant 360° coverage. Executive jets such as the Dassault-Breguet Falcon 200, Gulfstream III and IAI Westwind have been modified, together with turboprops as diverse as the Beech Super King Air, CASA Aviocar, EMBRAER Bandeirante and GAF Nomad (Searchmaster), plus piston-engined Dornier 128-2s, Piaggio P.166s and Pilatus/Britten-Norman Islanders (Defenders). More are on the market or being offered by manufacturers, many of them with provision for light armament including rockets and machine-guns. Large converted transports in limited use for surface patrol and surveillance are the Lockheed C-130-MP Hercules and three Boeing 737 twin-jets fitted with side-looking radar for Indonesia.

Completing the maritime air picture, it must be recorded that some aircraft with little or no specialist equipment are assigned to sea reconnaissance roles as stopgaps and expedients. South Africa is using Douglas C-47 Dakotas for surveillance off the Cape of Good Hope after its last elderly Shackletons were withdrawn

Grumman HU-16 Albatross

Span: 29.46 m (96 ft 8 in)
Length: 18.67 m (61 ft 3 in)
Height: 7.87 m (25 ft 10 in)
Speed: 380 km/h (236 mph)
Range: 4345 km (2,700 miles)
Armament: depth charges

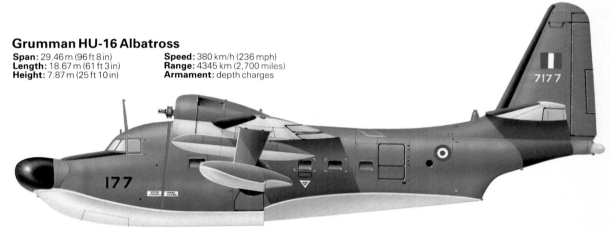

Greece is the last military operator of the Grumman HU-16 Albatross, and its aircraft are to receive turboprops to prolong life and improve performance.

Boeing 737 Surveiller

Span: 28.35 m (93 ft 0 in)
Length: 30.53 m (100 ft 2 in)
Height: 11.28 m (37 ft 0 in)
Speed: 856 km/h (532 mph)
Range: 4688 km (2,913 miles)
Ceiling: 12200 m (40,000 ft)
Armament: none

TNI-AU
INDONESIAN AIR FORCE

Indonesia's two Boeing 737s are employed for patrolling the myriad islands of that country. Lockheed C-130s are also used in this role.

in 1984, and Portugal assigns a normal transport C-130H Hercules to patrols in the Bay of Biscay, using only its limited search and weather radar. The RAF has given its fleet of target facilities BAC Canberras the task of visual maritime surveillance in an emergency such as the lead-up to war, yet does not envisage employing them as such in hostilities. Obviously, a broad spectrum of aircraft can undertake reconnaissance at sea, but as with most aspects of life, those demanding the best must pay the most.

Lockheed SP-2H Neptune

Span: 31.65 m (103 ft 10 in)
Length: 27.84 m (91 ft 4 in)
Height: 8.94 m (29 ft 4 in)
Speed: 649 km/h (403 mph)
Range: 5930 km (3,685 miles)
Armament: variations of 20-mm cannon, 12.7-mm machine guns, mines, torpedoes and depth charges

ARMADA

Argentina's Neptune fleet has been widely used for maritime purposes. Some were converted to electronic intelligence gatherers and were used in the Falklands.

Carrier Aircraft

If any diehard sailors continued to harbour the view during 1941 that the battleship was still the ruler of the oceans, their illusions were soon to be dispelled by the naval engagements in the Pacific between the USA and Japan. Most particularly, in May and June 1942, the Battles of the Coral Sea and Midway were fought by fleet aircraft, not big guns, and though the battleship retained a limited role, never again was it able to challenge the aircraft-carrier's versatility and long-range firepower.

During the years of comparative peace which have followed, the aircraft-carrier has consolidated its role in minor conflicts from Korea to Vietnam, and from Suez to Lebanon. In parallel, though almost all navies have been convinced of the type's worth, spiralling costs have resulted in membership of the 'carrier club' remaining almost static. If a carrier is defined as a vessel equipped with launch catapults and arrester wires, the total has diminished considerably as helicopters and the BAe Sea Harrier have given a useful potential to the smaller 'flat top'. Of those which have not dropped out of the club, the UK has abandoned its large-size carrier fleet in favour of the three 'Invincible' class vessels, popularly termed 'Harrier-carriers'.

The aircraft-carrier is built and equipped (as far as funding will allow) to reflect the duties of its parent service and, through that, its government. There are essentially but two types of navy: the one responsible for defence and the other force additionally tasked with power projection over the world's oceans. Smaller ships with restricted aircraft complements suffice for the former duty, but the latter demands a gigantic investment. Only the USA possesses a carrier force equal to the task of patrolling the globe, yet Soviet aspirations in this direction are clear.

Having taken upon itself the responsibility for defending its own interests, and those of its allies, on the high seas and the land bordering them, the USA has developed a fleet currently totalling 14 aircraft-carriers, mostly nuclear-powered. In order to accomplish missions in differing circumstances, the balance between aircraft types is variable within the typical limit of about 70 aeroplanes and 16 helicopters. Most importantly, however, the carrier must have the ability to embark a balanced force so that it can respond to all conceivable threats to itself and still have the excess capacity available for offensive operations. In the US Navy this means virtually a different type of aircraft for every duty: air defence, light attack, medium attack, anti-submarine warfare (medium-range with aeroplanes), anti-submarine warfare (short-range with helicopters), airborne early warning and COD (Carrier Onboard Delivery). Adaptations of the basic type additionally perform reconnaissance, electronic warfare and inflight-refuelling roles.

To state the obvious, carrierborne aircraft are diffe-

Above: Combining the strike role of the Vought A-7 with admirable air defence qualities, the McDonnell Douglas F/A-18 Hornet is a true multi-purpose aircraft.

Right: Carrierborne ASW coverage for the US Navy is handled by the Lockheed S-3 Viking. The new S-3B adds Harpoon anti-ship missile capability to its already extensive repertoire.

rent from their land-based brethren, to the extent that certain firms have traditionally specialized in their design. Grumman and McDonnell (Douglas) in the USA are typical examples now that British firms like Blackburn and Fairey have disappeared.

A prime requirement for a naval aircraft is its speed, though not the maximum, as may be at first thought, but rather the minimum. A land pilot viewing 3200 m (3,500 yards) of concrete runway will not be unduly concerned if a new aircraft has a landing speed of a few knots higher than its predecessor, but a carrier pilot attempting to catch an arrester wire on a heaving deck will call for the slowest possible approach. Great care has always been taken with the design of high-lift devices on carrier aircraft, with the typical result that (to take the example of the USAF and USN air-superiority fighters) the McDonnell Douglas F-15 Eagle approaches its airfield at 232 km/h (144 mph), whereas the heavier Grumman F-14 Tomcat is 19 km/h (12 mph) slower onto the deck.

Further complexities are introduced by the need to fold wings for stowage below – doubly if headroom is restricted. The landing gear must be robust enough for the 'firm' arrival on deck which is normal in carrier operations, and the whole airframe needs to be built to withstand the rigours of repeated catapult launches and arrested landings. The result is a weight penalty clearly demonstrated by the proposed Northrop F/A-18L land-based version of the McDonnell Douglas F/A-18A Hornet: at empty weight, the seagoing Hornet is over 1000 kg (2,205 lb) heavier than if it were to undertake the same fighter/attack role on land. Further tax-

Left: Despite the penalties of deck operations, the Grumman F-14 Tomcat is still among the world's finest fighters, and is certainly the most versatile, being able to bring to bear three types of missile and a gun on any airborne adversary. The most capable of the missiles is the Hughes AIM-54 Phoenix which is integrated with the Tomcat's AWG-9 radar. Together, this weapons system can track and kill six targets flying from 50 to 100,000 feet at ranges out to 100 miles. Here a VF-114 'Aardvarks' aircraft looses off a Phoenix during live trials.

Right: The British Aerospace Sea Harrier is an expedient method of putting capable airpower to sea without the need for large carriers. Proving itself in the Falklands, the Sea Harrier can perform both the fighter role needed for fleet defence and limited air-to-ground raids. This aircraft carries four Sidewinders: the FRS.Mk 2 version being developed will be AMRAAM-capable with look-down/shoot-down.

Carrier Aircraft

Left: The Soviet answer to the Sea Harrier is the Yakovlev Yak-38 'Forger'. This useful type cannot perform as well as the Sea Harrier as it has to carry two lift engines which are only used during STOVL operations. Anti-ship attack and limited air defence are its main roles.

Above: The Dassault-Breguet Super Etendard gained fame during the Falklands war as the launch vehicle for the Exocet missiles which sank British ships. The French navy uses the Super Etendard/Exocet combination from its two carriers *Clemenceau* and *Foch*.

ing the naval aircraft designer is the need to squeeze a quart into a pint pot, so that (say) submarine-hunting patrol from carrier decks is undertaken by the Lockheed S-3A Viking, whilst the same firm's far larger P-3 Orion does an identical job from the land.

The Soviet navy, as a logical progression of its rapid expansion from a coastal defence force, deployed the first of four 'Kiev' class ASW carriers in 1976, these being at some 38,000 tons only half the size of a typical US counterpart. Comparable in many ways to the UK's new carrier force, they have a complement of just 12 Yakovlev Yak-38 'Forgers' and up to 19 Kamov Ka-27 'Helix' helicopters. The gap between the air assets of the world's two greatest navies is still immense, although plans to narrow it are evident from the result of Western surveillance. A 65,000-ton nuclear-powered carrier is on the stocks at a Black Sea shipyard, to

be equipped with an angled flight deck, catapults and arrester wires, whilst deck operation evaluation is being conducted of the MiG-27 'Flogger', Mig-29 'Fulcrum', Su-25 'Frogfoot' and Su-27 'Flanker'.

Which of these (if any), and in what combination, are employed on the new Soviet carrier remains to be seen. If the present trend amongst carrier-owning nations is followed, dual-role capability will be preferred as a means of effectively doubling the number of fast jets on board under certain circumstances. Financial limits on the size of vessel to be built and the number of different aircraft types required for development has forced both the UK and France to condense fighter and attack roles in a single airframe. Admittedly, an 'Invincible' carrier with a wartime complement of up to a dozen Sea Harriers is unable to defend itself with 12 at the same time as dispatching 12 to attack enemy

targets. What it can do, however, is to allocate the greater proportion to attack when intelligence suggests that the ship is safe from retaliation, then reverse the balance when an enemy raid is expected. This is far from an ideal solution, but better than the alternative of opting out of the carrier business.

For the reasons outlined above, the only purpose-designed air-superiority fighter in general service is the Grumman F-14 Tomcat. Capable of all-weather flying (which is not exactly the same as all-weather carrier operation), the Tomcat is equipped with a sophisticated radar and the associated Hughes AIM-54 Phoenix AAM. Phoenix has the record-breaking range of over 200 km (124 miles), is the only active-radar AAM currently in Western service, and has a price tag appropriate to these attributes. One of the Tomcat's predecessors, the LTV F-8 Crusader, continues to defend France's two aircraft-carriers, but with the considerably shorter-range IR-homing Matra R.550 Magic AAM or older models of the AIM-9 Sidewinder.

Dual-role fighter/attack aircraft include the US McDonnell Douglas F-4 Phantom in decreasing numbers and the F/A-18 Hornet in correspondingly larger quantity. The US Marine Corps is the main Phantom user, even though it has a few squadrons recently converted to Hornets. Navy units may use the aircraft for air defence or light attack, in which latter case it is an alternative to the LTV A-7E Corsair. Suited only for attack, the Corsair has its US Marine parallels in the McDonnell Douglas A-4 Skyhawk and BAe/McDonnell Douglas Harrier. Popular despite its age, the Skyhawk is also the main general-purpose attack aircraft of the Argentine navy, despite losses whilst operating from land in the 1982 Falklands war. Argentina and, of course, France, fly the Dassault-Breguet Super Etendard interceptor and strike/attack aircraft from their carriers, and the latter also uses the first-generation Dassault Etendard IV for operational photo-reconnaissance, plus pilot training. Pending service entry of an RF-18 Hornet, the USN's reconnaissance needs are

Above: Vought's diminutive A-7E Corsair II, affectionately dubbed the 'Fruit Fly', still serves on the majority of the US Navy's carriers as a light attack aircraft. Due to be replaced eventually by the McDonnell Douglas F/A-18 Hornet, the A-7 has provided nearly 20 years of excellent service.

Below: Onboard ASW protection of the carrier battle group is handled by the Lockheed S-3 Viking. Principal sub-hunting sensors are sonobuoys carried in the bottom of the fuselage and dispensed via a series of tubes, and a retractable MAD sting, here seen deployed.

Grumman F-14 Tomcat

Radar
The Hughes AWG-9 radar is integrated with the Phoenix missile as an unequalled weapons system in terms of long range and multi-target capability

Cannon
For close-in work, the F-14 carries a six-barrelled rotary 20-mm M61 Vulcan cannon

Cockpit
As well as the pilot, the F-14 carries a radar intercept officer in the rear seat to operate the AWG-9 radar and to warn of other aircraft

Infra-red
This is an extremely sensitive infra-red detector for detecting aircraft beyond visual range

Phoenix missile
The AIM-54 missile has a range in excess of 160 km (100 miles). Maximum load is six

Yakovlev Yak-38 'Forger'

Span: 7.32 m (24 ft 0 in)
Length: 15.50 m (50 ft 10.25 in)
Height: 4.37 m (14 ft 4 in)

Speed: 1009 km/h (627 mph)
Range: 740 km (460 miles)
Ceiling: 12000 m (39,375 ft)

Armament: up to 2600 kg (5,730 lb) of stores including gun pods, AS-7 'Kerry' ASMs, rockets, bombs and AA-8 'Aphid' AAMs

The Yakovlev Yak-38 'Forger-A' serves aboard the Soviet navy's aircraft carriers. A two-seat trainer version 'Forger-B' also exists.

British Aerospace Sea Harrier

Span: 7.70 m (25 ft 3 in)
Length: 14.50 m (47 ft 7 in)
Height: 3.71 m (12 ft 2 in)

Speed: Mach 0.85
Range: 1500 m (920 miles)
Ceiling: 15600 m (51,200 ft)

Armament: usually two 30-mm Aden cannon and four Sidewinder or Magic AAMs; bombs, rockets, Harpoon or Sea Eagle can be carried; AIM-120 AMRAAM will be fitted

India is the only export customer so far for the excellent BAe Sea Harrier. These fly from the carrier *Vikrant*.

Vought F-8 Crusader

Span: 10.72 m (35 ft 2 in)
Length: 16.61 m (54 ft 6 in)
Height: 4.80 m (15 ft 9 in)

Speed: 1802 km/h (1,120 mph) at high level
Range: 1770 km (1,100 miles)
Ceiling: 17680 m (58,000 ft)
Armament: four 20-mm cannon.

Sidewinder, Magic or R530 AAMs for air-to-air operations; Zuni rockets, bombs or Bullpup missiles for air-to-ground

France protects its two carriers with the veteran Vought F-8E (FN) Crusader. These highly-capable yet outdated fighters can carry the Matra R530 missile.

McDonnell Douglas F/A-18 Hornet

Span: 11.43 m (37 ft 6 in)
Length: 17.07 m (56 ft 0 in)
Height: 4.66 m (15 ft 3.5 in)

Speed: Mach 1.8 at high level
Range: 3706 km (2,300 miles)
Ceiling: 15240 m (50,000 ft)

Armament: one M61 six-barrelled 20-mm cannon; 7710 kg (17,000 lb) of stores can include AIM-9 Sidewinder and AIM-7 Sparrow AAMs, bombs, rockets, Harpoon missiles, or extra fuel tanks

The two-seat version of the F/A-18A Hornet is used for conversion and continuation training, while retaining full combat capability.

Grumman F-14A Tomcat

Span: 19.54 m (64 ft 1.5 in) wings spread
Length: 19.10 m (62 ft 8 in)
Height: 4.88 m (16 ft 0 in)

Speed: Mach 2.34 at high level
Range: 3220 km (2,000 miles)
Ceiling: 15240 m (50,000 ft)
Armament: one M61 20-mm six-

barrelled cannon; usual mixed air-to-air load is four AIM-54 Phoenix, two AIM-7 Sparrow and two AIM-9 Sidewinder; air-to-ground stores can be carried

The Grumman F-14A Tomcat fulfils the air defence role on most US carriers, usually operating in concert with the Grumman E-2 Hawkeye AEW aircraft. This aircraft is from VF-143 'Pukin' Dogs', which saw limited action over Beirut while based on USS *Dwight D. Eisenhower*. It is depicted with a general air defence load, with an AIM-7F Sparrow and AIM-9L Sidewinder on each wing pylon and four AIM-54 Phoenix missiles under the fuselage. During combat, the wing sweep is automatically controlled by computer to give the optimum performance and airflow characteristics.

Wing pylons
These can carry a Phoenix missile, but usually carry one Sparrow and Sidewinder each

Ventral fins
These provide extra longitudinal stability at high angles of attack and low speed

With the specific task of covering beach assaults and protecting the beach-head, the US Marine Corps has procured the McDonnell Douglas/BAe AV-8C Harrier. Flying from the same amphibious assault ships that launch the beach assault, the Harriers are part of a highly capable total fighting machine.

being met by pod-equipped Tomcats and USMC RF-4B Phantoms.

The potential of BAe's Sea Harrier was demonstrated in unequivocal fashion in combat with Argentine fighters and fighter-bombers during 1982. The aircraft is closely linked to the British decision to maintain a diminished carrier force, and to Indian plans to retain its own vessel and possibly acquire a second. Italy has recently commissioned a ship purpose-built for the aircraft and is pursuing plans for an order. Spain bought the same first-generation (land) AV-8A Harrier as the US Marines and will follow that force in operating the much updated McDonnell Douglas AV-8B Harrier II. Harrier variants must be carefully distinguished, for only the Sea Harrier has radar and a limited all-weather air-defence capability with Sidewinders, the other being configured for attack.

When updated in the late 1980s with look-down/shoot-down radar and associated Hughes AIM-120 AAMs, the Sea Harrier will be considerably more potent in the interception role and retain the advantage that it can sometimes operate when conventional car-

Carrier Aircraft

McDonnell Douglas AV-8B

Span: 9.25 m (30 ft 4 in)
Length: 14.12 m (46 ft 4 in)
Height: 3.55 m (11 ft 8 in)

Speed: 1041 km/h (647 mph)
Range: 3929 km (2,441 miles)
Ceiling: 15240 m (50,000 ft)

Armament: one 25-mm, five-barrelled cannon; up to 7710 kg (17,000 lb) of air-to-air and air-to-ground stores, including Sidewinders, Mavericks and LGBs

The McDonnell Douglas AV-8B Harrier II has greatly increased all-round performance and load-carrying ability over the original version, and is currently in service with the USMC.

Dassault-Breguet Super Etendard

Span: 9.60 m (31 ft 6 in)
Length: 14.31 m (46 ft 11.4 in)
Height: 3.86 m (12 ft 8 in)

Speed: 1204 km/h (748 mph)
Range: 1300 km (808 miles)
Ceiling: 13700 m (45,000 ft)

Armament: two 30-mm DEFA cannon internally; one AN52 nuclear bomb, one Exocet missile or Magic AAMs; conventional stores to 2100 kg (4,630 lb)

Although not operating from a carrier during the Falklands campaign, Argentina's Dassault-Breguet Super Etendards stamped their mark on the conflict by sinking two British ships.

McDonnell Douglas A-4 Skyhawk

Span: 8.38 m (27 ft 6 in)
Length: 12.29 m (40 ft 4 in)
Height: 4.57 m (15 ft 0 in)

Speed: 1040 km/h (646 mph)
Range: 3219 km (2,000 miles)
Armament: two 20-mm cannon;

wide variety of stores, including nuclear bombs, rockets, ASMs and fuel tanks can be carried

Having seen service aboard the US Navy's carriers for many years, Argentina is the last seaborne user of the McDonnell Douglas A-4 Skyhawk.

rier aircraft are 'grounded' by adverse weather. The Sea Harrier is already far in advance of the non-radar Yak-38 'Forger', which relies on the old and inefficient system of separate lifting and forward-propulsion jets. It will be interesting to see if a 'Super Forger' is produced for the Soviets' big carrier, or even as a replacement for the current equipment.

Only the US Navy flies the heavy-attack Grumman A-6 Intruder and maritime reconnaissance Lockheed S-3A Viking. The previous Grumman S-2 Tracker is now the sole type of aeroplane to fly from Brazil's aircraft-carrier, whilst France and India still employ the ageing Breguet Alizé, in updated form in the case of the French Aéronavale. Again unique to the US in a naval context, Grumman's E-2 Hawkeye casts an airborne radar eye over the fleet to provide early warning of approaching aircraft as a parallel to the duties of the land-based Boeing E-3A Sentry AWACS and BAe Nimrod AEW.Mk 3. The US Navy even has a dedicated electronic jamming aircraft: the Grumman EA-6B Prowler, which is a considerably modified A-6 Intruder. Occasionally (and especially during an exercise) one of the USN's last remaining Douglas ERA-3B Skywarriors can be found operating in the electronic role from carrier decks.

The EKA-3B versions of the Skywarrior, which is the heaviest aircraft cleared for catapult/arrester operation, serve as tankers in the Naval Air Reserve, complementing KA-6D Intruders of the regular force. In France, it is the photo-reconnaissance Etendard IVP which has a secondary refuelling role with a 'buddy' pack assisting a few Super Etendards thus capable. Such a facility is of great importance at sea, when a combat aircraft's maximum take-off weight may be above catapult limits. Accordingly, attack aircraft can

Left: Carrier onboard delivery is the role for the Grumman C-2 Greyhound, flying from shore to ship with supplies and mail. The return journey takes back mail and crew needing hospitalization.

Below left: The McDonnell Douglas RF-18 is set to take over from TARPS pod-equipped Tomcats as the photo-reconnaissance element on board the US Navy's carriers.

Below: One of the most important types to be found on the US carriers is the Grumman EA-6B Prowler. This is a dedicated electronic warfare platform which can provide massive jamming power. This can be utilized in two principal ways: one is to accompany strike aircraft when they go on a mission to protect them, and the other is to electronically 'hide' the carrier from enemy radars.

Above: Still serving in small numbers and all but replaced by the larger C-2, the Grumman C-1 Trader is a COD version of the well-known S-2 Tracker carrierborne ASW aircraft.

Right: Carrier operations place an extraordinary strain on aircraft structures. This F-14 has just caught the arrester wire.

Left: The venerable Breguet Alizé still provides ASW coverage for the two French carriers *Clemenceau* and *Foch*. This aircraft also serves from the Indian carrier *Vikrant*.

be launched with maximum bombload and low fuel, then refuelled almost immediately afterwards. Naturally, the tanker is also available for a second or subsequent 'hook-up' if extreme range is demanded, and each attack squadron will include four KA-6s in addition to its A-6Es.

Finally, the COD aircraft is a combination of bumboat, liberty boat and admiral's barge. Morale at sea (not to mention operational efficiency) is improved by regular communications with the shore and allied carriers to bring mail and permit other privileges. Only the USN has the purpose-built Grumman C-2 Greyhound and the almost obsolete Grumman C-1 Trader for this task.

Naval aircraft weaponry is identical in almost all respects to their land-based compatriots. Fighters use the same AAMs for interception (there is nothing specifically naval about the Tomcat's Phoenix, despite its unique application) and attack aircraft employ bombs and rockets for missions against land targets and less heavily defended naval forces. There is, however, a preference for the anti-ship missile to confer stand-off capability, and the US complements the considerable all-weather potential of the Intruder with the McDonnell Douglas Harpoon. Equivalents elsewhere are Britain's BAe Sea Eagle (Sea Harrier), France's Aérospatiale AM.39 Exocet (Super Etendard), and the USSR's AS-7 'Kerry' (Yak-38 'Forger'). US Marine Corps needs for offensive support on the beach-head differ in some respects, so that the Harrier II is equipped to fire Hughes Maverick ASMs against high-value targets as well as dispense cluster and laser-guided bombs. Without doubt, the modern carrier is a veritable floating air force.

Above: Grumman's A-6 Intruder has served on the carriers as a heavy attack aircraft for years, and service is planned beyond the year 2000, thanks to constant update programmes.

Left: A Grumman E-2C traps aboard USS *America*, illustrating the size of this aircraft. The powerful turboprops and efficient wings make carrier operations with such a large aircraft relatively easy.

Below: Overview of an E-2C shows the size of the radome on the back of the aircraft. VAW-123 surely has the largest unit markings currently flying.

Naval Helicopters

The military helicopter is but half the age of the aeroplane, yet has become so firmly established in naval roles that it to some extent governs the evolution of the surface fleet and seaborne strategy. A helicopter platform and hangarage are items of warship design which are now taken as much for granted as were the cannon ports and rigging of an earlier age. Helicopters have replaced fixed-wing aircraft on certain duties as well as making new areas of operation possible, so that the need has been reduced for naval aeroplanes and the costly carriers from which they operate.

Special problems associated with the development of rotary-winged flight were not solved until the eve of World War II. Helicopters were wearing military markings by the time that conflict ended, and had landed aboard ships for trials purposes, the tasks restricted to SAR (Search And Rescue) and communications. For once, it was not an inability on the part of non-airmen to appreciate aviation potential which was to blame. The admirals had rapidly realized that the helicopter was an ideal adjunct to the destroyer in ASW (Anti-Submarine Warfare), and the hold-up was that it could not lift a worthwhile load of weapons.

War in Korea established the helicopter as an invaluable aid for rescuing downed pilots and evacuating casualties, whilst further developments on the R&D front saw the previously minimal margin steadily increase between empty and maximum weights. A major triumph was the fitment of sonar at this time and the associated carriage of torpedoes though not, at first, simultaneously. Naturally, the world's principal navies were the first to exploit the helicopter, flying it from the large numbers of carriers they had built for World War II. As the vessels grew old and governments baulked at the notion of one-for-one replacement, the frigate-based helicopter became extremely attractive. The UK, for example, having built an aircraft (the Short Seamew) to fly from carriers to deliver a torpedo at a spot selected by a destroyer's sonar, found that a helicopter operating from a platform welded onto the ship's stern would do equally well.

Today's naval helicopters are the descendants of those early days. As they have become larger (within the constraints of shipboard stowage) so avionics and weaponry have become more compact, masking the considerable increase in combat potential achieved in recent years. Not all are equipped with the full range of detection equipment and armament because their mode of employment, and the opponents they will meet, change from country to country.

Addressing the priorities for naval helicopter design in a logical order, the first aspect demanding consideration is the landing gear. Operation from shore bases creates no problems, yet landing upon the moving deck of an aircraft-carrier can cause some problems for the inexperienced. The large carrier wallows slowly in a high swell, compared with the more rapid gyrations of a destroyer's stern, and if the helicopter is to operate (bearing in mind that submarines are hardly inconvenienced by storms) special techniques are needed. It may at first seem strange that most naval helicopters have wheels instead of skids (the Agusta-Bell AB.212ASW is one exception) so increasing the risks of them rolling off the small stern platform. However, wheels are convenient for manoeuvring the helicopter into its hangar, a procedure often accomplished by manpower alone

Above: Among the smaller anti-submarine warfare helicopters is the Agusta-Bell AB.212ASW, which is used by several nations for this task. As well as a dunking sonar, it carries a search radar above the cabin.

Right: Principal transport helicopter for the US Marine Corps is the Boeing Vertol CH-46E Sea Knight. This type is found in large numbers aboard the amphibious assault craft of the US Navy, and is used for moving the Marines ashore and resupplying the beach-head. Sweden also uses the type from land bases for anti-submarine work.

and using strops and deck lashing points to prevent a disastrous breakaway.

A helicopter such as the Westland Lynx has a harpoon-like device protruding underneath its fuselage, which engages a metal grille set into the deck. Wheels are toed-in to permit the helicopter to pivot into the wind so that there is no need to change the ship's course. For take-off, full upward thrust is selected, then the harpoon released, resulting in a spectacularly rapid and safe departure whatever the deck is doing. Landing requires the pilot to judge the deck movement although, once down, the harpoon ensures that the Lynx stays down.

Canadian Sikorsky Sea Kings use a system known as the Beartrap which gives even greater foul-weather capability. Hovering a safe distance above the deck, the helicopter drops a lanyard and then draws up cable into its belly. With full thrust selected, the cable remains taut at all times as the Sea King is drawn onto the pitching deck by a winch. On touchdown a protruding harpoon is grasped in the manner of an animal trap, and the framework containing the jaws is winched on sunken rails into the hangar, taking the helicopter with it. The system, also bought by Italy, India and Japan, thus has the additional advantage of dispensing with manhandling.

Further aspects of naval helicopter design include a preference for two engines: indeed, single-engined Kaman SH-2A/B Seasprites were modified to this stan-

dard during service. Other types have boat-type hulls which allow them to alight on calm water, and many more are equiped with compressed-air flotation bags which inflate in an emergency.

Left: The Westland Lynx can perform all the tasks asked of a naval helicopter, including ASW, vertrep and missile guidance. For the anti-ship role, the Lynx can carry four BAe Sea Skua missiles.

Above: Latest version of the successful Sea Stallion family is the CH-53E, which adds a third engine for vastly increased lifting power. The type has been adopted by both the US Navy and Marine Corps, the former operating several MH-53E specialist mine countermeasures aircraft alongside CH-53E (illustrated) heavylift aircraft.

Above right: The trusty Sikorsky SH-3H serves on board the carriers of the US Navy for short-range ASW protection of the carrier battle group. It can carry torpedoes and depth charges for 'killing' subs and uses a dunking sonar to detect them. Search and rescue is another important task.

Right: France's major naval helicopter is the Aérospatiale Super Frelon, which conducts lift, ASW and SAR duties. One important task of the Frelon fleet is to ensure that French submarines leave port for their patrols without being followed by Soviet subs. Anti-ship capability comes in the form of the Exocet missile, seen here in a test firing.

Aérospatiale HH-65 Dolphin
Rotor diameter: 11.93 m (39 ft 2 in)
Length: 11.44 m (37 ft 6.5 in)
Height: 4.01 m (13 ft 2 in)
Speed: 280 km/h (174 mph)
Range: 880 km (546 miles)
Ceiling: 4575 m (15,000 ft)
Armament: none

Left: The most common form of submarine detection available to the helicopter is the dunking sonar. Seen here demonstrated by a Royal Australian Navy Sea King, the sonar is lowered into the water during a hover. These are active sonars, producing their own sound waves which bounce off a submarine and return to the sonar.

The US Coast Guard has adopted the Aérospatiale Dauphin II as its standard search and rescue helicopter, under the designation HH-65A Dolphin. For its role, it carries advanced avionics and detection gear, such as forward-looking infra-red.

Left: Principal helicopter aboard the ships of the US Navy is the Kaman SH-2F Seasprite. Slowly being replaced by the Sikorsky SH-60, the Seasprite is used for a variety of tasks, including ASW, cross-decking and SAR. This example is seen picking up a man overboard, using yellow dye to pinpoint his position.

Right: The Sikorsky Sea King and its Westland-built cousins are widely used around the world, performing anti-submarine work from both ship and shore. Canada's aircraft are employed for this task, keeping coastal waters clear from intruders.

Kamov Ka-25 'Hormone'

Rotor diameter: 15.74 m (51 ft 8 in)
Length: 9.75 m (32 ft 0 in)

Height: 5.37 m (17 ft 7.5 in)
Speed: 220 km/h (136 mph)
Range: 650 km (405 miles)

Ceiling: 3500 m (11,500 ft)
Armament: two torpedoes or nuclear depth charges for ASW missions

Kamov Ka-27 'Helix'

Rotor diameter: 15.90 m (52 ft 2 in)
Length: 11.30 m (37 ft 1 in)

Height: 5.40 m (17 ft 8.5 in)
Speed: 250 km/h (155 mph)
Range: 800 km (497 miles)

Ceiling: 600 m (19,685 ft)
Armament: torpedoes and nuclear depth dombs for ASW missions

Left: Kamov's Ka-25 'Hormone' helicopter has served on Soviet ships for years, employed in a similar way to Western helicopters. Specialist SAR and missile guidance versions exist.

Right: Replacing the Ka-25 on the larger ships is the more advanced Ka-27 'Helix'. This retains the co-axial rotor design, which allows the aircraft to fit into tight spaces on deck without the need for folding rotor blades.

Sensor equipment available to the ASW helicopter is similar in most respects to that of the maritime reconnaissance aircraft. There are radar, ESM (Electronic Support Measures) MAD (Magnetic Anomaly Detector) which is towed from a cable-drum, and the sonobuoy in its various types. In addition, the highly descriptive epithet 'dunking sonar' refers to the large listening device which can be lowered from a hovering helicopter into the water. This has its own onboard processing equipment and associated monitoring personnel. Furthermore, larger helicopters (and now, even some of medium size) carry consoles for interpreting signals from the sonobuoys they have laid, so achieving considerable autonomy from their parent vessel.

Lighter helicopters may have one or two sensors, but not the complete range, or they may forego some equipment in favour of armament. In this connection, it is of interest to note how frigate-based helicopters of the Royal Navy have become more complex in the passing of a single generation. When the Westland Wasp entered service in 1963, its principal combat function was to transport torpedoes from the ship to the vicinity of a suspected submarine. The Westland Lynx, which began to replace it from 1978 onwards, has radar, long-range anti-ship missiles, ESM and MAD. Some export Lynxes are also equipped with dunking sonar, and all this in an airframe slightly shorter than that of the Wasp.

Further naval helicopter roles, often accomplished with distinct subvariants, include ASV (Anti-Surface Vessel) attack, which is usually with missiles. Helicopters may also provide mid-course guidance for missiles launched from friendly ships hiding below the horizon of their target. Some Soviet helicopters have models optimized for this task with the appropriate radar and data links. Minesweeping is a role for the most powerful helicopters (including land-based, twin-rotor types) because of the requirement to tow heavy sleds and cables through the water. Since 1982 the UK has possessed a unique airborne early warning helicopter, the Westland Sea King AEW.Mk 2, to undertake vital duties previously assigned to specialist fixed-wing carrier aircraft. Finally, vertrep (vertical replenishment) at sea, SAR and medevac are general purpose tasks suited to almost any helicopter.

Throughout the West, the Mk 44 and newer Mk 46 homing torpedoes are by far the most common weapons employed in helicopter ASW, although the UK has deployed its Stingray since 1983 (pre-production versions of the last-mentioned seeing service in the 1982 Falklands War). Depth charges (such as the UK's Mk 11) are also available, but the greatest expansion has been in the area of air-launched anti-ship missiles.

Mil Mi-14 'Haze'

Rotor diameter: 21.29 m (69 ft 10 in)
Length: 25.30 m (83 ft 0 in)
Height: 6.90 m (22 ft 8 in)
Speed: 230 km/h (143 mph)
Range: 800 km (497 miles)
Ceiling: 4500 m (14,760 ft)
Armament: torpedoes and depth charges carried internally in the bottom of the hull

Shore-based ASW for the Soviet navy is carried out by the Mil Mi-14 'Haze'. This derivation of the Mi-8 transport carries a towed MAD 'bird' behind the main cabin. Despite its boat-shaped hull, amphibious capability is very limited.

Where once the wire-guided Nord/Aérospatiale AS.11 and AS.12 were the most potent such weapons available, Western naval helicopters now can choose from a range including the BAe Sea Skua and Sea Eagle, McDonnell Douglas Harpoon, Aérospatiale AM.39 Exocet and AS.15TT, OTO-Melara/Matra Otomat, and Sistel/Oto-Melara Marte. Other types of ASM are not suitable because they require a launch speed greater than that which can be achieved by a helicopter, although the Sea Eagle was in this category until optional booster rockets were devised.

Of all naval helicopters in current service, the Sikorsky Sea King is perhaps the best known. Additionally produced under licence in three countries, it has acted as a vehicle for different avionics suites, according to customers' specifications. Comparatively large for a naval helicopter, it flies from US Navy aircraft-carriers, whilst Kaman Seasprites are assigned to the smaller vessels from ASW and ASST (Anti-Ship Surveillance and Targeting). The Sikorsky SH-60B Seahawk is in prospect to replace the Seasprite and (probably later) the Sea King, but Anglo-Italian plans in the latter instance hinge on the European Helicopters EH-101. In the USSR, Kamov supplies the ship-based rotary-wing equipment and Mil's Mi-14 is employed in coastal roles from land bases.

Accompanying the purpose-designed naval helicopters are a plethora of converted civilian types, some (like the Agusta-Bell AB.212ASW) heavily modified, but others featuring minimum additions. Even the small Hughes 500 is employed, typically by the Spanish navy, for which it carries a single homing torpedo and MAD. Though basic, this equipment is quite sufficient to dispatch a submarine if the helicopter has been given its approximate position by other means. Once, only the aircraft-carrier and battleship had their own aviation support; now, even patrol boats may have a miniature air arm.

Attack Helicopters

As one of the most recent types of combat aircraft to evolve, the purpose-designed attack helicopter is a weapon which entered service only two decades ago. Closely associated with army aviation, it has already established itself firmly in the ranks of current users and is the object of study and development by those as yet lacking its unique attributes. Several European armies and those of the USSR and its allies are to receive helicopters optimized for battlefield attack roles within the next few years, as the USA progresses with its second-generation models. It is convenient to refer to all helicopters with an offensive role as being assigned to attack, but few of these are aircraft designed from the outset for the task they undertake. Armed helicopters existed before the specialized attack models appeared, and doubtless will continue to appear and find a market in many parts of the world.

The early use of helicopters in military units was, as explained elsewhere, in the areas of casualty evacuation and SAR. Gradually, however, duties close to the army front line were devised, notably the carrying of troops into battle, scouting and observation, the last-mentioned being a role formerly undertaken by fixed-wing aircraft. Enemy soldiers will naturally attempt to destroy an arriving helicopter before it has opportunity to deliver its load, and so to keep their heads down during the most vulnerable period of the helicopter's sortie, light armament was fitted. Similarly, the scout came in for unwelcome attention during its probing flights, and so it too began to carry arms. At about the same time, armies facing large numbers of tanks began fitting the new wire-guided anti-tank missiles to helicopters as a means of gaining additional flexibility.

In some respects, the helicopter was undergoing the same process of evolution as its fixed-wing forebear. Whereas it was World War I which forced aeroplanes to specialize, development of the military helicopter was accelerated by the Vietnam War. France had used helicopters to a limited extent during her abortive attempt to retain the South East Asia colonies, but when the USA began its increasing involvement on

One of the most heavily armed helicopters to appear is the Mil Mi-24 'Hind', which carries rocket pods and anti-tank missiles on the stub pylons allied to a rotary cannon in the nose turret.

behalf of the South Vietnamese government during the early 1960s, the helicopter became a vital element in pursuing the shadowy guerrilla armies of the Vietcong. Vietnam vindicated the army's faith in the helicopter and opened the floodgates of production, with quantities as large as 2,000 (Bell OH-58A Kiowas) being ordered at a time.

The USA's prime small transport helicopter in Vietnam was the Bell UH-1 Iroquois, known to one and all as the 'Huey'. UH-1s were soon in action armed as gunships as well as for self-protection, working in conjunction with scouts to flush out and destroy the elusive enemy. Typical fitments to the Huey included the XM16 system, comprising a clutch of four M60 7.62-mm (0.3-in) machine-guns mounted in a nose turret, plus a pair of XM157 or XM158 seven-shot launchers for 69.85-mm (2.75-in) 'Mighty Mouse' rockets. Alternative turret fitments were the XM5 with an M75 40-mm grenade-launcher and the XM21 which featured a GAU-2 six-barrel 7.62-mm Minigun. Heaviest firepower was provided by the XM3 system of two 24-round rocket-launchers, and most widely seen was the XM23 door-mounted M60.

These, and other weapon combinations (some of them field adaptations) were of immense value to US Army foot soldiers, and it was natural that lessons learnt should be incorporated in a helicopter optimized for fire support. The resultant AH-1 HueyCobra combined the proven dynamic systems of the UH-1 with a slim cabin which seated the pilot and weapon operator in tandem. This narrow profile, of only 91 cm (36in), allied to low cabin height, makes the AH-1 more difficult to hit with small-arms fire, and easier to camouflage on the ground. HueyCobras entered service in 1967, carrying combinations of Miniguns and 40-mm grenade-launchers in the nose turret, plus rockets and gun-pods on the four pylons attached to the stubwings. They quickly established a reputation for greatly improved response time and time-on-task compared

Left: Dramatic view of a McDonnell AH-64 Apache letting loose a salvo from its pylon-mounted rocket pods. Such weapons would be used against non-armoured positions such as troop concentrations or groups of soft-skinned trucks. Surprisingly, the AH-64 has not been developed with a mast-mounted sight, which means it has to leave the cover of the trees in order to aim its weapons. However, the type is extremely 'crash worthy', being designed around a cockpit shell that can take a heavy crash, hopefully protecting the occupants.

Above: The front view of the Bell AH-1S Cobra illustrates the extremely small cross-section which characterizes most gunships. This is to minimize the chance of being seen and the size of hittable target, and of course, to improve speed performance.

Above: The AH-64 Apache can carry the new Rockwell Hellfire fire-and-forget anti-armour missile (carried here on the inboard pylons). The engines of the AH-64 are heavily shrouded against heat emissions so as to present a low signature to the shoulder-launched, heat-seeking missiles which will be frequently fired at it over the battlefield.

Right: Scout helicopters form an important part of the airborne army, finding targets for anti-armour helicopters and often operating in hunter-killer teams. They are also used for designating targets for tactical aircraft. These are the widely used Bell OH-58 Kiowa, which often carries a rotary machine-gun for fire suppression.

Armed with wire-guided missiles for light anti-armour duties, the Westland Scout also lives up to its name, being employed for spotting duties. Many serve with the British Army, but are being gradually replaced by the Aérospatiale Gazelle.

Left: The US Army's anti-armour helicopter fleet can be deployed to any part of the world by C-5 Galaxy. These AH-1s are operating in Egypt.

Below left: This Pakistan army Bell AH-1S exhibits the classic gunship cockpit arrangement, with pilot in the rear and weapons officer in the front.

Above: The fearsome Mil Mi-24 'Hind' can be used to support amphibious operations, and is seen here on exercise in the Baltic Sea.

with the UH-1, and served in close-support and attack roles until the US pull-out from Vietnam in 1973.

Both types of attack-configured Huey included cockpit weapon sights to which turrets were slaved, so that the helicopter could engage targets away from its flight path. In the AH-1, the pilot (in the rear seat) was normally responsible for releasing armament from the stub-wing pylons and could also take over the turret when it was in the neutral (facing forward) position. Seating was, naturally, staggered in height to give the pilot adequate vision, yet it was the gunner who commanded the broader field of view.

With some changes, and equipment updated to reflect the progress in avionics during the intervening period, the HueyCobra currently serves in Europe with the US forces. The small size and speed which were of advantage in Vietnam are no less important in the NATO context, but the helicopter is assigned to operations in a more sophisticated military environment, in which all-weather combat capability is highly desirable. Most importantly, the HueyCobra had been adapted to carry anti-tank missiles (ATMs) in order to

offset the considerable numerical advantage in armour possessed by the Warsaw Pact. ATM capability is viewed as one of the essential requirements for any NATO attack helicopter.

Advances in the design of weaponry permit the helicopter to pack a punch out of all proportion to its size. Since France adapted the Nord AS.10 missile to the Sud (Aérospatiale) Alouette II in the 1950s, range and destructive power have multiplied, making the helicopter one of the most valuable battlefield assets. The later AS.11 and AS.12 missiles have now given place to second-generation weapons, whilst the first weapons in a third round of European ATMs are under development by an international consortium for deployment in the mid 1990s.

Two types of ATM dominate the current market for air-launched weapons: the Euromissile HOT and Hughes BGM-71 TOW. Four, six or eight such missiles mounted on the outrigger pylons might be the average armament of an anti-tank helicopter, complemented by a similar number of reload rounds if cabin volume permits (obviously not in the case of an optimized attack helicopter such as the HueyCobra).

With a range of some 4 km (2.5 miles), the average ATM will penetrate up to 800 mm (31.5 in) of solid armour, but a lesser thickness of the new-style composite armour. To overcome this shortcoming, ATMs are being updated with features such as larger warheads and nose probes which provide stand-off detonation of the shaped charge for optimum penetration. In the Eastern bloc, helicopters are normally equipped with AT-2 'Swatter' or AT-3 'Sagger' missiles, having penetrative powers of 500 mm (19.7 in) and 400 mm (15.75 in) respectively. Their range is up to 3 km (1.9 miles), although the later AT-6 'Spiral' may reach as far as 6 km (3.7 miles) according to some Western estimates. 'Spiral' is reported to have been temporarily withdrawn because of operational problems, but may now have returned to service. Certainly, the Pentagon has no illusions that the long-range helicopter-laun-

Left: The British Army's principal Westland Lynx AH.Mk 1, which uses the TOW missile as its main weapon. The large cabin can carry eight troops, making the Lynx an all-round battlefield weapon. Many are based in Germany, and will be augmented by the Lynx Mk 3 with greater performance.

Right: Light, extremely nimble and relatively inexpensive, the McDonnell (Hughes) Model 500 Defender is among the smallest of anti-armour helicopters. It has proved very popular with many operators, the majority of which cannot afford the complicated weapons used by the larger nations. This example test-fires a TOW from one of its four launchers.

A light helicopter employed by several nations for anti-tank duties is the Aérospatiale Gazelle. Most carry the Euromissile HOT weapon, including those of France, which is the largest user.

ched weapon will change the tactical situation on the battlefield. One of its reasons for cancellation in 1985 of the Sergeant York gun air-defence system for the US Army was that its shells would fall 2 km (1.24 miles) short of a helicopter attacking with 'Spirals' at maximum range.

This might afford some comfort to the Soviet crew, yet they would harbour no illusions that the battlefield is a safe place for the helicopter caught out in the open. An ATM takes some 17 seconds to fly 4 km, during which time the airborne gunner must follow the target with his sight to obtain a hit. Before that, the target has to be found, identified and checked for range, all of which takes time during which the helicopter is potential prey for guns, SAMs and airborne systems. Ultra-low level is now the operational height for the attack helicopter, as it flies in the 'nap of the earth' on its mission. Using natural features, hedges, woods and buildings for concealment, it thus attempts to locate the foe without being spotted and to hide in ambush until it pops up from cover just long enough to release and guide its ATM.

Even greater security is provided by the MMS (Mast-Mounted Sight) which replaces visual systems mounted on the cabin top or in the nose. Ungainly though it may be, the MMS is aviation's equivalent to the submarine periscope and almost eliminates the danger of a helicopter being seen from the direction of its potential victim. MMS systems are an extension (in two senses of the word) of the advanced sensors which are becoming increasingly common on attack helicopters. One of the more advanced of these, which is being fitted in the nose turret of the Hughes AH-64 Apache, is the TADS/PNVS (Target Acquisition Designation Sight/Pilot Night Vision Sensor). TADS provides the gunner with search, detection and recognition capability in night and adverse weather conditions through direct view optics, TV and FLIR. There is additionally a laser designation and rangefinding facility. PNVS is a second FLIR system which follows the pilot's head movements and projects an artificial image onto his helmet display (i.e. in a monocle immediately in front of his eye) to represent terrain which cannot be seen because of darkness, mist or smoke.

Further advances in attack helicopter technology incorporated in the Apache include the Rockwell AGM-114 Hellfire missile. As a 'fire-and-forget'

Bell AH-1S Cobra

Rotor diameter: 13.41 m (44 ft 0 in)
Length: 13.59 m (44 ft 7 in)
Height: 4.09 m (13 ft 5 in)
Speed: 227 km/h (141 mph)
Range: 507 km (315 miles)
Ceiling: 3720 m (12,200 ft)
Armament: eight TOW missiles
on outboard stations with rocket pods or gun pods on inboard pylons; chin turret mounts 20-mm M197 three-barrelled cannon

Many US-orientated nations have been supplied with the Bell AH-1. This AH-1S is used by Israel, whose aircraft have seen action against Syrian tanks.

Bell AH-1T Cobra

Rotor diameter: 14.63 m (48 ft 0 in)
Length: 14.68 m (48 ft 2 in)
Height: 4.32 m (14 ft 2 in)
Speed: 277 km/h (172 mph)
Range: 420 km (261 miles)
Ceiling: 2255 m (7,400 ft)
Armament: three-barrelled 20-
mm M197 cannon in turret; rocket pods, flare dispensers, grenade launchers, gun pods, Hellfire or TOW missiles on pylons

The US Marine Corps use a twin-engined version of the AH-1 for covering amphibious assaults. These fly from the assault ships.

Agusta A 129

Rotor diameter: 11.90 m (39 ft 0.5 in)
Length: 12.275 m (40 ft 3 in)
Height: 3.315 m (10 ft 10.5 in)
Speed: 315 km/h (196 mph)
Range: 480 km (300 miles) approx.
Ceiling: 3290 m (10,800 ft)
Armament: eight TOW missiles or optionally eight HOT or six Hellfire; provision for rocket and gun pods or Stinger AAMs

Developed for the Italian army, and a potential type for the British Army, the Agusta A 129 Mangusta carries eight HOT missiles.

Aérospatiale SA 342 Gazelle

Rotor diameter: 10.50 m (34 ft 5.5 in)
Length: 11.97 m (39 ft 5.5 in)
Height: 3.19 m (10 ft 5.5 in)
Speed: 260 km/h (161 mph)
Range: 710 km (440 miles)
Ceiling: 4100 m (13,450 ft)
Armament: four or six HOT missiles; rocket pods or machine gun and cannon pods

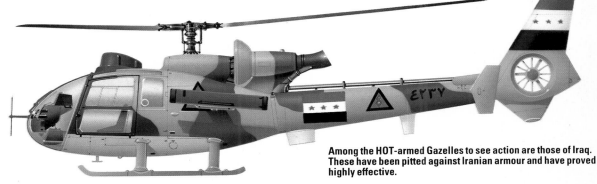

Among the HOT-armed Gazelles to see action are those of Iraq. These have been pitted against Iranian armour and have proved highly effective.

McDonnell Douglas Model 500 Defender

Rotor diameter: 8.03 m (26 ft 4 in)
Length: 7.62 m (25 ft 0 in)
Height: 2.64 m (8 ft 8 in)
Speed: 221 km/h (137 mph)
Range: 389 km (242 miles)
Ceiling: 4205 m (13,800 ft)
Armament: four TOW missile
can be replaced with rocket or gun pods and fuselage-mounted pylons

Typical of the third-world users of the McDonnell Defender is Kenya. The protuberance on the nose houses the TOW aiming sight.

Attack helicopters

Left: Four of the eight TOW tubes on this British Army Lynx are clearly visible. The sight is mounted above the left-hand (weapon aimer) seat.

Above: Afghanistan has seen widespread use of the gunship, with both Mi-24 'Hind' and Mi-8 'Hip' in action. This rear view of the former shows the rocket pods.

weapon, Hellfire obviates the requirement for target tracking during missile flight and is the first such ATM to see service. Helicopters like the Apache are also receiving air-to-air missiles for self defence, although they can additionally be used in an offensive manner to hunt enemy helicopters. AAMs derived from shoulder-launched army SAMs (SATCP, Javelin, Stinger, etc.) are well suited to aerial carriage with minimal modifications and will be seen in increasing numbers.

The more lightly equipped and agile scout helicopter is best suited to double up as a helicopter-killer, using cannon as well as SAMs. Several countries have equipped their helicopters with 20-mm cannon, sometimes in a 360° swivelling belly mounting for a range of duties, and larger 30-mm weapons are expected to achieve wider acceptance in future. The scout is being improved in other ways, transforming it from a visual reporter into an all-weather observer and target designator. Setting the trend in this direction is the US Army's programme to convert Bell OH-58A Kiowas into OH-58Ds with an MMS featuring TV, FLIR and laser designation. The refurbished Kiowas will have intelligence-gathering, surveillance and aerial reconnaissance tasks as well as directing artillery fire and supporting attack missions.

A common theme links almost all the large number of helicopters used throughout the world for the combat roles of attack, armed escort, anti-helicopter and

Left: A Bell AH-1S launches a TOW. This missile is guided by commands passed through a wire which trails out behind the missile during its flight. This means that the helicopter has to stay in sight of the target.

Mil Mi-24 'Hind-D'

Rotor diameter: 17.00 m (55 ft 9 in)
Length: 18.50 m (60 ft 8.5 in)
Height: 6.50 m (21 ft 4 in)
Speed: 320 km/h (199 mph)
Range: 350 km (218 miles)
Ceiling: 4500 m (14,750 ft)
Armament: four-barrelled 12.7- mm gun in nose; wing pylons usually carry four AT-2 'Swatter' ATMs and four UV-32-57 rocket pods

One of the most heavily armed helicopters in the world (the Mi-8 'Hip-E' takes the first prize), the Mi-24 'Hind-D' has very high performance. However, its large size makes it an inviting target over the battlefield and its effectiveness in a Central Front-type engagement may be limited. This is one of the many 'Hinds' ranged against NATO forces in Europe, being part of the Czech contingent.

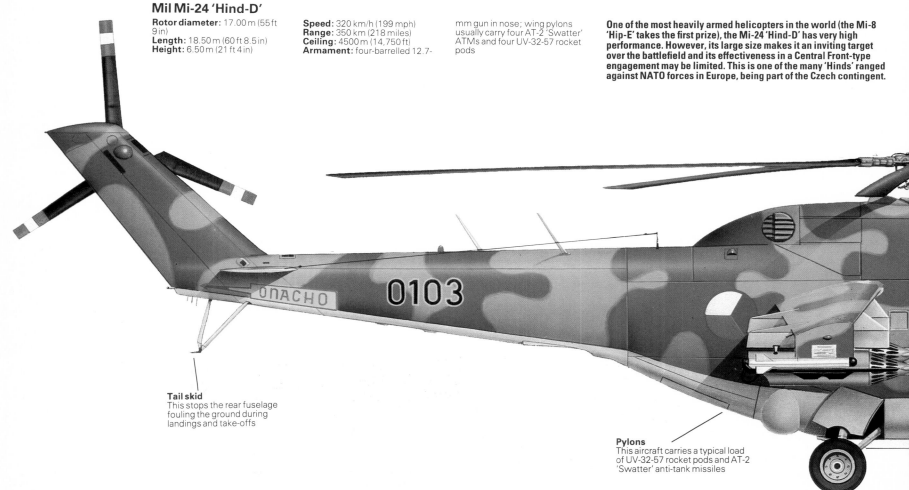

Tail skid
This stops the rear fuselage fouling the ground during landings and take-offs

Pylons
This aircraft carries a typical load of UV-32-57 rocket pods and AT-2 'Swatter' anti-tank missiles

scout. With the exception of weaponry and colour scheme, they are the same helicopters which will be found ferrying business executives, inspecting power lines and reporting on traffic jams for local radio stations anywhere between the UK and Japan. Reliance on a joint market has kept military helicopter development costs lower than would otherwise have been the case, but has meant that the product is sometimes less than robust enough for the battlefield. It is at last being fully appreciated that the attack helicopter must include armour and be able to withstand small-arms damage: no one previously sent to war protected from the enemy by a 0.5-cm (0.2-in) thick perspex bubble has been heard to raise a voice in dissent.

Thus the number of tandem-seat helicopters has rapidly increased during the 1980s in connection with

research into battle damage resistance and airframe strength. Following the HueyCobra and Apache have come the Agusta Mangusta, Eurocopter PAH-2 family and Mil Mi-28 'Havoc', the formidable Mi-24 'Hind' having been developed from an assault helicopter. There are even tandem-seat imitators based on the old Alouette III and Bell 47G airframes for armies with less financial resources. Advanced weapons, detection systems and vision enhancement will make this new wave of attack helicopters greatly more potent than their predecessors. Costs will be proportionately increased, yet partly offset by the use of acquired constructional details, powerplants and rotor systems in related scout and transport helicopters, such as with the US Army's plant for its LHX series due for deployment in the 1990s.

Two Japanese AH-1Ss traverse along a river. These carry eight TOW tubes, two rocket pods and the chin-mounted three-barrelled cannon each. The exhaust is upturned to deter heat-seeking missiles.

Before then, however, a new helicopter is likely to appear in the Soviet camp. Known to NATO only as the Kamov 'Hokum', this receives last mention because it has no parallel anywhere in the world and is the founder member of a new helicopter category: the purpose-designed fighter. Due in service later in the 1980s, 'Hokum' is an agile helicopter-killer with the extremely high maximum speed of 350 km/h (217 mph) compared with the 300 km/h (186 mph) which is the best the West can offer, in the form of the Apache. Nearly three-quarters of a century after its fixed-wing forerunner, the dogfighting helicopter is preparing to take to the battlefield.

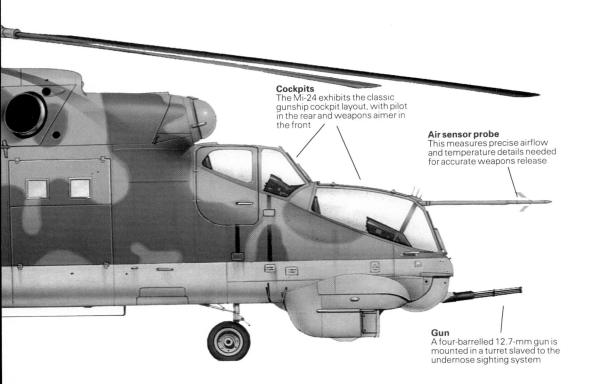

Cockpits
The Mi-24 exhibits the classic gunship cockpit layout, with pilot in the rear and weapons aimer in the front

Air sensor probe
This measures precise airflow and temperature details needed for accurate weapons release

Gun
A four-barrelled 12.7-mm gun is mounted in a turret slaved to the undernose sighting system

'Nap of the earth' flying is practised here by West German army MBB BO 105s. These light helicopters can carry six HOT missiles and are phenomenally agile, allowing every available bit of cover, such as a tree or river bank to be used.

Lift and Assault Helicopters

On 10 May 1940, three days before Igor Sikorsky made the initial untethered flight of the world's first practical helicopter, a spectacular mission by German gliderborne troops seized the mighty Belgian fort at Eben-Emael. Swift and unexpected, the airborne assault neutralized the fortress before it could fire a shot to impede the German army's march across Western Europe. Soon afterwards, parachute troops were landing at key objectives to facilitate the continued swift advance. After being used to gain similar advantages in the latter stages of the war, the glider fell into disuse, but gradually found a replacement in the form of the assault helicopter. Parachute units, too, often forsook the silk for a set of rotating wings to bear them into battle, and now few major armies are not dependent upon helicopters for battlefield transport.

It is the role of the assault helicopter to move troops rapidly to the point at which they are needed and (equally important) if necessary to sustain them there until other forms of supply can be established. This may mean not only a one-time dash into the battle zone to insert men, but a continuing resupply effort taking the helicopter into a hazardous area on numerous occasions. Typically, the West German army's air arm has the ability to airlift a reinforced air-mobile battalion of 1,000 men and 120 tonnes of equipment in a single wave of Sikorsky CH-53Gs, and thereafter to provide a brigade's daily needs in one wave of smaller Bell UH-1D Iroquois helicopters.

The majority of armies with assault helicopters assigned have these under their direct control, although there are exceptions. For example, in the UK the RAF is responsible for troop-carrying helicopters larger than the Westland Lynx, and in the Netherlands

Now used sparingly by the US Army, the Sikorsky CH-54 Tarhe is nevertheless a valuable asset, being able to lift awkward items without the need to sling them. Here the Skycrane straddles a truck.

army aviation is technically a part of the air force. Nor must be forgotten the marine corps' units which use the helicopter: notably the USMC which has its own air force, and the Royal Marines whose medium helicopter support is the responsibility of the Royal Navy. Whatever the technicalities of the command structure, it is clear that army aviation throughout the world has become almost totally helicopter-orientated. The aeroplane retains a hold in some forces as a means of liaison and observation, but fixed wings painted olive drab are a comparative rarity.

Three classes of helicopter are involved with provision of armies' logistic needs: light utility, medium lift (MLH) and heavy lift (HLH). By reason of its bulk, however, the HLH is not generally regarded as an assault vehicle in the sense of operating close to enemy forces. Early in the 1990s, a fourth category of support aircraft will appear when the convertiplane enters service with the US Army and Marines.

There are but five helicopters serving in military roles which may be considered HLH types, of which two are 'flying cranes'. The Sikorsky CH-54 Tarhe is the junior of the two, with a maximum loaded weight in the region of 19 tonnes, whereas the Mil Mi-10 'Harke' is exactly twice as heavy. Arguably, the Sikorsky helicopter is two in one, as it can operate in skeletal form for lifting underslung loads by cable, or can carry a purpose-designed container for mixed freight.

Also able to act as cranes, yet also able to carry

Left: Principal assault helicopter for the Soviet Union and its many client states is the Mil Mi-8 'Hip'. Built in vast numbers, these serve as general transports or as armed assault platforms.

Left: Following up the initial heliborne assault (by Bell UH-1 or Sikorsky UH-60), the US Army uses the Boeing Vertol CH-47 Chinook to move in heavy equipment such as artillery. The type is perfect for heavylift duties behind the front, being able to move supplies into difficult areas with great speed. Here, fuel bladders are uplifted.

Below: French troopers disgorge from an Aérospatiale Super Puma during trials with the army. The proximity of the tank shows the close tie-up between heliborne forces and the armour and infantry. Heliborne forces are usually employed ahead of the main land forces, securing positions and clearing enemy armour before the land forces can move up into safe territory.

Right: South Africa has used the helicopter widely during anti-guerrilla operations in Namibia and Angola. The chief types employed are the Aérospatiale Alouette III and Aérospatiale Puma, both of which are seen here. The fast-reaction, cross-country speed and lifting capabilities of the helicopter have been central to any successes the South Africans have had in the bush.

Soviet assault helicopters

Mil Mi-8 'Hip'

Rotor diameter: 21.29 m (69 ft 10.25 in)
Length: 25.25 m (82 ft 10 in)
Height: 5.65 m (18 ft 6.5 in)

Speed: 260 km/h (161 mph)
Range: 465 km (289 miles)
Ceiling: 4500 m (14,760 ft)
Armament: 'Hip-E' can carry one

12.7-mm machine-gun, six UV-32-57 rocket pods and four AT-2 missiles; other versions can carry various guns and rocket pods; 24 troops

The most numerous type in the Soviet air armies is the Mil Mi-8 'Hip', here exemplified by a 'Hip-E' armed assault craft.

Mil Mi-4 'Hound'

Rotor diameter: 21.00 m (68 ft 11 in)
Length: 16.80 m (55 ft 1.4 in)
Height: 5.18 m (17 ft 0 in)

Speed: 210 km/h (130 mph)
Range: 400 km (249 miles)
Ceiling: 6000 m (19,685 ft)

Armament: one 7.62-mm machine-gun and various rocket and gun pods

Not used by the Soviet Union, the Mil Mi-4 'Hound' is still in use with a number of client states, including Afghanistan.

Mil Mi-6 'Hook'

Rotor diameter: 35.00 m (114 ft 10 in)
Length: 41.74 m (136 ft 11.5 in)
Height: 9.86 m (32 ft 4 in)

Speed: 300 km/h (186 mph)
Range: 1000 km (621 miles)
Ceiling: 4500 m (14,750 ft)

Armament: some aircraft have one 12.7-mm machine-guns; up to 70 troops

Before the advent of the Mi-26, the Mi-6 'Hook' was the giant of the Soviet helicopter fleet. This example was supplied to Egypt.

Mil Mi-24 'Hind-D'

Rotor diameter: 17.00 m (55 ft 9 in)
Length: 18.50 m (60 ft 8.5 in)
Height: 6.50 m (21 ft 4 in)

Speed: 320 km/h (199 mph)
Range: 350 km (218 miles)
Ceiling: 4500 m (14,750 ft)
Armament: in addition to nose

gun and pylon-mounted rocket pods and missiles, eight troops can be carried

Although thought of primarily as a gunship, the Mi-24 'Hind' is also a useful assault ship, carrying eight troops. This aircraft flies with East Germany.

Currently the world's largest helicopter, the Mil Mi-26 'Halo' is employed by the Soviet forces for heavylift duties. This 'helicopter Hercules' will carry over 20 tonnes of cargo, including heavy vehicles which can be driven on through a rear loading ramp and clamshell doors.

considerable loads internally, are the Mil Mi-6 'Hook', Mil Mi-26 'Halo' and Sikorsky CH-53 Stallion family. Notably, all three have short landing gear and rear loading ramps to facilitate rapid transfer of cargo, particularly wheeled and tracked vehicles. Only the CH-53 can claim to include pure assault roles amongst its duties, as it is employed by the USMC to transport up to 55 fully-armed troops from assault ships to a beach-head, in addition to ferrying supplies and lifting downed aircraft. No firm evidence is available that the USSR intends to use the Mi-6 and Mi-10 in such forward roles, yet their impact would clearly be immense if thus employed.

The giant helicopter has been a favourite Soviet theme for decades, and records are held for producing the largest helicopter yet flown (Mil Mi-12 test vehicle) and the largest in current use (Mi-26). Described as a vertical take-off Lockheed Hercules, the Mi-26 tips any scales large enough to accommodate it at 56 tonnes, fully laden, and will carry 20 tonnes internally or externally, having demonstrated 25 tonnes in a record-breaking sortie. Mi-26s, some of which have been in military service since at least 1983, are able to hold medium tanks, whilst only marginally smaller loads are moved by the Mi-6. The latter, weighing over 42 tonnes all-up and lifting 12 tonnes internally, relegates the American CH-53 to fourth place in the HLH league, at 33 tonnes.

Record-breaking loads

Naturally, loads must be reduced from the theoretical maximum if they are to be moved any distance, but 'record-breaking' figures are closer to the reality of combat operations than in the case of the fixed-wing transport. Helicopters are used more for short-range missions, and in some cases the 'route' can be no more than a hundred or so yards across a river or other obstruction. An immense tactical advantage can thus be grasped by the imaginative use of the heavy helicopter.

Years of experiments into the convertiplane concept (now known as the tilt-rotor) are leading towards future deployment of the Bell/Boeing V-22 Osprey in military roles. Powered by a pair of rotating airscrews half-way between traditional propellers and rotors, the Osprey tilts its engine pods upwards for vertical take-offs and landings. However, because the rotating wing is incapable of matching the speed of its fixed equivalent, the engines turn to the horizontal for forward flight, which is sustained by short wings. This 'best of both worlds' aircraft will carry 24 combat troops at

Left: Pakistan is a user of the Mil Mi-8, as is its arch enemy India. Though lacking in frills, the Mi-8 is a rugged type which can take a lot of punishment. It is also designed for roughshod maintenance, ideal for service in wartime. An uprated version, the Mi-17, offers greater performance.

Above: Peru was one of the few nations to receive the giant Mi-6. The vast internal cabin can accommodate up to 90 passengers or 70 combat troops.

The extraordinary lifting capabilities of the Boeing Vertol CH-47 Chinook are illustrated by this Falklands shot of one airlifting another. The one RAF Chinook that survived the sinking of the *Atlantic Conveyor* put in sterling service before other aircraft could arrive following the cessation of hostilities.

Left: The Sikorsky CH-53 is used by a handful of nations for assault duties, notably Israel. They are used for inserting troops.

Above: The strange form of the Sikorsky CH-54 Tarhe shows how it can straddle large items to pick them up. Slung loads can be carried just as easily.

Left: The Grenada conflict saw the baptism of fire for the Sikorsky UH-60A Black Hawk. Casualty evacuation forms an important part of the battlefield helicopter's duties, these mostly being marked with a red cross.

Below: The UH-60A Black Hawk has been received into the US Army inventory to update the assault helicopter fleet, these augmenting the vast numbers of the existing Bell UH-1 Hueys. Many of these are based in Germany, and are often used by crack units such as the 101st Air Assault Division.

630 km/h (391 mph) compared with (say) 21 soldiers at 260 km/h (161 mph) in an Aérospatiale Super Puma, and deliver them to locations impossible for the aeroplane to reach.

It is this ability of the helicopter to obviate the uncertainties and dangers of glider and parachute transport, whilst additionally offering concentrations of personnel from the instant landing, which has made the helicopter so indispensable to armies. Those fortunate enough are equipped with the MLH, typified by the twin-rotor designs from the Boeing-Vertol family. Older Kawasaki-Vertol KV-107s and Boeing-Vertol CH-46 Sea Knights are still widely used, notably with the US Marines, yet it is the CH-47 Chinook which is perhaps the best known in Europe.

At a gross weight of just under 23 tonnes, the Chinook will carry 10.5 tonnes over 55 km (35 miles) and

Above: Derived from the naval ASW Sea King, Westland's Sea King HC.Mk 4 and Commando are dedicated assault and battlefield lift helicopters.

Right: The USMC uses the Sikorsky CH-53 widely for ship-to-shore assault duties. This example pumps out flares to decoy heat-seeking missiles.

12 tonnes over shorter distances. Like larger helicopters, it has a rear ramp for vehicles, cargo and troops, officially carrying 44 of the last-mentioned. The qualification is necessary in view of the fact that at least 81 fully-equipped soldiers were squeezed into an RAF Chinook during the Falklands war, and obviously could be again if an emergency arose. RAF Chinooks also provide a useful illustration of the sophistication to be found in assault helicopters of the current generation, for their crews have night-vision equipment, and aircraft operational aids include radar-warning receivers. Glassfibre rotor blades give longer maintenance-free life and greater resistance to battle damage, and a single-point pressure refuelling system cuts the time spent helpless on the ground at a forward fuel point on the edge of the battlefield.

Triple hook

Tactical operation is further assisted by the triple hook arrangement below the aircraft on which three cargo loads for dispersed points can be carried and individually delivered without the need for landing and manual off-loading. The forward and rear hooks can also act as steadiers for a large underslung load, whilst a Cruise Guide Indicator automatically selects optimum flight control settings for any load which the helicopter is asked to lift by comparing the torque of the two rotors. With a rotor at each end, the Chinook has a generous latitude for centre of gravity positioning, and the CGI makes full use of this in combat situations when loading sheets and other paperwork are discarded. (In any event, experience has taught air forces never to accept an army's weight declaration for anything.)

Single-rotor utility helicopters are employed to take troops into forward battle zones, and are more likely to carry light armament for secondary defence-suppression roles. They are available in sizes to suit various needs, from six seats in the original models of the Bell UH-1 Iroquois ('Huey') to the accommodation for 30 in Aérospatiale's Super Frelon. Like the Westland Commando (which holds 28 troops), the Frelon is a naval helicopter adapted for transport roles, although it has a rear loading ramp in place of the large side doors more common to the utility helicopter. Other British and French products used in the assault role are the

Aérospatiale Puma and Super Puma and the smaller Westland Wessex HU.Mk 5. Occupying the middle ground, developments of the Huey family are conveniently adapted to carry the usual basic army squad of 13 men.

Equivalents throughout the Soviet bloc are the Mil Mi-8 'Hip' and Mi-24 'Hind', the former taking some 30 or so troops and the latter eight. Progressive development has resulted in these receiving increasingly heavy armament, extending in the case of the 'Hip' to

The ubiquitous Huey is used worldwide as an assault helicopter, the US Army alone having over 4,000. These can also undertake lifting duties, with a cargo hook under the cabin floor.

no less than 192 rockets and four anti-tank missiles. Later models of the 'Hind', as clearly apparent, have adopted armoured tandem cockpits and all the aspects of a helicopter gunship, whilst retaining the ability to move troops. Such an aircraft illustrates well the priority given by nations such as the USSR to their assault helicopter forces.

Right: Employed as an all-round armed assault helicopter, the Westland Lynx serving with the British Army can accommodate nine combat-laden troops.

Below: Among the design constraints placed on the Black Hawk was that it should be able to fit the hold of the Lockheed Galaxy transport. Testament to that are these US Army aircraft taking part in Operation 'Bright Star', held in Egypt.

Heavy Transports

When, in 1948, the USSR imposed a total blockade on surface transport into West Berlin, the USA, UK and France launched their historic airlift to sustain the beleaguered city. For almost a year, until the USSR abandoned its attempt to starve the Western sectors into the communist empire, all requirements travelled by air. In came flour, coal and the other minimum requirements of human existence; out were flown exports to sustain the manufacturing industries. The USAF formed an Airlift Task Force equipped with eight squadrons of Douglas C-54s; the RAF committed a sizeable proportion of Transport Command's Douglas C-47s, Avro Yorks and new Handley Page Hastings; and civilian transports were also chartered to assist the herculean effort. As if on a heavenly conveyor belt, the transports droned down the corridors into Berlin every two or three minutes, 24 hours per day, split-second timing ensuring no disruption to those following behind. Today, the entire job could be handled by half a dozen Lockheed C-5 Galaxies.

There are few better examples than this of the growth in transport capacity within the world's air forces, a development which has run parallel to the burgeoning of civilian air travel and the appearance of ever-larger aircraft. The two trends have much in common, not least because they are self-sustaining movements. In the military sphere, the development of an aircraft to carry troops prompted calls for larger machines able to airlift armoured vehicles and small field guns. That accomplished, it was logical that heavier weapons should also have a means of air transport. Now, the giant military freighters in service with the superpowers can airlift main battle tanks and ready-to-fire intermediate-range nuclear missile systems.

Soldiering being essentially a labour-intensive operation, the early aeroplanes were of little value to military operations because of their limited capacity. However, between the wars, the RAF's contribution to policing the British Empire included the use of converted bombers and bomber derivatives to rush troops to trouble spots and even, on one occasion, evacuate large numbers of civilians from an encircled city. During World War II the comparatively vast increase in transport capacity resulting from large-scale deliveries of the legendary Douglas C-47/Dakota was a significant factor in Allied victories. For the first time, in Burma, major forces relied wholly upon air supply to sustain them during missions behind enemy lines, whilst US transports maintained a vital supply route to China over notoriously difficult terrain.

Transport aircraft have also acted as the spearhead of an assault by carrying paratroops into action. Germany and the USSR were early pioneers, the former gaining dazzling successes in campaigns during 1940-41. Thereafter, it was the Allies who used the troop carrier aeroplane in major operations, complementing it in the German fashion with expendable gliders to carry additional personnel and bulky equipment.

Although modern transports greatly exceed the lifting capacities of their forebears, the mode of employment differs little in some respects from the pattern established during World War II. Today's military forces rely heavily upon supplies to equip them for (and to sustain them in) battle. In peacetime the needs of troops stationed overseas are substantial, and transport aircraft a convenient means of satisfying them; in war, demands multiply many-fold, and rapid communications can often decide whether the outcome of a conflict will be victory or defeat.

When Argentina invaded the Falkland Islands, the first British aircraft to take up their wartime roles were

The most widely used transport is the Lockheed C-130 Hercules. This type forms the backbone of many Western tactical transport fleets, including that of the United States. This C-130, in desert camouflage, demonstrates its sprightly take-off performance from a rough sandy strip.

Hercules have seen action in many wars and conflicts in recent years, among them Grenada, where they provided tactical support to the invading forces. Their short and rough field performance allowed them into airfields that could not take the larger StarLifter.

not the Avro Vulcan bombers or BAe Sea Harrier fighters, or even the BAe Nimrod and BAe Victor reconnaissance and tanker aircraft. Out to the forward base at Ascension Island came a steady procession of Lockheed Hercules and BAe VC10 transports, bringing specialist logistics organizers and the material which the Task Force would need. Clearly, though lacking the popular appeal of the combat aircraft, transports are no less a part of modern military operations.

Heavy transport aircraft are flown in the strategic and tactical roles, and some aircraft types are suitable for either role. Generally, it is the largest aircraft which are defined as 'strategic', in that they have the potential to move large forces rapidly over great distances and so change the military balance for attack or defensive purposes. Tactical transports, usually a little smaller, are those operated within a theatre to redistribute assets. If (say) Norway came under threat of attack, British reinforcements would be flown in by RAF tactical aircraft; larger numbers of home-based US Army troops would come by USAF strategic transport.

Despite the similarities between civilian and military

Above: One of the main attributes of the Hercules is its amazing agility for an aircraft of its size. This RAF machine displays that agility during a typical tactical take-off.

Left: The long-range airlift of the United States is handled mainly by the Lockheed C-141B StarLifter. These have surprising rough field performance, allowing them to operate out of relatively unprepared strips.

Right: Giant of the USAF's transport fleet is the Lockheed C-5 Galaxy. Its gaping hold can accommodate main battle tanks, such as this M60 seen driving off down the integral ramp.

heavy transports, important differences do exist. Because the wise air force will buy enough aircraft for the demands of war, not the lesser needs of peace, military transports usually have a leisurely life compared with their hard-worked civilian counterparts. There is thus a reduced danger of them running out of fatigue hours for a considerable time although, as demonstrated by the Lockheed C-5A Galaxy, extensive fatigue rectification sometimes is found necessary. Air forces tend to keep their transports longer than do airlines, yet particularly at the tactical end of operations they can induce fatigue at a high rate with war zone manouvring of a kind which would terrify the average airline passenger.

Military transports must be able to work far from the 'luxuries' of civil aviation, such as comprehensive navigation aids and long, well lit runways. As far as is possible within the constraints of the loads to be carried, landing distances must be as short as possible in order to maximize the choice of landing sites. Wings are therefore liberally endowed with high-lift devices, and might even be designed for minimal landing distances to the slight detriment of cruise performance. Similarly, wheel loading must be as light as possible to assist the tactical transport to operate from earth surfaces instead of smooth, flat runways. Even when concrete is necessary for landing, it is as well to require as little thickness as possible. The mighty C-5A has a load classification number on concrete of 69, almost the same as the Airbus A300B2-200's 68, even though the

C-5's maximum take-off weight is 2.5 times greater. The C-5 has also been tested for its ability to taxi in deep snow and, doubtless, Soviet transports are likewise evaluated.

Inside, the decor of many military transports leaves something to be desired from the aesthetic viewpoint. Seating for troops is no more than canvas, and can be quickly removed to accommodate cargo. Interchangeability is the keynote of such aircraft, with floors designed for rapid cargo handling and stressed to withstand the weight of military equipment. Speed and convenience of access is a further aspect afforded high priority by the designer. Of strategic aircraft, only the RAF's VC10s (and, arguably, the USAF's McDonnell Douglas KC-10 Extenders, which have a partial transport assignment) have side freight doors which demand loading by lifting platforms or fork-lift trucks. Both were derived from civilian airliners.

Other heavy transports squat close to the ground on disproportionately short landing gear, of which only the wheels are often visible. They have full-size rear doors for access to the cavernous interior, these doors being of the clamshell or ramp types. The latter is preferable, as it dispenses with the need for even a short auxiliary ramp to be attached for vehicular access, and

can be opened in flight with minimal airflow problems. A swept-up rear fuselage allows large doors to be fitted, yet some aircraft have gone further and also have a lifting nose section. This roll-on/roll-off feature complicates design, but is obviously appreciated by any driver who is relieved of the need to reverse a tank or missile launcher for loading.

The weight brackets for strategic and tactical transports cannot be defined with the precision which classifies boxers. Upper ends of the strategic weight band are marked by the Antonov An-124 'Condor', which can leave the runway at up to 405 tonnes (399 tons), whilst the ubiquitous Hercules may be said to top the tactical range at 79 tonnes (78 tons). When comparing the cargo capacity of different aircraft, it is important to bear in mind that load and range vary in inverse proportion and that a reasonable balance between both provides the maximum operational flexibility. The An-124 has a maximum range of 16500 km (10,250 miles), yet can carry its full load of 150 tonnes (148 tons) only 4500 km (2,795 miles), which is nonetheless no insignificant distance. Were it to have inflight-refuelling capability, as do some other strategic aircraft, the An-124 would have even more impressive performance.

Turning to the tactical aircraft exemplified by the Hercules, a weight of up to 19 tonnes (19 tons) may be carried, with which the range is some 3800 km (2,360 miles). That range can be doubled, however, if a quarter of the load is replaced by additional fuel. The Hercules has also illustrated an unusual trend in military transports (but far more common in the civilian sector) of an optional fuselage stretch, which has been applied retrospectively to half the RAF's fleet. Generally, on loading military cargo, the transport 'weighs out' before it 'bulks out', that is to say, it reaches the maximum permissible weight when there is still space in the hold. Conversely, humans and some large-but-light cargoes take up all usable room whilst the aircraft is still far from maximum weight. The additional struc-

Lockheed C-5 Galaxy

Span: 67.88 m (222 ft 8.5 in)
Length: 75.54 m (247 ft 10 in)
Height: 19.85 m (65 ft 1.5 in)
Speed: 919 km/h (571 mph)

Range: 10410 km (6470 miles)
Ceiling: 10895 m (35,750 ft)
Armament: none; max payload is 118390 kg (261,00 lb)

LAPES (low altitude parachute extraction system) is used for depositing large items where there is no adequate landing strip. The system employs a large parachute which drags the palletized cargo backwards out of the hold.

Lockheed C-5 Galaxy

Nose door
The entire nose hinges upwards, while a ramp is lowered to reveal an opening as large as the cabin

Emergency door
The flight deck is way above the main cargo deck and requires separate escape hatches

Powerplant
These are General Electric TF39 turbofans each rated at 191.2 kN (43,000 lb st)

U.S. AIR FORCE

Nations around the world employ the Hercules, there being in the region of 50 users. Among those is Chile, whose aircraft have made infrequent trips to Europe to collect spares for other aircraft.

Aeritalia G222

Span: 28.70 m (94 ft 2 in)
Length: 22.70 m (74 ft 5.5 in)
Height: 9.80 m (32 ft 2 in)
Speed: 540 km/h (336 mph)

Range: 4633 km (2,879 miles) (maximum)
Ceiling: 7620 m (25,000 ft)
Armament: none; max payload is 9000 kg (19,840 lb)

Libya uses the Rolls-Royce Tyne-engined G222 for transport duties.

Transall C.160

Span: 40.00 m (131 ft 3 in)
Length: 32.40 m (106 ft 3.5 in)
Height: 11.65 m (38 ft 3 in)

Speed: 513 km/h (319 mph)
Range: 8858 km (5,504 miles) (maximum)

Ceiling: 8230 m (27,000 ft)
Armament: none; max playload is 16000 kg (35,275 lb)

Principal tactical transport of the West German Luftwaffe is the Transall C.160.

Lockheed C-141B StarLifter

Span: 48.74 m (159 ft 11 in)
Length: 51.30 m (168 ft 4 in)
Height: 11.98 m (39 ft 3.5 in)

Speed: 920 km/h (570 mph)
Range: 8500 km (5,000 miles)
Ceiling: 12200 m (40,000 ft)

Armament: none; max payload is 40440 kg (89,150 lb)

The Lockheed C-141B has an inflight-refuelling receptacle mounted above the forward fuselage, bestowing true global capability.

Lockheed C-130 Hercules

Span: 40.41 m (132 ft 7)
Length: 29.79 m (97 ft 9 in)
Height: 11.66 m (38 ft 3 in)

Speed: 602 km/h (374 mph)
Range: 7880 km (4,900 miles)
Ceiling: 10060 m (33,000 ft)

Armament: none; max payload is 19360 kg (42,675 lb)

ture used to stretch the fuselage reduces the payload by 1711 kg (3,772 lb), but means that 92 instead of 64 paratroops can be carried, and that a further light vehicle may perhaps be added to a load.

Strategic transports are generally expected to operate in the rear areas of a conflict, although there is a notable exception regarding US reinforcement plans for Europe. The first paratroops to arrive will climb aboard the C-5 Galaxies or Lockheed C-141 StarLifters in the USA and parachute out of them over West Germany after a nonstop flight. For sound tactical reasons, troops need to be dropped with maximum concentration in time and area, so position-keeping radar is needed when night operations are flown, and navigation must be to high standards.

Special tactics

Further skills are demanded of the tactical transport crew, one of the more spectacular results being the LAPES (Low-Altitude Parachute Extraction System) delivery of bulky loads mounted on pallets. Used when it is impossible or inadvisable for aircraft to land, LAPES requires a ramp-equipped transport to fly as low as some 2 m (6 ft) from the ground for the cargo to be drawn out by parachute. Similarly impressive is the 'Khe Sanh' tactical airfield approach, named after the South Vietnamese firebase supplied mainly by US Hercules during a Viet Cong siege: for a measure of security against light ground fire, the aircraft approaches high before diving for the runway and levelling out at the last moment before landing. Less common, but still employed occasionally, are techniques to pick up important packages from the ground and insert special forces into hostile territory.

With the exception of the Antonov An-22 'Cock', strategic transports have jet or turbofan power, whereas their tactical compatriots are generally turboprops. Differing efficiency values over long and short routes predetermine the designer's choice, yet the advent of

Once the world's largest aircraft, the Lockheed C-5 Galaxy remains unrivalled in the West. The vast fuselage virtually empty, the pivoting nose and rear ramp doors revealing a straight-through cargo hold. Ramps at both ends allow rapid drive-on/drive-off operations involving helicopters, fighters and even tanks.

Several of the RAF's Hercules fleet have had probes fitted, while others have had refuelling drogues installed to augment the tanker forces.

Wings
The C-5's wings incorporate many high-lift devices to reduce the high wing loading for take-off and landing

Tacan
The tactical airborne navigation system ensures accurate navigation around the Western world

Insignia
This C-5 carries both the shield of Military Airlift Command (MAC) and the 436th MAW

Rear doors
These are semi-clamshell, semi-ramp units which allow large vehicles to drive on or off

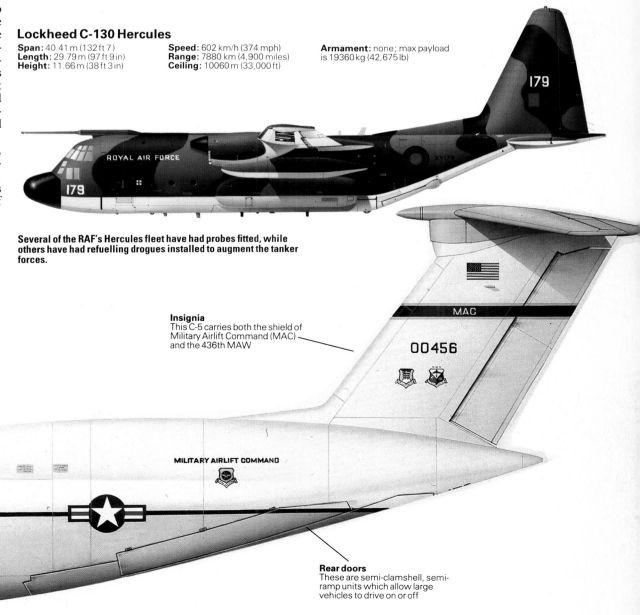

Heavy Transports

McDonnell Douglas DC-8 Series 62

Span: 45.24 m (148 ft 5 in)
Length: 47.98 m (157 ft 5 in)
Height: 12.93 m (42 ft 5 in)
Speed: 855 km/h (531 mph)
Range: 11620 km (7,220 miles)
Armament: none

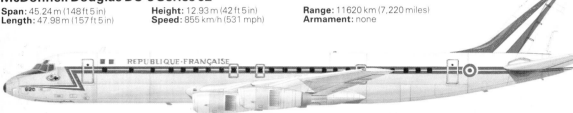

VIP transport for France is handled by the Douglas DC-8. One of these aircraft has been converted to a Sigint gatherer.

Above left: Currently the world's largest aircraft, the Antonov An-124 'Condor' has been developed for the state airline Aeroflot as well as the military forces. The distinction between Aeroflot and air force aircraft is unclear, as many Aeroflot transports have been seen on the military airlift to Afghanistan.

Above: The Royal Air Force employs the Vickers VC10 for its long-range passenger and high-priority cargo transport. These are based at RAF Brize Norton, and are often used for governmental and Royal Family transport.

Boeing Model 707

Span: 44.42 m (145 ft 9 in)
Length: 46.61 m (152 ft 11 in)
Height: 12.93 m (42 ft 5 in)
Speed: 966 km/h (600 mph)
Range: 12250 km (7,610 miles)
Armament: none

The Boeing Model 707 has provided an excellent base for long-range passenger transport, as well as strategic cargo transport. Many countries employ the type, including Australia, whose aircraft is shown here.

new turbofans, which are economic over short routes, and of the prop fan may result in future changes. Notably, the YC-14 and YC-15 designs, which were to have provided a Hercules replacement until abandoned, were turbofan twins. In the USSR, Antonov's tactical An-12 'Cub' (a Hercules equivalent) is being replaced by the four-jet Ilyushin Il-76 'Candid', which can carry twice its payload over five times the range and is thus clearly in what other nations would term the strategic bracket.

This account of heavy transports cannot end without brief mention of the many civilian aircraft which are taken into military use in small numbers by several air forces. Some of these are VIP transports, such as the two BAe 146s of The Queen's Flight and the Boeing 707 variant which is the USAF's 'Air Force One'. Military markings adorn other members of the Model 707 family and similar McDonnell Douglas DC-8 series, and further British airliners: the HS Trident, BAC One Eleven and Vickers Viscount. Venerable Douglas DC-4/C-54s, DC-6/C-118 and DC-7s are to be found in Latin America and elsewhere, and the

world's Marxist countries are supplied with Tupolev Tu-104s, Tu-134s and Tu-154s as well as Ilyushin Il-18s and Il-62s. A few twin-boom Nord Noratlas transports operate mainly in Africa. Far from the big league dominated by the An-124 and C-5, they are obviously of the size and price to suit their operators' needs, for it should not be forgotten that three average aircraft can sometimes be more valuable than one giant. Biggest is not always best, but there is no denying the fact that times have changed immeasurably since the Berlin Airlift.

Left: The United States' already vast transport fleet can be augmented by the many widebody airliners serving with that country's airlines. Here troops disembark from a Transamerica Douglas DC-10 during exercises in Egypt.

Right: Throughout the Soviet involvement in Afghanistan, nearly all matériel has been brought in by air, mostly into Kabul airport. Principal type on the airlift is the Ilyushin Il-76 'Candid', which has far better take-off and climb performance than other available transports. This is especially welcome when the Mujahideen are firing heat-seeking missiles at the aircraft leaving Kabul.

Soviet transport aircraft

Antonov An-12 'Cub'
Span: 38.00 m (124 ft 8 in)
Length: 33.10 m (108 ft 7.25 in)
Height: 10.53 m (34 ft 6.5 in)

Speed: 777 km/h (482 mph)
Range: 5700 km (3,540 miles)
Ceiling: 10200 m (33,500 ft)

Armament: two NR-23 cannon in tail turret; max payload is 20000 kg (44,090 lb)

Left: The Soviet equivalent of the Hercules is the Antonov An-12 'Cub', which has been supplied to many client nations. India is among these, using its aircraft on long-haul transport duties across the Himalayas to collect parts in support of the MiG licence production effort.

Above: The best-known VIP aircraft in the world is the VC-137C of the United States President. The aircraft operates under the call-sign 'Air Force One' when the President is on board, and can be seen regularly at major airports around the world.

Ilyushin Il-76 'Candid'
Span: 50.50 m (165 ft 8 in)
Length: 46.59 m (152 ft 10 in)
Height: 14.76 m (48 ft 5 in)
Speed: 850 km/h (528 mph)
Range: 6700 km (4,163 miles)
Ceiling: 15,500 m (50,850 ft)
Armament: two NR-23 cannon in tail turret; max payload is 40000 kg (88,185 lb)

Right: Although wearing a civilian scheme, the Ilyushin Il-76 transports of Iraqi Airways are regularly used by the air force for transport duties, and retain the rear gun turret found in the military versions of the type.

Antonov An-22 'Cock'
Span: 64.40 m (211 ft 4 in)
Length: 57.92 m (190 ft 0 in)

Height: 12.53 m (41 ft 1.5 in)
Speed: 740 km/h (460 mph)

Range: 10950 km (6,800 miles)
Armament: none; max payload is 80000 kg (176,350 lb)

Left: The Antonov An-22 'Cock' has for years been the giant of the Soviet air force, but is set to be dwarfed by the An-124. The An-22's hugely powerful turboprops and highly efficient wing give it impressive performance and, allied to its low-pressure tyres, allow it to take off from short, rough fields.

Antonov An-124 'Condor'
Span: 73.30 m (240 ft 5.75 in)
Length: 69.5 m (228 ft 0.25 in)
Height: 22.00 m (72 ft 2.25 in)
Speed: 865 km/h (537 mph)
Range: 16500 km (10,250 miles)
Armament: none; max payload is 150,000 kg (330,690 lb)

Right: The Antonov An-124 differs from the Lockheed Galaxy in having a fuselage mounted tailplane, but in other respects is similar, having an upward-pivoting nose and rear ramp door. It is marginally larger and has better rough field performance.

Light Transports and Liaison Aircraft

Such is the diversity of light transport and business aircraft on the civilian market that air forces have little need to commission purpose-designed equipment for moving small loads and personnel. As they are not intended for combat operations (but sometimes, by force of circumstances, find themselves in that unenviable position), conversion to military standards is a procedure requiring minimal changes. With the addition of appropriate radios and possibly IFF, and the optional removal of comfortable seats and interior fittings, almost any civil aircraft can adopt a military role of this kind. It should not be forgotten, though, that light transports of an earlier era were built with military duties in mind and are still widespread in their original use.

However versatile the heavy transport, its use is uneconomic for delivering small loads. Lighter, short-range aircraft are cheaper to purchase and operate, and can fly into airfields unavailable to their larger companions. For communications work, an at least reasonable standard of comfort is required: not many high-ranking officers and politicians are prepared to wear ear-plugs and sit on a canvas seat for air travel. There was, of course, a time when officers of medium rank had a base flight aircraft (the RAF's station flight 'hack') at their disposal, these having mostly disappeared by the 1960s.

Three broad strains of light transport may be seen to be in service with the world's air arms, being the STOL/rough-field, type, general-purpose and VIP. Most are twin-engined, and with a small number of exceptions, power is provided by a piston or turboprop engine. In the first category of aircraft, noted for their STOL (Short Take-Off and Landing) attributes, the name of de Havilland of Canada is pre-eminent. The firm's Beavers, Otters, Caribous, Buffaloes, Twin Otters, Dash 7s and Dash 8s are in service with (or have been ordered by) a host of air arms, particularly those in lesser-developed countries. Powered by between one and four engines, they cover the complete light transport range and provide some overlap with the bottom

end of the heavy bracket.

The USSR's standard STOL transport is unique in that it is a military biplane which is still in limited production abroad: the Antonov An-2 'Colt'. Widespread in its use, it is easily the most numerous of its genre, far outstripping the combined production of DH Canada, Australia's GAF Nomad and British products such as the Pilatus/Britten-Norman Islander/Trislander and Shorts Skyvan and Sherpa. Nevertheless, Shorts' reputation was further enhanced when the USAF chose its Sherpa for the EDSA (European Distribution System Aircraft) requirement in 1984. EDSA illustrates the way in which light transports can enhance operational readiness in an economical manner. A fleet of 18 Sherpas is available for short-notice distribution of spare components as large as a jet engine from European logistics depots (which have, of course, been stocked in part by strategic transports flying from the USA). The funds saved by not having a large holding of spares at each air base will more than pay for the aircraft involved.

Pride of place in the category of general-purpose

Above: Among the plethora of executive jets used by the military is the Canadair Challenger, which offers excellent range performance. This example serves with the Canadian Armed Forces.

Above: Still serving in large numbers around the world, the trusty Douglas DC-3/C-47 provides admirable load-carrying ability for knock-down price. Most of the users are Third World countries who cannot afford the high-tech aircraft used by the larger nations. The all-round ruggedness of the C-47 more than makes up for any lack of finesse.

Left: Many countries can afford to build their own light transports, Israel being no exception. The IAI Arava is used by that country's air force for many duties, including several electronic warfare conversions. This one is an export model for Ecuador.

Left: Featuring rough and short field performance, the GAF Nomad is an Australian design which has achieved minor export successes. This is a RAAF machine.

Above: The Gates Learjet is found in the inventories of many air forces. A military conversion of an executive jet, the Learjet can perform such tasks as mapping as well as its usual VIP role.

Britten-Norman Defender

Span: 14.94 m (49 ft 0 in)
Length: 10.86 m (35 ft 7.5 in)
Height: 4.18 m (13 ft 8.5 in)
Speed: 280 km/h (174 mph)
Range: 672 km (418 miles)
Ceiling: 580 m (17,000 ft)
Armament: wing pylons can carry 1050 kg (2,300 lb) of light stores, including rockets, bombs, torpedoes or ASMs

The rugged design and short take-off and landing of the Britten-Norman Defender have made it a favourite with Third World air forces. Mauritania is among the countries that fly armed versions, fitting rockets to the wings.

de Havilland Canada DHC-5 Buffalo

Span: 29.26 m (96 ft 0 in)
Length: 24.08 m (79 ft 0 in)
Height: 8.73 m (28 ft 8 in)
Speed: 467 km/h (290 mph)
Range: 3280 km (2,040 miles)
Ceiling: 5575 m (18,300 ft)
Armament: none; max payload is 8165 kg (18,000 lb)

Another popular design is the de Havilland Canada DHC-5 Buffalo, which combines a large hold with extraordinary STOL performance. This example is in the inventory of Togo.

Antonov An-26 'Curl'

Span: 29.20 m (95 ft 9.5 in)
Length: 23.80 m (78 ft 1 in)
Height: 8.575 m (28 ft 1.5 in)
Speed: 440 km/h (273 mph)
Range: 2550 km (1,580 miles)
Ceiling: 7500 m (24,600 ft)
Armament: none; max payload is 5500 kg (12,125 lb)

Universal in the transport fleets of Soviet client states and the Warsaw Pact is the Antonov An-26 'Curl'. This transport was derived from the well-known An-24 'Colt' but features a rear loading ramp allowing the carriage of light vehicles.

Fokker F.27M Troopship

Span: 29.00 m (95 ft 1.5 in)
Length: 23.56 m (77 ft 3.5 in)
Height: 8.50 m (27 ft 11 in)
Speed: 480 km/h (298 mph)
Range: 4390 km (2730 miles)
Ceiling: 9145 m (30,000 ft)
Armament: none; max payload is 6440 kg (14,200 lb)

A conversion of a successful airliner design, the Fokker F.27M Troopship offers cost-effective transport over medium ranges, with limited rough- and short-field capability. Finland is among the customers.

transports must be given to the ubiquitous Douglas C-47 Skytrain/Dakota, which remains in gainful employment over 50 years after its maiden flight. Seating up to some 30 personnel, the C-47 remains one of the larger aircraft of its type. Others may carry as few as six passengers, this end of the market being dominated by Cessna and Piper products. A common feature of many such aircraft is the ability to change the interior rapidly between passenger and freight configurations and the provision in some of a large side door or loading ramp. The latter will be found on STOL Caribous, Buffaloes, Sherpas and Skyvans, plus the IAI Arava, HS Andover C.Mk 1 and CASA C-212 Aviocar, amongst others.

The trend in general-purpose transports is towards turboprop power, notably in areas of the world where high octane fuel for piston engines is scarce. This is the case in lesser-developed countries, where the air force's principal role may be transport to remote regions. A few piston aircraft have been converted to turboprop power and others (like the Dornier Do 128) have been built in both versions.

However impoverished a nation, the national budget always seems able to provide a jet transport for senior government officials. In many cases, these are operated by the air force, possibly alongside similar models used for military purposes. Standard types of business jet are employed, the most common including the Canadair Challenger, Dassault Falcon series, HFB Hansa Jet, BAe 125, Piaggio-Douglas 808, Cessna Citation, Gates Learjet, Rockwell Sabreliner, Lockheed JetStar, Gulfstream II/III and Yakovlev Yak-42 'Codling'. Sabreliners and JetStars have long been widely used by the USAF, but that service has begun converting to Gulfstreams and Learjets, initially leased rather than bought.

Recently the light jet transport has been made more appealing to air forces by the availability of military versions from the factory. Offensive roles are foreseen for some, although the more common duties are those in the training area. Notably, Denmark bases one of its three Gulfstream IIIs in Denmark for fishery patrol, SAR and internal transport, thereby making full use of a costly asset. Other European air arms are appreciating the savings to be made by purchasing, chartering or leasing executive jets for target-towing, survey and ECM training now that the older combat aircraft relegated to these tasks are reaching the end of their useful lives.

Below: Something of a coup was gained by the Northern Ireland company Shorts when they received an order from the USAF for the C-23 Sherpa, for use as an EDSA (European Distribution System Aircraft).

Right: The Atlas Kudu is a licence-built conversion of the Aermacchi AL.60, and is widely used by the South African forces for spotting and airlifting small parties of troops.

Inflight Refuelling

From the twin viewpoints of operational potential and economy, all air forces need 'force multipliers': aircraft which allow greater use to be made of existing equipment. The aerial tanker is one such aeroplane which has become a vital aspect of military aviation, its practical career beginning as recently as the 1950s. Tankers large and small, old and new are in constant daily use throughout the globe but, remarkably, only one was designed from the outset for such operations.

The advantages to be gained from extending the range of aircraft without the need for an intermediate landing were appreciated when the aeroplane was in its infancy, yet it was not until 1924 that the first military experiments began in the UK. The initial problem to be overcome was establishing contact, something with which today's novice pilots may have difficulty, even though little else in the procedure is the same. Early schemes mooted included one requiring liberal quantities of rope and a grappling hook, plus some manual labour from the receiver's crew as the hose was hauled aboard for fuel transfer by gravity to begin. Air-to-air refuelling (AAR) was restricted to the experimental, record-breaking and 'flying circus' categories until the eve of World War II when a practical method was developed of refuelling Short S.30 Empire flying-boats from converted Handley Page Harrows.

AAR was one of the few aspects of military aviation which did not derive dramatic impetus from war. The USA relied on large bombers to cover the great distances involved in the Pacific theatre, and the RAF would have used the old line-hauling method to bomb Japan had not the conflict ended abruptly. Civil firms (notably the UK's Flight Refuelling Ltd) were left to perfect an improved technique, this resulting in standardization of the 'probe and drogue' method now employed by the RAF. Operational use on the V-bomber force began in 1958, by which time the US Air Force had also adopted the system, then discarded it for another.

AAR enabled the first generation of Western heavy nuclear jet bombers to be assigned to targets far inside the USSR, but other strategic uses rapidly evolved. With the aid of tankers, all types of appropriately equipped aircraft can be moved over great distances to new bases even when en route landing grounds do not exist or are unavailable for political reasons. The RAF

has deployed fighters to the Far East, and the USAF regularly practises the reinforcement of Europe with tactical aircraft flown over the Atlantic a squadron at a time with their escorting weather aircraft and tankers.

Even when flying on local duties, fighters appreciate the services of an AAR aircraft. Designed for brief combat and return, some are unable to undertake peacetime task such as the prolonged escort of an Elint snooper from the other side, without recourse to a tanker. The wasteful alternative is to dispatch a steady stream of relief fighters, such as Japan has to do (because refuelling capability was viewed until recently as 'offensive' in nature by local anti-militarists). Now, bombers, fighters, strike/attack aircraft and even some transports and maritime patrollers have refuelling equipment as a matter of course. In a small number of cases, receiver probes are neatly-designed retractable fitments; the rest have permanent or removable additions to the exterior of the airframe. In one unique

application, the USA extends the range of Sikorsky HH-53 rescue helicopters by refuelling them from a Lockheed Hercules. The close proximity of whirling rotor blades to the refuelling hose makes this an operation requiring more than the usual concentration.

Not all aircraft refuel in a like manner. The two principal systems are those evolved by the USAF and the RAF (the US Navy following the British method, rather than that of its sister force). The USAF techni-

Left: The Dassault-Breguet Etendard IV is used by the French navy for tanking, using a 'buddy-buddy' pod under the fuselage. The usual receiver is the Super Etendard strike aircraft.

Above: Saudi Arabia is one of the many countries that use the Lockheed C-130 as a tanker. The large volume and excellent load-carrying ability makes this an obvious choice for a tanker.

Below: The Lockheed HC-130 is a specialized tanker for use with the USAF's fleet of combat rescue helicopters, in this case the Sikorsky HH-53. This operation calls for maximum concentration.

Left: The US Marine Corps employs the Lockheed KC-130 Hercules to supply their tanking needs, and these are also available to Navy aircraft. The probe and drogue method allows the refuelling of two aircraft at a time, but calls for greater skill from the receiver pilots.

Right: The breathtaking Lockheed SR-71 reconnaissance platform uses a different fuel, JP-7, to other aircraft and consequently requires a separate force of tankers. These are designated KC-135Q, and carry extra navigation aids and communications gear for accurate rendezvous with the SR-71.

que is known as the 'flying boom' because the Boeing KC-135 tanker is equipped with a telescoping tube beneath the rear fuselage. Refuelling begins with the boom being extended and lowered as the recipient aircraft edges in behind and slightly lower than the tanker. At the end of the boom's outer casing is a pair of fins with which the whole structure can be manoeuvred by an operator in the rear of the KC-135. The pilot of the recipient aircraft has only to maintain formation as

the boom is manipulated into an orifice normally located behind his cockpit. Once it has locked in place, fuel transfer can begin.

'Flying boom' has the advantage that special skills and additional training are not required on the part of the pilot and his aircraft need not be fitted with a drag-producing probe or the additional weight of a retractable system (which can jam at an embarrassing moment). Its principal disadvantages are that only one

'client' can be fuelled at a time and the system is better suited to installation in large aircraft. The British 'probe and drogue' method involves the tanker carrying one or more hose-drum units, each comprising a rubber hose which is unwound from a drum and deployed in the airflow for refuelling to begin. The hose is compact enough to be housed in a pod, so that the tanker may have one (possibly with a spare) in the fuselage and two more on the wings. Two fighters can

Above: The US Navy relies heavily on the Grumman KA-6 for its tanking needs, using this converted strike aircraft as a permanent 'buddy' tanker. Other aircraft, such as the A-6 Intruder and A-7 Corsair II can carry buddy pods if so required.

Above: The Soviet Tupolev Tu-16 'Badger' employs a unique refuelling method, the receiver aircraft snagging the hose by means of a grapnel attached to the wingtip.

Below: The McDonnell Douglas KC-10 Extender represents a quantum leap in tanker capability, being able to carry all the spares and fuel necessary to deploy a fighter unit halfway round the world non-stop. Here a KC-10 tops up a Boeing B-52.

be refuelled simultaneously, but for safety reasons 'three's a crowd'.

It is left to the receiver aircraft's pilot to edge forward and make contact with the 'basket' mounted at the end of the hose. This is the most critical part of the operation, but once attached there is a little more latitude for relative movement than with the USAF system. The latter gains full marks for versatility, however, as demonstrated by the French purchase of C-135F tankers for its probe-equipped fighters and bombers. A short length of hose and a basket can be quickly added to a flying boom, but it is impossible for a USAF aircraft to receive fuel from a hose-equipped tanker. The USSR has adopted 'probe and drogue' for those of its Myasishchyev M-4 'Bison-As' converted to tankers,

Left: In the flying boom method, the receiver positions himself behind the tanker and moves slowly forward, until the boom operator is in a position to 'fly' the boom into the receptacle. Here a Fairchild A-10 takes up the pre-contact position.

but the Tupolev Tu-16 'Badger-A' relies on a unique wingtip-to-wingtip method.

Already, it will have become apparent that the USSR's two main tankers are converted bombers. Likewise, the RAF has relied to a greater or lesser extent on adaptations of all three V-bombers, of which the Vickers Valiant was withdrawn with fatigue problems and the HS Vulcan was an emergency project associated with (but not used operationally in) the Falklands war. Old bombers like the current Handley Page Victor have the advantage that they are already in service, with trained crews, and can have the necessary tanks and 'plumbing' installed in the redundant bomb bay. Some extra piping and pumps are required to link the existing fuel storage with the new fitments, so that most tankers can either use all the fuel themselves or (theoretically) give it all away.

Fuel management is also important in order to ensure that centre of gravity limits are not exceeded, and it will be seen that some tankers have receiver probes of their own. In some cases, it is useful to have this capability, a prime example being the bombing of Port

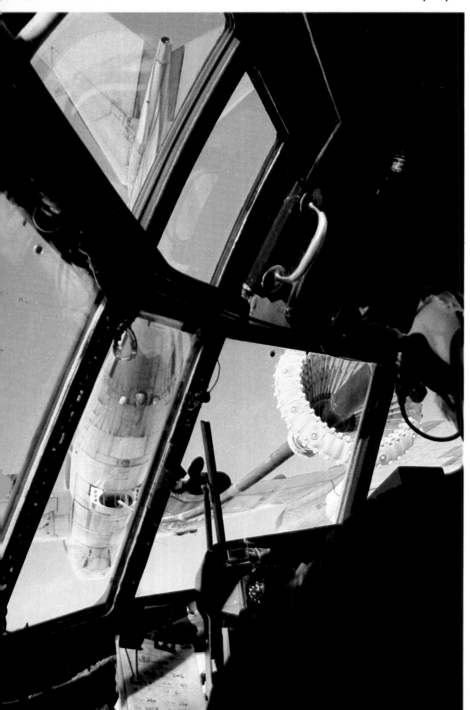

Left: The probe of this RAF Hercules can be seen clearly mated with the Victor's drogue. Such a contact requires high flying skills from the receiver pilot.

Above: A Grumman A-6E takes on fuel from a KC-10. The KC-10 carries a hose and drogue for refuelling non-USAF aircraft, as well as a large flying boom.

Boeing KC-135A

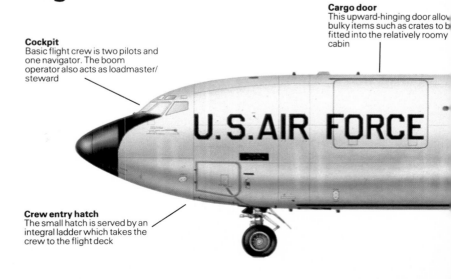

Cargo door
This upward-hinging door allow bulky items such as crates to b fitted into the relatively roomy cabin

Cockpit
Basic flight crew is two pilots and one navigator. The boom operator also acts as loadmaster/ steward

Crew entry hatch
The small hatch is served by an integral ladder which takes the crew to the flight deck

Handley Page Victor K.Mk 2
Span: 35.66 m (117 ft 0 in)
Length: 35.03 m (114 ft 11 in)
Height: 8.57 m (28 ft 1.5 in)
Speed: 982 km/h (610 mph)
Range: 7400 km (6,400 miles)
Armament: none; fuel load is 55880 kg (123,200 lb)

The ageing Victor fleet consists of converted nuclear bombers, and some retain their original camouflage.

Stanley by single Vulcans during 1982. Fourteen tanker sorties and 18 refuellings (10 of them between tankers) were necessary to support the bomber on its 12070-km (7,500-mile) journey and place Victors far enough out to give fuel when needed.

The USAF grasped the initiative in AAR when it called for a purpose-built aircraft for Strategic Air Command early in the 1950s. This, the Boeing KC-135 Stratotanker, formed the basis of the successful Model 707 airliner and the many 7-7s which have followed, although the prevailing trend is the conversion of transports for refuelling. Lockheed's KC-130H and a similar adaptation by the RAF of Hercules C.Mk 1s represent the rare prop-driven tanker, jets being more common. Strange to relate, ex-airline Model 707s have been fitted with hose-drum units for some customers, and a tanker version of the related Boeing E-3A Sentry built for Saudi Arabia. In the UK BAC VC10s retired from commercial use recently entered service.

Boeing 707s/KC-135s and VC10s have an asset additional to bombers in that they can transport some equipment and personnel as well as fuel. This capability has been taken one stage further in the wide-bodied tanker-transports operated by the USAF and RAF. The McDonnell Douglas KC-10A Extender is intended to accompany aircraft making a strategic deployment overseas, refuelling them and at the same time carrying ground crew and a large amount of support equipment. Lockheed TriStars being converted for the RAF have a similar capability, although they were specifically purchased to communicate regularly with the Falkland Islands and assist their reinforcement with fighters in an emergency. The USSR appears not to have a direct equivalent, yet is expected to deploy a tanker version of the Ilyushin Il-76 'Candid' heavy jet transport.

Discussion of such large tankers should not give the impression that all AAR aircraft are of this size. Navies, in particular, have smaller machines such as the Douglas KA-3B Skywarrior and Grumman KA-6D Intruder, whilst other aircraft not specifically designated can become instant tankers with the addition of the 'buddy-buddy' type of refuelling pod. This miniature hose-drum unit is attached to a 'wet' pylon of a tactical aircraft in order that it can sustain (usually) one of its fellows for a long distance sortie. It is also a tanker which can fly low and fast in a combat zone, unlike larger equivalents. Applications of the 'buddy-buddy' system include the HS Buccaneer, Dassault-Breguet Etendard IVP/Super Etendard and German navy Panavia Tornados, so supporting the view that no modern air arm can afford to be without tanker support.

This Victor K.Mk 2 is painted in the now standard hemp scheme of the RAF tanker fleet. The Victor has triple-point capability, although in practice two's company, three's a crowd.

McDonnell Douglas KC-10A Extender
Span: 50.41 m (165 ft 4.5 in)
Length: 55.35 m (181 ft 7 in)
Height: 17.70 m (58 ft 1 in)
Speed: 982 km/h (610 mph)
Range: 18500 km (11,500 miles)
Ceiling: 10180 m (33,400 ft)
Armament: none; maximum fuel load is 158,290 kg (348,975 lb) or 76843 kg (169,410 lb) of cargo

The KC-10 Extender can also perform long-range transport duties. Aircraft now carry a menacing dark grey paint scheme.

Boeing 707
Span: 44.42 m (145 ft 9 in)
Length: 46.61 m (152 ft 11 in)
Height: 12.93 m (42 ft 5 in)
Speed: 966 km/h (600 mph)
Range: 12250 km (7610 miles)
Armament: none; fuel load can exceed 55,880 kg (123,200 lb)

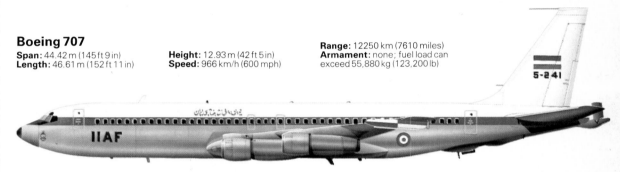

The Boeing 707 is used by Iran to tank its fleet of fighters, using both its drogue and flying boom.

British Aerospace VC 10 K.Mk 3
Span: 44.55 m (146 ft 2 in)
Length: 54.59 m (179 ft 1 in)
Height: 12.04 m (39 ft 6 in)
Speed: 885 km/h (550 mph)
Range: 8110 km (5,040 miles)
Ceiling: 12800 m (42,000 ft)
Armament: none; 102780 litres (22,609 Imp gall) of fuel

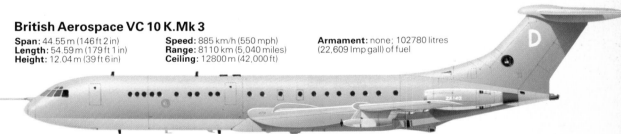

The Vickers VC10 is a triple-point tanker conversion of the well-known British airliner, serving with No. 101 Sqn at Brize Norton.

Boeing KC-135A
Span: 39.88 m (130 ft 10 in)
Length: 41.53 m (137 ft 3 in)
Height: 12.69 m (41 ft 8 in)
Speed: 982 km/h (610 mph) or Mach
Range: 11000 km (6,835 miles)
Ceiling: 10670 m (35,000 ft)
Armament: none; maximum fuel load is 90720 kg (200,000 lb)

Powerplant
The KC-135A has four Pratt & Whitney J57 turbojets which use full water injection during take-off, producing a great deal of smoke

With nearly 700 in service, the Boeing KC-135 Stratotanker is a common sight at USAF bases around the world. Its primary role is support of the SAC nuclear bomber fleet, but it spends most of its time supporting the other aircraft of the USAF, in particular tactical fighters. Using its empty hold, the KC-135 can also carry cargo, which is especially useful when it accompanies deployments of tactical aircraft, being able to carry their spares and ground crew.

Boom operator's station
Lying prone on a couch, the 'boomer' flies the boom with a joystick so that it is in the right position for mating with the receptacle

Flying boom
When not in use, the boom lies flat under the rear fuselage. It is lowered for use, suspended by cable. The two wings are controllable by the boomer

Avionics

Although the designers and manufacturers of avionics systems may deprecate the popular name 'Black Box' for their products, most of them continue to use a black metal casing to protect the highly complex devices which are so essential to modern aviation. Aviation electronics (avionics for short) account for at least one-third of the cost of an aircraft, greatly extending the abilities of its versatile but limited human crew. Flying is essentially a process of gathering, assimilating and using data, these all being areas in which electronic sensors and computers can excel.

Starting at the most basic level, the routine flight instruments of both military and civilian aircraft may be regarded as avionics. True, some of them still rely on direct air pressure and gyroscopes, but the movement is now away from a dial on the instrument panel and towards its representation on a multi-function TV screen which is the pilot's main source of data. It is well known that equipment has long been available to monitor flight parameters and keep the aircraft on an even keel and set course. The autopilot has now developed into an aid which will navigate the aircraft through a complex flight plan and land it automatically if weather conditions are poor at the destination.

Naturally, the en route autopilot is only as good as the aircraft's position-recording systems. The first generation of electronic aids such as the Loran, Tacan and Omega radio nets still perform a useful function, although the inertial navigation system (INS) is to be found on most advanced combat aircraft. Based on the movement-sensing properties of precision-built gyroscopes, the INS is accurate to within 3.2 to 4.8 km (2 to 3 miles) per flight hour, and can be even more precise if its computed position for the aircraft is updated by reference to a known geographic feature. Absolute navigational accuracy is demanded for strike/attack missions, so the INS of aircraft such as the Panavia Tornado can be updated by fixes taken with the on board radar to reduce errors to as little as 18 m (60 ft) per flight hour.

Seeking to evade detection, advanced strike/attack aircraft rely on radar to allow them to penetrate enemy defences at minimal altitude in all weathers. The first such avionics systems were known as Terrain Avoidance, in that they alerted the pilot to an obstacle ahead and required him to take appropriate action. Terrain-Following Radar (TFR), as now possessed by aircraft such as the Tornado, is an entirely automatic system which flies the aeroplane as low as 61 m (200 ft) and makes its own corrections for rising ground and power cables. In the flight test stage for later installation is the TERCOM (TERrain COntour Matching) system in which the outside view is matched electronically to a map stored in the aircraft's computer. Allied to the next generation of ring laser gyroscopes, TERCOM will produce unprecedented accuracy.

Useful though radar may be for TERCOM navigation, it has the military disadvantage of actively advertising the aircraft's position. The better solutions to seeing outside at night and in some types of poor weather are Low-Light-Level TeleVision (LLLTV) and Forward-Looking Infra-Red (FLIR). These pas-

Electro-optical aids in turret mounts are an increasingly common sight on battlefield helicopters. These are allied to helmet-mounted sights for low-visibility operations and weapon aiming.

sive electro-optic aids give no warning to the enemy, yet provide remarkably clear images of land or sea for both crew and computer. However, only recently have they been elevated from a target-acquisition aid to an important element in all-weather avionics.

It was the Vietnam War which brought FLIR to the forefront of military aviation, its first application being in a gunship during 1967. Now installations are multiplying, and even attack helicopters rely on thermal imaging (it no longer is restricted to looking just forward) to find their way about, day and night. The heat picture can be presented to the pilot projected upon a monocle positioned in front of one eye (the so-called 'helmet sight') or in his Head-Up Display (HUD), if it is one of the latest designs. HUD may be regarded as a logical extension of the reflector gunsight developed in the UK immediately before World War II, as it includes an angled transparent glass screen in the pilot's line of vision. As even clear glass has reflective properties, illuminated symbols can be projected into the pilot's line of sight whilst he is looking outside the aircraft.

At critical times of the sortie, such as weapon delivery or landing, the pilot can be distracted by the frequent need to refer to his instruments and change focus from a couple of feet to several hundred feet every few seconds. Readouts of important parameters projected on the HUD at infinity obviate this requirement, so the pilot is able to keep his head up, and attention outside the cockpit. En route, the HUD displays navigation data, then at the touch of a button changes to air-to-air combat or weapon-delivery modes. In advanced strike/attack aircraft, computers assume the greater proportion of the aiming task after the pilot or navigator has made a final position check at a landmark at the start of the final run in. The HUD displays the relative positions of aircraft and target as they close, and weapons are released at precisely the correct instant, after taking into account aircraft speed and height, wind speed and direction and the ballistic characteristics of different types of bomb.

Electronic countermeasures are more important than ever, and most combat aircraft carry ECM in one form or other. This Fairchild A-10 carries an ALQ-119 tactical jamming pod under the port wing.

In a high-priority programme, the USA is planning to augment the all-weather operating capability of several types of aircraft with an external podded system known as LANTIRN. Low-Altitude Navigation and Targeting Infra-Red for Night combines FLIR and TFR information in the pilot's HUD, so that he may operate day or night at low altitude and in bad weather. LANTIRN is a prime example of avionics considerably extending the combat potential of an aircraft. During the 24 hours of a European winter's day, a mere 20 per cent of the time is suitable, on average, for 'eyeball' flying, yet a night vision system such as FLIR adds a further 40 per cent to possible operating periods. Complementing this with TFR closes the remaining gap (13 per cent day and 27 per cent night) during which only an active radar system will permit flight. The UK has a less expensive system called Nightbird under development, relying upon FLIR displayed on the HUD for long-range sighting and pilot's Night Vision Goggles (NVG) providing for manoeuvring in flight. Nightbird allows aircraft operation for 60 per cent of the time, without costly TFR compoment.

Radar may also be obviated in attack aircraft if an alternative method can be found for pinpointing the target and accurately measuring its distance during the bombing run. The Laser Ranger and Marked Target Seeker (LRMTS) is such a device. If the pilot can see his target, he flies towards it as the LRMTS provides information from which the weapon-aiming computer can deduce the optimum moment of weapon release. However, when the aircraft is flying a close support sortie and a Forward Air Controller is on the gound with a laser designator, the FAC 'illuminates' the target as the aircraft arrives in his area. The LRMTS alerts the pilot, who then manoeuvres to begin the bombing run. Weapon release is automatic, even if the airman never catches sight of the target which the FAC has in his sights. The complete system can be further refined, with one aircraft carrying a laser designation pod and its companions equipped with laser-guided ('smart') bombs.

In the heat of battle, avionics assist in the vital aspects of warning against threats and preventing attack by 'friendly' units. Perhaps the most widely known of these functions is ECM (Electronic Countermeasures) which is typified by the jamming of

Left: The head-up display is found in nearly all of today's combat aircraft. It displays navigation or combat information in front of the windscreen, allowing the pilot to fly and fight without having to look down into the cockpit, an action which can have dire results in combat situations.

Above: Helmet-mounted sights and eyepieces give the modern helicopter pilot greater bad-visibility capability.

Above: Laser designation for attacks with laser-guided bombs can be accomplished either by ground troops or from the air. This Grumman A-6 carries a Pave Knife designator on the centreline.

The modern fighter cockpit (in this case a McDonnell Douglas F-15 Eagle) is dominated by the head-up display, where all necessary combat information can be displayed. The main flight instruments are located in the central console, while those for the armament are located to the left with engine instruments to the right. The two dark screens display radar returns (left) and defensive electronics (right).

enemy radio and radar signals. Some aircraft are specifically outfitted for this single task, and others carry podded or internal equipment to help them undertake the attack role. ESM (Electronic Support Measures) is the complete opposite, in that it listens for enemy signals in order to pinpoint their position. Thus can be seen the disadvantage of TFR and the value of passive IR and TV navigation at times when it is possible. The jamming aircraft, too, advertises its position, and must be circumspect in use of its equipment.

Related to ESM is the RWR (Radar Warning Receiver), whose antennae are normally found on fins and tailcones. RWR might be regarded as a personal ESM system. This warns a pilot that he is being 'painted' by an enemy radar and should initiate defensive moves in anticipation of attack. Some RWRs will automatically activate jammers or chaff/flare dispensers, having classified the type of radar reference to a data bank of signal characteristics. Operating in the opposite sense is the IFF Transponder (Identification Friend or Foe Transmitter/responder) which sends out a coded message (the 'password') when its carrier aircraft is interrogated by a friendly radar. NATO has recently decided to adopt a new, standard IFF to replace some of its ageing equipment, although the search for a completely secure and foolproof IFF has much in common with the

ancient alchemists' quest for the philosopher's stone.

These are by no means all the aviation electronics upon which a modern combat aircraft relies in order to execute its mission, but they are some of the more significant. Having been appraised of the capabilities of current and forthcoming avionics, the reader might be prompted to question the future of the human beings who are trained at taxpayers' expense to sit in the sharp end of military aircraft, seemingly just to monitor these black boxes as they go through their paces. Suffice to say this: three decades ago, when today's avionics bordered on science fiction, a British government defence review predicted the demise of the manned aircraft for combat operations within a few years. We are still waiting.

Above: Even the mighty Boeing B-52 has had to adopt large arrays of low-level avionics to perform its task in the modern combat environment. 'Eyelids' in the large protuberances below the nose reveal low-light-level TV and forward-looking infra-red for low-visibility, low-level operations.

Right: The 'thimble' nose of the British Aerospace Harrier GR.Mk 3 houses a laser ranger and marked target seeker, allowing it to achieve far greater weapons delivery accuracy against targets 'spotted' by laser by ground force.

Unguided Air-Launched Weapons

Combat aircraft exist for the prime purpose of firing or delivering their weapons. A remarkably broad spectrum of equipment is taken aloft by military aeroplanes and helicopters, and this can be grouped in several ways: air-to-air and air-to-surface; offensive and defensive; guided and unguided. The last-mentioned pair are convenient as a means of classifying aerial weaponry for examination, and here the systems without guidance are examined. To be pedantic, however, 'unguided' should describe weapons having no method of being influenced in their ballistic trajectory once it has left the aircraft. A cannon shell or bullet is most carefully guided during the first few feet of its path, and the chapter on avionics shows that great effort is expended in placing a bomber in precisely the right position for the weapons to be released. The distinction should therefore carefully be made between unguided and undirected.

It was not long into World War I before guns were added to aircraft; first to combat other machines, and then to attack ground targets. (The word 'strafe' is of German origin.) Guns are still widely used, ranging in calibres from 7.62 mm (0.3 in) to 30 mm, and very occasionally higher. The larger size is popular for fighter aircraft, as evidenced by the British Aden, French DEFA and Swiss Oerlikon 30-mm cannon types. Slight reduction has been evident in recent years, notably in the Panavia Tornado's 27-mm Mauser and the BAe Harrier GR.Mk 5's 25-mm Aden, showing that calibre is not the sole indicator of hitting power. For example, the Aden 24-mm weapon has a larger cartridge case, greater muzzle velocity and faster rate of fire than the old Aden 30-mm cannon.

Superpower small calibre

The USA and USSR have tended to stay with smaller calibres, the latter principally being associated with 23-mm weapons. American technology has been directed to achieving faster rates of fire in order to make the most of the fleeting fractions of a second during which the target is in the sights. This has brought about the multi-barrel weapons such as the Vulcan, which fires 6,000 20-mm shells per minute, compared with up to 1,850 25-mm rounds from the Aden 25 in the same period. Combining the best of both worlds, the GAU-8/A Avenger fitted to the Fairchild A-10A Thunderbolt fires at 4,000 rounds per minute, each 30-mm projectile having a tip of depleted (non-radioactive) uranium which spontaneously ignites on striking the target, so requiring no normal explosive filling.

Unguided rockets, usually housed in pods, are a favourite weapon of many air-to-ground crews, due to their accuracy and hitting power. Here a South African Blackburn Buccaneer lets fly with a full salvo.

Above: Cluster bombs form an important part of modern weaponry, these having maximum effect against soft targets across a wide area. This F-15E carries Rockeye units, as well as self-defence Sidewinders.

Left: The airborne gun is still a very viable weapon, especially when it is the GAU-8/A Avenger carried by the Fairchild A-10. This is a seven-barrelled weapon which fires depleted uranium ammunition.

Below: The effect upon a tank of a burst of the Avenger is shattering. The Avenger is the only airborne gun which can outshoot the deadly ZSU-23-4 SPAAG.

As an extension of the cannon shell, the rocket is a useful and powerful weapon. Even light aircraft are able to fire rockets without suffering the considerable airframe strains imposed by heavy cannon. Many calibres from 25 to 100 mm (1 to 3.94 in) are in regular use, occasionally on underwing rails, but more often in aerodynamic pods attached to aeroplanes and helicopters. Applications are generally against surface targets, and a generous variety of warheads is available to suit different purposes.

The bomb is no less ubiquitous. From the early hand-held devices, science has progressed to fission devices such as the American B57 which weighs less

Many modern attack aircraft have dispensed with the bomb bay, and so have to carry their weapons externally. This allows for greater flexibility of weapons options, but is crippling in drag. This is an Italian air force Tornado, loaded with GP bombs.

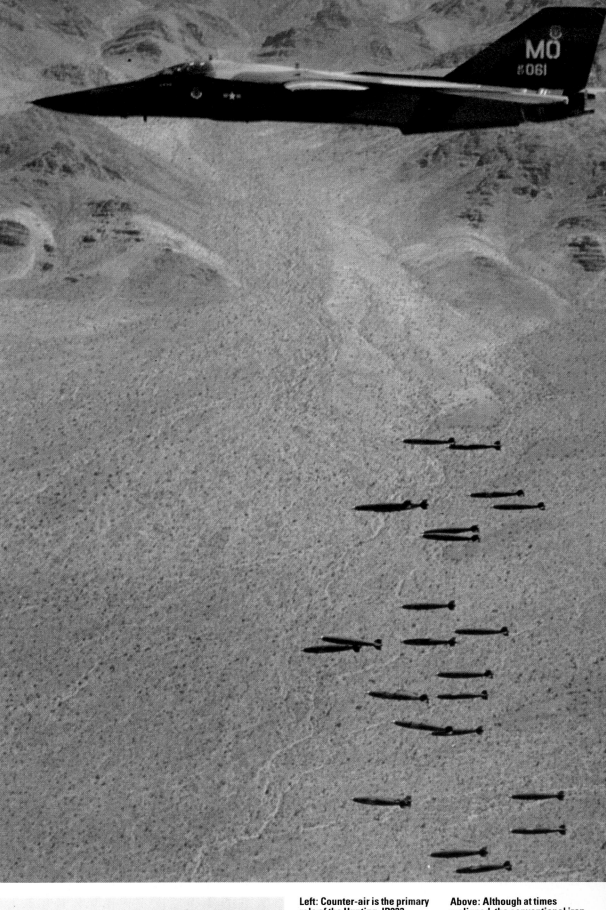

than 318 kg (700 lb) yet has the same destructive power as the Hiroshima weapon (20 kilotons). Strategic hydrogen bombs range above 1 megaton, although there are no present-day equivalents of World War II strategic conventional bombs like the 1814-kg (4,000-lb) or gigantic 9979-kg (22,000-lb) 'Grand Slam'. The 227-kg (500-lb) and 454-kg (1,000-lb) weapons are the most widely used, with smaller sizes available for light attack aircraft and larger weights for special missions. The 1000-kg (2,205-lb) size, made in both the USSR and France, is largest of the air-dropped weapons, but it should be remembered that the explosive content of bombs is only around 40-50 per cent of their total weight.

A further departure from tradition is to be noted in bomb delivery. In defended airspace it is too dangerous to fly at medium or high altitudes to release free-fall bombs, so low-level dropping at high speed is the norm. To prevent skidding along the ground, and give the aircraft time to put a little distance between itself and the explosion (a not unimportant consideration), retarding tails are fitted. These open out like an umbrella, or deploy a parachute, slowing the bomb and making certain that it strikes nose first. A slow arrival minimizes penetrative power, so different means are sometimes used for the important task of destroying the enemy's runways. The most spectacular and effective of these are the small bombs which are rocket-propelled deep into the concrete before exploding.

Indeed, the scattered 'bomblet' is in many cases far more lethal than a single weapon because of the large number carried by a single aircraft. A single 227 kg bomb a few feet off target is wasted, but the 147 sub-munitions scattered by a 227-kg (610-lb) BL755 cluster bomb stand a far greater chance of damaging battlefield and airfield targets. For the Tornado, the UK and West Germany have developed separate dispenser systems (JP233 and MW-1, respectively) containing both anti-runway bombs and anti-personnel mines for what are termed 'counter-air' missions. The MW-1 can also be used over the battlefield with a combination of different types of active and passive sub-munition effective against personnel and armour. Also in Germany, a system (VEBAL/SYNDROM) has been devised to eject bomblets from a pannier automatically each time the aircraft flies low over what its special detectors recognize as a large, warm metal object (i.e. a tank). Extremely accurate though this innovation may be, great interest is being expressed in giving scattered bomblets a form of terminal homing, so elevating them to the next level of sophistication: guided weapons.

Left: Counter-air is the primary role of the Hunting JP233 weapon, which uses small cratering mines and delayed action mines to take out enemy runways and then hinder repair work.

Above: Although at times maligned, the conventional iron bomb still plays a major part in air-to-ground weaponry. This General Dynamics F-111 lets fly with a heavy load during live drops in the desert.

Above: Rockets were used by the RAF's Harrier force in the Falklands, where they were found to be ideal weapons against Argentine positions. Cluster bombs were also used to great effect, both weapons possessing as important a morale-reducing factor as their explosive power.

Guided Air-Launched Weapons

Guided weapons have a long history of aerial deployment, in theory if not in practice. Germany was the first to employ a winged bomb steered by radio command, and might have fielded weapons more advanced still had World War II continued for a further year. It was then left to other nations, notably the USA, to persevere with the development of air-launched guided weapons. In this context, the word 'guided' is taken to imply some form of influencing a missile's trajectory once it has left its carrier. As will become apparent, that can be achieved by correction signals generated from equipment within the weapon as well as from messages transmitted by its parent aircraft. Once released, a missile is restricted in its ultimate options: it can either collide with another aircraft or strike an object on the ground or water. It is therefore an air-to-air missile (AAM) or air-to-surface missile (ASM).

The AAMs are carried both by fighter-interceptors and by aircraft seeking a measure of protection against enemy fighters as they go about other duties. In an extreme case they may be fitted to an unlikely carrier, such as the RAF BAe Nimrod maritime reconnaissance aircraft which took aloft Sidewinders during the Falklands war in case they happened upon an Argentine maritime reconnaissance Boeing 707 which had no defensive armament. Two principal groups of AAM present themselves for examination: IR-guided and radar-guided.

The notion of using infra-red (IR) as a method of detecting enemy aircraft predates airborne radar in fighters, but it was not until after World War II that practical heat sensors could be devised. Once that step had been achieved, the way was clear for development of a simple and comparatively cheap AAM which would go a long way towards replacing the cannon as primary equipment for air-to-air combat. By far the best known of these early weapons was the AIM-9 Sidewinder, greatly improved models of which are still coming off the assembly line. The USSR made a direct copy and mass-produced it as the K-13 (known to NATO as the AA-2 'Atoll').

By the time it got into its 'B' model, the Sidewinder was a reasonably reliable weapon, able to home on the hot exhaust of opponents' jetpipes from the rear quarter. Further advances in technology have given it (in its 'L' series) such sensitivity that when launched head-on it will seek the aerodynamically-generated warmth above a target's wings. Known as the 'all-aspect' weapon because the fighter pilot has few concerns as to the relative position of his opponent, the AIM-9L can even be equipped with filters so that it is not easily decoyed by flares released by its intended victim.

Weapons like the AIM-9, French Matra R.550 Magic, South African V3 Kukri and Israeli Shafrir/Python are termed short-range, or 'dogfight' AAMs, in that they are optimized for close engagements and fast manoeuvring at high speeds in the region of Mach 3. In such regimes the minimum range (say 300 m/984 ft for the Magic) can be as important as the maximum range (17.7 km/11 miles in the case of the AIM-9L).

For targets at longer distances, when interception is less of a dogfight and more a cold-blooded affair, a medium-range (MRAAM) missile is fired. The US AIM-7 Sparrow, French Matra Super 530 and British Sky Flash typify such weapons, by having semi-active radar homing (SARH). This means that they home onto the waves of their carrier aircraft's radar reflected from the target, at ranges of up to (Sparrow) 100 km (62 miles). It is not possible to classify all SARH mis-

Above: The AIM-7 Sparrow is carried in a semi-recessed fashion on many fighters, and the bay and lowered firing shoe can be seen on the F-14 Tomcat waiting for its deadly load.

Left: The McDonnell Douglas F-15 Eagle carries the well-known Sparrow (fuselage) and Sidewinder (wings) missiles into battle, this combination proving able to cover all but very long range engagements.

Below: This sequence shows an F-14 Tomcat taking out a QF-86 target drone with a Sidewinder missile. The Sidewinder homes in on the heat of the target's engine.

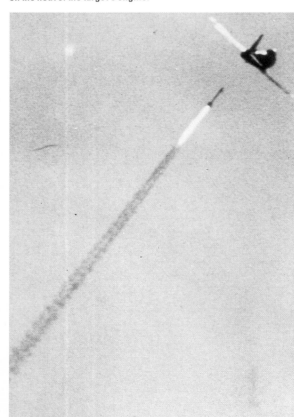

siles as MRAAMs, however, for the USSR is in the habit of making its missiles in both IR and SARH form and fitting fighters with at least one of each. France has also done this with versions of the older R.530.

Only the AIM-54 Phoenix, at nearly $1 million per unit, aspires to the long-range appellation, with a range of over 200 km (124 miles). This is a one-off missile, for AAM progress is directed more towards achievement of a broad height differential capability (snap up/snap down), operation in spite of ground clutter (in conjunction with pulse-Doppler 'look-down' radar) and fire-and-forget. The last-mentioned requires the AAM to have its own radar transmitter, as will the forthcoming Hughes AIM-120 AMRAAM. Deserving only passing mention, the LTV ASAT is an anti-satellite missile launched by a McDonnell Douglas F-15 Eagle, the aircraft acting merely as a launch vehicle, with no influence on the outcome of the mission.

Air-to-surface missiles

ASMs have even greater diversity of form than AAMs. There are general-purpose weapons, as well as those optimized for attacks against ships, tanks and radar stations. Some have a range of a few kilometres, other fly for over a hundred. Most basic are the anti-tank missiles (ATMs), usually carried by helicopters and often no more than a minimum-change version of a weapon carried by soldiers or fitted to a jeep. The Euromissile HOT, Hughes BGM-71 TOW and the Soviet AT-3 'Sagger' are in widespread use and all receive steering corrections by wire from their launcher until impact. Their range is up to 4000 m (4,374 yards).

Wire is also used for the Aérospatiale AS.12, a bigger weapon with a reach of 5000 m (5,468 yards) which is used against ships or similar large targets. Other anti-ship weapons, like the BAe Sea Skua and Aérospatiale Exocet, have longer range and are fitted with a radar altimeter to enable them to approach their targets at sea-skimming level for tactical surprise. When extra-long range is demanded, the traditional missile solid propellant motor is augmented by a miniature turbojet as a more efficient way of trading fuel for distance. The American AGM-84 Harpoon and BAe Sea Eagle are thus projected to distances of 100 km (62 miles) or so.

Like general-purpose ASMs such as America's AGM-65 Maverick, anti-ship missiles can employ more than one type of guidance, sometimes in different marks of the same weapon. Harpoon and Sea Eagle are fire-and-forget ASMs equipped with an inertial navigation system and active radar. After launch, they fly to the given target location (which can be supplied by a friendly unit other than the carrier aircraft) then engage radar for terminal guidance. Other anti-ship systems (the BAe Sea Skua for example) employ SARH like AAMs, requiring continuous target illumination. Television and imaging IR are alternative guidance methods, a crew member in the launch aircraft controlling the missile by radio from the pictures transmit-

Air-to-air missiles

AA-2 'Atoll' series

Length: 2.80 m (9 ft 2.24 in) (IR types)
Speed: Mach 2.5

Range: 8 km (5 miles)
Warhead: 6 kg (13.2 lb) HE fragmentation; impact and delay fuses

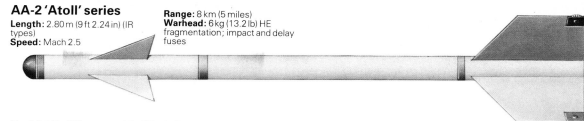

The AA-2 'Atoll' is a copy of the West's Sidewinder, and has undergone steady development, including a radar-guided model.

AA-7 'Apex'

Length: 4.20 m (13 ft 9.35 in) (IR version)

Speed: Mach 3.5
Range: 20 km (12.5 miles) (IR) or 55 km (34.2 miles) (SARH)

Warhead: 40 kg (88 lb) HE fragmentation; contact and proximity fuses.

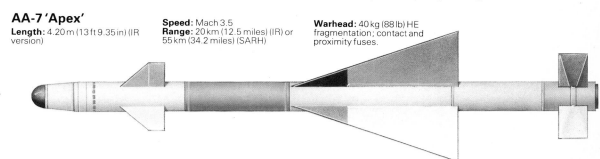

The AA-7 'Apex' can be considered a Sparrow equivalent, except that it is produced in both IR and SARH versions.

AA-6 'Acrid'

Length: 6.29 m (20 ft 7.64 in) (SARH)
Speed: Mach 4.5

Range: 25 km (15.5 miles) (IR) or 70 km (43.5 miles) (SARH)
Warhead: 90 kg (198.4 lb) HE blast fragmentation; contact and proximity fuses

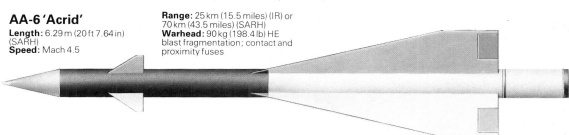

The giant AA-6 'Acrid' is the world's largest production air-to-air missile. It is carried only by the Mikoyan-Gurevich MiG-25 'Foxbat'.

Matra R.550 Magic

Length: 2.75 m (9 ft 0.25 in)
Speed: Mach 3
Range: 0.32-10 km (0.2-6.25

miles)
Warhead: 12.5 kg (27.56 lb) rod/ fragmentation type, containing

6 kg (13.2 lb) of HE; delay action, impact and IR proximity fuses

The Matra Magic is a popular missile, with particularly close ties with the Mirage family of fighters.

Matra Super 530

Length: 3.54 m (11 ft 7.4 in)
Speed: Mach 4.6
Range: 35 km (21.75 miles)

(R530F)
Warhead: HE fragmentation; radar proximity fuse

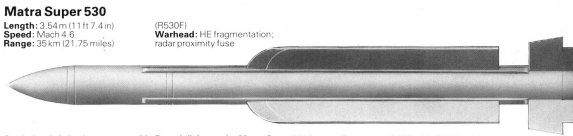

Carried mainly by the more capable French fighters, the Matra Super 530 is a medium-range AAM with SARH guidance.

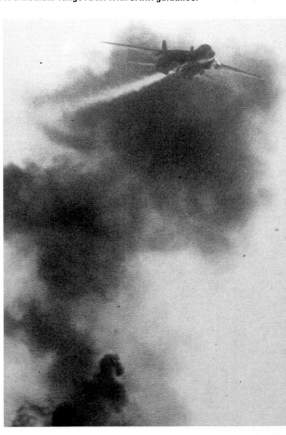

Above: Perhaps the best known of the anti-ship missiles, due to its Falklands exploits, is the Aérospatiale Exocet, seen here being released by a Dassault-Breguet Super Etendard.

ted by a camera in its nose.

More recently laser guidance has been practised by, amongst others, the Aérospatiale AS.30L, which flies down a beam of energy reflected from a designator pod. The multi-purpose Maverick, mentioned above, has TV, IR and laser versions. Lastly there is the anti-radiation missile (ARM) programmed to home onto enemy radar transmitters, presenting their operators with the option of switching off or being blown up. The Anglo-French Martel exists in ARM and TV versions, whilst the newest ARMs entering service include the Matra ARMAT, BAe ALARM and Texas Instruments AGM-88 HARM.

Air-breathing missiles (those with small turbojet engines) have been mentioned already, but are not restricted to anti-ship applications. Strategic nuclear air-launched missiles such as the Boeing AGM-86B ALCM cruise weapon are thus powered, and France's ASMP uses a kerosene-burning ramjet to achieve a range of 100 km (62 miles), rather less than the ALCM's 2500 km (1,555 miles). The USSR has long employed strategic air-launched cruise missiles, starting with the fighter-sized (9.00 m/29 ft 6 in wingspan) AS-3 'Kangaroo' of 1961 and progressing through to the smaller, faster AS-15 just being deployed.

In a new departure, the ASM is being developed as a carrier for sub-munitions of the type fitted in cluster bombs and the Panavia Tornado's MW-1 belly pack. Realizing the dangers of overflying the target to dispense the highly-efficient bomblets, designers have hit

Below: The Hughes TOW missile is the West's most important anti-tank weapon, being carried by the Bell AH-1S and Westland Lynx among others. Here an AH-1S fires a TOW, command guidance being supplied via a wire which unwinds as the missile is fired.

Right: The European equivalent of the TOW is the Euromissile HOT, which is carried by such helicopters as the Aérospatiale Gazelle (seen here firing). Future laser-guided missiles will allow the helicopter to fire and forget, enabling them to escape more rapidly.

Anti-ship missiles

AS-4 'Kitchen'

Length: 11.30 m (37 ft 1 in)
Speed: Mach 3.5

Range: 460 km (286 miles) (high altitude launch)

Warhead: 1000 kg (2,205 lb) high explosive or 350-kiloton nuclear

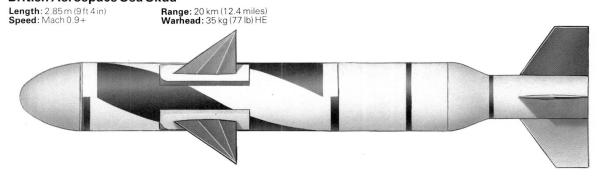

AS-4 'Kitchen' is a large anti-ship missile which can carry nuclear or conventional warhead. Intended for use against high-priority targets such as a carrier, the 'Kitchen' is carried by the Tu-26 'Backfire'.

McDonnell Douglas AGM-84 Harpoon

Length: 3.84 m (12 ft 7 in)
Speed: Mach 0.85

Range: 120 km (75 miles)
Warhead: 227 kg (500 lb) HE

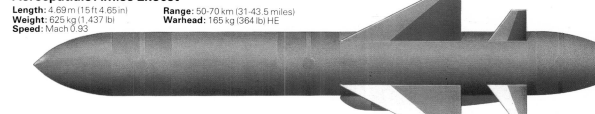

Harpoon is an anti-ship missile that can be launched from ship, submarine or aircraft.

British Aerospace Sea Skua

Length: 2.85 m (9 ft 4 in)
Speed: Mach 0.9+

Range: 20 km (12.4 miles)
Warhead: 35 kg (77 lb) HE

British Aerospace's Sea Skua is a light anti-ship missile often associated with the Westland Lynx. This combination proved itself in the Falklands.

Aérospatiale AM.39 Exocet

Length: 4.69 m (15 ft 4.65 in)
Weight: 625 kg (1,437 lb)
Speed: Mach 0.93

Range: 50-70 km (31-43.5 miles)
Warhead: 165 kg (364 lb) HE

The Aérospatiale Exocet is an air-breathing missile, which intakes air through an opening underneath the main fins.

Above: Anti-radiation is an increasingly important task for aircraft. The new HARM missile will provide greater capability in this field than has been achieved with the Shrike and Standard missiles currently in use. This Grumman A-6E carries a HARM during tests.

Above right: One of the most important general purpose missiles is the AGM-65 Maverick, which is guided by TV or imaging infra-red. Seen here being hoisted on to a Fairchild A-10, the Maverick is especially accurate, and is often used against armour.

Right: BAe's new anti-radiation missile is the ALARM, of which up to seven can be carried by the Tornado.

Below: Air-launched cruise missiles can be carried on the wing pylons of the B-52, 12 missiles being carried in this fashion.

Internally carried ALCMs are mounted on a rotary launcher in the B-52's bomb bay. As they drop, their tailplanes and wings pop out and their engines start.

upon the idea of a stand-off system. The UK, the US, France and West Germany are singly or in various combinations devising such weapons, typically the Franco-German Apache/CWS which will be fitted with an inertial navigation system. Apache/CWS has a common central section containing sub-munitions to which are bolted nose and tail units bestowing different options. The weapon will first be deployed for ballistic launching only, to a range of 15 km (9 miles); then have pop-out wings added to permit a glide to 30 km (19 miles); and, ultimately, a motor for ranges of 50 km (31 miles).

For all this sophistication, there is still a place in aircraft armament for the seemingly humble guided bomb. The laser-guided bomb (LGB) revolutionized conventional attack when first employed during the Vietnam War, and the type is stocked by most advanced air arms. It requires only a land or airborne laser designation source close enough to the target to illuminate it with a beam for the bomb's seeker head to follow. LGB systems, such as 'Paveway', comprise a seeker and a tail unit which may be simply 'clipped on' to any bomb to convert it to a 'smart' weapon. Similarly available are TV- or Imaging IR-guided weapons, typified by the American GBU-15 which augments a 2,000-lb (907-lb bomb with a nose camera/guidance unit and a tail section with autopilot, gyro unit and control module.

In conclusion, it remains to note one less obvious effect upon warfare of the latest generation of guided weapons, impressive though they may be. More than once in recent conflicts, aircraft have returned from an offensive patrol with weapons unused, even though the enemy was sighted and within range. The opposing unit was identified as a low-value target which would cost the enemy less to replace than the weapons which might have been used to destroy it. In addition to all his other attributes, must the modern combat pilot also be an accountant?

Laser-guided bombs have revolutionized the accuracy obtainable with large amounts of explosive, and this is amply illustrated by this 'Paveway' bomb hitting a truck. The Paveway equipment fits many standard bombs.

Sea Power

The scientific and tehnological revolution since the end of World War II has
had a considerable effect at sea, as it has on other fields of battle. Sophisticated weapons, detection and
communication systems have been crammed into platforms ranging from
nuclear-powered aircraft carriers through ballistic missile-armed submarines to the smallest of fast
attack craft, each type being much more capable (but considerably more
expensive) than vessels of preceding generations.

Contents

Ballistic Missile Submarines

Nuclear-powered submarines configured to fire long-range ballistic missiles (SSBNs) have a very special place in the strategy of nuclear deterrence. Operated by the USA, the USSR, the UK, France and China, they are not designed to make war upon the oceans by fighting other warships, in fact the opposite. they must run deep and run alone, and seek sanctuary out of the reach of hostile ASW forces. They are in effect floating missile silos made mobile by their nuclear powerplants, their very power to move giving them protection from the type of pre-emptive strike that so threatens the fixed-site land-based missile. For this reason the ballistic missile-firing submarine is the ideal instrument of deterrence. SSBNs cannot be eliminated in a first strike, yet their hydra-headed missiles could bring down devastating reprisal on a nuclear aggressor. There was the added factor that ballistic missiles launched from a mobile platform were inherently less accurate than fixed-site counterparts (although this is now no longer true). The first-generation missiles therefore did not have the accuracy to threaten pinpoint targets such as missile silos and command centres (so called 'counterforce targets') but only sprawling area 'countervalue' targets such as cities. In the past, therefore, submarine-launched ballistic missiles (SLBMs) provided the assured destruction component of the now discarded doctrine of 'mutually assured destruction' or MAD.

What has happened in the past decade is that guidance technology has matured to a degree whereby a new generation of SLBMs such as the US Trident II D-5 promises to be as accurate as a land-based missile. This has involved upgrades in the submarine's own SINS (Ship's Inertial Navigation System) which provides a continuous position plot, and navigation satellites which provide position fixes for both the launch submarine and the missile in mid-flight.

The first SLBMs were developed by the USSR. When the Soviets overran German secret weapon sites in the Baltic in 1945 they found giant containers designed to be towed behind U-boats: each one, if a plan called Project Laffarenz had ever come off, would have been used to fire a V-2 rocket at New York from positions off the US Atlantic coast. In a plan codenamed 'Golem' Soviet scientists tried to develop a similar concept but by 1955 had scrapped the towed containers and were conducting tests with ballistic missiles launched from a submarine itself. In 1955-6 seven 'Zulu' class submarines were rebuilt to accommodate two launch tubes running the depth of the keel and conning tower, each containing a purpose-designed missile report-named SS-N-4 'Sark' by NATO. These were followed by the purpose-designed diesel-powered 'Golf' class submarines each armed with three of these cumbersome liquid-fuelled missiles. At the same time the first of the nuclear-powered 'Hotel' class was under construction, also carrying three SS-N-4s each. These short-range (600km/373 mile) missiles, half of them mounted on non-nuclear powered submarines, accounted for much of the Soviet sea-launched strategic potential into the early 1970s.

The US Navy meanwhile got its first SLBM, the 2220-km (1,380-mile) range Polaris A-1, to sea in 1960 after a high-priority development programme driven through with great urgency by the US Navy and Lock-

Left: The 'Benjamin Franklin' class SSBN USS *Mariano G. Vallejo* was designed around A2 and A3 Polaris missiles, but by the time of commissioning was operating Poseidon C3 SLBMs. She was one of 12 'Poseidon' boats to be retrofitted with Trident I.

heed Space and Missile Co. The decision to go for solid-propulsion and cold gas underwater launch were crucial, while other new technologies mastered included small lightweight re-entry vehicles, miniaturized inertial guidance systems, advanced submarine navigation and many other critical breakthrough technologies. A new class of submarine was expediently devised by taking the existing 'Skipjack' class design of nuclear-powered attack submarine and literally grafting a 16-missile battery into it. The attack submarine USS *Scorpion* was sliced in two on the stocks, and a new section containing the missile launch tubes was added in the middle. The resulting SSBN, the USS *George Washington*, started its first deterrent patrol on 15 November 1960, and a new strategic era had begun.

Three classes of Polaris submarine were built for the the US Navy: the five 'George Washington' hunter/killer conversions, the five purpose-designed boats of the 'Ethan Allen' class armed with the 2780-km (1,725-mile) range Polaris A-2, and the 31 'Lafayette' class boats armed (from the eighth of class onwards) with the 4635-km (2,880-km) range Polaris A-3. From February 1969 to September 1977 the class underwent a conversion programme with larger launch tubes and a new Mk 88 fire-control system to accommodate the second-generation American SLBM, the Poseidon. First operational in March 1971, the Poseidon has the same range as the Polaris A-3 but a much bigger payload (10 Mk 3 MIRVs each with a yield of 50 kilotons) and much greater accuracy.

Far left: The 'Ohio' class are the new generation of US ballistic missile boats destined to carry the seaborne leg of the American deterrent triad well into the next century. Each submarine will be armed with 24 Trident D5 missiles.

Left: A test launch of Britain's much-modified Polaris A3 missile. These Royal Navy weapons have been the subject of a thorough updating programme, with new rocket motors and the 'Chevaline' modification has seen a dramatic increase in warhead penetration and accuracy.

Right: A 'Lafayette' class missile submarine undergoes a maintenance inspection. Some of her deadly cargo has been removed, but the white foam plastic covers on some tubes indicate that six missiles are still aboard. A similar operation aboard USS *Ohio* would reveal 24 tubes.

Ballistic Missile Submarines

Above: A finger on the button: this is the missile control station of USS *Ohio*, from where her 24 missiles would be launched if the unthinkable occurred. It has been said that a single 'Ohio' class boat is the third largest nuclear power in the world.

Left: A Trident C4 missile is launched from a refitted Poseidon boat during trials off the Florida coast. Each missile can carry up to eight warheads.

Above right: The missile compartment of the Trident missile submarine USS *Ohio* stretches into the distance. The 'Ohio' class are to be fitted with the larger Trident D5 missile, which for the first time will let submarines engage targets with precision.

Below: USS *Ohio* (SSBN 726) is shown at speed on the surface. While undoubtedly capable of high underwater speeds, such vessels carry out most of their patrols at low speeds.

In October 1979 the first operational patrol with the new Trident I SLBM was made with a converted Poseidon boat, the USS *Francis Scott Key*. The three-stage Trident with its 7000-km (4,350-mile) range vastly increases the searoom in which the launching submarine can hide, yet the addition of a stellar sighting technique to the Poseidon's inertial navigation means that it is no less accurate, even over these great ranges. By 1985 312 Trident Is had been retrofitted in Poseidon boats, with 304 Poseidon SLBMs remaining in service but slated for retirement between 1993 and 1999.

The first of the 18,750-ton submerged displacement 'Ohio' class boats, each to be armed with 24 Trident 11

D-5 missiles, completed trials in 1981 after a protracted and scandal-ridden construction period which went way over budget and schedule. Nevertheless 20 'Ohios' are planned by 1998, fitted with the Trident II D-5 SLBM from the ninth of class onwards while the others will be progressively retrofitted with this fourth-generation missile. The Trident II has even greater range and payload than the Trident I and can carry up to 15 MIRVs. What is even more significant is its accuracy, equivalent to that of a land-based ICBM. This 'assured second strike counterforce capability' as the US Department of Defence calls it, suits the new US notions of nuclear 'warfighting'. The targets of Trident submarines are rival weapons and command centres rather than cities, and the procurement of the weapon system confirms MAD's fall from favour.

Unlike the USAF and the specified purview of the Strategic Air Command, the US Navy's strategic submarine force is not under a single designated command (although its targeting is integrated with the Single Integrated Operational Plan or SIOP, the US strategic warmaking plan prepared at SAC's Omaha headquar-

ters). Operational control is exercised through LANT-COM, PACOM and EUCOM (Atlantic, Pacific and Europe Commands), answerable through the Joint Chiefs to the National Command Authority, who alone can authorize a launch.

A launch order would arrive as an Emergency Action Message. Only by mating it with its coded counterpart in the captain's safe would he begin a launch sequence. In certain circumstances a commander could arm and fire his weapons without coded instructions, even though it would need the co-operation of most of the crew. Just how that message would arrive is another important consideration. The essence of SSBN operations is stealth: the boats must come to the surface as infrequently as possible yet must be in a position to receive emergency action messages. US submarines communicate by a variety of means and on a span of frequencies all ultimately reaching back to the National Military Command Center via the most secure pathways of the Defence Communication System. The US Navy currently relies on satellites and shore transmitters to make contact with submarines trailing antennas

USS *Ohio* is seen entering port at Cape Canaveral during her initial Trident C4 launch trials. The C4 is a three-stage solid-fuelled weapon carrying eight independently-targetted re-entry vehicles, each with a single 100-kiloton warhead. The bigger D5 missile will carry 10 warheads, each of 475-kiloton yield.

some 10 to 20 m (33 to 66 ft) below the surface, a depth to which a very low freqency (VLF) radio signal can penetrate. There are also 18 TACAMO (Take Charge and Move Out) Lockheed EC-130Q aircraft, of which two are constantly aloft (one over the Atlantic and the other Pacific) to communicate on VLF through trailing aerials 8 km (5 miles) long. Even by these means a submarine has to come close to periscope depth or trail a radio buoy, while communications are intermittent. For many years therefore research has been conducted on Extremely Low Frequency (ELF) submarine communications systems with the power to reach the depths where SSBNs would normally operate, and the construction of such a system, with an 80-km (50 miles) long ground antenna begun in 1982, has been an important part of the US strategic arms modernization programme.

Ballistic Missile Submarines

Developed from the 'Yankee' class, the 'Delta I' was designed to launch the SS-N-8 missile, although only 12 tubes were fitted instead of the 16 of the earlier class. Although into its fourth variant, the 'Deltas' retain many of the characteristics of the 'Delta I' illustrated. The size of the missiles and the relatively small-diameter hull necessitate the distinctive missile casing abaft the fin.

Below: The mammoth *Typhoon* SSBN is thought to be comprised of two 'Delta' class hulls in a side-by-side configuration with the missile tube compartment forward of the sail. A true monster of the deep, the *Typhoon* has been designed for operations under the polar ice. Its huge size enables it to be armed with missiles capable of hitting the continental USA without ever having to leave northern Soviet waters.

The Soviet navy, which had first put a ballistic missile to sea in the 1950s but had then been rapidly overtaken by American developments, made great efforts to catch up from 1970 onwards, but still has far fewer strategic warheads at sea than does the USA and a much smaller percentage (23 per cent) of its total. Because of problems of serviceability and geography the Soviet navy can deploy only a fifth of its SSBN force at any one time compared with the US Navy's 50 per cent, while its boats are much noisier and tactically more vulnerable. The command and control network is cruder: the naval command was able to communicate with submerged submarines only from 1983 onwards using specially modified aircraft, a technique the US Navy had long perfected.

The pioneer nuclear-powered 'Hotel' class was followed by the mass-produced 'Yankee' class from 1967 onwards with 12 or 16 launch tubes armed with SS-N-6 'Sawfly' missiles with a range of up to 4000 km (2,485 miles). The 'Delta' class units, operational from 1972 onwards, each carry 16 SS-N-8 missiles with a 6000-km (3,730-mile) range. The 'Delta III' class boats each carry 16 SS-N-18 liquid-propellant missiles with two stages and a triple MIRV warhead. In 1979 a new missile, reporting-named SS-NX-20, was tested. It is thought to carry 12 MIRVs and arm the huge new submarines of the 'Typhoon' class, the first of which was launched in 1980 with two more by 1985. The 'Typhoon' is 170 m (558 ft) long (that is two and a half Boeing 747s) and displaces 33,000 tons submerged. Propelled by two nuclear reactors, despite its size the Typhoon is designed not to venture far from home but rather to act as a huge mobile floating silo screened from searching ASW forces by friendly forces or by surface ice.

US intelligence reported a new SLBM under test from 1983 onwards. Reporting-named SS-NX-23, it is expected to be deployed in a new 'Delta IV' class and feature accuracy over previous systems, plus multiple warheads.

The UK has operated a submarine-based deterrent force since 1969 based on four SSBNs armed with 64 US-supplied Polaris A-3 SLBMs. A secret and very expensive programme codenamed 'Chevaline' was put in hand through the 1970s to upgrade the 'front end' of the Polaris A-3s with a triple semi-MIRV system. Missiles thus modified are designated Polaris A3TK. It is current UK government policy to acquire the Trident II D-5 with British-developed warheads in a US MIRV bus. Four new SSBNs of the 'Vanguard' class will be built in the UK, each 150 m (492 ft) long, displacing 15000 tonnes and powered by a new pressurized water reactor that is also being developed to power the 'Trafalgar' class hunter/killer SSNs.

The French Force Océanique Stratégique (FOST) is based on the Ile Longue naval base in Brest Bay and consists of six SNLEs (Sousmarins Nucléaires Lance

Engins), the first of which *Le Redoubtable* was launched in 1967 and the latest *L'Inflexible* launched in 1985, with a seventh building. Each can launch 16 3000-km (1,865-mile) range M-20 missiles with a new 4000-km (2,485 mile) MIRV missile, the M-4, phasing in from 1985.

The People's Republic of China tested its first SLBM in 1982 and in 1985 it was thought that the CSS-NX-3 was nearing operational status. Deployed aboard a possible 12 'Xia' class submarines, the missile is reported as having a single 2-megaton warhead and a range of 2800 km (1,740 miles).

'Delta III' nuclear-powered ballistic missile submarine

Below: For many years the world's largest underwater vessel, the 'Delta III' class of ballistic missile submarine is a mainstay of current Soviet strategic capability. At least 15 have been built at Severodvinsk, with several more under construction in a modified form to take the next-generation SS-NX-23 missile.

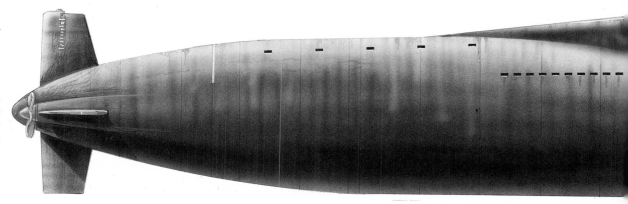

'Lafayette' and 'Benjamin Franklin' classes

Originally designed to carry Polaris A2 missiles, the 'Lafayette' class were successively converted to launch Polaris A3 and Poseidon C3 missiles. The last 12 units built to the 'Lafayette' SSBN design were officially designated the 'Benjamin Franklin' class because they were completed with quieter propulsion machinery. Of these vessels, six have been converted to carry the C4 Trident I SLBM.

Displacement: 7,250 tons surfaced and 8,250 tons dived
Dimensions: length 129.5 m; beam 10.1 m; draught 9.6 m

Propulsion: one pressurized water-cooled reactor powering two steam turbines driving one shaft
Speed: 28 kts surfaced and 25 kts dived
Diving depth: 350 m operational and 465 m maximum

Armament: 16 launch tubes for 16 Trident I C4 or for 16 Poseidon C3 submarine-launched ballistic missiles, and four 533-mm (21-in) bow tubes for 12 Mk 48 ASW/anti-ship torpedoes
Complement: 140 ('Lafayette') or 168 ('Benjamin Franklin')

'Ohio' class

The 'Ohio' class represents the latest in American technology, and is designed to defeat all foreseeable ASW threats that the Soviets are known to possess or believed to be capable of developing. Destined to become the mainstay of the American SSBN fleet in the next decade and after, the 'Ohio' class will eventually carry the D5 Trident II SLBM.

Displacement: 16,764 tons surfaced and 18,750 tons dived
Dimensions: length 170.7 m; beam 12.8 m; draught 10.8 m
Propulsion: one pressurized

water-cooled natural-circulation reactor powering a turbo-reduction drive to one shaft
Speed: 20 kts surfaced and 24 kts dived
Diving depth: 300 m operational and 500 m maximum

Armament: 24 launch tubes for 24 Trident I C4 submarine-launched ballistic missiles, and four 533-mm (21-in) bow tubes for an unknown number of tube-launched weapons
Complement: 133

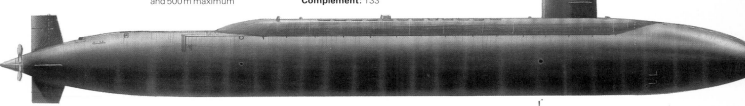

'Resolution' class

Although constructed in the United Kingdom, the four 'Resolution' class SSBNs have a considerable amount of their internal systems based on American components that were used in the 'Lafayette' class. They have been re-armed with the upgraded Polaris A3TK Chevaline system designed to penetrate Soviet ABM defences around Moscow.

Displacement: 7,500 tons surfaced and 8,400 tons dived
Dimensions: length 129.5 m; beam 10.1 m; draught 9.1 m
Propulsion: one pressurized water-cooled reactor powering two steam turbines driving one

shaft
Speed: 20 kts surfaced and 25 kts dived
Diving depth: 350 m operational and 465 m maximum
Armament: 16 launch tubes for 16 Polaris A3TK submarine-

launched ballistic missiles, and six 533-mm bow tubes for an unknown number of tube-launched weapons
Complement: 135

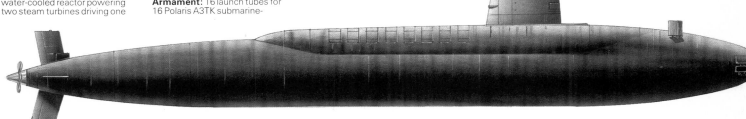

'Typhoon' class

While the 'Typhoon' class is of about the same length as the US Navy's 'Ohio', the unusual hull form almost doubles the beam of its American contemporary. The SS-NX-20 missiles are solid-propelled, and are believed to have payloads of up to nine RVs and a range of some 8300 km.

Displacement: 26,000 tons surfaced and 30,000 tons dived
Dimensions: length 170.0 m; beam 23.0 m; draught not known

Propulsion: four pressurized water-cooled reactors powering four steam turbines driving two shafts
Speed: 20 kts surfaced and 30 kts dived

Diving depth: 400 m operational and 600 m maximum
Armament: 20 launch tubes for 20 SS-N-20 submarine-launched ballistic missiles, and six 533-mm bow torpedo tubes
Complement: 150

'Redoutable' class

First of the French strategic missile submarines was *Le Redoutable* (S611), commissioned in December 1971. She and her sisters were designed and built in France without any help from the Americans, unlike the British Polaris boats, which were based on the US Navy's 'Lafayette' class.

Displacement: 8,045 tons surfaced and 8,940 tons dived
Dimensions: length 128.7 m; beam 10.6 m; draught 10.0 m
Propulsion: one pressurized water-cooled reactor powering

two steam turbines driving one shaft
Speed: 18 kts surfaced and 25 kts dived
Diving depth: 250 m operational and 330 m maximum

Armament: 16 launch tubes for 16 M20 submarine-launched ballistic missiles, and four 550-mm bow tubes for 18 L5 ASW and F17 anti-ship torpedoes
Complement: 135

'Delta III' class

Displacement: 9,750 tons surfaced and 11,000 tons dived
Dimensions: length 152.7 m; beam 12.0 m; draught 8.7 m
Propulsion: two pressurized water-cooled reactors powering

four steam turbines driving two shafts
Speed: 20 kts surfaced and 24 kts dived
Diving depth: 400 m operational and 600 m maximum
Armament: 16 launch tubes for 16 SS-N-18 SLBMs and six 533-mm bow tubes for up to 12 anti-ship/ASW torpedoes
Complement: 140

Nuclear-Powered Attack Submarines

The nuclear-powered submarine may seem to be the most potent warship of all, but in fact its military utility is limited. As seen in the preceding section, ballistic missile submarines (SSBNs) have one distinct doomsday deterrent role and must seek solitude rather than make open warfare upon the oceans. The nuclear-powered attack submarine (SSN) and guided-missile-firing nuclear-powered submarine (SSGN) are designed in contrast to make war upon the oceans, to seek out and destroy the enemy with deadly efficiency. Although they are not (yet) armed with long-range strategic land-attack missiles, SSNs and SSGNs are in many ways the most powerful warships at sea, but they cannot do everything. For example, they cannot transport and land an amphibious task force, or enforce a blockade in anything but the highest-intensity warfare. Nor can submarines as yet affect the battle for air superiority or contribute to fleet air defence, although autonomous vertical-launch missiles are under development which might allow them to do so.

But the nuclear-powered attack submarine is the deadly enemy of the surface ship, able to cripple an aircraft-carrier not only with torpedoes, but with a salvo of cruise missiles launched from over the horizon with a high-flying aircraft or even a satellite providing the target information. In similar manner a vital replenishment convoy coming for example from the USA to reinforce European NATO in time of crisis could be decimated by a couple of Soviet cruise-missile submarines. Even without the awesome destructive power of the ballistic missile submarine, it is not surprising that the composite sea power of today (and the technology that supports it) is written around the sub-surface threat, either making it more effective or dedicated to hunting it down. An important aspect of this process is that, in certain applications, the most effective adversary of the submarine is another submarine, the so-called 'hunter-killer'.

Post-1945 the lessons of the Battle of the Atlantic (how it was lost and how it was won) were eagerly examined by the Western Allies and the Soviets, and experiments were conducted with the prototypes of the Kriegsmarine's last weapons in the battle (including homing torpedoes, 'Type XXI' high-speed 'Electro-Boats' and 'Type XVII' peroxide-fuelled boats). Although Soviet wartime sub-surface operations had not been significant, the submarine was judged the ideal instrument with which to challenge the West, and the construction of a mighty submarine force has been undertaken with complete continuity of purpose.

Soviet attack submarines

In the early development phase of this formidable force, the Soviet emphasis was on defence, with submarines designed as 'carrier-killers' to attack the US Navy's aircraft-carriers which in the early 1950s were significant instruments of any postulated strategic nuclear attack on the USSR's. In fact the Soviet navy got a ballistic missile to sea in a submarine first, with the comparatively crude SS-N-4 of 1955, three of which could be fired from the surface by a conventionally-powered 'Zulu V' boat, but when the US Navy began to deploy the much more sophisticated Polaris submarine-launched ballistic missile (SLBM) in strength

in the early 1960s, the Soviet emphasis shfited to anti-submarine operations. Then when the Soviet navy got its own SLBMs to sea in nuclear-powered boats (with the mass production of the 'Yankee' class SSBN), the emphasis on ASW continued, the assumption being made early on that the most effective way to stalk and destroy an enemy submarine was to use another submarine.

USS *Jacksonville* is one of the 'Los Angeles' class attack submarines that are destined to serve with the US Navy into the 21st century as the primary underwater ASW platform. They carry Mk 48 torpedoes, Harpoon and Tomahawk SSMs and will be fitted for the ASW/SOW (ASW Stand-Off Weapon) system to replace their SUBROC missiles.

Left: A windfall for Western naval intelligence, this Soviet 'Victor III' class SSN got into difficulties off the North Carolina coast in November 1983. The vessel had to be towed to Cuba for repairs after becoming the most photographed submarine in the Soviet navy. The pod on the top of the upper rudder is for a towed sonar array, the first such installation on a Soviet submarine. To match the sonar's long range, the class carries both SS-N-15 and 16 ASW missiles.

Right: A 'Victor I' class SSN is photographed by a P-3 Orion of the US Navy as it passes through the straits of Malacca en route to the Soviet Pacific Fleet in 1974. The Victors were the first Soviet boats designed as 'hunter/killers' of other nuclear submarines.

The first Soviet nuclear-powered submarines, the 'November' class laid down in 1958 at Severodvinsk, were designed from the outset as anti-submarine warfare hunter-killers. When the USA deployed longer-range SLBMs from submarines which could lurk in the open oceans, the task of searching the Atlantic while NATO looked on was beyond the powers of the Soviet surface ASW units. The solution was to build more hunter-killer submarines with range and endurance to wait near the enemy's home ports and stalk their prey to the deep ocean patrol areas.

The 'Victor' class was designed for this role and was followed in 1968 by the 'Charlie' class which also had a considerable anti-surface ship capability. This class caused a wave of near-panic in the West when its units first appeared, by virtue of the sight of eight ports in the bow casing covering vertical launch tubes for an anti-shipping missile designated SS-N-7. This was reported as a 40-km (25-mile) range SSM which would break surface after launch and fly a sea-skimming trajectory to its target. If a submarine could penetrate a carrier task group's ASW screen, then the SS-N-7s comparatively short range could be used to advantage to pick off surface targets without warning.

Above: The 'Alpha I' class introduced a titanium alloy hull into Soviet navy service. This is a notoriously difficult material to weld, and at least one 'Alpha' has been photographed by US reconnaissance satellites in dry dock with damage caused by hull cracking.

Below: The single 'Papa' class cruise missile submarine could well be the precursor of a series of submarines designed to take on the US Carrier Battle Group, as she is apparently a development of the 'Charlie' class incorporating some of the advanced technology of the ultra-high-speed 'Alpha' class.

'Alpha I' class

The 'Alpha' class are the fastest, deepest-diving and just possibly the most expensive submarines in the world. Known as 'The Golden Whale' to Soviet sailors, the 'Alphas' are thought to achieve their very high speed by using an automated liquid-metal cooled reactor of advanced design.

Displacement: 2,800 tons surfaced and 3,680 tons dived
Dimensions: length 81.0 m; draught 8.0 m
Machinery: one liquid-metal reactor powering two steam turbines driving one five-blade propeller
Speed: 20 kts surfaced and 45 kts dived
Diving depth: 600 m operational and 1000 m maximum
Torpedo tubes: six 533-mm, two with 406-mm liners, all bow
Basic load: maximum of 18 533-mm torpedoes, but normally a mixture of eight 533-mm anti-ship or ASW, 10 406-mm ASW, and two 533-mm anti-ship 15-kiloton nuclear torpedoes plus two SS-N-15 anti-submarine 15-kiloton missiles, or a total of 36 AMD-1000 ground mines
Complement: 45

'Charlie II' class

A total of 20 'Charlie' class SSGNs have been built in three sub-classes since 1967 at the Gorki shipyard. Primarily used for surprise pop-up missile attacks on high-value surface targets such as carriers, the 'Charlie' SSGNs also have a useful secondary ASW capability.

Displacement: 4,500 tons surfaced and 5,500 tons dived
Dimensions: length 103 m; beam 10 m; draught 7.8 m
Machinery: one pressurized-water reactor powering two steam turbines driving one five-bladed main propeller
Speed: 20 kts surfaced and 26 kts dived
Diving depth: 400 m operational and 600 m maximum
Torpedo tubes: two 618-mm, six 533-mm (two with 406-mm liners) all in bow
Basic load: eight SS-N-7 'Siren' anti-ship missiles (four with 500 kg HE warheads, four with 200 kiloton nucler warheads); up to 12 533-mm torpedoes, or a combination of eight 533-mm dual purpose, six 406-mm ASW and two 533-mm 15 kiloton nuclear torpedoes; two SS-N-15 15 kiloton ASW missiles; two 609-mm Type 65 wake-homing very long range anti-ship torpedoes.
Complement: 110

Above: Similar in many respects to the preceding 'Swiftsure' class, HMS *Trafalgar* is the first Royal Navy submarine to be covered with anechoic tiles that reduce underwater radiated noise.

Right: USS *Birmingham* (SSN695) shows off an emergency surfacing drill during her sea trials. Note the large volumes of water pouring from her sail and the sail-mounted diving planes. A normal surfacing is achieved gradually by selective blowing of ballast tanks.

The investment in attack submarines continued during the 1970s, the cruise missile 'Charlie' and torpedo-armed 'Victor' classes being developed through improved models, while the boats of the 'Alpha' class with titanium-alloy hulls began to appear with a reported very deep diving capacity (over 900 m/2955 ft) and a very high submerged speed (42 kts) which provided ASW problems of an entirely new order. While Western navies devoted vast resources to weapon systems that could get to grips with deep-diving 'Alphas', the boats themselves were reportedly not a success and several have been seen by satellite reconnaissance in the process of being dismantled. New-generation SSNs include the 'Mike', 'Sierra' and 'Akula' classes armed with ASW torpedoes and SS-N-15/16 missiles and possibly SS-N-21 cruise missiles. The latest SSGN is the huge 14,000-tonne submerged displacement 'Oscar' class carrying 24 SS-N-19 anti-ship missiles with a range of 550 km (342 miles).

Western SSNs

The US Navy put the world's first nuclear-powered submarine to sea (in the form of the USS *Nautilus* which sailed for the first time in January 1955) followed by the 'Skate' and 'Skipjack' classes, the latter incorporating the 'teardrop' hull section and in place of a conning tower the slim 'sail' that has characterized subsequent US nuclear-powered submarines. The latest SSN in US Navy service is the 'Los Angeles' class, the first of which entered service in 1976. A total of 44 had been authorised by the Congress to 1985, with 20 more requested to support the US Navy's plan to have 100 first-line multi-mission SSNs. The 'Los Angeles' class boats are much larger than previous SSNs with a higher submerged speed. They are equipped with BQQ-5 long-range acquisition and BQS-15 close-in sonars, plus a towed array sonar, and can operate SUBROC, Sub-Harpoon and Tomahawk cruise missiles as well as conventional and wire-guided torpedoes. From 1984 onwards new-build 'Los Angeles' class boats have had a vertical launch system for missiles and modifications for operations under ice. An advanced computer-processing and sensor programme is being developed called SUBACS (SUB-marine Advanced Combat System) to be installed in new boats of the class. And according to the US Department of Defense's 1985 report, 'to meet the Soviet submarine threat of the 21st century, we have begun development of a new attack submarine incorporating the latest advances in technology. A key design objective is to make improvements in sound quieting ... improved sensor systems and ability to operate under ice more effectively ... now in a preliminary design stage, the submarine is scheduled for initial production in FY 1989.'

The Royal Navy also has a requirement for a new generation of nuclear-powered attack submarines, the first of which (HMS *Trafalgar*) was launched in 1981. The 'Trafalgars' will be armed with US supplied Sub-Harpoon SSMs, and the older SSNs of the 'Valiant', 'Churchill' and 'Swiftsure' classes will be retrofitted with the weapon. The Royal Navy is the only navy to have experience of live warfare employing nuclear-powered attack submarines: they were the means by which the original exclusion zone around the Falklands Islands was enforced in 1982, arriving long before the

'Sturgeon' class

Essentially an enlarged and improved 'Thresher/Permit' design with additional quieting features and electronic systems, the 'Sturgeon' class SSNs built between 1965 and 1974 were the largest class of nuclear-powered warships built anywhere until the advent of the 'Los Angeles' class boats. Like the previous class they are intended primarily for ASW, and employ the standard American SSN amidships torpedo battery aft of the fin, with two tubes firing diagonally outwards from the hull on each side.

Displacement: 4,266 tons surfaced and 4,777 tons dived
Dimensions: length 89.0 m (first 28 boats built) or 92.1 m (last 9); beam 9.65 m; draught 8.9 m
Machinery: one pressurized-water reactor powering two steam turbines driving one shaft
Speed: 18 kts surfaced and 26 kts dived
Diving depth: 400 m operational and 600 m maximum
Torpedo tubes: four 533-mm amidships with 17 Mk 48 533-mm torpedoes and six SUBROC anti-submarine missiles (being modified to 11 Mk 48 torpedoes, four Sub-Harpoon missiles, four Tomahawk cruise missiles and four ASW/SOW)
Complement: 121-134

surface warships of the Task Force. The sinking of the elderly Argentine cruiser *General Belgrano* by HMS *Conqueror* was the first and only overt act of war by a nuclear-powered boat. The British submarine picked up the cruiser and its escorts first on a Type 2024 towed-array passive sonar and was then able to close to short range because the Argentine escorts were not fitted with stand-off ASW weapons (such as ASROC) or with helicopters. The risk of a torpedo attack was

acceptable if made at high speed even if the old Mk 8s actually used were much shorter ranged (4 km/2.5 miles) than the wire-guided Tigerfish also carried by *Conqueror* but which had a reputation for unreliability.

France began building SSNs in the mid-1970s, the first of which (the *Rubis*) was commissioned in 1982 with four more on order. The new class derives much (including sonar, armament and fire control) from the 'Agosta' class conventional boats and, as this is the

smallest class of SSNs ever designed, there has clearly been a great reduction in the size of the 48-megawatt reactor compared with the original 'Le Redoubtable' SSBN class of the 1960s. Missile armament is the encapsulated SM.39 version of the Exocet anti-ship missile.

The Chinese navy is reported to have had two SSNs of the 'Han' class operational since the mid-1970s, but further detail and new building information are sparse.

'Los Angeles' class

The high underwater speed of the 'Los Angeles' class boats allows them to be the first American SSN units to be capable of providing an effective underwater escort capability for American carrier battle groups. Previous SSNs were too slow for most of the missions assigned to such escorts.

Displacement: 6,000 tons surfaced and 6,900 tons dived
Dimensions: length 109.7 m; beam 10.1 m; draught 9.85 m
Machinery: one pressurized-water reactor powering two

steam turbines driving one shaft
Speed: 18 kts surfaced and 31 kts dived
Diving depth: 450 m operational and 750 m maximum
Torpedo tubes: four 533-mm amidships
Basic load: 26 533-mm weapons (Mk 48 torpedoes, SUBROC anti-

submarine missiles to be replaced by ASW/SOW, Sub-Harpoon anti-ship missiles and Tomahawk cruise missiles) or 52 Mk 57, Mk 60 or Mk 67 mines
Missiles: (from 34th boat onwards) 15 Tomahawk cruise missiles in vertical launch tubes
Complement: 127

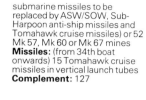

'Rubis' class

Currently the smallest of the world's front-line SSNs, the 'Rubis' class is powered by a French-developed and built 48 mW integrated reactor-heat exchanger system that fits well into what is essentially a heavily modified conventional 'Agosta' class submarine design. At present two squadrons of these SSNs are planned by the French navy, one based at Brest to cover the SSBN base and the other at Toulon.

Displacement: 2,385 tons surfaced and 2,670 tons dived
Dimensions: length 72.1 m; beam 7.6 m; draught 6.4 m
Machinery: one pressurized-water reactor powering two turbo

alternators driving one shaft
Speed: 18 kts surfaced and 25 kts dived
Diving depth: 300 m operational and 500 m maximum
Torpedo tubes: four 550-mm all bow

Basic load: 14 F17 wire-guided anti-ship and L5 mod. 3 active/passive ASW torpedoes, or 28 TSM3510 ground mines; from 1985 will be 10 F17/L5 mod. 3 and four SM.39 or 28 mines
Complement: 66

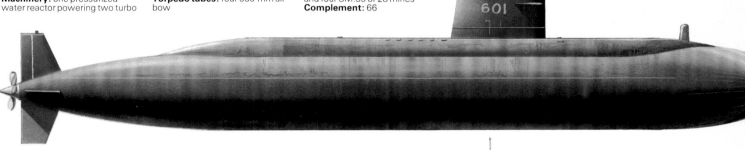

'Swiftsure' class

Quieter than their predecessors, the 'Swiftsure' class have proved to be excellent ASW platforms in service. The sonar fit is being upgraded and will eventually include the Type 2046 towed array as successor to the Type 2024. To match the detection ranges of the sonars all Royal Navy submarines will carry the Marconi Spearfish heavyweight torpedo.

Displacement: 4,200 tons surfaced and 4,500 tons dived
Dimensions: length 82.9 m; beam 9.8 m; draught 8.2 m
Machinery: one pressurized-water reactor powering two steam turbines driving one shaft

Speed: 20 kts surfaced and 30 kts dived
Diving depth: 400 m operational and 600 m maximum
Torpedo tubes: five 533-mm (21-in) bow

Basic load: 20 Mk 8 or Mk 24 Tigerfish 533-mm torpedoes plus five Sub-Harpoon anti-ship missiles, or 50 Mk 5 Stonefish and Mk 6 Sea Urchin mines
Complement: 97

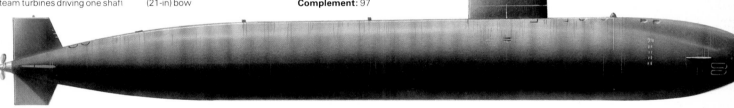

The clean external lines of USS *Sturgeon* (SSN 637) have no unnecessary protuberances that could cause cavitation (local low-pressure areas or vacuums), which is a prime cause of noise underwater. *Sturgeon* is armed with the 10-kiloton nuclear ASW missile SUBROC (to be replaced by ASW/SOW in the future), the use of which has to be approved by the President.

Conventionally-Powered Submarines

Above: Many smaller nations obtained their first submarines from the USA as the US submarine force went nuclear. This is the 'Guppy' class *Santa Fe* of the Argentine navy after her capture in 1982.

Above right: The 'Foxtrot' class is used all over the North Atlantic by the Soviet Northern Fleet, as shown by this 'Foxtrot' at anchor in the Gulf of Mexico, some 80 nautical miles west of the American port of Key West, Florida.

Right: 'Kilo' class medium-range boats have been entering service with the Soviet Pacific Fleet since 1980. This boat was seen in transit to the Indian Ocean from the important Soviet base at Cam Ranh Bay in Vietnam, where it is thought to have replaced one of two much less capable 'Foxtrot' class boats.

In the age of the nuclear-powered hunter/killer submarine, what role do 'conventionally' powered diesel-electric submarines have? First of all, nuclear-powered boats are very expensive indeed, to the extent that only superpower navies or those with perceived global intervention missions can afford them. Secondly, conventional boats have advantages for certain missions: they are useful for coast defence and for clandestine reconnaissance and minelaying, for they have the advantage over SSNs of being able to go completely quiet whereas a nuclear submarine must always circulate coolant through the reactor core.

Great technical advances were made by German U-boat designers in the closing stages of World War II. While the 'Type XXI' U-boat with its streamlined hull form, snorkel air mast and high underwater speed arrived too late to have any operational impact, development effort on the hydrogen peroxide-fuelled Walther turbine pointed the way to the true submarine independent of surface-derived oxygen. Several 'Type XVII' HTP (high test peroxide) boats fell into Soviet hands at the end of the war and the Royal and US Navies each got one, but their highly volatile propellant proved of more danger to their crews than they might be to any potential enemy and this line of development was terminated, the nuclear reactor proving the key to the true 'submarine' (capable of unlimited underwater operations independent of fuel and air from the surface) rather than the mere 'submersible'.

One of the most important aspects of the 'Type XXI' was the streamlined hull form, and the deletion of deck guns, conning tower platforms and the other features of wartime submarines configured as much to transit and fight on the surface as underwater. While development of peroxide-fuelled boats fizzled on and the first nuclear-powered submarines were on the drawing board, the major navies set about adapting the last German ideas to their wartime boats which still existed in large numbers. The American GUPPY (Greater Underwater Propulsive Power) programme reworked older boats by removing deck guns and obstructions and inserting a new battery section to double the available power. A large number of war-built boats were modified to 'Guppy I', 'Guppy II' or 'Guppy III' standard with progressive upgrades in weapon and sensor fit. 'Guppy IIIs' had the Mk 45 Astor nuclear torpedo, since withdrawn. Although now superseded in the US Navy by SSNs, the 'Guppies' continue to serve in minor navies and will continue to do so for some time.

The British navy modified its wartime 'A' class boats in similar ways, removing guns and external obstructions and remodelling the hull with high streamlined 'sail' conning towers. The first 'modern' purpose-built Royal Navy submarine was the 'Porpoise' class of 1958-61, capable of great diving depth and long-range underwater operations at high submerged speed, and possessing advanced features such as air- and surface-warning radar operable at periscope depth and air scrubbers to recycle oxygen when submerged. The

success of the 2400-tonne submerged displacement 'Porpoise' class led to the follow-on 'Oberon' class, of which 13 were built for the Royal Navy 1957-67, six for Australia, three for Brazil, three for Canada and two for Chile. Armament is eight 533-mm (21-in) torpedo tubes, six at the bow and two at the stern, and the class has an excellent reputation for quietness in spite of the age of the design.

The first of a new class of diesel-electric submarine, the 'Type 2400', was ordered for the Royal Navy from Vickers in late 1983. The first of the class, bearing the historic name *Upholder*, is due for commissioning in 1987 with competitive tender issued for three more.

The Soviet navy set out a hugely ambitious plan in 1948 to build 1,200 submarines between 1950 and 1965, in three broad classes, long-range, medium-range and short-range, the last powered by Walther turbines. The medium-range boats were the 'Whiskey' class, the first of which was commissioned in 1951 and designed very much along principles established by the last generation of wartime U-boats. About 240 'Whis-

kies' were built in 1951-7 in six types (the earliest models having deck guns) and large numbers were transferred to Soviet bloc and client navies. The larger longer-ranged 'Zulu' class boats were built at the same time, but in much smaller numbers, and six of the class were converted to carry a primitive first-generation submarine-launched ballistic missile.

While in the 1960s the US Navy's submarine fleet was switching to all-nuclear powerplants, the Soviet navy persisted with conventionally-powered patrol submarines, deploying in succession the short-range coastal 'Quebec' class, the 'Romeo' class which was basically an improved 'Whiskey', the 60-strong 'Foxtrot' class, and from 1973 onwards the 18-strong 'Tango' class. In 1980 a new 'Kilo' class was identified, shorter than the 'Tango' and apparently designed specifically for inshore operation. There are also the specialized 'Bravo' class which acts as target boats for underwater weapons trials, the 'India' class rescue (clandestine operation) submarine, and the 'Lima' class research vessels.

'Foxtrot' class submarine

A total of 62 'Foxtrot' class units were built from the late 1950s onwards in several subgroups. Of the total, two have been written off due to accidents whilst some of the older units which are in their 25th year are believed to have entered the reserve fleet to be reactivated only in the case of general war. Surprisingly, even after this period of time the basic design is still being built for the export market, with new-build ships being transferred to India, Libya and Cuba, albeit with downgraded electronic systems.

Displacement: 1,950 tons surfaced and 2,500 tons dived
Dimensions: length 91.5 m; beam 8.0 m; draught 6.1 m
Propulsion: three diesels delivering 4474 kW with three electric motors driving three shafts
Speed: 18 kts surfaced and 16 kts dived

Diving depth: 300 m operational and 500 m maximum
Torpedo tubes: 10 533-mm located as six at the bows and four at the stern
Basic load: 22 533-mm anti-ship and anti-submarine torpedoes, or 44 AMD-1000 influence ground mines
Complement: 80

A 'Foxtrot' class conventional attack submarine of the Northern Fleet is shown with a 'Kashin' class large anti-submarine ship of the Black Sea Fleet during their deployment with the Soviet Mediterranean Squadron.

Australian submarine forces consist of six British-designed 'Oberon' class diesel patrol boats, based at HMAS Platypus, Neutral Bay, Sydney. HMAS *Otway*, seen entering Sydney Harbour, is typical, and has been refitted with new electronics and Harpoon anti-ship missiles.

Evolved from the 'Foxtrot' class, the 'Tango' class long-range patrol submarine has been in service since the early 1970s. The example seen here was photographed off the US coast during the Soviet navy's 24th deployment to the Caribbean, in transit to Havana during late December 1984.

'Foxtrots' carry a 'Snoop Tray' search radar and a mast mounted 'Stop Light' ECM system.

Most Soviet boats designed in the 1950s carry a cluster of sonars in the bow. It would be reasonable to assume that both active and passive systems are carried, possibly with a short range upward scanning system for under-ice operation.

The number of free flood holes make the 'Foxtrot' class more noisy than western boats of the same period, but they are still much quieter than Nuclear boats.

Conventionally-Powered Submarines

The 2400-tonne submerged displacement 'Foxtrot' class has been widely exported (notably to India and Libya), while for a long time they formed the bulk of the Soviet submarine force in the Mediterranean to which they are better suited than big nuclear boats.

The 26-strong French 'Daphné' class contends with the British 'Oberons' and Soviet 'Foxtrot' for export success, with South Africa, Pakistan, Spain and Portugal among the customers for this small submersible (just over 1000-tonne submerged displacement). Armament is 12 550-mm (21.7-in) torpedo tubes (eight bow plus two internal and two external stern tubes). There are, however, no reloads. In 1971 the *Hangor*, a Pakistani submarine of the 'Daphné' class, sank the Indian frigate *Kukri* with a torpedo.

Ironically, perhaps, it is German dockyards who have had the most success with conventional submarine exports, led by the products of IKL (Ingenieurkontor Lubeck) and the design leadership of Professor Ulrich Gabler. The West German navy's first submarine was a wartime Type XXI scuttled off Flensburg in May 1945, raised and rebuilt in 1958-9 and recommissioned for experimental purposes in 1960. This ghostly echo of the huge wartime U-boat fleet was followed by the first IKL design, the 'Type 205' of 370-tonne displacement with a crew of 21, six of which were commissioned in 1961-8. These were followed by 18 'Type 206s' (*U-13* to *U-30*) built in 1971-4 and armed with eight 533-mm torpedo tubes. During their refit in 1977-8 these boats were fitted with the same minelaying gear as fitted to the earlier class, in an annular system with mines disposed on the outside of the pressure hull in a ring. The 48-m (157-ft) boats are built largely of non-magnetic steel alloy developed in response to the threat of magnetic mines in the shallow waters of the Baltic. Minelaying is one of the most important functions of conventionally-powered coast-defence submarines.

The IKL designs are small but powerfully armed. Without the constraints of designing for the West German navy with its mission in the Baltic Sea, IKL came up with a stretched but still very compact design aimed

at export markets, and the 54-m (177-ft) long 1350-tonne submerged displacement 'Type 209' has proved very successful, over 30 being sold to the navies of Argentina, Colombia, Ecuador, Greece, Indonesia, Peru, Turkey and Venezuela. The 'Type 209' can make 10 kts on the surface and 22 kts submerged from its 5000-shp (3730-kW) diesel-electric powerplant. There are eight 533-mm torpedo tubes and, despite the boats' small size, eight reloads are carried.

The Swedish navy deploys conventional submarines of an interesting indigenous design. The 'Nacken' class has a short, stubby teardrop hull with an unusual X-form rudder arrangement claimed to give better manoeuvrability than the usual cruciform type. The class is

The West German navy's 450-ton diesel-electric 'Type 206' submarines carry eight 533-mm (21-in) torpedo tubes. Crewed by four officers and 18 men, they have the uniquely German feature of a hull built of high-tensile non-magnetic steel. *U-29* was commissioned in 1974 and can make 10 kts surfaced and 18 under water.

a development of the original 'Sjoormen' design but with greater emphasis on automation and fire control, the boat requiring a crew of only 19. Armament is eight wire-guided Tp 61 peroxide-fuelled torpedoes with four bow tubes.

The most successful Western export submarine of the post-war period is the West German 'Type 209', which has been sold to navies in all parts of the world.

'Daphné' class

Of the nine remaining units of the 'Daphné' class, only the name ship has not undergone a full mid-life modernization which changes the shape of the bow area by adding a large sonar. Once the 'Daphné' class units wear out they will not be replaced, as the French navy will concentrate on building only nuclear attack submarines for the future.

Displacement: 869 tons surfaced and 1,043 tons dived
Dimensions: length 57.8 m (189.6 ft); beam 6.8 m (22.3 ft); draught 4.6 m (15.1 m)
Propulsion: two diesels delivering 1825 kW (2,448 hp) with two electric motors driving two shafts
Speed: 13.5 kts surfaced and 16 kts dived
Diving depth: 300 m (984 ft) operational and 575 m (1,886 ft) maximum
Torpedo tubes: 12 550-mm (21.7-in) located as eight in the bows and four in the stern
Basic load: 12 550-mm (21.7-in) anti-submarine and anti-ship torpedoes, or 24 ground influence mines
Complement: 45

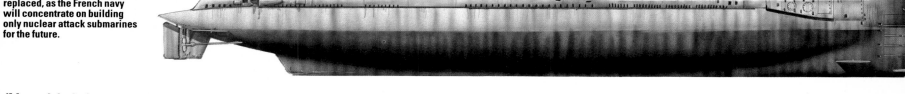

'Yuushio' class

The 'Yuushio' class is the mainstay of a projected 15-boat submarine fleet that will eventually be armed with the American Sub-Harpoon anti-ship missile. All the classes incorporate Japanese-built equipment, weapons and electronics into their designs.

Displacement: 2,200 tons surfaced and 2,730 tons dived
Dimensions: length 76.0 m; beam 9.9 m; draught 7.5 m
Propulsion: two diesels delivering 2535 kW (3,400 hp) with one electric motor driving one shaft
Speed: 12 kts surfaced and 20 kts dived
Diving depth: 300 m operational and 500 m maximum
Torpedo tubes: six 533-mm amidships
Basic load: 18 anti-submarine and anti-ship torpedoes
Complement: 75

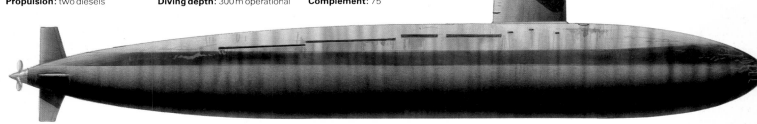

'Upholder' class

To meet a requirement for a new conventional submarine class for the Royal Navy, Vickers Shipbuilding and Engineering Ltd has developed the 'Type 2400' or 'Upholder' class. As with most new submarine classes, the emphasis has been placed on standardization and automation to reduce crew numbers.

Displacement: 2,160 tons surfaced and 2,400 tons dived
Dimensions: length 70.3 m; beam 7.6 m; draught 5.4 m
Propulsion: two diesels with one electric motor driving one shaft
Speed: 12 kts surfaced and 20 kts dived
Diving depth: 300 m operational and 500 m maximum
Torpedo tubes: six 533-mm bow
Basic load: 18 533-mm anti-submarine and anti-ship torpedoes, or 36 influence ground mines
Missiles: Sub-Harpoon underwater-to-surface anti-ship missiles
Complement: 44

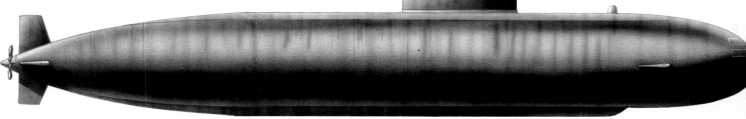

'Tango' class

Production of the 'Tango' class is now believed to be ended at the Gorki shipyard. The design appears to be an improved 'Foxtrot' but with the sensors and SS-N-15 ASW missiles of the third generation nuclear vessels. The later units were apparently built slightly longer in order to accommodate all the systems associated with the ASW missile fire-control and targeting functions.

Displacement: 3,000 tons surfaced and 3,700 tons dived
Dimensions: length 92.0 m; beam 9.0 m draught 7.0 m
Propulsion: three diesels delivering 4474 kW (6,000 hp) with two electric motors driving two shafts
Speed: 16 kts surfaced and 15.5 kts dived
Diving depth: 300 m operational and 500 m maximum
Torpedo tubes: eight 533-mm located as six in the bows and two at the stern
Basic load: 18 533-mm anti-submarine and anti-ship torpedoes, or 36 AMD-1000 influence ground mines
Missiles: two SS-N-15 underwater-to-underwater anti-submarine missiles

'Enrico Toti' class

The 'Enrico Toti' class was designed specifically for the shallow water areas found around the Italian coastline. Armed with four bow torpedo tubes for the wire-guided A184 heavyweight torpedo, the four vessels have a top speed of 20 kts submerged for a short time, but can sustain 15 kts for one hour.

Displacement: 524 tons surfaced and 591 tons dived
Dimensions: length 46.2 m; beam 4.7 m; draught 4.0 m
Propulsion: two diesels delivering 1641 kW (2,200 hp) with one electric motor driving one shaft
Speed: 14 kts surfaced and 15 kts dived
Diving depth: 180 m operational and 300 m maximum
Torpedo tubes: four 533-mm bow
Basic load: six A184 dual-role wire-guided torpedoes, or 12 ground influence mines
Complement: 26

'India' class

The 'India' class rescue submarines are equipped to carry and operate two deep submergence rescue vessels, and are believed to operate in support of the naval Spetsnaz special operations brigades when not being used in their primary role. Of the two 'Indias' one is in the Northern Fleet and the other in the Pacific Fleet.

Displacement: 3,900 tons surfaced and 4,800 tons dived
Dimensions: length 106.0 m; beam 10.0 m; draught not known
Propulsion: three diesels delivering 8948 kW (12,000 hp) to two electric motors powering two shafts
Speed: 15 kts surfaced and 12.5 kts dived
Diving depth: mother craft 300 m operational and 500 m maximum; DSRVs 1000 m operational
Armament: demolition charges, small arms etc
Complement: 70 crew plus 120 passengers/divers

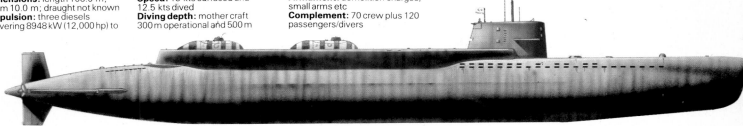

Aircraft-Carriers

The big CTOL (Conventional Take-Off and Landing) aircraft-carrier remains the primary instrument of maritime air power if no longer the supreme arbiter of sea power, the position it won during World War II. It has become the subject of controversy, however, with several question marks raised over its future: how long it would survive in all-out warfare in the face of submarine-launched anti-ship missiles, does it justify its enormous expense, and would the money and resources be better spent spread round a larger number of smaller, more austere 'sea-control' warships. Nevertheless a fixed-wing aircraft-carrier is a very powerful piece on the naval chess-board. Sea-based air power can be used to establish local sea control by shooting down or driving off enemy aircraft and by destroying any submarines within its anti-submarine reach. At the same time it is the most formidable instrument of power projection, able to carry massive strike power to any point on the globe.

Today only the US Navy can afford to build and put to sea the enormous concentration of military assets that large nuclear-powered carriers represent plus the large number of smaller warships that act as a carrier battle group's escort, but candidate members of this very exclusive club are waiting to join. Having put to sea the two ASW helicopter carriers of the 'Moskva' class in the 1960s and the V/STOL carriers of the 'Kiev' class in the 1970s, the Soviet navy is building its very first CTOL carrier, which will be nuclear-powered, and France has ambitious plans to build two CVNs by the end of the century. The Royal Navy has adopted the V/STOL solution with the 'Invincible' class while navies such as Argentina, Brazil and India meanwhile get by with ageing early postwar vintage hulls adapted as ASW platforms.

One of the key advantages of big CTOL carriers is the ability to operate role-dedicated aircraft types. A US strike carrier, for example, carries a wide range of specialized aircraft for various functions. A typical CVN air wing of 87 aircraft comprises four Grumman E-2C Hawkeyes for airborne early warning, 24 Grumman F-14A Tomcats for dedicated air-defence armed with long-range AAMs, 10 Lockheed S-3A Viking ASW aircraft, six Sikorsky SH-3 Sea King ASW helicopters, 24 McDonnell Douglas F/A-18A Hornets or Vought A-7E Corsair II light attack aircraft (two squadrons), 10 Grumman A-6E Intruder medium attack/strike aircraft (one squadron), four Grumman EA-6B Prowler ECM aircraft, four Grumman KA-6 tankers and a Grumman C-2A utility aircraft. This mix of types and role allows independent operations as well as composite fleet air and anti-submarine defence.

By contrast in the Falklands fighting the Royal Navy with slender resources but with remarkable success had to fulfil the gamut of essential tasks ranging from the securing of sea control by deflecting attacks in air to air combat and taking the war to the enemy on the ground with a single type of aircraft and without airborne early warning.

The Royal Navy had abandoned CTOL in 1978 with the paying off of HMS *Ark Royal* (HMS *Hermes*, which was the Falklands Task Force flagship, had her fixed wing capability removed in 1973, but was converted in 1980 to operate BAe Sea Harriers and Westland Sea King ASW helicopters), but showed the potential and the flexibility of V/STOL naval air operations to advantage in the Falklands when RN Sea Harriers and RAF Harriers performed brilliantly, operating from the two carriers and from improvised merchant ship platforms.

It was the transition in the early 1950s from piston-engined to high-performance jet naval aircraft that raised the stakes. Supersonic jets required bigger and bigger platforms from which to operate, and a nuclear powerplant became almost obligatory. As carriers grew in size the smaller navies of the world (including the Dutch, Canadian, Australian and finally Royal Navies) were squeezed out by cost and had either to switch to land-based maritime air power or to look at the alternative that V/STOL seemed to offer.

In spite of the British retreat from the CTOL business, three postwar British inventions proved crucial in solving the problems of operations with high-performance jets. After experiments in the 1950s with flexible rubber decks, the angled flight deck presented itself in a simple solution allowing an aircraft to land clear of the forward parking/take-off area, and so made possible continuous landing/take-off operations. This saved a large number of crashes into the barrier and allowed a touch and go landing if the hook failed to trap the arrester wire. The mirror landing sight automated and made much clearer the landing information presented to a pilot on final approach, and the steam catapult allowed much heavier aircraft to be launched even if the carrier was not moving into wind.

The next step was nuclear power, which was an

Top: An increasingly common sight on the world's oceans, this Soviet carrier group includes *Kiev*, a 'Kresta' class ASW cruiser, a 'Kashin' class SAM destroyer, and a fast support vessel.

Left: HMS *Illustrious* (nearest the camera) takes over from HMS *Invincible* near the Falklands after the former had hurriedly been readied for sea during the course of the South Atlantic War. The escort is the guided missile destroyer HMS *Bristol*.

Right: USS *Constellation* undergoes replenishment from a 'Mars' class combat stores ship in the South China Sea during the late 1970s. Commissioned in 1961, *Constellation*, her sisters *Kitty Hawk*, *America*, and the modified *John F. Kennedy* are the ultimate expression of conventional, fossil fuelled air power at sea.

Aircraft-Carriers

American innovation. Such a powerplant imparted a global range and provided masses of steam to operate the catapults, but a big CVN was and is terrifyingly expensive both in the capital cost of the ship and its air group and in the manpower needed to run it (446 officers and 5,758 men, for example on board the USS *Nimitz*).

After design studies begun in 1950, the world's first nuclear-powered carrier, the USS *Enterprise*, was commissioned in 1961, at the time the largest warship ever built and with eight pressurized water-cooled reactors, their uranium cores providing enough power for 483000 km (300,000 miles) of steaming. The *Enterprise* as built was characterized by a distinct top to her island configured for an ECM system. This was removed in her 1979-81 refit and replaced by a mast similar to that of the 'Nimitz' class ships. The USS *Nimitz* was ordered nearly a decade after the *Enterprise*, and two years of delays resulting from problems with her propulsion plant delayed her commissioning to 1975, her sisters the USS *Dwight D. Eisenhower* and USS *Carl Vinson* following in 1977 and 1982, and three more following in the later 1980s. The 'Nimitz' class is powered by two pressurized water-cooled reactors which can push the 93,000-ton displacement warship through the water at over 30 kts, their cores estimated to be able to provide enough energy for 1.61 million km (1 million miles) of steaming.

The design of US supercarriers, both nuclear and conventionally propelled, has been heavily influenced by the needs of strike warfare. As US strategic policy changed from the idea of the massive nuclear threat (in the late 1940s carrier aircraft were considered an important means of bringing Soviet targets within range of nuclear attack) to the doctrine of 'flexible response', so aircraft-carriers became floating airfields able to sustain prolonged conventional campaigns against ground targets. And in such circumstances the consumption of fuel and ordnance can be prodigious: the A-7 carries over five tons of bombs on a typical mission and in a three-day high-intensity campaign can expend over 45 tons. A strike air group of 36 thus consumes 1,650 tons of air to ground munitions in three days. The logistic needs of large-scale strike warfare in Vietnam saw carriers become huge floating bomb dumps, moored at semi-permanent offshore stations, while planners also had an eye on potential war in Europe where carrier aircraft might have to supplant land-based aircraft whose airfields had been destroyed, making attacks with conventional weapons against Soviet tactical targets.

The Royal Navy was squeezed out of the nuclear-powered carrier business as long ago as 1966 when when its revolutionary new CTOL carrier CVA 01 was cancelled because of cost. With the CTOL carriers' days numbered, the Royal Navy developed a hybrid ASW/AAW-dedicated ship at first known for the purpose of political camouflage as a 'through-deck cruiser' then as a 'command cruiser' and finally as an 'ASW cruiser'. Originally based on design for a sea control ship with area-defence SAMs and ASW helicopters, the ability to operate the Sea Harrier V/STOL aircraft (being developed in parallel) was bravely incorporated into the design. The new ship was designed to operate at the 'fleet speed' of 28 kts powered by four Rolls-Royce Olympus gas turbines generating 112,000 shp

Above: The nuclear powered super carriers USS *Eisenhower* and USS *Nimitz* are seen during the Indian Ocean Battle Group change over in 1980. Escorted by such vessels as the nuclear powered cruiser USS *California* (CGN 36) the modern Carrier Battle Group is capable of sailing at sustained speeds of over 30 kts for almost unlimited periods.

Right: Smoke and fire erupts from USS *Enterprise*'s flight deck off Oahu on 14 January 1969. CVW-9 aircraft were fully loaded with fuel and ordnance when a Zuni missile was accidently fired into the pack, resulting in 28 deaths and more than $50 million damage to the ship.

(83,510 kW). The massive slab-sided funnels contain the trunking for the gas turbines which are provided with integral hoists to allow them to be removed. Armament consists of a twin Sea Dart launcher forward and Phalanx CIWS added as a result of the South Atlantic fighting. While under construction a 7° 'ski jump' was built into the flight deck, a brilliantly simple

invention that allows the Sea Harrier to take off with a greater payload in a shorter length. By the time of the Falklands campaign any niceties about type name could be forgotten and HMS *Invincible* went to war as what she was: an aircraft-carrier operating 10 Sea Harriers and nine Sea King helicopters with great pugnacity and skill.

'Nimitz' class aircraft-carrier

Built to survive in a nuclear environment, USS *Nimitz* is well capable of delivering its own nuclear strike; it carries 100 or more nuclear weapons in its magazines for tasks ranging from destroying a nuclear submarine to devastating a large city. Its aircraft can attack in all weathers at all altitudes over long distances, and as such would make *Nimitz* a priority target for Soviet forces in the event of war.

'Nimitz' class

Displacement: 81,600 tons standard, 91,487 tons full load or (*Theodore Roosevelt* onwards) 96,351 tons full load
Dimensions: length 332.9 m; beam 40.8 m; draught 11.3 m; flightdeck width 76.8 m or (*Theodore Roosevelt* onwards) 78.4 m
Machinery: four-shaft geared steam turbines (two nuclear reactors) delivering 280,000 shp (208795 kW)
Speed: 35 kts
Aircraft: 24 F-14A Tomcat, 24 A-7E Corsair, 10 A-6E Intruder, 4 KA-6D Intruder, 4 EA-6B, 4 E-2C, 10 S-3A, 6-8 SH-3H and provision for 1 C-2A
Armament: four 20-mm Phalanx close-in weapon systems (CIWS)
Complement: 3,300 plus 3,000 air group

'Midway' class

Displacement: *Midway* 51,000 tons standard, 64,000 tons full load; *Coral Sea* 52,500 tons standard, 63,800 tons full load
Dimensions: length 298.4 m; beam 36.9 m; draught 10.8 m; flightdeck width 72.5 m
Machinery: four-shaft geared steam turbines delivering 212,000 shp (158090 kW)

Speed: 30.6 kts
Aircraft: approx 70
Armament: two octuple Sea Sparrow SAM launchers (no reloads) in *Midway* only, three 20-mm Phalanx CIWS in both
Complement: *Midway* 2,615 plus 1,800 air group; *Coral Sea* 2,710 plus 1,800 air group

'Midway' class

Because of their smaller size, the two vintage World War II (but modified) 'Midway' class ships have to operate with reduced air groups when compared to later US carriers.

'Forrestal' class

Displacement: (first two) 59,060 tons standard, 75,900 tons full load; (second two) 60,000 tons standard, 79,300 tons full load
Dimensions: length (first) 331 m, (second) 324 m, (third) 326.4 m and (fourth) 326.1 m; beam 39.5 m; draught 11.3 m; flightdeck width 76.8 m
Machinery: four-shaft geared steam turbines delivering 260,000 shp (193880 kW) in *Forrestal* and 280,000 shp (208795 kW) in others

Speed: 33 kts (*Forrestal*) or 34 kts (others)
Aircraft: as for 'Nimitz' class
Armament: three octuple Sea Sparrow SAM launchers (no reloads), three 20-mm Phalanx CIWS
Complement: 2,790 plus 2,150 air group

'Forrestal' class

Introduced in the 1950s, the 'Forrestal' class represented an enormous leap in carrier capability as well as forming the basis for subsequent US carrier design.

'Kitty Hawk', 'America' and 'John F. Kennedy' classes

Displacement: first two 60,100 tons standard, 80,800 tons full load; third 60,300 tons standard, 81,500 tons full load; fourth 61,000 tons standard, 82,561 tons full load
Dimensions: length (first two) 318.8 m, (third) 319.3 m and (fourth) 320.7 m; beam 39.6 m; draught (first three) 11.3 m or (fourth) 10.9 m
Machinery: four-shaft geared steam turbines delivering 280,000 shp (208795 kW)

Speed: 33.6 kts
Aircraft: see 'Nimitz' class
Armament: three octuple Sea Sparrow SAM launchers (no reloads), three 20-mm Phalanx CIWS
Complement: 2,900 plus 2,500 air group

'Kitty Hawk' class

Essentially built to an improved 'Forrestal' design, the 'Kitty Hawk' class carry an air group similar in size and composition to the 'Nimitz'.

'Kiev' class

Displacement: 36,000 tons standard, 44,000 tons full load
Dimensions: length 275 m; beam 50 m including flightdeck and sponsons; draught (31 ft 2 in)
Machinery: four-shaft geared steam turbines delivering 180,000 shp (134225 kW)
Speed: 32 kts
Armament: four twin SS-N-12 'Sandbox' SSM launchers (16 missiles), two twin SA-N-3 'Goblet' area-defence SAM launchers (72 missiles), two twin

SA-N-4 'Gecko' short-range SAM launchers (36 missiles, not in third vessel), two twin 76-mm (3-in) DP, eight 30-mm ADG-630 six-barrel 'Gatling' CIWS, two 12-barrel 250-mm (9.84-in) MBU 600 ASW rocket-launchers, one twin

SUW-N-1 ASW launcher (20 FRAS-1 and SS-N-14 'Silex' carried) and two quintuple 533-mm ASW torpedo tubes
Aircraft: 32 (20 helicopters)
Complement: 1,200 excluding air wing

'Kiev' class

The first of a 4-ship class, the *Kiev* was laid down in September 1970, launched in December 1972 and commissioned in October 1976 after extensive trials.

'Clemenceau' class

Displacement: 22,000 tons standard, 32,185 tons full load (*Clemenceau*) or 32,780 tons full load (*Foch*)
Dimensions: length 265 m; beam 31.7 m with bulges; draught 8.6 m
Machinery: two-shaft geared steam turbines delivering 126,000 shp (93960 kW)
Speed: 33 kts
Armament: eight 100-mm DP
Aircraft: 40
Complement: 1,338

'Clemenceau' class

The 'Clemenceau' class were the first French vessels to be designed from the outset as aircraft carriers, incorporating all the design lessons learned in the 1950s.

Veinticinco de Mayo

Displacement: 15,892 tons standard, 19,896 tons full load
Dimensions: length 211.3 m; beam 24.4 m; draught 7.6 m; flight deck width 42.4 m
Machinery: two-shaft geared steam turbines delivering 40,000 shp (29830 kW)
Speed: 24.25 kts
Armament: nine single 40-mm AA
Aircraft: 22

'Veinticinco de Mayo'

The main target for the British SSN force during the Falklands war was *Veinticinco de Mayo*, the flagship of the original task force that invaded the islands.

Right: The British light carrier HMS *Invincible* steams at speed in the South Atlantic operational area during the 1982 Falklands War. A minimum of 15-20 kts was maintained at all times to avoid submarine attack, whilst a defensive zig-zag pattern was followed.

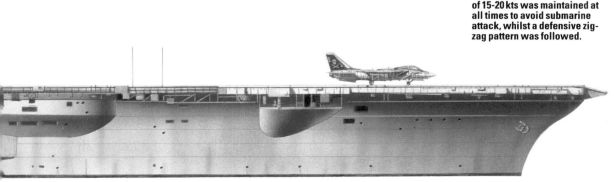

Aircraft-Carriers

Left: A recent view of *Minas Gerais* with four S-2E Trackers, four SH-3D Sea Kings, two Lynx and an Ecureuil ranged on the flight deck. A more modern V/STOL carrier design is currently under study to replace her.

Right: Seen entering Nice, *Clemenceau* and her sister provided air support to the French contingent in Lebanon in 1983. After recent modifications the two 'Clemenceau' class carriers will serve on until the 1990s.

Below: USS *California* (CGN 36) acts as a 'goalkeeper' escort to the carrier USS *Nimitz* (CVN 68), defending her against any aircraft that leak through the outer defences.

Carrier-Based Naval Air Power: A Summary

Argentina

The Argentine navy operates 14 Super Etendards but whether or not they operate from the *Veinticinco de Mayo* is unresolved. The navy's flagship is the former British 'Colossus' class carrier HMS *Venerable*, acquired from the Netherlands in 1969, but she took no effective part in the Falklands campaign. The *Veinticinco de Mayo* operates 21 aircraft, a variable complement of McDonnell Douglas A-4 Skyhawks, Grumman S-2A Trackers and Sea King ASW helicopters.

Brazil

The *Minas Gerais* commissioned in the Brazilian navy in 1960 (ex-HMS *Vengeance*) is an ASW platform operating only seven S-2A Trackers and four Sea Kings.

France

The French navy's two CTOL carriers *Foch* (1963) and *Clemenceau* (1961) were given extensive refits in the early 1980s and will serve until the 1990s with Super Etendard aircraft in the strike and air-defence roles. On present plans construction of a new nuclear-powered carrier, the *Charles de Gaulle*, will begin in 1986 with a second to follow.

India

The carrier *Vikrant* (ex-HMS *Hercules*) commissioned in 1961 has recently been modernized by the addition of a ski-jump. Eight Sea Harriers have been delivered, replacing old Sea Hawks, and the ASW role is undertaken by four Breguet Alizés. HMS *Hermes* has been acquired from the Royal Navy together with more Sea Harriers.

Italy

The Italian navy operates the helicopter carrier *Giuseppe Garibaldi* commissioned in 1984 and equipped with 16 ASH-3 Sea Kings although it is also V/STOL capable. More ASW helicopters are deployed around various naval vessels and at shore bases.

Spain

In 1973 the Spanish navy became the third in the world to operate V/STOL aircraft when it acquired eight AV-8As from the US Marine Corps. Originally the World War II light carrier USS *Cabot*, the *Dedalo* was joined in 1986 by the *Principe de Asturias* light V/STOL carrier, purpose-built from the US sea-control ship design. The new carrier has a ski jump and hangarage for 20 aircraft.

UK

Plans to run down the Royal Navy's organic fixed-wing air capability were dramatically reversed by the Falklands crisis. Instead of selling her carriers abroad, the Royal Navy has three such ships (HMS *Invincible*, HMS *Illustrious* and HMS *Ark Royal*), the old warhorse HMS *Hermes* having been paid off in 1985. There are 24 Sea Harriers in service with 14 more on order while the original batch began to receive a mid-life systems update from 1985.

USA

Under the Reagan administration the US Navy has a goal of 15 deployable carrier battle groups with the full complement of escorts, support ships and 90-95 carrier aircraft each. The thirteenth carrier, the nuclear-powered *Carl Vinson*, became operational in 1982 with the fifth CVN, the USS *Theodore Roosevelt*, building. By the end of the decade the sixth CVN, the *Abraham Lincoln*, will give the navy its 15 carriers while in late 1991 the USS *George Washington* will replace the USS *Coral Sea* (commissioned 1947), which will become a training carrier. Under the SLEP (Service Life Extension Program) the older large-deck carriers, will have their original 30-year design life extended by 15 years. The first such extension, the USS *Saratoga* (1956) was completed in 1984 and the USS *Forrestal* (1955) began her SLEP refit in the same year. Other US carriers not mentioned above are CVNs USS *Enterprise* (1961), *Nimitz* (1975) and *Dwight D. Eisenhower* (1977), CVs (conventionally-powered aircraft-carriers) USS *John F. Kennedy* (1968), USS *America* (1965), USS *Constellation* (1961), USS *Kitty Hawk* (1961), USS *Independence* (1959), USS *Ranger* (1957), USS *Saratoga* (1956) and USS *Midway* (1945).

USSR

So far Soviet aircraft-carriers have been configured as ASW platforms only with small numbers of the relatively crude Yakovlev Yak-38 'Forger' V/STOL aircraft for reconnaissance. The helicopter-carrying ASW cruisers *Moskva* and *Leningrad* were commissioned in 1968-9, and the aircraft-carriers *Kiev*, *Minsk*, *Novorossiisk* and *Kharkov* from 1975-85. A nuclear-powered carrier was laid down in 1982, and this is expected to operate navalized versions of land-based aircraft, possibly the Sukhoi Su-24 and Su-27.

Above: USS *Nimitz* (CVN 68) with CVW 8 embarked returning home after the unsuccessful attempt to free the Embassy hostages in Teheran. Many of her aircraft wear special markings for contingency operations during the raid.

Left: Deployed on several occasions to the Mediterranean, *Kiev* uses her Yak-36MP 'Forger-A' VTOL fighters as maritime patrol aircraft interceptors.

Right: USS *Kitty Hawk* (CV 63) is seen towards the end of the Vietnam War. Carrier-based air power played a major part in that conflict, and the big carriers proved their worth, being able to operate larger aircraft much more intensively than the modified World War II 'Essex' class which had been active in the early years of American involvement.

Above: An early photograph of the British light carrier HMS *Invincible*, with five Sea Harriers from No. 899 Squadron, which is the Navy's training unit. It was not long before both ship and aircraft were blooded in the battle for the Falkland Islands.

Left: *Novorossiysk*, the third of the Soviet 'Kiev' class ASW carriers, is seen on her maiden voyage in the North Atlantic. While she differs slightly in weapon and electronic fit from *Kiev* and *Minsk*, the mission of the class remains the same: in wartime a highly potent ASW vessel possessed of great surface action capability, and in peacetime a power-projection symbol with extensive command and control facilities suitable for intervention in small wars worldwide.

Right: In spite of the growth of the Soviet surface fleet, the aircraft carriers of the US Navy remain the ultimate expressions of seaborne power. USS *America*, seen transitting the Suez Canal, is just one of what will be a supercarrier force 15-strong in the 1990s, each Carrier Battle Group being more powerful than many of the world's air forces.

Cruisers and Destroyers

In the decade following the end of World War II, while one by one the great battleships were towed away to the breaker's yard, it seemed for a while as if their lesser sisters, the cruisers, might follow them: in 1945 the Royal Navy had 60 cruisers, by 1955 23 and by 1968 four. It seemed that this large class of ship, superior in self-contained fighting power to anything but a battleship, with a balanced mix of defensive and offensive weapons and the ability to cruise unrefuelled halfway across the world, was now redundant. However the first generation of shipborne guided weapons, such as the SAMs which became operational in the 1950s were so bulky that they needed ships of cruiser size to accommodate them. In the USA, for example, a number of war-built hulls were converted to operate the big Talos and Terrier air-defence SAMs. Cruisers' size also made them ideal platforms for task force radars and their accommodation and communications fits made them useful flagships. The US Navy and Marine Corps in particular were also reluctant to give up their large number of gun cruisers because of their amphibious fire support capability, which was shown to effect in the Korean and Vietnam wars.

Enduring asset

Thus the cruiser did not disappear from first-division navies. Its endurance and balanced defensive/offensive armament made it a considerable naval asset even in the age of the missile, while its size made incorporation of new technology that much easier. The US Navy thus embarked on a new-build programme of nuclear cruisers (originally classified as guided missile frigates) from the mid-1950s onwards with the USS *Long Beach*. The Soviet navy has also used ships of cruiser size to prove technical innovations, the 'Kynda' class of Raketny Kreyser (rocket cruiser), for example, was built in 1961-2 and ushered in the era of the anti-ship cruise missile. And the first Soviet nuclear-propelled surface warship was a very large cruiser, the 25,000-tonne *Kirov* which sailed from her Leningrad building yard to join the Northern Fleet in 1981.

The era of the modern missile-armed cruiser began in 1952 when work was started in the USA on converting the heavy cruisers USS *Boston* and USS *Canberra* to

accommodate twin Terrier SAM launchers in place of the after 203-mm (8-in) gun mountings. In 1956 work began on six cruisers of the 'Cleveland' class, which were equipped with Terrier or Talos SAMs in place of their aft 152-mm (6-in) gun turrets and the US *Little Rock*, USS *Oklahoma City*, USS *Providence* and USS *Springfield* were fitted as fleet flagships. The last of the conversions were the heavy cruisers USS *Albany*, USS *Columbus* and USS *Chicago*, all very extensively rebuilt with 'double ended' missile armament (Talos and Tartar SAMs fore and aft), a very capacious bridge for the flagship role and two lofty 'macks', combined masts and funnels.

The nuclear-powered cruiser USS *Bainbridge* executes a high-speed turn to port. *Bainbridge* is essentially similar to the 'Leahy' class cruisers, but has larger dimensions and tonnage to accommodate the two D2G pressurized-water cooled reactors that give her a 38 kts speed and virtually unlimited range.

While these missile gun/hybrids provided useful lessons in the development and operational practice of missile-armed ships, a brand new cruiser was on the drawing board which would push existing technology to the limits in all directions. The *Long Beach*, laid down in 1957, was the first ship with all-missile armament (Talos/Terrier), was the first nuclear-powered

Left: USS *Long Beach* was the first US surface warship to have nuclear power. During the Vietnam War in 1967-8 her long range Talos SAM systems engaged North Vietnamese MiGs on seven occasions, shooting down two at ranges in excess of 120 km (75 miles).

Above: The experimental SAM missile crusier *Dzerzhinsky*, fitted with a navalized version of the Soviet army's SA-2 'Guideline' missile, which proved unsuccessful in service. She was placed in reserve with the Black Sea Fleet in the late 1970s.

Below: The guided missile cruiser USS *Albany*, a converted World War II 'Baltimore' class heavy cruiser, made a rare multiple missile launch on 30 January 1963. Talos missiles were fired fore and aft and a Tartar was launched from amidships.

Left: For the inner defence role USS *California* carries two single-rail Mk 13 SAM launchers for the Standard SM2-MR missile, which can engage targets out to 74 km at heights up to 24390 m. A nuclear-tipped Standard with a W81 fission warhead is under development for service in the 1990s.

Below: This photograph of six US nuclear-powered cruisers steaming together is a rare sight. Normally operating singly or in pairs to provide air cover to nuclear carriers, they were involved in Exercise 'READEX I-81' in the Caribbean on 26 February 1981.

surface warship, and was equipped with a very powerful phased-array radar with its characteristic antennas giving the ship its distinctive square box superstructure. The ship grew further in the design stage to accommodate strategic systems, the Regulus II cruise missiles and eight Polaris SLBMs, neither of which was ever fitted. *Long Beach* was followed by the nuclear powered 'frigates' USS *Bainbridge* and USS *Truxtun* (reclassified in 1975 as cruisers). But the US Navy's plans to go all-nuclear proved too ambitious, for the cost of these ships was crippling. Thus the conventionally-powered guided-missile frigates of the 'Belknap' and 'Leahy' classes (built 1962-7 and also reclassified later as cruisers) armed with Standard SAMs and ASROC anti-submarine missiles continued to be the backbone of fast carrier task force escorts.

Nuclear power

But nuclear power came back into fashion in the late 1960s, and when the carrier USS *Nimitz* was ordered in 1967 she was followed by two new nuclear-powered frigates (DLGN). Named USS *California* and USS *South Carolina*, they were reclassified as cruisers soon after their commissioning. The design is a development of the 'Truxtun' with helicopter pad on the fantail and twin towers in place of lattice masts carrying the multiplicity of sensor and ECM arrays. Armament is two 127-mm (5-in) guns, Harpoon SSMs in two quadruple launchers, fore and aft Mk 13 Standard SAM launchers each with magazines for 40 missiles, single Mk 16 eight-tube 'pepperbox' type ASROC launcher and two Phalanx CIWS. The four ships of the 'Virginia' class completed in 1976-1980 differ in improved anti-air warfare capability (two twin Mk 26 launchers for Standard MR SRAMs, electronic warfare equipment and anti-submarine fire control, plus a helicopter hangar under the quarterdeck. The use of the dual-purpose Mk 26 launcher for ASROC and SAMs allowed the ships to be 3 m (10 ft) shorter.

Below: USS *Jouett* of the conventionally powered 'Belknap' class. During the Vietnam War USS *Biddle* and USS *Sterett* of this class shot down four MiGs and one Styx SSM in two separate incidents.

Right: The first dedicated guided missile cruisers to be built for the Soviet navy were the four 'Kynda' class, built at Leningrad. They were designed for surface action, unlike contemporary US Navy vessels.

Cruisers and Destroyers

Left: A Soviet navy 'Kara' class Large Anti-Submarine Ship (BPK). These serve only with the Black Sea and Pacific fleets, where they have a command capability. The extremely heavy weapon and sensor fit is characteristic of Soviet practice, and contrasts strongly with the almost stark appearance of their American contemporaries.

Thirty years after the end of World War II most traditional gun cruisers in world navies had been scrapped or laid up, but some went through missile/ASW conversion programmes while other navies experimented by building hybrid helicopter-carrying 'escort cruisers' from scratch. The prewar Italian cruiser *Giuseppe Garibaldi* was converted with a twin Terrier launcher aft in 1962 and the French cruiser *Colbert* (commissioned originally in 1959) was converted in 1970-2 with a twin Masurca SAM system in place of the aft 127-mm gun mounting. The Royal Navy's cruisers HMS *Tiger* and HMS *Blake* were converted in 1965-72 to operate four Westland Sea King ASW helicopters from a large hangar and flight deck installed aft, in place of a twin 152-mm gun mounting. In 1964 the Italian navy commissioned the pioneering purpose-built *Andrea Doria* and *Caio Duilio*, missile/gun-armed light cruisers with a large helicopter deck aft, and in 1970 these were followed by the bigger *Vittorio Veneto* with twin Terrier/ASROC launcher and a rear flight deck for nine helicopters.

A handful of traditional war-built gun cruisers lingered on in third-world navies. The old light cruiser HMS *Achilles* built in 1933 went to the Indian navy in 1948 as the *Delhi*, followed in 1957 by the 'Colony' class cruiser HMS *Nigeria*, which was renamed *Mysore*. Two more 'Colonys', HMS *Newfoundland* and *Ceylon*, went to Peru in 1960 and the light cruiser HMS *Diadem* to Pakistan in 1957 as the *Babur*. The Swedish *Göta Lejon* went to Chile in 1971 and the Dutch *De Ruyter* and *De Zeven Provincien* went to Peru in 1973 and 1976. Six 'Brooklyn' class cruisers of the US Navy were transferred in 1951 (two each to Chile, Brazil and Argentina). It was the 43-year old cruiser *General Belgrano* of this class, a survivor of Pearl Harbor, that the Royal Navy submarine HMS *Conqueror* torpedoed in the opening moves of the Falklands campaign.

Below: Originally to have been a third 'Andrea Doria' class hybrid cruiser/helicopter carrier, the *Vittorio Veneto* was much enlarged, as it became clear that the earlier vessels were too small for their tasks..

Right: USS *Mississippi*, the third 'Virginia' class cruiser, was designed as a highly capable carrier escort. Each of the twin missile launchers is capable of firing a variety of missiles.

'California' class nuclear-powered guided missile cruiser

Displacement: 9,561 tons standard and 11,100 tons full load (CGN 36)
Dimensions: length 181.7 m; beam 18.6 m; draught 9.6 m

Propulsion: two pressurized-water cooled reactors powering geared steam turbines delivering 60,000 shp (44740 kW) to two shafts
Speed: 39 kts
Complement: 563
Aircraft: none embarked
Armament: two quadruple Tomahawk SSM launchers, two quadruple Harpoon SSM launchers with eight missiles, two single Standard SM2-MR SAM launchers with 80 missiles, one octuple ASROC ASW launcher with 24 missiles, two 127-mm DP guns, two 20-mm Phalanx CIWS mountings, and four 324-mm torpedo tubes with 16 Mk 46 torpedoes

Classed initially as missile cruisers and then as *frégates*, the *Suffren* (D602) and *Duquesne* (D603) were the first French warships designed from the outset to carry surface-to-air missiles. Their primary mission is to act as an ASW and anti-air warfare escort for the two French fixed-wing aircraft carriers, *Clemenceau* and *Foch*.

'Kresta II' large ASW ship

Displacement: 6,000 standard and 7,600 tons full load
Dimensions: length 158.5 m; beam 17.0 m; draught 6.0 m
Propulsion: geared steam turbines delivering 100,000 shp (74570 kW) to two shafts
Speed: 34 kts
Complement: 400
Aircraft: one Kamov Ka-25 'Hormone-A' ASW helicopter
Armament: two quadruple SS-N-14 'Silex' ASW launchers with eight missiles, two twin SA-N-3

'Goblet' SAM launchers with 48 missiles, two twin 57-mm DP guns, four 30-mm ADG6-30 CIWS mounting, two 12-barrel RBU 6000 ASW rocket-launchers, two six-barrel RBU 1000 ASW rocket-launchers, and two quintuple 533-mm ASW torpedo tube mountings

A Soviet 'Kresta II' class BPK (Bolshoi Protivolodochnye Korabl', or large ASW ship), armed with SS-N-14 'Silex' ASW missiles in two quadruple launcher boxes each side of the bridge. The class also has a useful anti-ship capability in its 'Silexes' and SA-N-3 'Goblet' SAM missiles.

'Kara' class large ASW ship

Displacement: 8,200 tons standard and 9,700 tons full load
Dimensions: length 173.0 m; beam 18.6 m; draught 6.7 m
Propulsion: COGAG gas turbine arrangement delivering 120,000 shp (89485 kW) to two shafts
Speed: 34 kts
Complement: 525
Aircraft: one Kamov Ka-25 'Hormone-A' anti-submarine helicopter
Armament: two twin SA-N-3 'Goblet' SAM launchers with 72 missiles (except in *Azov* which has only one SA-N-3 system plus one SA-N-6 SAM system), two twin SA-N-4 'Gecko' SAM

launchers with 36 missiles, two quadruple SS-N-14 'Silex' ASW launchers with eight missiles, two twin 76-mm DP guns, four 30-mm ADG6-30 CIWS mountings, two 12-barrel RBU 6000 ASW rocket-launchers, two (none in *Petropavlovsk*) RBU 1000 ASW rocket-launchers, and two quintuple 533-mm ASW torpedo tube mountings

A total of seven 'Kara' class were built at the 61 Kommuna, Nikolayev North Shipyard on the Black Sea. One, the *Azov*, acted as trials vessel for the SA-N-6 vertical launch SAM system in the Black Sea, where she has remained since being built.

'Krasina' class guided missile cruiser

Displacement: 11,550 tons standard and 13,000 tons full load
Dimensions: length 187.0 m; beam 22.3 m; draught 7.6 m
Propulsion: gas turbines
Speed: 36 kts
Complement: 650
Aircraft: two Kamov Ka-27 helicopters (one 'Helix-A' anti-submarine helicopter and one 'Helix-B' missile-guidance helicopter)
Armament: eight twin SS-N-12 'Sandbox' SSM launchers with 16 missiles, eight SA-N-6 SAM

launchers with 64 missiles, two twin SA-N-4 'Gecko' SAM launchers with 36 missiles, one twin 130-mm DP gun, six 30-mm ADG6-30 CIWS mountings, two 12-barrel RBU 6000 ASW rocket-launchers, and two quadruple 533-mm ASW torpedo tube mountings

The 'Krasina' class of RKR (Raketnye Kreyser, or missile cruiser) is the follow-on to the 'Kara' class. Powered by gas turbines, they can manage 36 kts at full power and have a main battery of eight twin SS-N-12 'Sandbox' SSM missile launchers.

Although primarily an anti-air warfare ship, USS *California* also has a useful ASW armament in its SQS-26CX low-frequency sonar (with a range of 18.28 km in the direct path and up to 64.02 km in the bottom-bounce or convergence-zone operating modes), ASROC missiles with either a 5 kt Mk 17 nuclear depth charge or a Mk 46 ASW torpedo as the payload, and torpedo-tube fired, 11-km range 45 kt Mk 46 torpedoes.

Cruisers and Destroyers

Both France and the UK purpose-built missile-armed light cruisers in the 1960s. The *Suffren* and *Duquesne*, completed in 1967-70, are armed with the Masurca SAMs and the Malafon stand-off ASW system, and have a large three-dimensional air surveillance radar enclosed in a big golfball radome forward. The Royal Navy's Type 82 HMS *Bristol* (1973), armed with the Sea Dart SAM and Ikara anti-submarine system, was a one off designed to escort the new CVA-01 class fleet carrier which was never built. The seven light cruisers of the 'County' class that preceded it (the lead ship HMS *Devonshire* was completed in 1962) had combined gas and steam turbine propulsion, and were the first British warships to be armed with guided weapons, the beam-riding Seaslug SAM. The last four of the class have been armed with Exocet SSMs in place of the second forward 114-mm (4.5-in) gun mounting.

Postwar Soviet cruiser development began with three ships of the 'Chapaev' class built from a prewar design and the 14 powerful cruisers of the 'Sverdlov' class built from 1951 onwards, each with 12 152-mm guns in triple turrets. Like their US contemporaries, in the 1960s some were reworked with aft SAM launchers and extended flagship facilities.

The four ships of the 'Kynda' class appeared in 1962-5 and marked a great leap forward in Soviet and world warship design with their multiple missile armament including two quadruple launchers for the SS-N-3, the first long-range anti-ship SSM. The four ships of the 'Kresta I' class laid down in 1964-6 were originally given the Soviet designation Bolshoy Protivolodochnye Korabl' meaning large anti-submarine ship (changed in 1978 to missile cruiser) and were provided with a helicopter landing pad and hangar for the first time in a Soviet ship. The 10 'Kresta IIs' laid down in 1966-74 added the SS-N-14 system to the class's powerful anti-submarine reach. The bigger gas turbine powered 'Kara' class (10,000-ton displacement at full load) were built in parallel and added twin 76-mm (3-in) guns amidships and SA-N-4 SAMs to the already powerful armament of the 'Kresta' class, so displaying the typically Soviet design practice of packing armament and sensors into a hull at the expense of crew habitability and below-deck control room space.

In 1980 a warship of an entirely different order of capabilities joined the Soviet fleet. Possibly displacing as much as 30000 tonnes and nuclear-powered, the battle-cruiser *Kirov* is armed with a formidable mix of SSMs, SAMs and ASW weapons. The *Kirov* (second of class *Frunze* was commissioned in 1983 and one more is building) could act as the focus of a task force in its own right, or alternatively support the new CVN. The ships of the 'Slava' or 'Krasina' class (three commissioned in 1982-6) are a smaller edition of the 'Kirovs' designed as a conventionally-powered back-up for that class. The Slavas are characterized by an massive deck-mounted battery of 16 SS-N-12 surface-to-surface missiles.

Above: The 'Sverdlov' class cruiser *Dzerzhinsky* was altered in the early 1960s, being fitted with an SA-N-2 launcher in place of its X-turret. Presumably the conversion was not a great success, as no other 'Sverdlov' was so converted. Although potentially fine NGS (Naval Gunfire Support) ships, the 'Sverdlovs' remain vulnerable to modern weaponry and, since there is no sign of the Soviet navy updating their missile defences by the addition of close-in weapon systems, it may be that these large, impressive vessels are being retained as training ships and 'flag-showers'.

Right: The Soviet battlecruiser *Kirov* is seen in the Baltic in 1980. *Kirov* and her sisters are the largest warships (apart from carriers) to have been built since World War II and are the heaviest armed Soviet surface combatants to date. Their extensive electronic fit allows them to act as command and control centres for surface action groups.

Above: Conceived as an escort to the cancelled British 'CVA-01' carrier, HMS *Bristol* was the first vessel to be armed with the Sea Dart missile system. The cancellation of the carrier, and cost constraints, meant that her successors would be the much smaller and less capable 'Type 42' class.

Left: Almost certainly an interim class between the 'Kynda' and 'Kresta II' designs, the anti-ship RKR 'Kresta I' class carries two twin launchers for the SS-N-3B 'Shaddock' SSM each side of the bridge. To target the missiles they carry their own Kamov Ka-25 'Hormone-B' helicopter in a stern-mounted hangar.

Right: Classed initially as a missile cruiser and then as a *frégate*, the *Suffren* (D602) was the first French warship designed from the outset to carry surface-to-air missiles in order to act as an ASW and anti-air warfare escort for the two French fixed-wing aircraft carriers, *Clemenceau* and *Foch*.

Cruisers and Destroyers

Destroyers

The 'destroyer' in the sense of its original role as a 'torpedo boat destroyer' was so successful that the steam-powered torpedo boat which seemed to pose such a threat when it first appeared in the 1890s did not survive for longer than a decade. So successful in fact was the new, fast gun- and torpedo-armed class of warship designed to counter the threat of the torpedo boat that it both drove the torpedo boat from the seas and usurped its function of surface torpedo attack.

In two world wars however the destroyer established its place very much as an anti-submarine warship, equipped with the sensors and weapons to hunt and destroy underwater predators in the open ocean, and fast enough to outrun them. The old torpedo surface-attack function withered away, and by the early years of World War II the advent of gun-control radar made even night attacks against capital ships virtually suicidal.

The postwar generation of destroyers was very different from its wartime predecessors. The new threat of the nuclear submarine, the advances in sonar and long-range anti-submarine warfare systems, the advent of guided missiles and the adding of an air dimension in the shape of light anti-submarine helicopters meant much larger and much more complicated ships. The term destroyer became applied to a very wide range of warships, the more specializecd roles of 'submarine' destroyer or 'aircraft' destroyer being understood.

New-built destroyers optimized for fleet air defence with first-generation SAMs stretched to the size of light cruisers. The US Navy's Terrier-armed 'Coontz' class built in 1957-61 is nearly half as long overall again as a 1944 'Gearing' class destroyer, while today's 'Spruance' class destroyer at 171.7 m (563.2 ft) overall is in fact longer than a Royal Navy 'Colony' class cruiser. The older war-built gun-armed destroyers continued to serve alongside the new missile-armed ships, although they were turned over more and more to the ASW escort role as their size ruled out the installation of big SAM systems. Then in 1960 the US Navy, faced with the block obsolescence of its older ships, began the huge Fleet Rehabilitation And Modernization (FRAM) programme to save a large number of 'Fletcher', 'Allen M. Sumner' and 'Gearing' class units from the breaker's torch by arming them instead with ASW systems such as ASROC. While they have disappeared from US Navy service, several FRAM destroyers linger on in smaller navies. The US Navy's first postwar destroyers, the 'Forrest Sherman' class laid down in 1953-6 and originally built with gun and torpedo armament, were similarly converted to either Tartar SAM or ASROC in the late 1960s, but have now been pulled out of the front line with engineering problems.

The 23 ships of the 'Charles F. Adams' class built in 1958-64 took the overall 'Forrest Sherman' design but built in Tartar and ASROC armament from the beginning. Three were built for Australia, and three of a heavily modified version for West Germany as the 'Lütjens' class. These successful ships were extensively refitted in the early 1980s with Standard SM-1 SAMs and Harpoon surface-to-surface missiles.

The latest large-class US destroyers are the ships of the 'Spruance' class, the lead ship of which was laid down in 1972, and which will provide the backbone of the US Navy's surface ASW force well into the next century. This in itself is significant because from the outset the 'Spruance' was designed very much as a weapons platform, big and adaptable enough to accommodate mid-life electronic and weapon system updates. When they first appeared these large, ungainly warships were immediately controversial, apparently grossly underarmed yet of outsize proportions built in prefabricated modular sections using mass production techniques. Another innovation was the use of twin gas turbines, each exhausting through massive square cut funnels. Ten years after the class entered service, the original concept was proven sound when refits began to incorporate digital sonar, LAMPS III helicopter facilities, Tomahawk and Mk 41 vertical missile launch systems.

The first of a new class of guided-missile destroyer, the 'Arleigh Burke' class designed as replacement for the 'Charles F. Adams' and 'Coontz' classes, was laid down in 1985. The primary mission is anti-air warfare with Standard SM-2 SAMs, but the new ships will be smaller than the Aegis cruisers of the 'Ticonderoga' class (see the section on naval SAMs) which they will supplement, though with considerable ASW and surface strike capability armed with VLS ASROC, Tomahawk and Harpoon.

Above: Although their hulls are simply bigger versions of the 'Impavido' class, *Audace* and *Ardito* of the Italian navy are much more effective vessels.

Right: The US Navy's 'Spruance' class destroyers such as USS *Elliott* were designed with plenty of room for extra or replacement systems.

In contrast with the US design philosophy of outsize destroyers, the Royal Navy's 'Type 42' destroyers displace less than half the tonnage of the 'Spruance' class and pack in the maximum fit of weapons and sensors into a compact hull. The primary weapon system of the gas turbine-powered 'Type 42' is the Sea Dart long-range area-defence SAM, with target illumination supplied by two Type 909 radars positioned fore and aft for all-round coverage and a large mast-mounted 'bedstead' Type 1022 air-warning radar. A single Mk 8 114-mm gun is mounted forward. ASW weapons are the STWS automated anti-submarine torpedo system and a Westland Lynx helicopter. The first of the class, HMS *Sheffield*, was lost to an air-launched Exocet in the Falklands fighting together with sister ship HMS *Coventry*, hit by low-level bombing attacks. Survivors have been retrofitted with 30-mm and 20-mm cannon for close-in air defence. From Batch 3 (10 of class HMS *Manchester* commissioned in 1982) the design was radically stretched by 12.8 m (42 ft) overall to improve speed and seakeeping and provide space for improved weapon systems.

After building large numbers of traditional gun-armed destroyers in the 1950s, in 1962 the Soviet navy put into service the first gas turbine-powered operational warships in the world. These 'Kashin' class destroyers are typically Soviet in being crammed with sensors and weapons. Modernization and mid-life updates have apparently been difficult for that very reason, and as the ships have not proved seaworthy enough for North Atlantic operations are kept rather in the Black Sea and Mediterranean. In 1980 two new classes of large destroyer began to appear. The 'Sovremenny' class is optimized for surface warfare with eight SS-N-22 SSMs and SA-N-7 SAMs. The 'Udaloy' class is similar in size and layout but designed as a specialist submarine killer with eight SS-N-14 ASW missiles and a large variable-depth sonar.

Left: The 'Kashin' class first entered service in the early 1960s with the last of 20 units commissioning in 1972 and were the world's first major warship class to be powered by gas turbine. Surprisingly, only six have undergone extensive modifications during that time to form the 'Kashin Mod' sub-class, whilst the others have undergone only normal refits.

The first post-war US destroyer design, the 'Forrest Sherman' class, dates from the mid-1950s. Originally gun-armed destroyers, four were converted to guided missile configuration in the mid-1960s. USS *Somers* was the last of the class to be modified, recommissioning in 1968.

Below: Fitted with eight launchers for a new vertical launch point defence SAM system plus the usual variety of Soviet ASW weapon systems, the 'Udaloy' class of ASW destroyer is well capable of taking care of itself in unfriendly waters whilst prosecuting a submarine contact. This class, according to the latest American intelligence reports, is being constructed at a very fast rate with up to six units operational and another five either being built or fitted out at two different shipyards.

The first of the stretched 'Type 42s', HMS *Manchester* (D95). These vessels are designed to remedy the shortcomings of the original class by restoring the length cut-off and increasing the beam slightly. However, as originally conceived they would have suffered from the same lack of armament as HMS *Sheffield*.

'Sovremenny' class destroyer

Perhaps the most impressive of the new generation of Soviet surface warships of destroyer size is the 'Sovremenny' class, built for the surface strike role. Latest American intelligence reports indicate that at least four are operational, with another five on the slipways being built or fitted out.

Displacement: 6,200 tons standard and 7,800 tons full load
Dimensions: length 155.6 m; beam 17.3 m; draught 6.5 m
Machinery: geared turbo-pressurized steam turbines delivering 100,000 shp (74570 kW) to two shafts
Speed: 36 kts
Aircraft: one Kamov Ka-25 'Hormone-B' missile-guidance/Elint helicopter

Armament: two quadruple SS-N-22 SSM launchers (no reloads), two single SA-N-7 SAM launchers (48 missiles), two twin 130-mm DP guns, four 30-mm ADG6-30 CIWS mountings, two RBU1000 300-mm ASW rocket launchers, two twin 533-mm ASW torpedo tubes, and 30-50 mines (according to type)
Complement: 350

Escorts, Frigates and Corvettes

In structuring their ASW (Anti-Submarine Warfare) forces, the NATO and Soviet navies have followed two distinct strategies screening and hunter-killing. The classic expression of the screening tactic is the convoy with escort forces shepherding a mass of merchant ships through dangerous submarine-infested waters, while a newer expression is the creation of sanctuaries in which ballistic-missile-firing submarines can operate, like batteries of floating silos immune from direct attack. Screening means waiting for the enemy to come to you, whereas the hunter-killer role means what it says: seeking out and destroying enemy sub-surface units as rapidly and effectively as possible.

ASW surface units such as frigates designed for convoy escort need not be as sophisticated and expensive as those designed for offensive hunter-killer operations in contested waters, or at least in theory that is the case. One problem, however, is the great size and complexity of modern long-range active sonars which demand comparatively large vessels to accommodate them and their associated electronics, and thus the distinction between the relatively small and simple escort vessel and the big open-ocean submarine hunter begins to break down. The need to operate one or sometimes two helicopters pushes up the size, as does the need for some kind of self protection in the shape of anti-ship missiles and short-range SAMs. The result is that a frigate of the 1980s, like the Royal Navy's 'Broadsword' class, can be considerably bigger than warships rated as destroyers.

There is confusion inherent in the very name 'frigate'. In the 17th century a frigate was a small single-deck warship, but by the time of the Napoleonic wars, frigates had grown greatly in size: big enough, in fact, to operate independently for long periods and battle-worthy enough to take on all but the biggest warships. The early 19th century frigate was a multi-purpose vessel: a scout for the fleet, an escort and a commerce raider (in short a 'cruiser'), and from the mid-century onwards 'cruiser' began to supplant the old and noble expression frigate, which fell into complete disuse.

Then during the criticial year of the Battle of the Atlantic, 1942, the Royal Canadian Navy and RN introduced a big new class of twin-screw escort known as the 'River' class, a greatly enlarged version of the 'Flower' class corvettes of 1939-40 which had been found to be too small and too slow for operations in the Atlantic. The 'Rivers' were first classified as twin-screw corvettes, but the RCN began to call them frigates and the RN soon followed, eventually bringing a whole range of mid-size ASW escort ships into the newly rediscovered category.

By the 1960s the term meant any seagoing ship intended for escort and ASW operations, but the Americans further stirred the pot by classifying their big destroyers as frigates while other navies kept the term for small coastal escorts. Since then the US Navy has reclassified its bigger destroyers as cruisers and put destroyer escorts (DEs) of the 'Brooke', 'Knox', 'Garcia' and 'Bronstein' class into the frigate (FFG/FF) category. In other navies the term corvette has been revived to cover small escorts and coastal patrol craft which are not capable of deep-water operations.

The 'River' and 'Loch' classes of 1942-45 laid down a pattern of design priorities for frigates which has held broadly true to this day: open-ocean seaworthiness and good crew habitability with fuel efficient engines for long-endurance missions. However, with the high underwater speeds of the last generation of U-boats, and by implication the new Soviet submarines that would be faced in the 1950s, postwar frigate designers reintroduced steam turbines in place of fuel-efficient diesels to provide pursuit speeds above 25 kts. In the UK alarming cost increases forced a compromise: the twin-screw 'Type 12s' of the 'Whitby' class (the lead ship of which was laid down at Cammell Laird in 1952) and the single-screw 'Type 14' utility frigates of the 'Blackwood' class completed between 1955-8. The 'Whitbys' were very successful and could make 30 kts on 75 per cent power with a very efficient and weatherly hull form. This had a raised flared forecastle to throw

aside spray, a V-section forward, and a deep mid-section for sustained high speed in bad weather. These ships were followed by nine 'Rothesay' class ships, which incorporated detail modfications into the 'Type 12' design.

In 1959 were laid down the first of a new class of 'General Purpose Frigate', which radically stretched the original 'Type 12' design, reflected the concurrent developments in the range of sonar and ASW weapon systems, included a degree of anti-aircraft (AAW) armament. The resulting 'Leander' class achieved a very useful increase in the amount of equipment carried including long-range air-warning radar, improved sonar, a small ASW helicopter and (from HMS *Naiad*, the ninth of class onwards), Seacat short-range SAMs. In the 'Leander' rework of the 'Type 12' design, internal weight was moved downwards, the forecastle deck was extended right back to the stern and many other detail improvements were made.

Quartier Maitre Anquetil **is one of the 'D'Estienne d'Orves' class of coastal escorts of the French navy. Three were built for Argentina, one being badly damaged by small arms fire and anti-tank rockets from Royal Marines on South Georgia. They are austere, economical vessels, not suitable for deep water ASW.**

HMS *Broadsword*, **first of the 'Type 22' class frigates, provides 'Goalkeeper' protection to the carrier HMS** *Hermes*. **The fitting of Seawolf missiles has made the class potent close air defence vessels. Intended for ASW operations in the North Atlantic, Batch 3 vessels will receive a 4.5-in gun and two CIWS.**

USS *Roark* is one of the 46 strong 'Knox' class dedicated ASW frigates of the US Navy. Criticized for their single screw propulsion and solitary gun, they have been systematically refitted during the 1980s, acquiring Harpoon SSMs and Phalanx 20-mm CIWS.

Below left: Completed in 1965, HMS *Arethusa* was converted to carry an Ikara ASW rocket launcher during a major refit completed in 1977. Eight of the original Batch 1 'Leander' class vessels have been altered in this way.

Below: From the seventeenth 'Leander' the design was amended by increasing the beam. HMS *Andromeda* was the first of five broad-beamed 'Leanders' to be fitted with Seawolf and Exocet missiles, re-commissioning in 1980.

Escorts, Frigates and Corvettes

A high-speed turn is made by HMS *Broadsword*, first of the 'Type 22' class. These vessels, with their two Lynx helicopters, were designed to counter modern high-performance nuclear submarines, and do so in the harsh seas north and west of the British Isles.

Below: HMS *Arrow* saw considerable action in the South Atlantic, bombarding enemy positions near Port Stanley, rendering assistance to the stricken HMS *Sheffield*, and firing in support of 2 Para during the attack on Goose Green.

With the run-down of the Royal Navy's CTOL aircraft-carriers, the task group escort role of single-purpose ASW/AAW ships changed: such ships themselves had now to have some ability to engage hostile surface ships. For the surface strike role the second batch of 'Leanders' was retrofitted with Exocet SSMs, losing their forward twin 114-mm (4.5-in) guns in the process. A further eight ships of the class were also converted to carry the Ikara stand-off ASW missile. Twenty-six Leanders were built for the Royal Navy and six more by the Dutch, two each for the Australian, Chilean, and New Zealand navies and six for India. The Royal Australian Navy has modified its 'Rothesay' class to the same standard but without the helicopter hangar, while RN Leanders are still the subject of an improvement programme including the fitting of Seawolf SAMs on the final 1967-72 production batch of eight.

By the late 19050s the Royal Navy was already outlining its requirements for a successor to the 'Leander' class, and as the new design progressed it was shaped by further technical advances in weaponry and sensors, the changing nature of the Soviet threat and long-term shifts in NATO's overall anti-submarine strategy. The resulting 'Type 22' frigate of the 'Broadsword' class emerged as a very large escort indeed, capable of independent mid-ocean hunter-killer operations with all-missile MM.38 Exocet SSM and Seawolf SAM armament plus two Westland Lynx helicopters. The use of gas turbine engines in a coupled cruise/full-power arrangement gives high acceleration, a top speed of over 30 kts and a maximum range of over 7000 km (4,350 miles) on the cruise engines. The use of gas turbines with their need for massive trunked intakes and easy access for removal also gives the class their characteristic boxy appearance. The 'Type 22s' deployed in the Falklands fighting, HMS *Broadsword* and HMS *Brilliant* with their Seawolf SAMs, proved amongst the most battleworthy of any warships involved in the campaign. Fourteen 'Type 22s' had been built or were on order by the beginning of 1985. The six Batch 2 ships (from HMS *Boxer* commissioned 1984 onwards) are 12.5 m (41 ft) longer overall. Batch 3 ships (HMS *Cornwall* laid down June 1985 onwards) will be armed with Harpoon SSMs and operate Westland Sea King or EH101 ASW helicopters.

While the big 'Type 22s' were under development, the Royal Navy accepted a commercial design from Vosper Thornycroft for eight much smaller patrol frigates of the 'Amazon' class completed in 1974-8. While the 'Broadswords' are approximately the same size as the 'Leander', their use of gas turbines virtually doubles the power, and they have a respectable fit of sensors and weapons including Type 184 hull-mounted sonar, a single 114-mm Mk 8 gun, Seacat SAMs, four Exocets and a Lynx helicopter. Two of the class, HMS *Ardent* and HMS *Antelope*, were lost in the Falklands fighting.

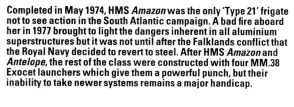

HMS *Amazon*

Completed in May 1974, HMS *Amazon* was the only 'Type 21' frigate not to see action in the South Atlantic campaign. A bad fire aboard her in 1977 brought to light the dangers inherent in all aluminium superstructures but it was not until after the Falklands conflict that the Royal Navy decided to revert to steel. After HMS *Amazon* and *Antelope*, the rest of the class were constructed with four MM.38 Exocet launchers which give them a powerful punch, but their inability to take newer systems remains a major handicap.

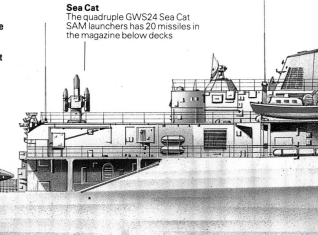

Sea Cat
The quadruple GWS24 Sea Cat SAM launchers has 20 missiles in the magazine below decks

'Type 22' 'Broadsword' class

Batch 3 variants of the 'Broadsword' class will be highly capable ships, although the frigate designation may seem incongruous for a vessel nearing 5,000 tons equipped with significant air, surface and ASW capabilities.

Displacement: 3,500 tons standard and 4,400 tons full load
Dimensions: length 131.1 m; beam 14.8 m; draught 6.1 m
Propulsion: COGOG arrangement with two Rolls-Royce Olympus TM3B gas turbines delivering 37285 kW

(50,000 hp) and two Rolls-Royce Tyne RM1A gas turbines delivering 6338 kW (8,500 hp) to two shafts
Speed: 29 kts
Armament: four single MM.38 Exocet surface-to-surface missile launchers with four missiles, two sextuple GWS25 Sea Wolf

surface-to-air missile launchers with 60 missiles, two single 40-mm AA guns, two single 20-mm AA guns, and (F90 and F91) two triple 324-mm STWS1 ASW torpedo tubes with Mk 46 and Stingray torpedoes
Aircraft: one or two Westland Lynx HAS.Mk 2/3 ASW/anti-ship helicopters
Complement: 223 normal and 248 maximum

'Maestrale' class

Comparable to the Dutch 'Kortenaer' class or the West German 'Bremens', the Italian 'Maestrale' class vessels are faster than most other Western frigates and are comprehensively equipped with modern ASW technology including both a hull and towed variable-depth sonar.

Displacement: 3,040 tons standard and 3,200 tons full load
Dimensions: length 122.7 m; beam 12.9 m; draught 8.4 m
Propulsion: CODOG arrangement with two General Electric/FIAT LM2500 gas turbines delivering 38478 kW (51,600 hp) and two GMT B230 diesels delivering 10,146 hp

(7566 kW) to two shafts
Speed: 32 kts
Armament: four single Otomat Mk 2 surface-to-surface missile launchers with four missiles, one octuple Albatros surface-to-air missile system with 24 Aspide

missiles, one 127-mm DP gun, two twin 40-mm Dardo CIWS, two single 533-mm torpedo tubes for A184 torpedoes, and two triple 324-mm ILAS-3 ASW torpedo tubes for Mk 46 and A244/S torpedoes
Aircraft: two Agusta-Bell AB.212 ASW helicopters
Complement: 213

'Bremen' class

The West German navy is to receive six 'Bremen' class frigates, general-purpose vessels carrying two Westland Lynx helicopters for ASW purposes. The 'Bremens' were developed from the Dutch 'Kortenaers' and have the same hull form but diesel cruising engines instead of turbines.

Displacement: 2,900 tons standard and 3,750 tons full load
Dimensions: length 130.5 m; beam 14.4 m; draught 6.0 m
Propulsion: CODOG arrangement with two General Electric/FIAT LM2500 gas turbines delivering 38478 kW (51,600 hp) and two MTU 20V TB92 diesels delivering 7755 kW (10,400 hp) to two shafts

Speed: 32 kts
Armament: two quadruple Harpoon surface-to-surface missile launchers with eight

missiles, one octuple NATO Sea Sparrow surface-to-air missile launcher with 24 RIM-7M

missiles, two 24-round RAM point-defence surface-to-air missile launchers with 48 missiles (being fitted), one 76-mm DP gun, and four single Mk 32 324-mm ASW torpedo tubes for Mk 46 torpedoes
Aircraft: two Westland Lynx HAS.Mk 88 ASW helicopters
Complement: 204 normal and 225 maximum

'Wielingen' class

Wielingen has no helicopter facilities but is well armed for a vessel of her size. The first of four such frigates, it is armed with an 100-mm dual-purpose gun plus a 30-mm Goalkeeper CIWS. This class will provide Belgium with her only ocean-going escort capability.

Displacement: 1,880 tons standard and 2,283 tons full load
Dimensions: length 106.4 m; beam 12.3 m; draught 5.6 m
Propulsion: CODOG arrangement with one Rolls-Royce Olympus TM3B gas turbines delivering 20880 kW (28,000 hp) and two diesels

delivering 4474 kW (6,000 hp) to two shafts
Speed: 29 kts

Armament: four single MM.38 Exocet launchers, one octuple NATO Sea Sparrow SAM launcher with 24 missiles, one 100-mm DP gun, one 30-mm Goalkeeper CIWS, one sextuple 375-mm ASW rocket launcher and two single ASW torpedo launchers with 10 L5 torpedoes
Complement: 160

Search radar
Type 92Q air- and surface-search radar is the main sensor for the onboard action information organization system

Fire control radar
The RTN-10X fire control radar is part of the digital fire control system which operates the Sea Cat missile system and the 4.5-in (115-mm) gun

Exocet
Most of the 'Type 21s' are fitted with four MM.38 Exocet anti-ship missiles, which have a range of over 40 km

Dual-purpose gun
The 4.5-in (114-mm) DP Mk 8 DP gun is fully automatic, and can fire at a rate of 25 rounds per minute out to a range of 22 km

'Amazon' class

Displacement: 2,750 tons standard and 3,250 tons full load
Dimensions: length 117.0 m; beam 12.7 m; draught 5.9 m
Propulsion: COGOG arrangement with two Rolls-Royce Olympus TM3B gas turbines delivering 37285 kW (50,000 hp) and two Rolls-Royce Tyne RM1A gas turbines delivering 6338 kW (8,500 hp) to two shafts

Speed: 32 kts
Armament: four single MM.38 Exocet surface-to-surface missile launchers with four missiles (not in F169 and F172), one quadruple GWS24 Sea Cat surface-to-air missile launcher with 20 missiles, one 114-mm DP gun, four single 20-mm AA guns, and two triple 324-mm STWS1 ASW torpedo tubes with Mk 46 and Stingray torpedoes
Aircraft: one Westland Lynx HAS.Mk 2 ASW helicopter
Complement: 177 normal and 192 maximum

Escorts, Frigates and Corvettes

In 1978 the first of the Dutch 'Kortenaer' class frigates was completed, a warship developed against the background of a NATO requirement for a standard hull which could be manufactured in European shipyards to a common specification. The 'Kortenaer' was a purely Dutch design but it matched the 'NATO Frigate' requirement so well that the West German navy decided to adopt it as the 'Fregatte 122' (later 'Bremen' class) but with various modifications, for example replacing the original design's Rolls-Royce Olympus/Tyne gas turbine combination with US-supplied General Electric LM2500 gas turbines plus twin MTU 20V TB92 diesels for cruising. Two Lynx helicopters provide the primary ASW reach, and two quadruple Harpoon launchers supplemented by two single OTO-Melara 76-mm guns serve in the surface-to-surface role. Short-range air defence is provided by Sea Sparrow SAMs.

After lengthy consideration and wrangling over cost, the first of the new 'Type 23' frigates was ordered by the Royal Navy in 1985 (the lead ship of this 'Duke' class is HMS *Norfolk*, due for commissioning in 1989). Similar in size to Batch 1 'Type 22s', the new frigate will be powered by Rolls-Royce Spey gas turbines with diesels for cruising. Armament will be Harpoon SSMs, vertical-launch Seawolf and the 30-mm Goalkeeper CIWS. An EH101 helicopter will be the primary ASW system.

US Navy frigate development was influenced by the need to replace the wartime generation of escorts which became obsolescent en masse during the 1960s. The chosen solution was to design a utility escort suitable for mass production but without the complex and expensive missile armament of contemporary destroyers. The resulting 'Knox' class with single-shaft steam turbine propulsion was originally criticized for an over-austere armament fit, but subsequent reworking to carry the LAMPS-type Kaman SH-2 Seasprite helicopter combined with an eight-cell ASROC launcher made the 'Knoxes' very capable ASW platforms; fitting of Sea Sparrow SAMs gave them a measure of short-range air defence.

The successor to the 46-strong 'Knox' class, the 'Oliver Hazard Perry' class is also a utility design configured for mass production with over 50 in service by 1986. The superstructure is built up of slab-sided boxes, with a diminutive rear-mounted funnel for the twin gas turbines that turn a single screw. Two LAMPS helicopters are shipped, and these can be armed with anti-ship missiles for surface strike as well

Left: The Dutch 'Kortenaer' class frigate HNLMS *Callenburgh* (F808) preceeds HNLMS *Tromp* (F801). The 'Kortenaers' have a well balanced armament fit, primary ASW weapons being the two Westland Lynx helicopters carried.

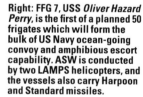

Right: FFG 7, USS *Oliver Hazard Perry*, is the first of a planned 50 frigates which will form the bulk of US Navy ocean-going convoy and amphibious escort capability. ASW is conducted by two LAMPS helicopters, and the vessels also carry Harpoon and Standard missiles.

as homing ASW torpedoes. There is a Standard SAM/Harpoon SSM/Tomahawk cruise missile launcher forward, and a Mk 75 lightweight 76-mm (3-in) gun between funnel and mast. A Phalanx 'Gatling' mounted above the helicopter hangar provides close-in defence.

Left: USS *Lockwood*, one of 46 'Knox' class frigates operated by the US Navy, launches a Harpoon anti-ship missile from the dual-purpose octuple Harpoon/ASROC launcher. Criticized by some for their single-screw propulsion, the 'Knox' class forms the backbone of US frigate strength.

Escorts, Frigates and Corvettes

Other significant European frigates are the Italian 'Lupo' and 'Maestrale' classes, designed with an eye on export markets. In 1975 two customers (Venezuela and Peru) ordered six and four respectively of the new 'Lupo' class before even the lead ship was complete. The high speed of 35 kts maximum and a heavy weapon load (including Otomat SSMs, Aspide SAMs, single 127-mm/5-in and twin 40-mm guns, plus twin triple ASW torpedo tubes) made the 'Lupo' attractive, but to the point of overloading. To remedy this the 'Maestrale' class developed in parallel has the same propulsion and virtually the same payload (exchanging one Otomat launcher for an extra Agusta AB.204 helicopter) while the hull is stretched by 1.6 m (5.25 ft) in beam and 9.5 m (31 ft) in length for better seakeeping, a fixed rather than telescopic hangar and variable-depth sonar in the transom.

The Soviet navy built a large class of frigates in the 1950s, and this was allocated the name 'Riga' by NATO. Many have now been transferred to other navies or put into reserve. The 'Rigas' had a comparatively heavy surface-to-surface armament and only light ASW depth charge mortars. Some have been modernized by the removal of the torpedo tubes and the augmentation of the radar fit. But the latest Soviet frigates (Storozhevoy Korabl', or escort ship) of the 'Krivak' class are much more formidable with heavy ASW and AAW armament including SA-N-4 SAMs and SS-N-14 anti-submarine missiles plus twin 12-barrel RBU 6000 depth charge mortars. The gas turbine-driven 'Krivaks' have an extensive sensor fit including air-search radar, plus hull-mounted and variable-depth sonars.

The term 'corvette' now mainly applies to small general-purpose ships with ASW capacity for use on coastal waters. The French 'd'Estienne d'Orves' or 'A69' class is a good modern example: it is under 1,000 tonnes standard displacement and powered by twin diesels for a top speed of 24 kts. The design is well balanced, with a 100-mm (3.94-in) gun forward, a combined mast/exhaust stack amidships flanked by two or four Exocet launchers, and a six-barrel ASW mortar aft. The Soviet 'Petya' class corvettes also carry a heavy armament on a small hull: two 76-mm guns, ASW torpedoes and multi-barrel mortars, plus variable-depth sonar. These coastal escorts were followed by the 20-strong 'Mirka' class.

Above: The 'D'Estienne d'Orves' class frigate *Second Maitre le Bihan* is seen with (aft of the flag) her sextuple ASW rocket launcher elevated. She also carries four single torpedo tubes for L3 or L5 ASW torpedoes.

Left: *Galapagos* is the fifth unit of the 'Esmerelda' class of 685-ton corvettes built in Italy for Ecuador. Carrying six MM.38 Exocets, quadruple Albatros SAM launcher and guns and torpedoes, they are more heavily armed than many frigates.

Above: *Maestrale* is a stretched version of the Italian 'Lupo' class frigates with greater emphasis on ASW. Good sea boats, the eight 'Maestrales' carry two light helicopters with dunking sonar. The ships themselves carry 25000-m range ASW torpedoes.

Above: The Brazilian 'Niteroi' class ASW vessel *Uniao* has a Branik missile launcher system aft, which fires the Australian Mk 44/46 torpedo-equipped Ikara missile. The magazine carries a total of 10 such missiles, which are targetted by both the bow sonar and the VDS system.

'Krivak II' class patrol ship

The 11 'Krivak II' class vessels differ from their 21 predecessors in having single 100-mm guns in place of twin 76-mm weapons in the two aft turrets. Classified by the Soviets as *Storozhevoy Korabl'* (SKR, or patrol vessel), the 'Krivak' is designed to hunt and kill nuclear submarines in the deep waters of the world's oceans. The class is faster and much more heavily armed than Western contemporaries.

Displacement: 3,000 tons standard and 3,700 tons ('Krivak I') or 3,800 tons ('Krivak II') full load
Dimensions: length 123.5 m; beam 14.0 m; draught 4.7 m
Propulsion: COGAG arrangement with four gas turbines delivering power to two shafts
Speed: 32 kts
Armament: one quadruple launcher for SS-N-14 'Silex' anti-submarine missiles, two twin launchers for 36 SA-N-4 'Gecko' SAMs, two twin 76-mm DP ('Krivak I') or two single 100-mm DP ('Krivak II') guns, two 12-barrel RBU6000 250-mm ASW rocket-launchers with 120 rockets, two quadruple 533-mm tube mountings for anti-submarine torpedoes, and between 20 and 40 mines according to type
Aircraft: none
Complement: 220

Single 100-mm gun turret
This is carried only by 'Krivak II' frigates; 'Krivak I's had twin 76-mm guns, and 'Krivak IIIs' have a helicopter hangar in place of both rear turrets.

'Dubna' class replenishment tankers can refuel from either beam and the stern; here all lines are in use to refuel three 'Krivak' class frigates. The first two batches of 'Krivaks' have limited endurance for ASW operations on the high seas.

'Yubari' class frigate

Yubari is highly automated, which allows her to operate with only a small crew. Designed to operate under a protective umbrella of land-based aircraft, the design has little anti-aircraft capability, although Phalanx CIWS is being fitted.

Displacement: 1,470 tons standard and 1,690 tons full load
Dimensions: length 91.0 m; beam 10.8 m; draught 3.6 m
Propulsion: CODOG arrangement with one Rolls-Royce/Kawasaki Olympus TM3B gas turbine delivering 28,390 hp (21170 kW) and one Mitsubishi 6DRV diesel delivering 4,650 hp (3468 kW) to two shafts
Speed: 25 kts

Armament: two quadruple Harpoon surface-to-surface missile launchers with eight missiles, one 76-mm DP gun, one 20-mm Phalanx CIWS (being fitted), one quadruple 375-mm Bofors ASW rocket launcher, and two triple 324-mm Mk 68 ASW torpedo tubes with Mk 46 torpedoes
Aircraft: none
Complement: 98

'Mirka' class anti-submarine ship

'Mirkas' of the Soviet Black Sea fleet are regularly deployed to the Mediterranean squadron to provide ASW protection for its high-value surface units and the many deep water anchorages.

Displacement: 950 tons standard and 1,150 tons full load
Dimensions: 82.4 m; beam 9.1 m; draught 3.0 m
Propulsion: CODAG arrangement with two diesels and two gas turbines delivering power to two shafts
Speed: 35 kts
Armament: two twin 76-mm DP

guns, four ('Mirka I') or two ('Mirka II') 12-barrel RBU6000 250-mm ASW rocket-launchers with 240 or 120 rockets, and one ('Mirka I') or two ('Mirka II') 533-mm quintuple tube mountings for five or 10 anti-submarine torpedoes
Aircraft: none
Complement: 98

'Jianghu' class frigate

The People's Republic of China has built the 'Jianghu' class frigate in three discrete versions. Still in production, the Egyptian navy has recently purchased two 'Jianghu I' units with revised gun armament.

Displacement: 1,568 tons standard and 1,900 tons full load
Dimensions: length 103.2 m; beam 10.2 m; draught 3.1 m
Propulsion: ('Jianghu I' and 'Jianghu III') two diesels delivering power to two shafts
Propulsion: ('Jianghu II') probably a CODOG arrangement delivering power to two shafts
Speed: 26.5 kts for 'Jianghu I' and 'Jianghu III', and 30 kts for 'Jianghu II'

Armament: two twin container-launchers for Shanghou-Yihou 1 anti-ship missiles, two single (or twin in 'Jianghu III') 100-mm DP and six twin 37-mm AA guns, two or four 12-barrel RBU1200 250-mm ASW rocket-launchers with 100 or 200 rockets, two racks for 60 depth charges, and between 40 and 60 mines according to type
Aircraft: none
Complement: 195

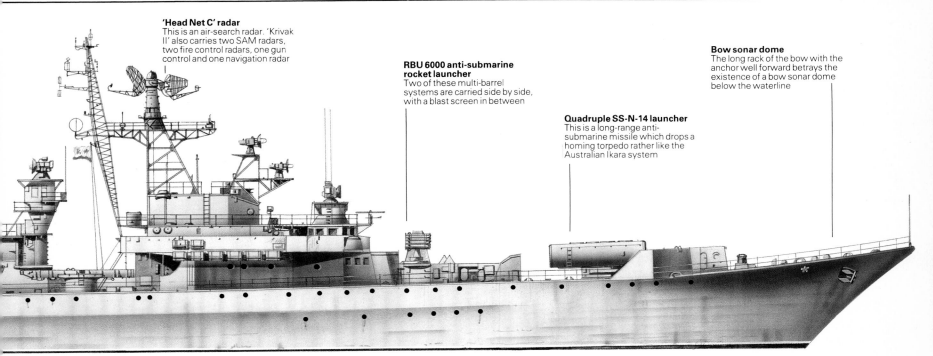

'Head Net C' radar
This is an air-search radar. 'Krivak II' also carries two SAM radars, two fire control radars, one gun control and one navigation radar

RBU 6000 anti-submarine rocket launcher
Two of these multi-barrel systems are carried side by side, with a blast screen in between

Quadruple SS-N-14 launcher
This is a long-range anti-submarine missile which drops a homing torpedo rather like the Australian Ikara system

Bow sonar dome
The long rack of the bow with the anchor well forward betrays the existence of a bow sonar dome below the waterline

Fast Attack Craft

Twice in the comparative recent history of warship development the advent of a new weapon has given David a chance against Goliath, giving small warships the ability to challenge their apparently much mightier brethren. Today it is the sea skimming anti-ship missile, whereas in the 1870s it was the Whitehead torpedo launched from a fast, steel-hulled steam-powered torpedo boat that sent navies into a panic. It seemed that these new naval mosquitoes could swarm into the battle line and blow up lumbering battleships almost with impunity. In fact that other new class of late-19th century warship, the torpedo boat 'destroyer', rapidly rendered the small torpedo boat ineffective and usurped its surface torpedo attack role in fleet actions. But high-speed motor gun and torpedo boats did not disappear. British Coastal Motor Boats (CMBs) served resolutely through World War I and in the 1919 War of Intervention against the new Bolshevik regime, in which a British CMB sank the Soviet cruiser *Oleg* off Kronstadt. The Italians also pugnaciously operated torpedo-armed motor boats in the Adriatic sinking several Austro-Hungarian warships including the dreadnought *Svent Istvan*.

The Germans began experimenting with the Schnellboot (fast boat) concept in 1930, and by 1939 had built up a useful force of very potent motor torpedo boats developed by Lürssen powered by Mercedes or MAN high-speed diesels. Known as E-boats to the British (for 'enemy boats') and as S-Boot to the Germans, these craft clashed on many occasions in the Channel and North Sea with British MTBs and MGBs, but the actual amount of shipping sunk by the fast attack craft of each side was in fact quite low. The same was true in the Pacific, where Japanese torpedo boats achieved very little although the US Navy had some success in the Solomons with the PT boat (evolved from a British MTB design by Hall-Scott).

The Soviet staff took MTBs seriously from its earliest days, the first designs (done under the direction of A.N. Tupolev the aircraft designer) appearing in the late 1920s. They were advanced craft for their time with aluminium or duralumin hulls employing aircraft construction techniques. In the decade before the war a large MTB fleet was built up and a number of boats were supplied to Nationalist Spain. During World War II Soviet-built MTBs proved of limited fighting value, but from 1943 large numbers of US-built Elco and Higgins Lend-Lease boats began to arrive. Most of these survived the war and formed the backbone of the Soviet light forces in the immediate post-war years. Then in 1951 came the first of the 'P6' class armed with two 533-mm (21-in) torpedoes and four 25-mm AA guns. In 1960 an extensive conversion programme began to fit a first-generation naval SSM, the SS-N-2 'Styx' to the 'P6', the conversion being known in the west as the 'Komar' class. Unlike a gun, a missile has no recoil and is relatively easy to mount on the light hull of small attack craft.

When the elderly Israeli destroyer *Eilat* was sunk in 1967 by four 'Styx' SSMs fired from two Egyptian 'Komar' class missile boats, world navies behaved very much as they had done 100 years before when faced by the steam torpedo boat, vastly overestimating the actual threat posed by the new weapon. In December 1971 Indian 'Osa' class missile boats sank a Pakistani destroyer and several merchant ships using 'Styx' missiles, but the reputation of the Soviet-supplied fast attack craft (FACs) plummeted in October 1973 when Israeli missile craft armed with Gabriel SSMs devastated a force of Syrian 'Komars' and 'Osas' without loss to themselves.

While the USSR had been developing shipborne SSMs since the mid-1950s, Western navies were far slower to wake up to the potential of the anti-ship missile. But after the sinking of the *Eilat*, designs for new FACs began to proliferate, all built round the new Western SSMs such as the Exocet and Otomat then themselves just progressing from the prototype state. But just as the first torpedo boats were chased from the sea by torpedo boat destroyers, so it was realized that a modern FAC is only as effective as the weapon system it carries. In reacting to the success of the 'Styx'-armed Soviet-designed boats, Western navies had credited the missile with far more effectiveness than it actually possessed. The 'Styx' which had first entered service in 1960 employed easily jammable command guidance and its original victims were not fitted with even half-adequate ECM.

Two generations of fast attack craft are seen in this photo of Iskraeli boats off the cost at Haifa. The 'Dabur' class torpedo boat in th background carries two Mk 46 lightweight torpedoes together with 20-mm cannon and machine-guns. The 'Saar 3' class boat in the foreground is a modified Lürssen deaign, and Gabriel III and Harpoon missiles make it an opponent to be feared in battle.

'Osa' class missile craft provide the backbone of Soviet coastal forces. Operating in 24-vessel brigades, they can launch attacks from over 17 km range. Soviet training emphasizes massed night attacks on enemy major units in coastal waters or convoys. Missile craft are used to engage warships while torpedo boats deal with merchant ships.

'Huchuan' class fast attack craft

The 'Huchuan I' class of torpedo-armed hydrofoil has been built in large numbers by the People's Republic of China; some 140 are estimated to be in service. Introduced some 20 years ago, they have been exported to Albania, Pakistan, Romania and Tanzania.

Displacement: 39 tons full load
Dimensions: length 21.8m; beam 4.9m or 7.5m when foilborne; draught 1.0m or 0.31m

when foilborne
Propulsion: three M50 diesels delivering 3,600hp (2685kW) to three shafts
Maximum speed: 54 kts
Complement: 12-15
Armament: two 533-mm anti-ship torpedo tubes and two twin 12.7-mm heavy machine-guns
Electronics: one 'Skin Head' radar

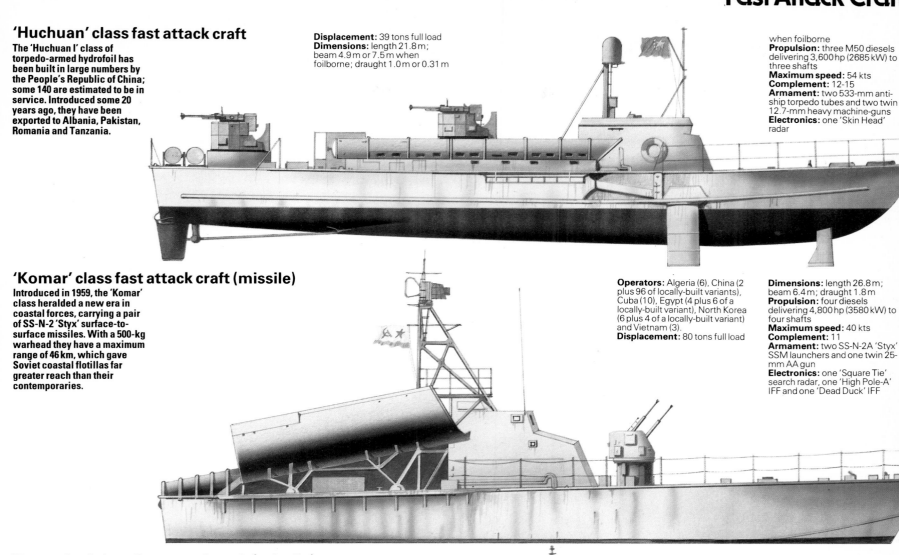

'Komar' class fast attack craft (missile)

Introduced in 1959, the 'Komar' class heralded a new era in coastal forces, carrying a pair of SS-N-2 'Styx' surface-to-surface missiles. With a 500-kg warhead they have a maximum range of 46km, which gave Soviet coastal flotillas far greater reach than their contemporaries.

Operators: Algeria (6), China (2 plus 96 of locally-built variants), Cuba (10), Egypt (4 plus 6 of a locally-built variant), North Korea (6 plus 4 of a locally-built variant) and Vietnam (3).
Displacement: 80 tons full load

Dimensions: length 26.8m; beam 6.4m; draught 1.8m
Propulsion: four diesels delivering 4,800hp (3580kW) to four shafts
Maximum speed: 40 kts
Complement: 11
Armament: two SS-N-2A 'Styx' SSM launchers and one twin 25-mm AA gun
Electronics: one 'Square Tie' search radar, one 'High Pole-A' IFF and one 'Dead Duck' IFF

'Ramadan' class fast attack craft (missile)

After breaking with the Soviet Union, Egypt turned to Western industry to supply its defence needs. Vosper Thornycroft won a £150 million contract to supply six FACs. All in service by 1982, they are the most capable vessels of their type in Egyptian service.

Displacement: 312 tons full load
Dimensions: length 52.0m; beam 7.6m; draught 2.0m
Propulsion: four MTU diesels delivering 17,150hp (12795kW) to four shafts
Maximum speed: 40 kts
Complement: 40

Armament: four Otomat SSMs, 1 single 76-mm DP gun forward and a twin 40-mm anti-aircraft mount aft
Electronics: one S820 radar, one S810 radar, two ST802 radars, one Sapphire fire-control system and one Cutlass ECM suite

'Reshef' class fast attack craft (missile)

The loss of the Israeli destroyer *Eilat* to missile boat attack spurred the Israelis into building similar vessels of their own. After having several classes built in France, they produced the 'Reshef' steel-hulled boats, of which two were ready in time for the 1973 Yom Kippur war.

Displacement: 450 tons full load
Dimensions: length 58.1m; beam 7.6m; draught 2.4m
Propulsion: four Maybach (MTU) diesels delivering 14,000hp (10440kW) to four shafts
Maximum speed: 32 kts
Complement: 45

Armament: two/four Harpoon and four/five Gabriel III SSMs, two single 76-mm DP guns (although some boats have a 40-mm gun in place of the stern 76-mm), two single 20-mm and three twin 12.7-mm machine-guns

Electronics: one Thomson-CSF Neptune TH-D1040 radar, one Selenia Orion RTN-10X radar, one Elta MN-53 ECM system, chaff launchers and (in some craft) ELAC sonar

'Tarantul' class missile corvette

Built at Leningrad, the 'Tarantul I' was completed in 1978 and a 'Tarantul II' appeared three years later. One 'Tarantul I' has been transferred to the Polish navy and one has been built without its full set of electronics, presumably for export to a Soviet client state.

'Tarantul' class
Operators: Soviet Union, Poland
Displacement: 580 tons full load
Dimensions: length 56.0m; beam 10.5m; draught 2.5m
Propulsion: two gas turbines delivering 30,000hp, two diesels delivering 2,000hp to two shafts

Maximum speed: 36 kts
Complement: 50
Armament: four SS-N-2C 'Styx' SSM launchers ('Tarantul I'), four SS-N-22 ('Tarantul II'), one quadruple SAM-5 launcher, one 76-mm gun, two 30-mm Gatling guns

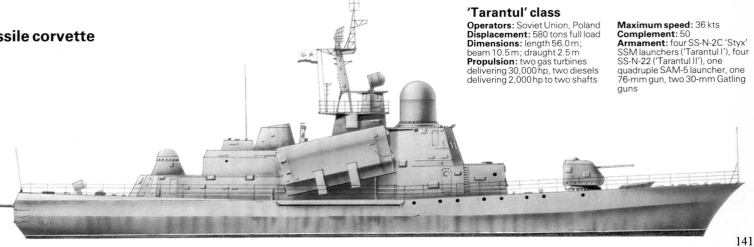

Fast Attack Craft

Although SSM guidance technology has made great strides since the '60s, the other apparent attractions of FACs are also open to question. While many navies large and small have invested in them as an alternative to the big expensive frigate, FACs cannot take their firepower very far from home. The problem with downsized warships is that they cannot maintain lengthy patrols in open water, and their crew and equipment are likely to be shaken to pieces in rough weather. Another problem is that the FAC makes a poor platform for line-of-sight sensors and cannot operate helicopters.

While thus limited to coastal waters and short-range actions, at the same time FACs are not cheap. Their internal volume is of necessity packed with electronics and sensors, all requiring maintenance and much more difficult to modernize than on a big platform. The cost of a missile-armed FAC can exceed that of a 3,000-ton frigate, and all navies who operate such craft have found them very expensive to maintain.

Nevertheless a wide range of FACs is in service with world navies, and there is a lively and hard-fought for export market. The Soviet 'Osa' class has been widely transferred to the navies of client states including Cuba, Egypt, Syria, India and Somalia plus the Warsaw Pact states. The 'Osa' class was the first purpose-built FAC(M) of the Soviet navy, bigger than the 'Komar' conversions (200 tonnes displacement full load) and carrying four 'Styx' missiles. The 'Osa I' class can be distinguished by box-section missile launchers, the 'Osa II' by cylindrical containers. There are twin 30-mm AA guns and some craft have launchers for SA-7 IR-homing short-range SAMs. Propulsion is by diesel with a top speed of over 30 kts. India is also a customer for the much bigger 'Nanuchka' class missile-armed corvette first identified in 1969. The 850-tonne displacement 'Nanuchkas' are also diesel powered, armed with six SS-N-9 SSMs, twin SA-N-4 SAMs with a pop-up launcher on the forecastle, and twin 57-mm guns aft.

Syrian 'Osas' fought an action with Israeli FAC(M)s during the 1973 Yom Kippur War. Israel order her first modern strike craft in 1965: the 45-m (148-ft) 'Saar 2/3' class designed in West Germany but built in France. The first arrived in 1969 to be armed locally with Israeli-developed Gabriel SSMs. The Israeli-developed 'Reshef' class stretched the original design to 58 m (190 ft) enough to mount an extra 76-mm (3-in) gun along with six Gabriel launchers. Two boats of the 'Reshef' class fought an action which accounted for 14

A Soviet-supplied 'Osa-I' missile boat of the Egyptian navy. Most Egyptian vessels of this type have now undergone refits, with Western electronic equipment in place of the Soviet systems. They also carry SA-N-5 SAMs.

Syrian FACs off Lattakieh using Gabriel 1 missiles with half the range of the opposing SS-N-2s. This disadvantage was offset by skilful tactical handling and capable ECM. More of the enlarged 'Reshef II' type have been built in Israel and in South Africa and these boats have shown exceptional open-water performance. The current armament fit consists of 30-km (18.6-mile) range Gabriel II and US-supplied Harpoon SSMs.

Following the transfer of West German technology to French yards with the Lürssen-designed 'Saar' class for Israel, the French expeditiously capitalized on the design and grabbed a large share of the world FAC market with the 47-m (154-ft) 'La Combattante II' and 56-m (184-ft) 'La Combattante III' types supplied to West Germany, Greece, Iran, Libya, Malaysia, and Nigeria amongst others. Usual armament is an OTO-Melara Compact 76-mm gun forward with four Exocet or Harpoon launchers angled outwards amidships. The longer 'La Combattante IIIs' have an extra 76-mm gun.

The Swedish 'Spica' class of 1966-76 introduced gas turbine propulsion, and with three Bristol Siddeley Proteus engines these FACs can make 40 kts in calm water. The 'Spicas' were originally armed with six wire-guided 533-mm torpedoes for surface attack, but in 1982 a conversion programme began to fit them with RBS 15 SSMs. The boats of the slightly smaller 'Hugin' class commissioned in 1978-82 were designed from the outset with six RBS 15s and a 57-mm gun. The two boats of the 'Spica III' class commissioned in 1985-6 have variable sonar and anti-submarine torpedoes as well as eight SSMs, and are designed to act as flotilla leaders for smaller FACs.

For all their apparent promise, hydrofoils have proved a disappointment in the FAC role, proving too complex, expensive and unreliable. The US Navy began experiments with the Boeing-built *High Point* hydrofoil as early as 1962, but never got really serious about this class of high-speed craft which rises out of the water on planing foils. Six 'Patrol Combatant Missile' craft (PHMs) were commissioned 1977-82 each armed with two quadruple Harpoon launchers and intended to be the first of a major NATO-wide class, but plans for 30 more were dropped, the original batch serving in an experimental tactical squadron at Key West, Florida. The Royal Navy operated an experimental Boeing hydrofoil as HMS *Speedy* in 1979-82 but also remained unconvinced. Only the Italian navy has become a regular hydrofoil user with seven of the 'Sparviero' class operational in the Mediterranean since 1980. The Chinese navy uses many semi-hydrofoils, with foil-lifted bows and planing sterns, in the FAC role.

The 'Spica' classes form the backbone of the Swedish navy's fast attack craft forces. They are designed as multi-role vessels with the capability of switching armament fits according to the proposed mission. This Spica II carries four container/launcher boxes for Bofors RBS 15 SSMs.

Above: The British Wellington Mk 5 is a supremely capable hovercraft able to make 58 kts. The Iranians have made good use of their troop-carrying model, which can take 170 infantrymen. This model can carry four Exocet SSMs.

Above: British shipbuilders, Vosper Thornycroft built six 'Ramadan' class fast attack craft for Egypt to replace Soviet-built boats lost in the 1973 Yom Kippur war. Armed with an OTO-Melara 76-mm gun, twin Breda 40-mm AA guns and four Otomat SSMs, the 'Ramadans' are as good as any Israeli vessel they may encounter.

Left: Built entirely of aluminium, the 'Sparviero' class hydrofoils of the Italian navy are capable of 50 kts and carry a pair of Otomat SSMs. In the confined waters around Italy their short range and limited armament are not a serious disadvantage.

Below: USS *Pegasus* is seen in company with a USN VC-1 composite squadron Sikorsky SH-3G Sea King helicopter and McDonnell Douglas TA-4J Skyhawk two-seat operational attack trainer off Hawaii. Six 'Pegasus' class boats are based at Key West, Florida.

Assault Landing Ships

'There will never be an occasion for British forces acting alone to face an opposed landing.' That was first said in 1966 and repeated in subsequent British defence estimates. The Royal Navy's commando carriers HMS *Albion* and HMS *Bulwark* converted from 'Centaur' class aircraft-carriers in 1959-61 were duly scrapped in 1972 and 1976. Then came the Falklands campaign and the need to land, support and supply a fighting force 12875 km (8,000 miles) from the UK. It looked like an impossible logistic nightmare but turned out as a triumph, existing plans merging with brilliant extemporization to land 5,000 men and 8,000 tons of stores.

A particular aspect of the campaign was the use of merchant ships 'taken up from trade' for purposes varying from troop transport to tanking, from aircraft ferrying to mine sweeping. The majority of ships were used for the purpose for which they had been designed: for example tankers and tugs were minimally modified (simply the ability to replenish at sea) but a few, such as the container ships and roll off ferries used as aircraft platforms and troopships, were more extensively modified, with V/STOL landing pads for example.

Over 60 such 'STUFT' vessels were engaged in the campaign and they were right in the firing line, as proved by the loss of the container ship *Atlantic Conveyor* to an air-launched Exocet missile. The success of the hastily improvised merchant fleet was ironic in the sense that in the previous year a British defence review had announced plans to axe the Royal Navy's own two purpose-built large amphibious assault ships HMS *Intrepid* and HMS *Fearless* whose usual role would be to transport the Royal Marines to support NATO's northern flank in Norway. Reprieved in February 1982, they were saved from the axe again after the Falklands fighting although no replacements have been ordered. Two smaller Royal Navy logistic landing ships, *Sir Galahad* and *Sir Tristram*, were also lost in the fighting to air strikes leaving four of their class still in commission. A Norwegian and a Canadian ro-ro (roll-on, roll-off) ship were commissioned in 1983 as replacements for the lost ships.

Fearless commissioned in 1965 and her sister *Intrepid* two years later, and reflect general design principles for assault ships with the special feature of also being in effect floating docks. The origins of such ships lie in the tank landing craft (LCTs) of World War II which, from Anzio to Iwo Jima gave the Allies the ability to make direct attacks on defended coastlines and land troops and *matériel* over beaches rather than rely on capturing a port. The Landing Ship, Dock (LSD) pioneered by the Americans represented a further development, in effect an ocean-going self-propelled floating dock. The bow was conventional, but aft was a bottom-hinged gate giving access to the internal dock. Built-up superstructure bridged the docking well at the forward end and machinery was crammed into the narrow side spaces flanking the dock.

Fearless, classified as a Landing Platform, Dock (LPD), has a docking well able to accommodate four Landing Craft, Mechanized (LCMs) two by two. Each LCM can accommodate 100 tonnes of stores, the equivalent of two main battle tanks. The middle of the ship is given over to vehicle and stores stowage, and the forward part to crew spaces while troop accommodation is largely in the lower superstructure. To undock

HMS *Fearless* signals HMS *Antrim* prior to the San Carlos landings. The run to the Falkland Sound was made at night, with the first troops landing at 0400 hours on 21 May 1982. *Fearless* and her sister *Intrepid* made the Falklands campaign possible, yet were to have been deleted under the infamous 1981 Defence Review.

the LCMs, the ship takes aboard 5,000 tons of seawater by the stern, taking the deck of the docking well (in normal trim above the water) below the waterline. With the stern gate lowered, the LCMs can back out under their own power. They can re-enter two abreast and run up to a ramp at the head of the dock leading straight to the tank deck, enabling armoured vehicles to drive straight onto them. Other vehicles (a specimen load would include 15 tanks, seven 3-ton and 20 quarter-ton trucks) can be transferred from other decks to

the loading dock via ramps including the after deck which forms the roof of the docking well. Slung beneath davits two to a side are four LCVPs (Landing Craft, Vehicle/Personnel) each with a 5-ton capacity, enough for 35 troops or two Land Rovers.

Fearless can accommodate up to five Wessex-size helicopters on the open after deck. There is no hangar accommodation, as a helicopter flight is attached only for a specific mission, such as establishing an airhead which would be reinforced by landing over the beach.

'Fearless' class

The two 'Fearless' class vessels are tasked to provide amphibious assault lift capabilities, using an onboard naval assault group/ brigade headquarters unit with a fully equipped assault operations room from which the force commander can mount and direct all the air, sea, and land force assets required for the operation.

Displacement: 12,210 tons full load
Dimensions: length 158.5 m; beam 24.4 m; draught 6.2 m
Propulsion: two geared steam turbines delivering 22,000 shp to two shafts
Speed: 21 kts
Complement: 617 (37 officers, 500 ratings and 80 Royal Marines)
Troops: 330 normal, 500 overload and 670 maximum

Cargo: maximum 20 MBT, one BARV, 45 4-ton trucks with 50 tons of stores, or up to 2,100 tons of stores; four LCUs and four LCVPs; five Westland Wessex HU.Mk 5 or four Westland Sea King HC.Mk 4 plus three Aérospatiale Gazelle or Westland Lynx helicopters
Armament: four GWS20 Quadruple Sea Cat SAM launchers, two Mk 9 40-mm AA guns plus variable number of 7.62-mm GPMGs and Blowpipe hand-held SAM launchers

Left: HMS *Fearless* (right) refuels at sea from one of the Royal Fleet Auxiliary's old 'Leaf' class support ships. On the left is the LSL (Landing Ship Logistic) *Sir Tristram*, which was badly damaged by Argentine air attack later in the campaign.

Above: HMS *Fearless* under attack from an Argentine Dagger in San Carlos water. The camouflaged aircraft can be seen passing just in front of the main mast and almost at bridge level. By the bridge house can be seen one of *Fearless*'s two 40-mm L/70 anti-aircraft guns.

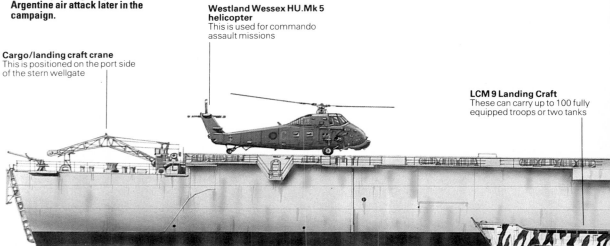

Westland Wessex HU.Mk 5 helicopter
This is used for commando assault missions

Cargo/landing craft crane
This is positioned on the port side of the stern wellgate

LCM 9 Landing Craft
These can carry up to 100 fully equipped troops or two tanks

HMS *Intrepid* takes on more men and stores from the carrier HMS *Hermes* before parting company to steam for San Carlos. *Intrepid* can be distinguished from *Fearless* in photos of the Falkland campaign by the absence of SCOT satellite communication antennae (large black domes halfway up the mainmast).

'Sir Lancelot' class Landing Ship Logistic (LSL)

Sir Lancelot was ordered in 1963 as a prototype LST, a modified design. *Sir Bedivere* followed and a further four LSLs were built to this pattern. The bow and stern have ramps built into them for roll-on/roll-off capability and interior ramps connect the two cargo decks.

Displacement: L3029 5,550 tons and rest 5,674 tons full load
Dimensions: length 125.1 m; beam 19.6 m; draught 4.3 m
Propulsion: two diesels delivering 9,400 bhp (L3029 9,520 bhp) to two shafts

Speed: 17 kts
Complement: 69 (18 officers and 51 men)
Troops: 340 normal, 534 maximum
Cargo: maximum 18 MBTs and 32 4-ton trucks plus 90 tons of general cargo, 120 tons of petrol,

oil and lubricants, and 30 tons of ammunition (L3029 the same except only 16 MBTs and 25 4-ton trucks); two Mexeflottes; three Westland Wessex HU.Mk 5 or two Westland Sea King HC.Mk 4 or three Aérospatiale Gazelle or Westland Lynx helicopters

Armament: two Mk 9 40-mm AA guns plus variable number of 7.62-mm GPMGs and Blowpipe hand-held SAM launchers (normally no armament is carried)

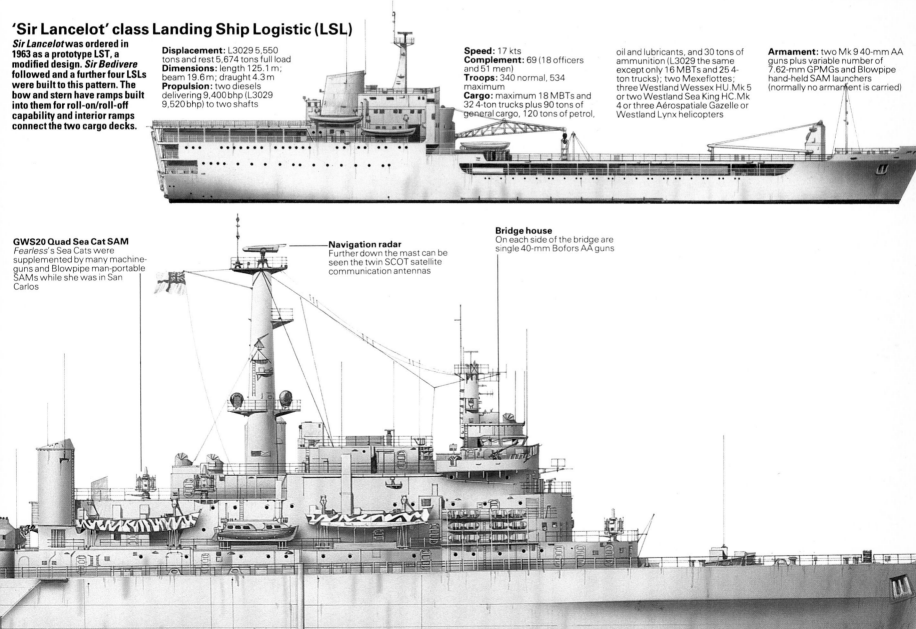

GWS20 Quad Sea Cat SAM
Fearless's Sea Cats were supplemented by many machine-guns and Blowpipe man-portable SAMs while she was in San Carlos

Navigation radar
Further down the mast can be seen the twin SCOT satellite communication antennas

Bridge house
On each side of the bridge are single 40-mm Bofors AA guns

Assault Landing Ships

A 'Frosch' class LST of the East German navy on exercise in the Baltic Sea. Similar to the Soviet 'Ropucha' class, the German vessels sport a forest of aerials, suggesting that they are used in a command role.

Below: The Soviet amphibious transport dock *Ivan Rogov* photographed from a US aircraft. Capable of carrying a battalion of Soviet Naval Infantry, she also operates four or five Kamov Ka-25 'Hormone-C' helicopters, and several air cushion vehicles.

Each ship is fitted out as a Naval Assault Group/ Brigade Headquarters with an Assault Operations Room from which naval and military commanders can control the progress of an assault operation. The ships' tall mainmast supports the necessary communications aerials for its headquarters role. Point AA defence is provided by four quadruple Seacat launchers (one at each corner of the superstructure) and twin 40-mm Bofors on the bridge wings. For countering sea-skimming missiles, twin nine-barrelled Corvus launchers can fire chaff or IR flares.

Running amphibious assault ships is an expensive business, but their usefulness in the Falklands fighting allied to the UK's defence policy makers' perception of the role of British armed forces (both in direct support of NATO's northern flank or 'out of area' where an opposed landing might be faced once more) has earned them a qualified reprieve.

If there should be a war in Europe, one of the opening moves might indeed be a Soviet thrust into northern Norway or at the Baltic approaches guarded by Denmark. Soviet Naval Infantry would be at the forefront of any such attack, an elite force whose strength and capabilities have steadily increased over the past decade. In 1978 the first Soviet LPD appeared, the 14000-tonne displacement *Ivan Rogov* with a second ship following in 1982. The ships have a high built-up superstructure surmounting a 159-m (522-ft) long hull with opening bow doors forward and a flooding dock aft capable of accommodating two 'Lebed' assault hovercraft and an 'Ondatra' class LCM. A helicopter pad forward has a flying-control station and the after helicopter deck is similarly fitted, the ship being capable of operating up to five Kamov Ka-25 'Hormones'. Armament includes SA-N-4 SAMs, two twin 76-mm guns, four 30-mm 'Gatlings' for close-in defence and twin 20-barrel BM-21 rocket-launchers for shore bombardment. With a capacity for a battalion of naval infantry (522), up to 40 tanks (if the dock capacity is used), trucks and other vehicles, the 'Ivan Rogov' class has been judged to provide the Soviet navy with long-range self-sustaining assault capability of far greater potential than any previous Soviet ship. The new LPDs are supported by LSTs of the 'Ropucha' and 'Alligator' classes, which operate regularly in the Mediterranean, in the Indian Ocean and off West Africa with naval infantry units embarked, and the smaller LSMs of the 'Polnochniy' class. In addition the large Soviet merchant fleet features a high degree of special equipment for inbuilt military compatibility. Unlike the British merchant fleet in the Falklands campaign, they could transform themselves onto a war footing as auxiliary amphibious assault ships straight away.

Mention should be made of the Soviet development of air cushion vehicles (ACVs) in the amphibious assault role: as pointed out above, the 'Ivan Rogov'

'Aist' class amphibious assault hovercraft

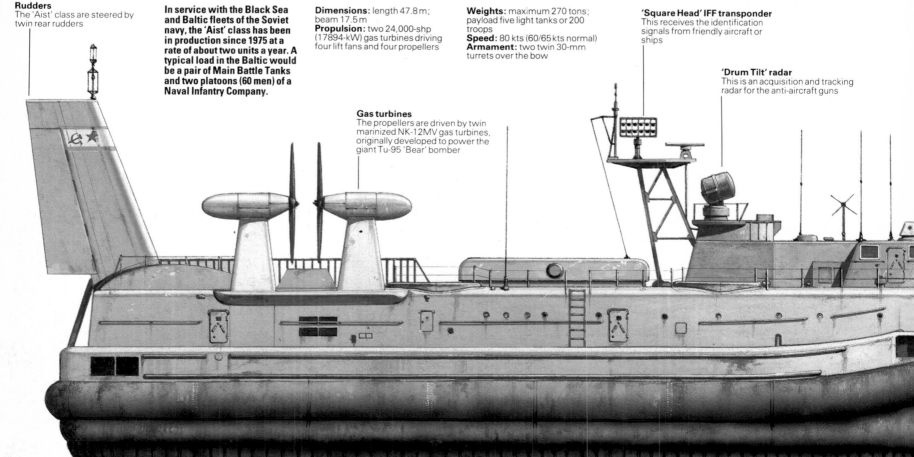

Rudders
The 'Aist' class are steered by twin rear rudders

In service with the Black Sea and Baltic fleets of the Soviet navy, the 'Aist' class has been in production since 1975 at a rate of about two units a year. A typical load in the Baltic would be a pair of Main Battle Tanks and two platoons (60 men) of a Naval Infantry Company.

Dimensions: length 47.8 m; beam 17.5 m
Propulsion: two 24,000-shp (17894-kW) gas turbines driving four lift fans and four propellers

Weights: maximum 270 tons; payload five light tanks or 200 troops
Speed: 80 kts (60/65 kts normal)
Armament: two twin 30-mm turrets over the bow

'Square Head' IFF transponder
This receives the identification signals from friendly aircraft or ships

'Drum Tilt' radar
This is an acquisition and tracking radar for the anti-aircraft guns

Gas turbines
The propellers are driven by twin marinized NK-12MV gas turbines, originally developed to power the giant Tu-95 'Bear' bomber

class ships each operate two 'Lebed' class ACVs and the Soviet navy has persisted with the development of military hovercraft while other navies had less success. The Royal Navy, having established an inter-service military hovercraft trials unit in 1970 and operated ACVs in the Falklands (1977) and in Hong Kong, abandoned further work with hovercraft in 1985, judging them too noisy, too thirsty for fuel and too unreliable for all-weather military operations. The Soviets in contrast have developed a range of standardized ACVs, the 27-tonne 'Gus' class deployed to all fleets except the Northern, the 87-tonne 'Lebed' class which can accommodate two light tanks or 120 troops, and the big 220-tonne 'Aist' class which can carry five tanks or 200 troops. Two gas turbine engines drive four axial lift

Ivan Rogov **was the first Soviet LPD; a second unit,** *Alexandr Nikolaev*, **was completed in 1982 at Kaliningrad. It is expected that the Soviets will eventually build four such vessels, one for each of their fleets, lifting Soviet out-of-area amphibious capability considerably.**

'Aist' class air cushion vehicles are capable of carrying four or five PT-76 light tanks and 150 Naval Infantry. With a maximum speed of 120 km/h and complete amphibious capability, the 'Aists' are an important element in Soviet amphibious tactics.

fans and four propeller units for forward propulsion at the speed up to 64 kts. Twin 30-mm AA guns are mounted to the sides of the blunt bow with its opening ramp.

In spite of the Soviet build-up of its amphibious forces and the technical innovation in equipping them,

they are small in comparison with the US Marines and the large number of specialized ships which support them, enough to lift one and one-third Marine Amphibious Forces (MAFs). A MAF consists of three reinforced battalions plus an air wing, a total of 45,000 marines and 6,300 US Navy personnel. Although the MAF is used as a measurement criteria for amphibious lift, a more realistic benchmark is the number of reinforced battalions that can be maintained afloat in forward areas, primarily the Mediterranean, Western Pacific and lately the Indian Ocean supported by maritime prepositioning ships. The US Navy can keep two reinforced battalions continuously afloat in WesPac and one in the Mediterranean. In addition a reinforced battalion is intermittently deployed in the Atlantic.

Lead ship of the LHA class, USS *Tarawa* **is seen about to recover a Marine Corps V/STOL AV-8A Harrier during an exercise in the Philippines. The 'Tarawas' are the largest amphibious warfare ships yet constructed; nine were planned, but post-Vietnam war cuts reduced this to five.**

Port twin 30-mm AA guns
Each 'Aist' has two distinctive 'Dalek'-shaped turrets for Gatling-type AA guns

Assault Landing Ships

Left: USS *Ogden* (LPD 5) is one of the 'Raleigh' class Amphibious Transport Docks which can accommodate up to 20 LVTP-7 amphibious armoured personnel carriers in their cavernous stern well. There are no hangar facilities, but up to six helicopters can be operated from the stern deck for short periods.

Right: US Marines board USS *Guadalcanal* (LPH 7), one of the seven 'Iwo Jima' class amphibious assault ships. These were the first vessels to be designed at the outset to operate helicopters. Although they look like an aircraft carrier, they carry no arrester gear and no catapults. 'Iwo Jimas' have accommodation for a battalion of US Marines and 24 helicopters.

The 60 active and six reserve ships include big Amphibious Assault Ships (LHAs) that look like downsized aircraft-carriers, Landing Platform Helicopter (LPHs), Command and Control Ships (LCCs), Amphibious Transport Docks (LPDs), Landing Ships, Dock (LSDs), Landing Ships, Tank (LSTs) and Amphibious Cargo Ships (LKAs).

The five ships of the 'Tarawa' LHA class are, at almost 40000-tonne displacement full load, the largest purpose-built assault ships in the world. First ordered in 1969 and commissioned in 1976-1980, the 'Tarawas' can accommodate a reinforced battalion, 19 Sikorsky CH-53 Sea Stallion helicopters and a large number of fighting vehicles and palletized stores. Beneath the full-length flightdeck are two half-length hangar decks connected by lifts. Beneath the aft elevator is a large floodable docking well capable of accommodating four LCU1610 landing craft. There are also extensive hospital facilities and storage for 37855 litres (10,000 US gal) of vehicle petrol and 1.514 million litres (400,000 US gal) of JP-5 helicopter fuel.

Displacing half the tonnage of the 'Tarawa' class, the seven LPH ships of the 'Iwo Jima' class commissioned in 1961-1979. There is no docking well as the vessels were the world's first assault ships designed and constructed specifically to operate helicopters: 11 CH-53 Sea Stallions or 20 Boeing-Vertol CH-46 Sea Knights. Each LPH can carry a US Marine battalion landing team, its artillery, vehicles and equipment plus a reinforced squadron of assault helicopters. Like the later ships there are extensive hospital facilities aboard plus aviation fuel storage. Anti-aircraft defence is provided by Sea Sparrow SAMs and Phalanx CIWS.

The proposed replacement for the two 'Iwo Jimas' will be 10 LHDs of the 'Wasp' class (first laid down in 1985 and due for commissioning 1989), larger than the 'Tarawa' class and carrying a mix of assault helicopters and McDonnell Douglas AV-8B Harriers plus assault ACVs. Sixty-six such Landing Craft Air Cushion (LCAC) to be built by Bell Aerospace are on order for

the US Navy, the first having been delivered at the end of 1984.

Classed as LCCs are the two amphibious command ships of the 'Blue Ridge' class. They are based on the hull and machinery arrangement of the 'Iwo Jimas', but their internal spaces are packed with control rooms, communication equipment and three separate computerized tactical data-handling systems, while their decks bristle with antennae and masts.

The 12 'Austin' and two 'Raleigh' class ships are amphibious transport docks, similar in layout to the British LPDs with rear flooding docking wells covered by a helicopter platform and berthing accommodation for about 1,000 men. The eight 1950s' vintage 'Thomaston' class dock landing ships are due for replacement by the 15000-tonne 'Whidbey Island' class LSDs, the first two of which were commissioned in 1985. These latter are capable of operating both helicopters and AV-8B V/STOL aircraft.

Above: An LVTP-7 comes ashore from a US amphibious squadron which includes USS *Saipan* (LHA 2) and a 'Newport' class tank landing ship.

Left: This US amphibious squadron can transport and land up to 4,000 Marines. Nearest is USS *Inchon* (LPH 12).

The US Navy plans to build 90 Landing Craft Air Cushion (LCACs). This is the prototype, testing with USS *Spiegel Grove*.

Mine Warfare

The same kind of technology that has made homing torpedoes and underwater warfare systems so effective also applies to the humble mine. Mines have in fact never really been that humble: their role in sea warfare has always been important (it was mines with influence fuses laid in British coastal waters that came close to winning the first round of the Battle of the Atlantic for Germany as much as the submarine) and they remain very important today. At one end of the strategic spectrum mines can be used as political tools for enforcing blockades. Further up the curve of warfare intensity, mines sown by aircraft or submarine can be used to choke off a vital seaborne trade artery, warship transit area or replenishment route. And in all-out war, nuclear mines can be laid offensively to bottle up known submarine operating bases or to create barrier defences for ballistic-missile firing submarine sanctuaries.

The simplest type is the bottom mine, which can be sown in water up to 70 m (230 ft) deep and which awaits the overhead passage of a recognizable target before rising to meet it. The older type of moored mine can be used at depths beyond the limits of the continental shelf, extending their effective target acquisition range by using acoustic, pressure or magnetic effects or a combination of fusing techniques. Soviet mines are known to fall into four categories. The first comprise defensive moored mines of the conventional spherical shape used for coastal ASW barrier: fusing is either by antenna contact or by an acoustic fuse with an effective range of 30 m (100 ft). The second category covers offensive bottom mines capable of laying by submarine, ship or aircraft with normal laying depths between 70 and 200 m (230 and 655 ft); they are thought to have multiple-influence fusing built in for the maximum resistance to countermeasures including magnetic, acoustic and pressure sensitivity. The third category, and one which has caused a particular stir with NATO navies, is the offensive moored ASW mine. The majority are so-called rising mines designed to attack transit and choke points frequented by NATO submarines and surface warships: one such, allocated the reporting name 'Cluster Bay' by NATO, is designed for use on the continental shelf while a second, reporting name 'Cluster Gulf', is intended for deeper waters. Both are described as tethered torpedo-shaped devices fitted with an active/passive target-detection system. If the target is confirmed by the weapon's guidance computer as being in a cone above it, a rocket motor is fired and the mine powers its way towards the target (surface ship or submarine), its active guidance taking over in the terminal phase. In fact it functions like a short-range 'sleeping' torpedo. For operations in European waters, Soviet conventionally-powered submarines with their ability to move very quietly are the primary offensive minelayers, while nuclear-powered SSNs range much farther. Rective and renewal minelaying could be accomplished by the Soviet naval air force with Tupolev Tu-16 'Badger', Tu-22 'Blinder' and Tu-26 'Backfire' aircraft. The Soviet navy is also considered to have a number of nuclear mines (with yields between 5 and 20 kilotons) for use against high-value targets.

France, Belgium and the Netherlands have combined to produce a minehunter design to replace the old US-built minesweepers supplied during the 1950s. All three navies have now taken delivery of their respective sub-classes, and the French navy has used two, *Eridan* and *Cassiopée*, in action during the international operation to clear the Red Sea of mines laid by a Libyan freighter in 1984. The Dutch *Alkmaar* and one of her sister ships are seen here on an exercise. The latter is lowering one of her PAP-104 mine disposal vehicles over the side by hydraulic crane; guided by a cable link to the suspect mine, it can deposit the explosive charge beneath its belly as directed by its operator.

The USA has an extensive mine warfare programme with the same aim: rapid creation of defensive or offensive barriers. Current US stocks of sea mines consist of the aircraft-laid Mks 52, 55 and 56 and the submarine- or warship-laid Mk 57 moored mine. The US Navy also employs a range of general-purpose aircraft bombs which can be delivered without parachutes after modification with influence fuses for use in shallow water against coastal targets. A development programme called 'Quickstrike' is under way to produce a new generation of these comparatively simple weapons.

A far more exotic developmental mine warfare programme is called CAPTOR, short for encapsulated torpedo. CAPTOR is a bottom-moored mine which can be laid at great depths (by submarines, surface ships or aircraft) to release a Mk 46 anti-submarine homing torpedo once activated. The detection and control unit has the reported ability to distinguish between surface ships that pass over its field of influence and submarines which it can classify by their acoustic signature.

Faced with this degree of sophistication, MCM (Mine CounterMeasures) vessels have become the seaborne equivalent of 'stealth' aircraft in that their signatures as presented to mine activation systems have been made as low as possible. Hulls are therefore made of wood or glassfibre, while extensive degaussing keeps remaining magnetic signatures low. Hulls are further designed to minimize pressure and noise, while variable-pitch propellers and general noise-damping keep down acoustic signatures and vibration.

'Natya' class ocean-going minesweeper

The Soviet Union constructed 34 'Natya I' class minesweepers between 1969 and 1980, and although their minesweeping equipment might not be as effective as that of Western equivalents the sheer number of these ships will make up for any such deficiency. They are more heavily armed than many Western mine warfare vessels, mounting two quadruple SA-N-5 SAM launchers, two five-barrel RBU 1200 ASW rocket launchers, and 25-mm and 30-mm AA guns. Built as a successor to the 'Yurka' class, the 'Natya I' design of *Morskoy Tralshchik* (seagoing minesweeper) is still in slow series production for export. The Indian, Libyan and Syrian navies have seven (plus five building), seven and one respectively.

Davits
A pair of hydraulically-powered davits are used to deploy both sweeping gear and MCM mini-subs

Deck
While the sides of the poop deck are filled with equipment containers, the deck itself is clear to allow the crew to work

30-mm cannon turret
The automatic twin 30-mm cannon turret is a standard fit on Soviet light forces

25-mm cannon mounts
The twin 'over-and-under' 25-mm cannon are fitted in two mounts in echelon on either side of the funnel, the port mount being further forward

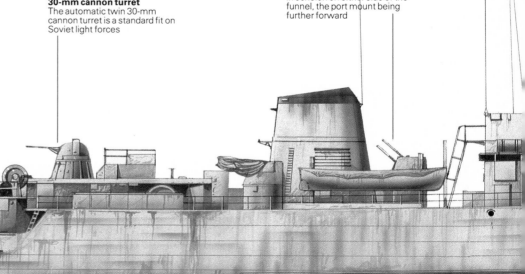

The aluminium alloy-hulled 'Yurka' class of sea-going minesweepers is fitted for magnetic and acoustic sweeping operations. To improve their self-defence capabilities the class is currently being refitted with SA-N-5 'Grail' SAM launchers. The 'Drum Tilt' fire control radar is carried at the top of the mainmast above the IFF systems and the 'Don 2' navigation radar. Surprisingly for Soviet ocean-going minesweepers, this class does not have any ASW systems, which are fitted to earlier and later classes.

'Avenger' class MCMV

The US Navy's lack of appreciation of mine warfare has become obvious, as only 14 'Avenger' class have been ordered. This is utterly inadequate to deal with the Soviet minelaying forces, although the innovative 'Cardinal' class of surface effect ship may be a harbinger of a more realistic approach.

Displacement: 1,040 tons standard and 1,240 tons full load
Dimensions: length 68.3 m; beam 11.9 m; draught 3.5 m
Propulsion: four diesels delivering 1790 kW (2,400 hp) to two shafts

Speed: 14 kts
Armament: two 12.7-mm machine-guns
Electronics: one SQQ-30 minehunting sonar, and one MNS mine-disposal system
Complement: 72

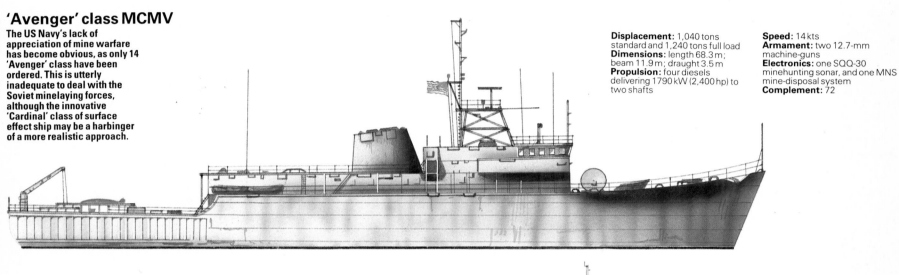

'Lerici' class MCMV

The 'Lerici' class mine countermeasures vessels are equipped to carry the Italian MIN-79 minehunting submersible and six divers, who will use CAM mine destructor charges. Built in the early 1980s, the GRP-hulled ship is the first of a probable 12 for the Italians, with another four being built for the Malaysian navy and one for Nigeria.

Displacement: 470 tons standard and 502 tons full load
Dimensions: length 50.0 m; beam 9.6 m; draught 2.6 m
Propulsion: one diesel delivering 1372 kW (1,840 hp) to one shaft
Speed: 15 kts
Armament: one 20-mm AA gun
Electronics: one SQQ-14 minehunting sonar, and one MIN-79 mine-disposal system
Complement: 40

'Drum Tilt' radar
This is a pedestal-mounted fire control radar common to many Soviet small surface combatants. It probably has acquisition and tracking functions

'Square Head'
This is thought to be an IFF (identification friend or foe) interrogation system, although it may be a missile targeting system

Rocket launchers
Soviet 'Natyas' are equipped with a pair of five-barrel RBU 1200 ASW rocket launchers, which give the type a secondary capability as coastal ASW escorts

'Natya' classes

Displacement: 650 tons standard and 765 tons full load
Dimensions: length 61.0 m; beam 10.0 m; draught 3.5 m
Propulsion: two diesels delivering 3729 kW (5,000 hp) to two shafts
Speed: 18 kts
Armament: ('Natya I') in most units two quadruple SA-N-5 'Grail' SAM launchers with 16 missiles, two twin 30-mm AA and two twin 25-mm AA guns, two 250-mm five-barrel RBU1200 ASW rocket-launchers with 50 rockets, and between 10 and 20 mines depending on type
Armament: ('Natya II') two quadruple SA-N-5 'Grail' SAM launchers with 16 missiles, and two twin 30-mm AA guns
Electronics: one 'Tamir' minehunting sonar
Complement: 60

Mine Warfare

MCM roles divide into further specialities: the minesweeper whose task is to cut the cable of bottom-moored mines or detonate ground mines harmlessly, the deep sweeper which is typically a deep-water stern trawler equipped to cut the cables of moored mines at depths close to the edge of the continental shelf, and the less traditional minehunter which locates mines on the seabed via sonar then neutralizes them with a remotely-controlled submersible. The French PAP 104 is an important example of such a system. It is a submersible 2.7 m (8.86 ft) long and capable of operating at depths down to 500 m (1,640 ft). In an operational engagement, the MCM vessel's minehunting sonar first identifies a potential target, then the PAP 104 is launched and, under guidance received through trailing wires, closes on the target. The submersible carries a TV camera for positive target identification, and a system for placing an explosive charge next to the target mine to destroy it. Battery power is sufficient for five missions and maximum speed is 5.5 kts. The PAP 104 has been ordered for nine navies, and operator vessels include the joint Dutch-Belgian-French GRP-hulled tripartite minehunter type. The Royal Navy uses the PAP in the new coastal minehunters of the 'Hunt' class (commissioned 1982-5).

The system will also be used in the MCM ships ordered by the US Navy in two big construction programmes: the 'Avenger' class with hulls of composite wood/GRP construction and the very unconventional 'Cardinal' class which uses GRP construction in a surface effect twin-hull design.

The West German Troika system is another variation on the remotely-controlled unmanned vessel theme, but this time operating on the surface. It consists of a control ship and three unmanned minesweep-

A Type 351 Troika minesweeping drone control ship of the West German navy is seen with her three charges in front. For passage to a sweep area, the drones carry a crew of three which is taken off for operations. The unmanned vessels are then used mainly for magnetic minesweeping.

ing vessels designed to be as resistant as possible to underwater explosions, each one powered by a diesel-driven hydraulic system driving a combined rudder and propeller. Each unmanned sweeper has coils to generate a magnetic field plus two acoustic hammers for medium-frequency noise and one towed low-frequency acoustic displacer. Sophisticated electronics allow precision control of each sweeper via a UHF link while images of the swept channels are generated by radar in the control vessel.

Aircraft are important platforms for minelaying and potentially for minesweeping. The US Navy, for example, has no surface minelayers, but instead uses submarines, plus carrier- and land-based aircraft including Boeing B-52s. The US Navy has also led the technology of minesweeping from the air, deploying the large Sikorsky RH-53D Sea Stallion helicopter which tows an MCM sled through the water. An improved MCM helicopter, the MH-53E, began operations in 1984.

The Tripartite minehunters are an unusual exercise in collaboration: Belgium provides most of the electronics, France the minehunting equipment, and the Netherlands the propulsion systems. This is *Eridan*, the first Tripartite to enter service with the French navy.

Right: The Sikorsky RH-53D and the current MH-53 series of minesweeping helicopter have been one of the major MCM resources available to the US Navy in the last couple of decades. The RH-53D has been used operationally on a number of occasions, including operation 'End Sweep' (clearing the waters of Haiphong harbour), clearing the Suez Canal and most recently in the Red Sea.

Left: The *Eridan*, with a maximum speed of 15 kts, could take days to reach an operational area. This is one of the penalties that modern mine countermeasures vessels have to put up with, because large propulsion plants for high speeds cause excessive magnetic and acoustic signatures.

Right: The 'Hunt' class are the largest and most expensive GRP-hulled ships in the world, and have minimal acoustic and magnetic signatures. *Ledbury* and *Brecon* swept up Argentine mines off Port Stanley in the Falklands.

Naval Auxiliaries

Assessing naval power is not just a question of count-ing attack submarines, carrier aircraft and missile-armed destroyers. Just as effective land power needs the correct balance of 'teeth and tail', so sea power depends on a complex web of land bases, dockyards and repair facilities. If a navy is to venture far from its own shores it also need specializing naval vessels con-figured to support its fighting units when they are far from home bases, to refuel, rearm and revictual them. This is the primary function of naval auxiliaries, although the distinction is blurred by the use of mer-chant ships 'taken up from trade' to support military operations in time of war. In the Falklands campaign, for example, 60 such 'STUFT' vessels accompanied the Task Force together with 22 ships of the Royal Fleet Auxiliary. It would have been impossible to land and supply the ground force and keep the fighting ships operational without them.

Any major navy claiming a role more than coast defence must thus have a highly developed fleet auxili-ary whose numbers parallel those of its 'fighting ships' proper. In the mid-1950s the Soviet navy, before it had truly begun its rise to world status, had only 15 support ships, mostly converted merchant ships and ex-Ger-man vessels. Now it has 70 depot, support and repair ships and as many replenishment and support tankers. In addition the state-controlled Soviet merchant marine has 350 tankers and 1,375 highly-automated modern cargo ships which may be diverted to fleet support at any time. Over half the Soviet navy's out-of-area support is from merchant tankers.

The Soviet navy's support ships are purpose-built and fully militarized. The missile support ships of the 'Lama' class, for example, were built in 1963-1979 and are armed with up to eight 57-mm guns, and have their engine spaces aft to leave room for a capacious hold amidships for missile and submarine spares. There are mooring points along the hull for submarines to come alongside.

The 400000-tonne full load 'Berezina' class reple-nishment ships are designed to support 'Kiev' class aircraft-carriers, carrying up to 16000 tonnes of fuel, 3000 tonnes of provisions and 500 tonnes of fresh water, with four heavy cranes to handle transfers plus an amidships liquid-fuelling gantry. In contrast with Western practice, these ships are heavily armed in their own right with four 57-mm and four 30-mm 'Gatling' guns, a twin SA-N-4 SAM launcher and multi-barrel anti-submarine mortar. It also operates two Kamov Ka-25 'Hormone' helicopters for vertical replenish-ment (vertrep) ship-to-ship supply capacity plus an anti-submarine reach. There is a considerable fit of sensors including air-search radar, missile and gun fire-control radars, and hull-mounted sonar.

Above: The Soviet replenishment ship *Berezina* refuels a 'Kiev' class carrier and a guided missile cruiser. It is believed that the *Berezina* was constructed for the carrier support role, and may well be testing the concept for a new generation of replenishment vessels that will be built for the Soviet fixed wing carriers now under construction.

Right: An enlarged development of the 'Don' class, 'Ugra' class submarine support ships can provide base facilities for a flotilla of eight to 12 submarines. Two vessels serve as training ships. Apart from being submarine depot ships, 'Ugra' class vessels can also serve as command and control ships for task groups and provide significant local defence for a replenishment area.

Left: A view from astern of a 'Riga' class frigate of the Soviet refuelling technique of towing the warship whilst it takes on fuel. Although this method has some advantages it makes both ships highly vulnerable to attack during the operation, as it is very slow to execute.

'Berezina' class underway replenishment oiler

The only Soviet replenishment ship comparable to the US Navy's large AOR/AOE ships is the replenishment oiler *Berezina*, which can supply petroleum products, munitions, stores and fresh water to ships on each side and fuel to a ship astern. Armament is extremely heavy for a ship of this type, comprising a twin SA-N-4 SAM launcher, two twin 57-mm guns with four Gatling-type 50-mm close-in weapon systems, and two RBU 4500A six-barrelled ASW rocket launchers. If the two Kamov Ka-25 'Hormone' helicopters carried retain their ASW capacity, then *Berezina* has a considerable defence against hostile submarines.

Cranes
Ten-ton capacity cranes are used for loading stores and servicing ships moored alongside

Solid cargo transfer rigs
Solid cargo transfer while under way is handled by two slide-and-stay constant-tension transfer rigs on each side

'Bass Tilt' radar
This is a fire control radar, directing the fire of the 30-mm Gatling type close-in weapons to be found on the aft superstructure

Kamov Ka-25 'Hormone-C' helicopters
These are operated from the flight deck astern. The utility helicopters may have some ASW capability

'Stromboli' class replenishment tanker

Commissioned in 1975 and 1978, the two replenishment tankers of the 'Stromboli' class are capable of transferring up to 3,000 tons of fuel oil, 1,000 tons of diesel, 400 tons of JP 5 aviation fuel and up to 300 tons of other stores. No hangars have been fitted, although a helicopter flight deck allows for Vertrep operations.

Type: replenishment tanker
Displacement: 3,556 tons light and 8,706 tons full load
Dimensions: length 129 m; beam 18 m; draught 6.5 m
Propulsion: two diesels delivering 7160 kW (9,600 hp) to a single shaft

Speed: 18.5 kts
Armament: single 76 mm/62 (Compact) with mounts for two single 40 mm (not shipped)
Aircraft: none, but helicopter flight deck is fitted
Complement: 115

'Poolster' class fast combat support ship

The Royal Netherlands Navy's 'Poolster' class fast combat support ship is unique in NATO navies in having an ASW armament of depth charges to go with a helicopter group of up to five Westland Lynx ASW helicopters. The stores she carries include lightweight torpedoes and conventional depth bombs for use by the helicopters.

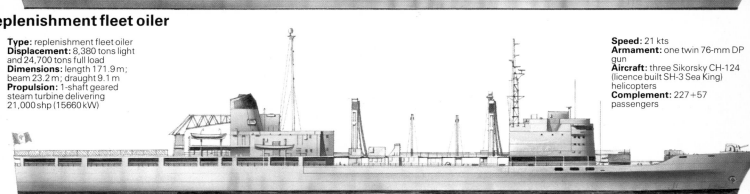

Type: fast combat support ship
Displacement: 16,836 tons full load
Dimensions: length 169.6 m; beam 20.3 m; draught 8.2 m
Propulsion: 1-shaft geared steam turbine delivering 22,000 shp (16405 kW)
Speed: 21 kts
Armament: two single 40-mm AA guns, and two depth-charge racks
Aircraft: between one and five Westland SH-14 Lynx helicopters
Complement: 185

'Protecteur' class replenishment fleet oiler

Given the US Navy AOR designation, the 'Protecteur' class can carry diesel and aviation fuel in addition to fuel oil. Unusually, it also carries four LCVPs, and can accommodate up to 50 troops for commando operations. Up to three licence-built Sikorsky SH-3 Sea King ASW helicopters can be used as spare aircraft by an ASW hunter-killer task group as well as being able to provide vertical replenishment of ammunition, dry stores and fuel.

Type: replenishment fleet oiler
Displacement: 8,380 tons light and 24,700 tons full load
Dimensions: length 171.9 m; beam 23.2 m; draught 9.1 m
Propulsion: 1-shaft geared steam turbine delivering 21,000 shp (15660 kW)

Speed: 21 kts
Armament: one twin 76-mm DP gun
Aircraft: three Sikorsky CH-124 (licence built SH-3 Sea King) helicopters
Complement: 227+57 passengers

'Rhein' class depot ship

'Rhein' class depot ships of the Federal German navy are designed for operations in the restricted waters of the Baltic and German North Sea. Serving as depot ships of Fast Patrol Craft and diesel submarines, the armament fit enables the vessels to operate in place of frigates or as training ships.

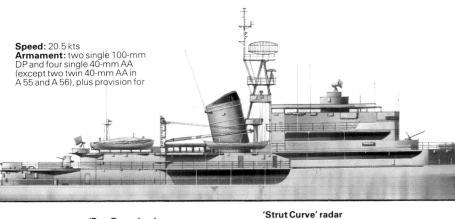

Type: depot or training ship
Displacement: 2,330/2,400 standard and 2,940/3,000 tons full load (depending upon type)
Dimensions: length 98.2/98.6 m depending upon type; beam 11.83 m; draught 5.2 m
Propulsion: 2-shaft diesels delivering 14,400 hp (10738 kW)

Speed: 20.5 kts
Armament: two single 100-mm DP and four single 40-mm AA (except two twin 40-mm AA in A 55 and A 56), plus provision for

up to 70 mines according to type
Electronics: one DA-02 air- and surface-search radar, two WM-45 fire-control radars, one Kelvin Hughes 14/9 navigation radar, one hull sonar
Complement: 153 except A 55 and A 56 114, A 61 and A 68 163, and A 65 and A 67 125

Type: underway replenishment oiler
Displacement: 14,000 tons light and 40,000 tons full load
Dimensions: length 212.0 m; beam 26.0 m; draught 12.0 m
Propulsion: 2-shaft diesels delivering 54,000 hp (40268 kW)
Speed: 22 kts
Armament: one twin SA-N-4 'Gecko' SAM launcher with 18 missiles, two twin 57-mm AA and four 30-mm ADG6-30 AA guns, and two RBU 1000 anti-submarine rocket launchers
Aircraft: two Kamov Ka-25 'Hormone-C' helicopters
Complement: 600

Liquid cargo transfer rig
'Berezhina' can refuel two vessels simultaneously by means of the central rig

'Pop Group' radar
This fire control radar directs the twin SA-N-4 SAM launcher mounted in pop-up fashion in a silo abaft the twin funnel

'Strut Curve' radar
This medium-range air-search radar is able to detect aircraft flying at medium altitude at about 60 km

'Muff Cob' radar
Similar to 'Bass Tilt', this is more often associated with 57-mm guns than any other system

Rocker launchers
As with most vessels of the Soviet navy, 'Berezhina' has an integral ASW capability in the shape of two six-barrelled RBU-1000 rocket launchers

Gun turrets
The two turrets at the bow each contain twin 57-mm guns, primarily for use in the anti-air role but capable of engaging surface targets

Naval Auxiliaries

The Royal Navy or more properly the Royal Fleet Auxiliary operates fleet tankers of equivalent size but without armament. The RFA's three 'Ol' class, two 'Tide' class and three 'Appleleaf' class tankers are designed for underway replenishment (unrep) alongside or by helicopter, each ship being able to operate up to four Westland Sea Kings. The fleet tankers of the 'Rover' class are much smaller (11500 tonnes full load) and can operate a single Sea King. The fleet replenishment ships of the 'Fort' class are not tankers but have four capacious holds for up to 3500 tonnes of dry cargo and armament. They can operate up to four Sea Kings either in the vertrep role or as a dedicated ASW platform. These ships are thought to have special weapon exclusion areas for nuclear depth bombs.

As befits the world's most powerful navy, the US Navy's auxiliary forces are very large. There are both the auxiliary ships of the navy proper and the vessels of Military Sealift Command (MSC) which operate under naval command but with civilian crews and are unarmed in peacetime. Most US defence cargo is carried in commercial merchant ships under charter to the government through MSC.

The auxiliary ships of the US Navy are divided into two broad categories, so-called unrep ships and fleet support vessels. The unrep ships carry out direct support in forward operational areas. The number of unrep ships available should be enough to support deployed carrier or amphibious task groups in up to five locations simultaneously while MSC ships carry fuel, ammunition and so on from the USA for transfer to the unrep ships at overseas bases. Fleet support ships, such as submarine and destroyer tenders, tugs, salvage vessels and so on, rarely venture far from harbour either in the USA or at overseas bases. These unrep and fleet support ships are armed and are mainly navy-crewed, but an increasing number are operated by the MSC with civilian crews.

The modern unrep fleet oilers of the 'Cimarron' class, for example, commissioned from 1981 onwards and are sized to provide two complete refuellings of a conventionally-powered aircraft-carrier and eight escorting destroyers. These ships have a sizeable helicopter platform aft, and are fitted with chaff launchers and two Phalanx close-in weapon systems.

Above: Seen passing through the Suez Canal, *Gold Rover* is one of a class of small fleet tankers designed to deploy with and replenish destroyer- or frigate-sized vessels. She has a capacity of 6,600 tons of aviation and diesel fuel, lubricating oil, fresh water, and a small amount of dry and refrigerated stores. A helicopter pad is fitted permitting VERTREP, but there is no hangar.

Below: The RFA *Blue Rover* takes part in a replenishment-at-sea (RAS) during the early stages of the campaign to retake the Falklands. The *Blue Rover* was the only one of her class to serve in the Total Exclusion Zone, and apart from RAS duties she supplied fuel and ammunition to the army from San Carlos Water between 1 June and 22 June.

Above: *Fort Grange* can store up to 3,500 tons of dry and refrigerated foods, stores and munitions on pallets in her four holds, and can handle cargo in both underway and vertical replenishment. This Westland Sea King HAS.Mk 5 has just taken off from the *Fort Grange* on a VERTREP mission with an underslung load of ammunition for the army ashore on the Falklands.

USS *America* replenishes from the 'Sacramento' class combat support ship USS *Seattle*. These extremely expensive vessels are designed to provide an entire carrier battle group with the fuel, stores, victuals and ammunition required for several days' combat operations in one single replenishment.

The fast combat support ship USS *Detroit* is seen while steaming alongside one of the US Navy's carriers. An idea of her size can be gauged from the fact that she dwarfs the 'Spruance' class destroyer USS *Peterson* (DD969), which is being replenished. These ships have proved very effective, but such is their cost that only four have been completed.

Seen during a NATO exercise making an underway replenishment of (left) a 'Knox' class frigate of the US Navy and (right) a Canadian 'Iroquois' class destroyer, the 'Rover' class small fleet tanker can carry over 6,000 tons of fuel products.

Above: HMS *Fearless* and the LSL *Sir Tristram* undergo alongside refuelling at speed from one of the RFA's old 'Leaf'-class support ships. These 'Leaf' class vessels are not purpose-built ships, but commercial tankers chartered by the RFA under normal contract arrangements, and are principally used to move bulk fuel loads from oil terminals to MOD storage farms, as well as to replenish the fleet tankers at sea.

Above: The ammunition ship USS *Flint* as seen by USS *Chicago* during a replenishment operation. *Flint* can also provide vertical replenishment using its two UH-46 Sea Knight helicopters.

USS *Sylvania*, a 'Mars' class combat store ship, has five holds (one refrigerated) to carry its 4,000 tons of supplies. Here a Boeing Vertol UH-46D Sea Knight VERTREP helicopter of Helicopter Combat Support Squadron 4 moves away with some of these supplies slung beneath its fuselage.

Naval Surface-to-Surface Missiles

The big-gun battleship was a launch platform for surface-to-surface missiles: large-calibre armour-piercing shells propelled for ranges up to 29 km (18 miles) by the power of the propellant detonated in their massive main armament. During World War II, however, bombs and torpedoes delivered by aircraft toppled the big-gun warship as the arbiter of seapower, while the first primitive air-to-surface guided missiles such as the German Fritz-X, which sank the battleship *Roma* in 1943, made their operational debut. It is not surprising that warships were among the first effective targets for guided missiles, for they are massive chunks of floating metal moving on a relatively flat surface while at the same time their radar, optical and IR signatures are great and they also pump out their own electromagnetic radiation. They move relatively slowly and cannot take violent evasive action. It is not surprising therefore that the naval SSM (Surface-to-Surface Missile) has proliferated in the last 20 years and caused searching questions to be asked about the surface warship's ability to survive in the face of an ever more sophisticated threat. The destruction of HMS *Sheffield* by an air-launched surface-skimming Exocet anti-ship missile during the sea battle for the Falklands served further to emphasize the vulnerability of surface warships in the age of missile warfare.

The Exocet, designed and developed in France, is typical of the sea-skimming missiles developed from the late 1960s onwards to be launched from a wide range of platforms including major warships, fast patrol boats, high-performance aircraft, helicopters and submarines. Because any such platform can pose a threat whether it be an aircraft or a destroyer over the horizon or an undetected submarine, the defence priorities are the same: find the launch platform and destroy it before it can fire. If that fails, be prepared to destroy the weapon launched at you or baffle it with ECM (Electronic CounterMeasures). To do that, the technology of the threat must be understood.

The Exocet is a very good working example. In its ship-launched MM.38 and improved MM.40 versions, the target may be acquired by a variety of ways, by mast-mounted surface radar for example or fed in over the horizon by air reconnaissance. The target's approximate co-ordinates are then fed by the ship's fire-control system into the missile's inertial guidance system, the assembly of accelerometers and gyros spun up several minutes before launch. After launch the missile flies towards the point designated, the onboard computer remembering where the missile was launched and where it was told to go, making it a true 'fire-and-forget' system. In mid-flight the missile descends to a height a few metres above the wavetops, using a down-looking radar altimeter to maintain height and the radar clutter of the wavetops to hide from the target's defensive radar system. In the last stage of flight the missile's active homing head switches on, bringing the missile electronically live and therefore visible to the target's electronic support measures equipment but with only a few seconds of the flight

Using a variety of command-guided and semi-active homing techniques, the Gabriel Mk I was used extensively in the 1973 Yom Kippur War by the Israeli navy, and sank a number of Syrian and Egyptian craft.

now left. The terminal seeker directs the missile to home on the biggest source of radar returns, namely the metallic 'barn-door' represented by the target warship.

The AM.39 air-launched version functions in exactly the same way in that the target co-ordinates are imparted by the launch aircraft's surface search radar, and the missile does not need a booster as the aircraft supplies the launch speed. An SM.39 submarine-launched version has been developed which is all but identical to the air-launched version, using a pop-out capsule for underwater launch from torpedo tubes.

The Soviet navy pioneered anti-ship SSMs, and has put several generations of such weapons into service. In 1967 the Israeli destroyer *Eilat* was sunk by hits from Soviet-supplied SS-N-2A 'Styx' missiles fired from an Egyptian fast attack craft, an event which caused Western navies to sit up suddenly and take notice of the potential of SSMs. For many years the long-range SS-N-3 'Shaddock' launched from Soviet surface warships

The MBB Kormoran uses an active or passive radar-homing seeker mode to target itself on a point just above the waterline of its victim. The Kormoran Mk 1 is used by the Marineflieger and by Italian anti-shipping units. A Mk 2 version is already under development for the West German navy to arm its Tornado strike aircraft.

and SSGNs was unmatched by Western navies. The latest SSM in the Soviet inventory is the SS-N-19, which has been identified as a vertically-launched system deployed both on the nuclear-powered battlecruiser *Kirov* and the very large missile-firing 'Oscar' class submarines. NATO analysts credit the missile with a speed of Mach 2.5 and a range of no less than 500 km (311 miles), suggesting that land-based aircraft, helicopters or satellites would be used for midcourse guidance before the missile's autonomous terminal homing came into play. A new shorter-range SSM, given the reporting designation SS-N-22 and using an unknown guidance system and operational profile, was identified aboard cruisers of the 'Sovremenny' class in 1985.

Above: Seen here being launched from an 'Osa' class fast patrol craft, SS-N-2 'Styx' sank the Israeli destroyer *Eilat* in October 1967, and India sank the Pakistani destroyer *Khaibar* in 1971.

Right: Improvements to the sustainer motor and container-launcher of Exocet have resulted in the evolution of the larger MM.40 variant. This has increased range, and also allows a larger number of rounds to be carried.

The RBS 15, manufactured by the Saab-Bofors missile corporation, will become one of Sweden's most effective anti-ship assets in the next decade. In ship-launched form it will equip the 'Spica' class Fast Attack Craft of the Swedish navy, while the air-launch variant will be fitted to the AJ-37 and SH-37 Viggen and to the new JAS 39 Gripen when it enters service in the 1990s.

Right: Designed as a simple low risk technological programme, the Harpoon anti-ship missile has developed into a versatile system capable of being launched from a ship, submarine or aircraft. Since its operational debut, it has demonstrated exceptional reliability and effectiveness in defeating the total spectrum of naval surface ship targets in adverse weather and in severe ECM environments.

The US Navy got into the SSM business relatively late, not getting the RGM-84 Harpoon anti-ship missile operational until 1977. Since then, however, Harpoon has been widely deployed in applications across the US fleet from the demothballed battleships of the 'Iowa' class via cruisers, destroyers and frigates to patrol hydrofoils. Harpoon is a sea-skimmer using mid-course inertial guidance followed by active radar guidance in the terminal phase. It has extensive inbuilt ECCM (Electronic Counter-Counter Measures) and the ability to engage targets taking high-speed evasive action. It had also been developed as the AGM-84 for air launch from land-based aircraft such as the Lockheed P-3 and carrier-based aircraft such as the Grumman A-6, and in encapsulated form as the UGM-84 for submerged launch from submarines. Sub-Harpoon has also been supplied to the Royal Navy, though the Exocet remains that service's principal surface-to-surface weapon.

The anti-ship Harpoon has a range of more than 90 km (56 miles). Capabilities of a different order are the preserve of the Tomahawk sea-launched cruise missile, with a range of 2500 km (1,555 miles) in its land-attack version. Tomahawk is a system which blurs the distinction between tactical weapons (for warfare against rival naval forces) and a strategic bombardment weapon which potentially gives the destructive firepower of a nuclear ballistic missile submarine to the simplest of warships. The anti-ship version of Tomahawk has been engineered with either nuclear or conventional warheads. Range is reduced to 450 km (280 miles), however, and the terminal guidance is a modified version of the Harpoon's active radar system.

Several countries have developed indigenous surface-to-surface anti-ship missiles, and air-launched or coast defence variants have often been developed in parallel. Among those not mentioned above are the Chinese C801 (bearing a close resemblance to the French Exocet), the Franco-German ANS (under development as a supersonic Exocet replacement), the Franco-Italian Otomat, the Israeli Gabriel (with a range of 200 km/124 miles for the latest version), the Italian Sea Killer, the Norwegian Penguin, the Swedish RBS 15 and RB08, the Taiwanese Hsiung Feng (thought to be a version of the Israeli Gabriel), the Soviet SS-N-9 'Siren' and SS-N-12 'Sandbox', and the British Sea Eagle SL (the ship-launched variant of the air-launched anti-ship missile).

Right: A Penguin is launched from one of the Norwegian navy's five 'Oslo' class frigates. Developed as the first Western anti-ship missile system, the Penguin has undergone considerable improvement over the years. The ship-launched versions are carried in simple container-launcher boxes that weigh about 650 kg complete with missile.

Naval Artillery

The big naval gun reached its highest state of the development during World War II, the conflict which proved that the day of the big gun battleship was over in the age of air power. But the giants have not all slipped away: the US Navy retains four battleships of the 'Iowa' class, two of which were brought out of mothballs in the 1980s and equipped with powerful batteries of Harpoon and Tomahawk missiles while significantly retaining their 406-mm (16-in) main armament. The guns fire a massive shell weighing 1225 kg (2,700 lb) over 40 km (25 miles) with a barrel elevation of 45°, and there are estimated to be at least 18,000 rounds of wartime manufacture still serviceable. During the US debacle in the Lebanon in 1983 the US *New Jersey* sent 406-mm shells crashing into the hills behind Beirut in a futilely symbolic but nevertheless deadly display of rage. Far more effectively, during the British recapture of the Falkland Islands in 1982 precision-directed firepower from the 25 rounds per minute 114-mm (4.5-in) Mk 8s of Royal Navy warships on the 'gun-line' (guided by forward observation officers ashore) proved of vital importance in softening Argentine defensive positions. Over 8,000 shells were fired, giving an idea of how intense was the bombardment.

Experience (not always happy) with missiles over the last few decades, and the effectiveness of naval artillery for such roles as shore bombardment indicated above, have led to a revival in naval guns, though 20 years ago it seemed their day was over for good. In the anti-ship role, for example, it was soon realized that firing a surface-to-surface missile was an expensive way of putting 'a shot across the bows' of a suspect ship: a gun was a more cost-effective alternative, and much more useful in low-intensity 'junk bashing' operations. On a small ship it is also easy to run low on SSMs but correspondingly harder to run out of gun ammunition.

In the anti-air role the surface-to-air missile rules supreme at long range, but at short range guns can be brought into action very rapidly and put up a very high rate of fire (see section on Close-In Weapon Systems). Again the Falkland experience showed hurried conversions before the Task Force sailed, frigates' seaboats being replaced by 20-mm rapid-fire Oerlikon cannon (declared obsolete in 1945) and GP machine-guns being lashed to ships' rails in an effort to put as much firepower as possible in the face of low-level air attacks.

In such situations high rates of fire are important, but most modern warships look underarmed compared with their World War II ancestors. While warships of 1945 bristled with guns of all calibres, a modern destroyer generally has a single, apparently small-calibre weapon mounted forward. But that single mounting is radar-directed under computerized fire control and has an entirely automated loading and fire sequence. The US Navy, for example, after World War II began to develop a 127-mm (5-in) 38-calibre weapon in a twin mounting with each barrel firing at 18 rounds per minute. As in several other rapid-fire weapons, the designers decided to replace twin barrels with twin feed mechanisms alternately feeding a single barrel. The only penalty in such an arrangement is the possibility of a higher failure rate. The latest 127-mm mounting entering service on US Navy warships, the 54-calibre Lightweight Mk 45, is designed to incorporate all the

The 'Type 21' frigate HMS *Active* in action during the Falklands campaign. The supposedly outdated medium gun proved itself invaluable in the shore bombardment role, and post-Falklands 'Type 22s' were redesigned to carry a gun.

improvements made since the development of the 127-mm/38.It requires about one-third the crew (six instead of 14 men), and with a single operator in the control centre can fire a drum load of 20 heavy shells.

Computerized fire control has progressed at the same rate as missile guidance, and radar directors often have an overlap with semi-active missile guidance. The Royal Navy uses the same radar director to control its 114-mm guns and Sea Dart long-range SAMs, and in some recent US ships the Mk 86 fire-control system has a similar capability directing Mk 45s and Standard SAMs. The Mk 86 additionally has an advanced indirect shore bombardment capability for targets which are not within view of radar or optical sensors. Known target and own ship co-ordinates are entered at the weapon's control console while the ship's movements and position are automatically updated during an engagement.

Guided projectiles may be the next change in naval gun fire, particularly laser guidance for use against surface and shore targets as well as slowly-manoeuvring small targets such as sea-skimming anti-ship missiles.

Above: Commissioned in 1980, *Niels Juel* is the nameship of a three-strong class of Danish frigates armed with Harpoon SSMs and an OTO-Melara 76-mm gun, which is one of the most widely used naval guns, fitted to the warships of over 40 different navies.

Left: *Second Maître de Bihan*, based in the Channel, displays her bow-mounted 100-mm main armament, which has a rate of fire of 60 rounds a minute and is capable of engaging either surface or aerial targets including sea-skimming anti-ship missiles.

Above: USS *New Jersey* is an unrivalled instrument of power projection. Brought out of mothballs for the Vietnam War, she is now modernized; the white domes of Phalanx CIWS can clearly be seen in this photograph. Her nine 16-in (406-mm) guns fire shells containing nearly a ton of high explosive.

Above: The 'Sverdlov' class cruisers of the Soviet navy carry a varying number of 152-mm guns in triple turrets. They are used for shore bombardment by the Baltic fleet and may now have tactical nuclear capability.

Right: USS *New Jersey* opens fire with one of her forward 16-in guns. The bombardments of Lebanon revealed the need for more modern ammunition (she is still using up old stocks left over from World War II) but the threat of her awesome firepower was enough to cow the most fanatical of the Lebanese militias.

Fleet Air Defence

The Falklands campaign of 1982 demonstrated just how vulnerable surface warships are to air attack. If the fuses had been set differently on the bombs delivered by Argentine air force McDonnell Douglas A-4 Skyhawks in suicidally low-level attacks on the British Task Force in San Carlos Water, far fewer bombs would have failed to explode and many more British warships might have been sunk, and the outcome of the campaign might thus have been very different. Nevertheless it was attacks like that made by Argentine navy Dassault-Breguet Super Etendards armed with air-launched Exocet anti-ship missiles that caught the headlines. It was the cold and deadly efficiency of attacks made from over the horizon by an unseen enemy that seemed so chilling.

The threat of such attack by the surface-skimming anti-ship missile, (air, surface- or submarine-launched) demands a huge technological effort in fleet defence, both in sensors (to detect and identify targets at maximum range) and in weapons (long-range defensive systems to hit the hostile launch platform before it fires its missile and a CIWS or Close-In Weapons System to shoot down the missile if all else fails). Moreover, because hostile submarines are likely to make attacks with surface-skimmers rather than with torpedoes, anti-submarine screening becomes analogous to air defence: it is imperative to destroy or deter the launch platform before it gets a shot in. One air-launched Exocet (whose warhead failed to explode) was enough to gut the 'Type 42' class destroyer HMS *Sheffield*. It has been estimated that six SS-N-7s as launched by Soviet 'Charlie' class submarines would certainly sink a US supercarrier. Of course, just one nuclear-tipped example of this missile would be enough on its own.

The US Navy, with its seapower built around hugely expensive carrier task groups, is not surprisingly equipped on a lavish scale with such systems, and well rehearsed in the doctrines for their use. The solution developed over many years is defence in depth with three distinct zones of operation and weapon effectiveness.

Land-based maritime aircraft and attack submarines patrol the perimeter of the outer zone on ASW duties, their operations co-ordinated with the fixed ASW sensor networks and land-based radars. Meanwhile in the 'air envelope', fleet air-defence fighters such as the Grumman F-14A Tomcat armed with very-long-range Phoenix air-to-air missiles screen the fleet from cruise missile-armed bombers or aircraft able to provide mid-course guidance for submarine-launched missiles. Carrier-based AEW aircraft such as the Grumman E-2B Hawkeye provide long-range target detection and direct the combat air patrols to maximum effect.

In the middle zone surface warships provide a second ring of ASW protection using towed-array sonars and directing helicopters to investigate contacts.

Sea Dart was used on several occasions in the Falklands, but Argentine familiarity with the system (which arms their two Type 42 destroyers) ensured that most attacks were made outside the missile's performance spectrum, with the result that Sea Dart was not as successful as had been expected.

It is in this zone that long-range missile defence begins to cover the fleet.

In the inner zone, close-in point defences and electronic countermeasures are the last defence against air threats which by this stage include supersonic cruise missiles and sea-skimmers.

In the US Navy the technology of missile-based fleet air defence has developed in step with the doctrine of layered defence and the evolving nature of the threat, while smaller navies with less assets nevertheless still strive to apply the principles of layered defence. The critical problems are detection capacity, multiple target capability, reaction time, firepower, area coverage, reliability and resistance to electronic countermeasures. The US Navy's solution is called Aegis, technologically a very ambitious programme 20 years in development, to provide a 'leakproof' umbrella for carrier battle groups. The heart of Aegis is the SPY-1A phased-array radar capable of the simultaneous detection and tracking of multiple targets and linked to four powerful computers which co-ordinate the targeting and launch of extended-range Standard SM-2 missiles while the fire-control system and its associated radar illuminate the target.

The long-range (55-km/34-mile) Standard missile uses semi-active terminal guidance, that is it has a radar receiver in its nose able to home on energy generated by the shipborne target-illumination radar and reflected

A 'Kashin' class destroyer launches an SA-N-1 'Goa'. The engagement envelope of the Mach 2.1 missile is between 6 and 22 km at heights ranging from 90 to 15250 m. The 60-kg warhead can be high explosive or low-yield nuclear.

by the target. A nuclear warhead for the SM-2 is under development to replace the dual-capable Terrier naval SAM first deployed with a W45 nuclear warhead in 1958. The nuclear Standard SM-2N has a W81 fission warhead with a low kiloton yield.

For short-range applications the much simpler CLOS (Command to Line of Sight) guidance system has its attractions: the ship's radar tracks both the target and the missile itself after launch (or the missile is tracked optically via a TV camera), and the fire-control system sends the missile signals via a data link to come into the line of sight to the target. The command-guided Seawolf missile fitted to the destroyers HMS *Broadsword* and HMS *Brilliant* proved a tremendous asset in the Falklands fighting, but though no Seawolf-equipped ship was lost they came close to being overwhelmed by mass attacks. Each ship had only a dozen missiles ready to fire, while the CLOS guidance system meant that the Seawolf could not engage targets that were not approaching the ship on which the Seawolf was mounted, and when missiles came in parallel or away from the ships, the Seawolf point-defence system was largely ineffective.

Left and above: A Seawolf missile is launched from a Type 22 frigate. The missile is highly effective, but with ancillary radar, launch and command systems the Seawolf system is rather heavy, and to operate two launchers effectively the Type 22 frigates have to be larger than Type 42 destroyers.

Above: Off San Juan, the 'Belknap' class cruiser USS *Wainwright* fires an SM-2ER missile. The extended range version of the Standard is capable of ranges in the region of 150 km.

Right: Terrier has been largely superseded by Standard, but for many years it provided air defence for the US Navy. The RIM-2E had a maximum range in excess of 70 km.

Left: In between the Mks 10 (seen above) and 26 twin-rail launchers, the single-rail Mk 13 system was fitted to missile destroyers as well as to the two nuclear cruisers *California* and *South Carolina* and to the 'Oliver Hazard Perry' class frigates. The Mk 13 can handle Terrier, Standard and Harpoon missiles.

Right: The French destroyer *Georges Leygues* is seen tied up alongside the wharf in Beirut while providing support for the ill-omened Multi National Force in 1982. The eight-round Crotale launcher and its associated radar systems are prominent at the top of the photograph.

Right: Silhouetted by the dawn, the twin Mk 26 launcher of the nuclear-powered cruiser USS *Mississippi* is loaded with two Standard SM-1 MR missiles. The GMLS Mk 26 is the fastest and most versatile launcher in US Navy service today. Fully automatic, the Mk 26 can handle Standard SAMs, Harpoon SSMs and ASROC ASW missiles, from magazines of 24, 44 or 64 round capacity. It equips the first Aegis cruisers, but will be superseded by vertical launch systems.

Left: The first of the Aegis-equipped cruisers, USS *Ticonderoga* (CG47). The heart of the Aegis system is the two paired SPY-1A fixed-antenna radars that provide simultaneous surveillance, target-detection, and target-tracking to well over 160 km distance.

Above: The ADF6-30 30-mm cannon is in widespread use throughout the Soviet navy, ranging from the eight mounted on *Kirov* and *Kiev* (two of *Kiev*'s being seen above, fitted forward of the bridge) to the single units fitted to smaller vessels. The same mount is used for a twin 30-mm gun.

The Aegis system combines aspects of both semi-active and CLOS guidance. The Standard missile has an autopilot which the Aegis fire-control computer sets before firing (directing the missile to the target area), while the system also provides some mid-course correction via a command guidance link, the missile receiving the signals via rear-facing antennae. Because the shipborne illuminating radar need operate only in the terminal phase its target load capability is increased. Furthermore, the missile's energy-efficient path (made possible by steering the missile to the likely position of the target on impact rather than following it on line of sight) means that the slant range the missile can fly to the target is effectively doubled. The first Aegis cruiser, USS *Ticonderoga*, joined the fleet in 1983 and a further 23 are planned to become operational by the early 1990s. Later Aegis ships will have VLSs (Vertical Launch Systems) offering much more efficient use of shipboard space and also all-weather operability. It is planned that US shipborne weapons should conform to a common module compatible with the Mk 41 VLS now in a state of advanced development.

Vertical-launch capability offers great operational advantages, allows more efficient ship design and is a feature of virtually all new-generation naval SAMs while being re-engineered into existing ones. The French are working on a new 10-km (6.2-mile) range VLS missile called SAN 90 for service in the 1990s and intended ultimately to replace the conventionally launched short-range Naval Crotale and medium-range Masurca. The Canadian navy is converting its Sea Sparrow-armed frigates to VLS configuration, while a VLS Seawolf GWS 26 will arm the Royal Navy's new 'Type 23' frigates. The Soviets have long been specialists in VLS SAM installations, with the SA-N-6 (operational in the battle-cruiser *Kirov* since 1980) and two new and unknown systems identified subsequently as the SA-N-8 and SA-N-9 in the US DoD system.

Barak is an Israeli-built naval self-defence system. Although originally designed with missile, radar and guidance system on a single mount, as here in a test launch from a 'Reshef' class missile boat, the production system is likely to use VLUs (Vertical Launch Units) containing up to eight missiles each.

Goalkeeper is a Dutch-designed system with a 30-mm Gatling type cannon manufactured by General Electric in the USA, with electronics by Hollandse Signaalapparaten. The system has been chosen by the Royal Navy for new-build vessels.

An urgent lesson of the Falklands fighting was the desperate need for short-range firepower to destroy or deter threats which had penetrated the outer and middle defences. Several Royal Navy warships have subsequently had their seaboats replaced by twin 30-mm rapid-fire cannon, while Phalanx systems were expeditiously acquired from the USA for installation in the ASW carriers HMS *Illustrious* and HMS *Invincible*. The Phalanx is a radar-guided multiple cannon firing at a cyclical rate of 3,000 rounds per minute. The actual projectiles are 20-mm rounds of exceptionally dense depleted uranium which are designed literally to put a wall of metal in the path of an incoming sea skimmer. Phalanx is widely deployed throughout the US Navy, and the Soviets have a similar 30-mm Gatling type CIWS plus associated radar installed on major surface units. Similar radar-guided fast-slewing CIWS have been developed by a US-Dutch consortium (Goalkeeper) and Switzerland (Seaguard). The Spanish have developed a novel system called Meroka grouping 12 20-mm Oerlikon cannon barrels in a single unit with a theoretical rate of fire of 9,000 rounds per minute.

Left: The General Dynamics Phalanx system makes use of the 20-mm Vulcan cannon developed for aircraft use in the 1950s. Primary CIWS for the US Navy, the Phalanx has been fitted to the Royal Navy's 'Invincible' class carriers.

Above: The RAM, or Rolling Airframe Missile, employs components from both the Sidewinder AAM and the Stinger portable SAM, added to a passive radar seeker. This is the first test launch of RAM over water.

Underwater Weapons

The battle between submarine and surface escort has been one of the most testing of all in the story of military technology during the present century. Several times during the Battle of the Atlantic, perhaps the most important campaign of World War II, a technological breakthrough by each side swung the balance of the actual fighting: high-frequency direction-finding, ahead-throwing launchers for depth charges and schnorkelling are all good examples. By the end the Germans were putting to sea very fast, dangerously capable U-boats which could outrun surface escorts, but as the war on land was almost over these advanced boats were far too late to have any real effect. But the lessons were clear: ASW (Anti-Submarine Warfare) forces would in the future need a whole new range of underwater weapons which would not simply be dropped over the stern of a destroyer, but of necessity delivered by systems that would take them to the target, if necessary many kilometres away from the escort. There were further developments in the 1950s and 1960s, in the form of nuclear depth bombs with their terrifying power, and the development of the hunter-killer submarine as a primary ASW platform, designed to penetrate defended seaspace and seek out and destroy ballistic missile submarines in their sanctuaries.

Today the principal anti-submarine warfare weapon employed by hunter-killer submarines is the wire-guided torpedo, best described perhaps as an underwater guided missile. Target acquisition and mid-course guidance are handled by the submarine's own sonar, which detects and plots a target's position very much as a fighter aircraft's air-to-air radar might do, and by the fire-control computer which transmits guidance commands down trailing wires until the weapon's own short-range active sonar takes over in the terminal phase. The torpedo must of course be faster than the submarine it is set to chase, a fact which poses particular design problems when faced with the submerged top speed of over 40 kts attainable by some Soviet submarines.

The Mk 48 heavyweight torpedo, arming all US Navy attack and fleet ballistic missile submarines, has a speed of 55 kts and a range of almost 40 km (25 miles). It was the recognition in the late 1970s of the apparent high-speed and deep-diving capabilities of the Soviet

'Alfa' class SSNs that led to a development programme called ADCAP (ADvanced CAPabilities) to boost performance of the conventionally armed Mk 48. A nuclear-armed torpedo called Astor was developed as a last-ditch self-defence weapon for submarines, but it was credited with a kill probability of 2:0 (the target and the launch submarine).

That is also the problem with nuclear depth bombs: they have to be taken to the target well clear of the launching vessel, whether surface ASW escort or another submarine. As well as wire-guided torpedoes, US Navy nuclear-powered attack submarines carry a system called SUBROC, which is a guided missile launched underwater from forward torpedo tubes to follow a short underwater path, break surface and fly up to 56 km (35 miles) before releasing the warhead, a Mk 57 nuclear depth bomb (as carried by fixed-wing ASW aircraft including the Lockheed P-3 Orion and

Lockheed S-3 Viking) with a 1-kiloton yield and a lethal radius of up to 8 km (5 miles). Soviet submarines are known to operate a system similar to the SUBROC, known in the West as the SS-N-15, equipping boats of the 'Papa', 'Alfa', 'Victor III' and 'Tango' classes.

Under present plans SUBROC will be replaced in the US Navy by a system called ASW/SOW (Anti-Submarine Warfare Stand-Off Weapon), which will carry a lightweight homing torpedo as an alternative payload to a nuclear depth bomb. ASW/SOW will also replace the ASROC system on US Navy escorts as the primary shipborne anti-submarine weapon, employing an operational profile very similar to the current weapon but with greater technical sophistication and over-the-horizon range. On surface ships the weapon will be stored in ready-use canisters for firing from VLS (Vertical Launch Systems) on guided-missile cruisers and destroyers. For submarine launch the missile will be carried by capsule to the surface before the solid-propellant rocket motor ignites to propel it to the target area.

ASROC has been operational since 1961 and consists of a short-range missile (range between 2 and 10 km/ 1.2 and 6.2 miles) carrying a 1-kiloton yield Mk 17 nuclear depth bomb or a Mk 46 acoustic homing torpedo. The Mk 46's method of operation is typical of the type: immediately on entering the water it begins a descending helical search pattern, sweeping a 'lethal volume' within which its own autonomous terminal homing will operate. If it fails to acquire a target it starts again, and is capable of multiple consecutive attacks. An upgrade called NEARTIP (NEAR-Term Improvement Program) is in hand for the Mk 46, significantly designed to restore its acquisition range (estimated at some 450 m/1,475 ft) in the face of Soviet sound-reduction technology and in particular the use of anechoic (sound-absorbing) submarine coatings, code-named 'Clusterguard' by the US Navy.

Left: In concept, ASROC is simply a ballistic rocket designed to drop a homing torpedo or nuclear depth charge into the approximate position of an enemy submarine. Once in the water, the torpedo's homing mechanism or the nuclear weapon's huge kill radius does the rest.

Below: Designed for launch from surface ships, helicopters and aircraft, the Whitehead A244 is capable of both active and passive operations in a wide variety of attack patterns. The weapon has also been adapted as a potential warload for the Ikara anti-submarine missile system.

ASROC and the ASW-SOW system planned to replace it are ballistic missiles technically capable of all-weather operation. Faced with the problem of taking the weapon to the target, other navies have developed small robotic aircraft to carry homing torpedoes out to the likely target area. With their wings and cruise motors they have longer range but are bulkier and less all-weather capable. Typical systems are the French Malafon, the Australian Ikara and the Soviet SS-N-14 'Silex', all with homing torpedoes as the payload. The Ikara, in service with the Royal Australian and Royal Navies since the 1960s, was adapted in 1982 to carry the Stingray, the UK's latest lightweight torpedo designed principally for launch from helicopters or fixed-wing shore-based aircraft. After a expensive development programme, Stingray is claimed to have unique capabilities, be equally effective in shallow or deep water, and is equipped with an onboard computer which enables it to make its own tactical decisions about which homing mode to select and response to target behaviour. The weapon is also reported to have an advanced directed-blast warhead capable of penetrating the improved outer pressure hulls of deep-diving submarines.

A passive homing torpedo may not be able to home on a diesel-electric submarine lying silent on the sea bed, however, and an active homer might not pick it out from the background. In modern ASW firepower, therefore, there is still room for the old mortar-fired depth bomb of the British 1950s' vintage Limbo type.

Above: SUBROC exits the water at the start of its flight, its rocket motor having ignited once it was a safe distance away from the launching submarine. Target data has been fed into its inertial guidance system, the 6.4-km lethal radius of its nuclear warhead allowing for a wide margin of error.

Right: A Soviet 'Petya' class patrol vessel, seen cruising off the Philippines, has twin 12-barrel RBU 6000 anti-submarine rocket launchers aft of her gun turret. The rockets are not guided, but fired in salvoes to bracket a target.

Above: An engineering model of ASW/SOW is launched by Boeing in Washington's Puget Sound. The production missile will carry either a Mk 50 Barracuda Advanced Lightweight Torpedo or a nuclear depth charge. ASW/SOW will have a speed in excess of Mach 1.5.

Right: The best hunter of submarines is often another submarine armed with a high speed heavyweight torpedo. Here a Mk 24 'Tigerfish' wire-guided torpedo is loaded into a 'Churchill' class nuclear fleet submarine of the Royal Navy. 'Tigerfish' is the end result of an incredibly protracted development programme dating back to 1959.

Land Power

In one respect, warfare has changed little over the centuries. In the final
analysis, it is the quality of the soldiers on the ground that decides the course of war. But this is not to
say that technology has had no impact on the battlefield; from the use of night
vision devices and 'smart' weaponry which for the first time allows battles to be fought 24 hours a day,
through man-portable equipment of unprecedented capability to the new
command, control and communications systems, the electronic revolution has taken its place on the
land battlefield with a vengeance.

Contents

Main Battle Tanks

For all their expense and technical sophistication, a strike aircraft or nuclear-armed missile cannot take a surrender. At the end of the day it is land forces that must move forward, seize and hold ground if any high intensity military operation is to achieve a successful conclusion and today, as for the last five decades, the cutting edge of land power is the MBT (Main Battle Tank). It has been said many times that the era of the tank was over, that first tactical nuclear weapons and then the 'new lethality' of infantry-operated precision-guided weapons had rendered them obsolete. But faced with the probability of operations on a battlefield dominated by the threat of tactical nuclear weapons, the Soviet army concluded long ago that the mass and hardness of tanks was the only chance. The build-up of the Warsaw Pact's vast force of armoured fighting vehicles has been the result.

Western armies too have concluded that the most potent enemy of the tank is another tank and, although hedging its bets by the deployment of advanced anti-tank systems, has also invested much in the development of super-sophisticated main battle tanks dripping with electronics and fire-control systems that would shame a battleship. But however sophisticated the technology, the designer of main battle tanks is faced with the old problem of striking the right balance between mobility, firepower and protection, the eventual mix reflecting national traditions and the perception of how any future wars might be fought. That perception of course is not static, and with a modern MBT costing over $3 million and having a service life of 30 years, the pressure on MBT designers to get it right in the first place is very strong.

The great testing ground of the tank was World War II and in particular the great mobile armoured battles on the Eastern Front. The Soviet T-34/76, perhaps the most significant tank in history, represented a brilliant balance of mobility, firepower and protection, and (an especially important factor) it was comparatively easy to mass produce, appearing in great numbers from early 1942 onwards to turn the tide of mobile warfare on the Eastern Front. The Germans, having considered the desperate measure of manufacturing a direct copy of the new Soviet tank, produced the PzKpfw V Panther, one of the best tanks of World War II and a key prototype for subsequent Western tank development.

Since the end of World War II, Soviet armour design has had the virtues of simplicity, ruggedness and low silhouette when compared to any Western contemporaries, although the Arab/Israeli wars indicate that it is the training of the tank crews that is the deciding factor in battle. Nonetheless, the increasing sophistication of such systems as this East German T-72 (fitted with KMT-5 mine-clearing ploughs) presents NATO with a significant problem, especially when considered against the large number in production.

Below: Roaring out of a blazing forest, this T-62 keeps its fully stabilized 115-mm gun trained on the target. The contemporary of the US M60 series, the T-62 has seen much action in the Middle East. Although being replaced in the Red Army by the T-72, it remains a formidable MBT and will continue in front-line service for many years to come.

Mainstay of Pakistan's armoured forces is the T-55 and its Chinese derivative, the T-59. Schemes are now afoot to modernize this 30-year-old design, one option under consideration being to replace the dated D-100T 100-mm gun with a British L7 series 105-mm weapon.

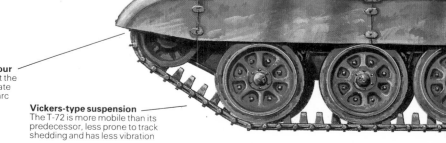

T-72 M1980/81 Main Battle Tank

This improved model of the T-72 was first observed at a parade in Berlin in 1981, and it subsequently appeared at the November parade in Moscow. Early T-72s had a pronounced hood in front of the right-hand (commander's) cupola, its absence on this model indicating that optical equipment has been replaced by a laser rangefinder.

Crew: 3
Weights: empty 39000 kg; loaded 41000 kg
Powerplant: one V-12 diesel developing 582 kW
Dimensions: length, gun forward 9.24 m and hull 6.95 m; width without skirts 3.60 m; height with machine-gun 2.37 m
Performance: maximum road speed 60 km/h; range 480 km; fording 1.4 m; vertical obstacle 0.85 m; trench 2.8 m; gradient 60%; side slope 40%

125-mm smoothbore gun
This has an automatic loader which allows the crew to be reduced to just three men

Advanced frontal armour
It is widely assumed that the Soviet T-72s have laminate armour over the frontal arc

Vickers-type suspension
The T-72 is more mobile than its predecessor, less prone to track shedding and has less vibration

Above: With its automatic loader and laser rangefinder, the T-72 undermined NATO's cosy belief in the qualitative superiority of its armour. The T-72 was probably in service by 1975 but more details have only just emerged, and Western analysts still lack the critical details of its construction. Finland is the latest country to receive the T-72.

Right: The Peoples' Republic of China still relies on its copy of the T-54/55, the T-59. Early models lacked main armament stabilization and infra-red night vision equipment, but more recent models have made good these deficiencies and some have been seen with what is probably a laser rangefinder.

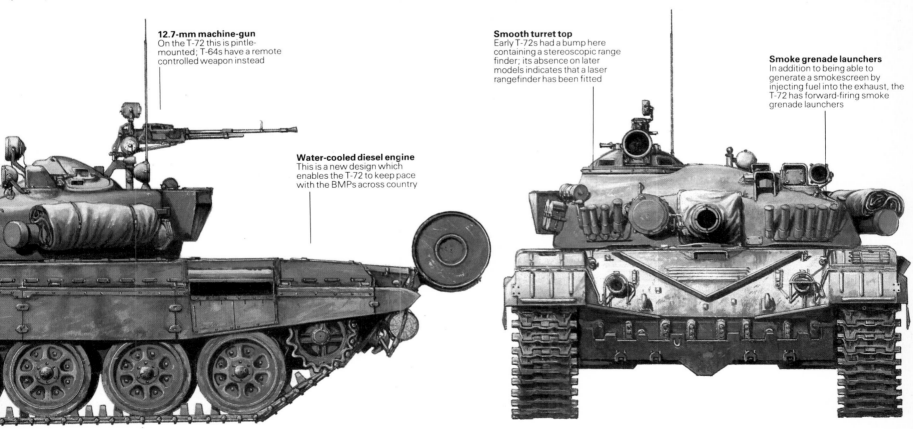

12.7-mm machine-gun
On the T-72 this is pintle-mounted; T-64s have a remote controlled weapon instead

Water-cooled diesel engine
This is a new design which enables the T-72 to keep pace with the BMPs across country

Smooth turret top
Early T-72s had a bump here containing a stereoscopic range finder; its absence on later models indicates that a laser rangefinder has been fitted

Smoke grenade launchers
In addition to being able to generate a smokescreen by injecting fuel into the exhaust, the T-72 has forward-firing smoke grenade launchers

Main Battle Tanks

The M1 Abrams is the first MBT to enter production powered by a gas-turbine engine. Much smaller than a diesel of comparable power, this type of engine suffers from a much higher fuel consumption, making a greater fuel capacity essential. This model has been fitted with a laser gunnery training simulator, used in order to save expensive live ammunition while on exercise.

Below: Mainstay of the US tank force in the 1960s and 1970s, the M60 has also been exported to a number of countries, including Iran, Israel, Egypt, Jordan and Saudi Arabia. In spite of the arrival of the M1 Abrams in US Army service, it will remain the major armour asset of the US Marine Corps for some years to come. This is a Marine M60A3 seen during amphibious landing exercises.

The original T-34 design itself was capable of stretch. From 1943 onwards the characteristic hooded turret with 76-mm (3-in) gun was replaced by a new turret mounting a powerful 85-mm (3.35-in) gun. Henceforward Soviet armour developed in a direct lineal line, first with the T-44 of 1945 which married the T-34/85 turret with a new lower hull and suspension. Then came the T-54 of 1949 which combined this hull with the D-100T 100-mm (3.94-in) main armament, and by 1955 an improved version of this weapon had been combined with an uprated powerplant and suspension to produce the T-55. The T-62 of 1961 further improved hull and suspension design, but now incorporated the new U-5T smoothbore 115-mm (4.53-in) gun with auto-loading and integrated fire control.

The T-64 first identified in service in 1970 combined a more powerful 125-mm (4.92-in) version of the T-62's main armament in a new hull, but this design seems to have been an intermediate stage towards the definitive T-72, the most important Soviet MBT of the 1980s. Keeping step with Western technology, the latest Soviet MBT is the T-80 incorporating composite armour, advanced computerized fire control and 125-mm smoothbore main armament firing high-velocity fin-stabilized ammunition.

Standard armament

Western tank main armament became standardized on 105-mm (4.13-in) calibre, the British L7 rifled gun of 1950s vintage being the prototype mounted in the Centurion, the Swedish S-tank and standardized as the US M68 on the West German Leopard 1, the US M60 and the early-model US M1 Abrams. The switch to 120-mm (4.72-in) came in the 1970s, in the forms of British rifled L11 in the Chieftain and Challenger, and the German Rheinmetall smoothbore Rh-120 used on the Leopard 2 and M1A1.

A gun is only as effective as the ammunition it fires and the fire-control system by which it is brought to bear on its target. World War II vintage fire-control systems slaved the gun to an optical sight which the gunner lined up to the target, determining range with an optical rangefinder and using a simple mechanical computer to determine elevation. Post-war the use of ranging machine-guns firing tracer speeded up the process, but the big breakthrough was the application of laser rangefinders and the development of micro-electronic ballistic computers. Very accurate range data could now be allied with automatice fire-control data fed automatically into a stabilized gun-laying system with (in some instances) automatic ammunition feed, allowing fire from the move and much faster engagement sequences.

Abrams is fitted with a pair of British designed six-barrel smoke dischargers, one on either side of the turret

Abrams is protected by a variant of the British-developed Chobham laminated armour, which is considerably more effective than conventional armour plate

Merkava Main Battle Tank

Certainly the most experienced armoured force in the world today, the Israelis have made use of their extensive experience in the design of the Merkava (Hebrew for 'Chariot'). Emphasis has been placed on protection and survivability, with the whole front of the vehicle devoted to engine, transmission and armoured fuel tanks, providing protection to the crew over and above the tank's own armour.

Crew: 4
Weight: 56 tonnes
Powerplant: V-12 diesel developing 671 kW
Dimensions: length (with gun forward) 8.36 m; length (hull) 7.45 m; width 3.72 m; height (roof) 2.64 m
Performance: maximum road speed 46 km/h; maximum range 500 km; gradient 60%; vertical obstacle 1 m; trench 3 m

M60A3 Main Battle Tank

The M60A3 is the most widely used American-built MBT and is the ultimate expression of a line of vehicles stretching back to the M26 Pershing heavy tank of World War II. It is armed with the 105-mm M68 gun (developed from the British L7) and has an advanced fire control system incorporating stabilization, passive night vision equipment, a laser rangefinder and a ballistic computer.

Crew: 4
Weight: 48.98 tonnes
Powerplant: Continental AVDS-1790-2A 12-cylinder diesel developing 560 kW
Dimensions: length (with gun forward) 9.436 m; length (hull) 6.946 m; width 3.631 m; height 3.27 m
Performance: maximum road speed 48.28 km/h; maximum road range 500 km; fording 1.219 m; gradient 60%; vertical obstacle 0.914 m; trench 2.59 m

Cadillac-Gage Stingray

The Cadillac-Gage Stingray light tank weighs little over 17 tons, but has the firepower of an MBT. Costs have been minimized by the use of running gear already in production – the suspension, for instance, is the same as that of the M109 self-propelled howitzer. The gun is a development of the British Royal Ordnance 105-mm weapon, suitably adapted for use from a relatively light vehicle.

Crew: 4
Weights: empty 17237 kg; loaded 19051 kg
Powerplant: one Detroit Diesel Model 8V-92 TA diesel developing 399 kW
Dimensions: length, gun forward 9.35 m and hull 6.30 m; width 2.71 m; height overall 2.54 m
Performance: maximum road speed 69 km/h; range 483 km; fording 1.22 m; vertical obstacle 0.76 m; trench 1.69 m; gradient 60%; side slope 30%

FMC Close Combat Vehicle-Light

The major reorganization of the US Army which has seen the formation of a new concept light division has also prompted manufacturers to develop new equipment suitable to the new units. The three-man CCV-L (Close Combat Vehicle-Light) has been designed by the FMC's ordnance division around the standard M68 105-mm gun, with a West German low recoil system.

Crew: 3
Weights: empty 17509 kg; loaded 19414 kg
Powerplant: one Detroit Diesel Model 6V-92 TA 6-cylinder diesel developing 412 kW
Dimensions: length, gun forward 9.37 m and hull 6.20 m; width 2.69 m; height 2.36 m
Performance: maximum road speed 70 km/h; range 483 km; fording 1.32 m; vertical obstacle 0.76 m; trench 2.13 m; gradient 60%; side slope 40%

M1 Abrams Main Battle Tank

The M1 Abrams is one of the most advanced tanks currently in production. Currently fitted with the M68 derivative of the British L7 105-mm rifled gun, as illustrated, the first of the M1A1 variant is armed with the smoothbore 120-mm gun developed by Rheinmetall for the Leopard 2. Fire control systems are of the highest order, as witnessed by the success of the Abrams in NATO's annual tank gunnery competitions.

For anti-aircraft protection the M1 is fitted with the venerable but still highly effective M2HB 12.7-mm heavy machine-gun

The Avco-Lycoming gas-turbine is more powerful than contemporary diesels, which explains the exceptional performance of such a heavy tank

The tank commander has six periscopes on his cupola, giving 360 vision. He also has a ×3 telescopic sight for his M2 MG

Main Battle Tanks

Left: The first native German tank design to enter service with the Federal German army since its formation, the Leopard has seen a series of improvements culminating in the Leopard 1A4, currently in service. Although being replaced by the next-generation Leopard 2, the total build in excess of 6000 vehicles will ensure the original Leopard's presence in several armed forces' inventories for years to come.

Below: An early model Leopard 1 of the Norwegian army fires a shot from its 105-mm main armament. As with many tanks, the gun is the well-proven Royal Ordnance Nottingham L7 rifled model, and the Norwegians use the standard varieties of ammunition.

While high-velocity APDS rounds are designed to destroy rival tanks by smashing through their armour, HEAT rounds are designed to achieve the same results by burning through armoured hulls. HEAT rounds have hollow noses backed by a convex HE charge detonated by a base fuse which will produce a devastating jet of superheated gas and metal moving at 20000 m (65,615 ft) per second on impact. HEP (High Explosive Plastic) and HESH (High Explosive Squash Head) rounds also have frangible nose cones and base fuses, but instead splatter against the surface of the armour on impact, detonating against it to send a shock wave into the tank's interior and blasting off a scab or metal inside to do the internal damage. Squash-head projectiles can be countered with spaced armour, and their effectiveness depends on angle of impact. HEAT rounds are more effective but they too have been countered by the development of composite armour laminations of armour plate with energy dissipating ceramic and other materials. Composite armour has given the current fourth-generation MBTs their characteristic slab-sided appearance with maximum protection going to the turret and the frontal arc.

Typical maximum armour thicknesses range between 120 and 200 mm (4.72 and 7.87 in), the degree of thickness (and therefore weight) reflecting the design philosophy behind the tank. Of the 1960s generation, for example, the West German Leopard 1 was relatively thinly armoured, its weight of 39 tonnes reflecting the emphasis on mobility compared to the British Chieftain's 200-mm maximum armour and operating weight of 55 tonnes. The Soviet T-62 at 37.5 tonnes again was lightly armoured while the T-72 with 200-mm steel frontal armour weighed in at 41 tonnes. The current generation with compound armour is appreciably heavier with the Challenger at 61 tonnes, the Abrams at 54.5 tonnes and Leopard 2 at 55 tonnes, and the Soviet T-80 catching up the heavyweights at an estimated 48.5 tonnes.

Design for protection is not limited to armour. Great efforts have been made to design 'survivability' into MBTs right from the start with internal layouts designed to protect critical systems, fire-suppression devices, blow-out doors to deflect blast, special ammunition stowage arrangements and so on while the switch to diesel fuel in self-sealing tanks further diminishes the tankman's nightmare of 'brewing up' once hit.

Leopard 1A4 Main Battle Tank

250 examples of the Leopard 1A4 were built for the Bundeswehr. It was the final Leopard 1 variant, incorporating all the updating of previous versions as well as the new turret of the A3 model. This version also has a much more effective fire control system and considerably enhanced electronics.

Crew: 4
Weight: 40 tonnes
Powerplant: MTU 10-cylinder diesel developing 619 kW
Dimensions: length (with gun forward) 9.543 m; length (hull) 7.09 m; width 3.25 m; height (overall) 2.613 m
Performance: maximum road speed 65 km/h; maximum range 600 km; gradient 60%; vertical obstacle 1.15 m; trench 3 m

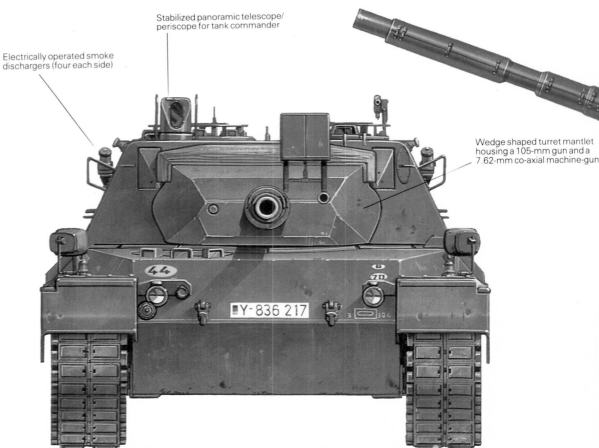

Stabilized panoramic telescope/periscope for tank commander

Electrically operated smoke dischargers (four each side)

Wedge shaped turret mantlet housing a 105-mm gun and a 7.62-mm co-axial machine-gun

Leopard 2 Main Battle Tank

The Leopard 2, in spite of its name, is an entirely different tank from its predecessor. Advanced Chobham-type laminated armour, a 120-mm smoothbore gun whose APFSDS-T round can penetrate the frontal armour of the latest Soviet tanks, advanced fire control systems and an engine of greatly increased power mean that it is a considerable improvement on the Leopard 1.

Crew: 4
Weight: 55.15 tonnes
Powerplant: MTU 12-cylinder multi-fuel developing 1119 kW
Dimensions: length (with gun forward) 9.668 m; length (hull) 7.772 m; width 3.7 m; height (overall) 2.79 m
Performance: maximum road speed 72 km/h; maximum range 550 km; gradient 60%; vertical obstacle 1.1 m; trench 3 m

Biber Armoured Bridgelayer

The Leopard, far more than most tanks, has been the progenitor of a series of specialized variants. The Biber (Beaver) bridgelayer is shown in travelling order, with the stabilizer/dozer blade under the nose of the tank. The bridge can be positioned in less than five minutes, and can span gaps of up to 22 m. It has been acquired by several Leopard users including Canada, Australia, the Netherlands and Italy as well as West Germany.

Crew: 2
Weight: with bridge 45300 kg
Powerplant: MTU MB 838 Ca.M500 10-cylinder multi-fuel developing 618.9 kW
Dimensions: length (with bridge) 11.82 m; width (with bridge) 4.00 m; height (with bridge) 3.57 m
Performance: maximum road speed 62 km/h; maximum range 550 km; fording 1.2 m; gradient 60%; vertical obstacle 0.7 m; trench 2.5 m

Leopard Armoured Engineer Vehicle

The Leopard armoured engineer vehicle is almost identical to the armoured recovery version, both being based upon the Leopard 1 hull and built by Krupp MaK of Kiel. The crane traversed forward has been fitted with an auger (normally carried along the back of the hull) and is able to drill holes 70 cm in diameter and to a maximum depth of 2 m.

Crew: 4
Weight: loaded 40800 kg
Powerplant: one MTU MB 838 Ca.M500 10-cylinder diesel developing 618.9 kW
Dimensions: length (overall) 7.98 m; width (overall) 3.75 m; height (with MG) 2.69 m
Performance: maximum road speed 65 km/h; maximum range 850 km; gradient 60%; fording 2.10 m; vertical obstacle 1.15 m; trench 3 m

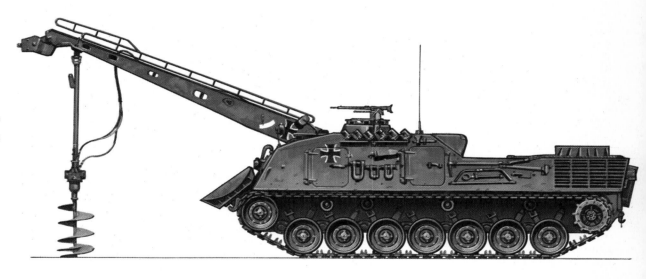

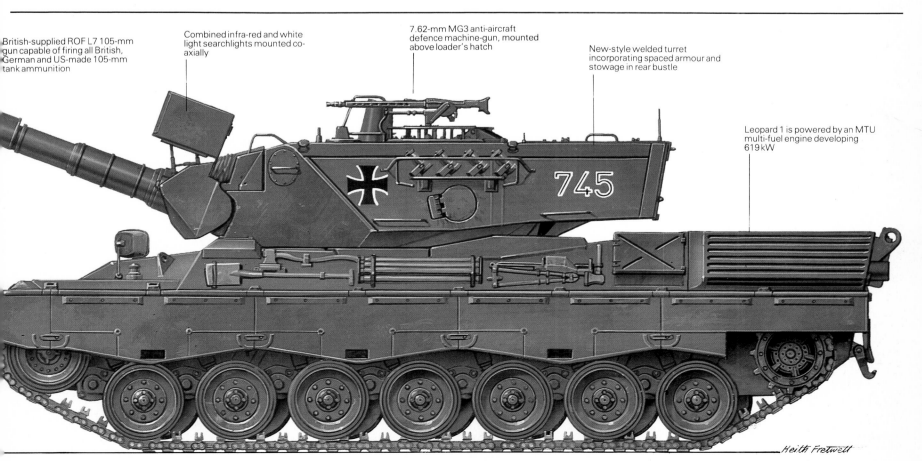

British-supplied ROF L7 105-mm gun capable of firing all British, German and US-made 105-mm tank ammunition

Combined infra-red and white light searchlights mounted co-axially

7.62-mm MG3 anti-aircraft defence machine-gun, mounted above loader's hatch

New-style welded turret incorporating spaced armour and stowage in rear bustle

Leopard 1 is powered by an MTU multi-fuel engine developing 619 kW

Keith Fretwell

Main Battle Tanks

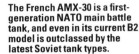

The French AMX-30 is a first-generation NATO main battle tank, and even in its current B2 model is outclassed by the latest Soviet tank types.

Armed with the ubiquitous ROF L7A1 105-mm rifled gun, the Japanese Type 74 is unusual in that it has adjustable hydro-pneumatic suspension.

Computerized fire-control systems are the heart of a modern MBT, and the high degree of sophistication of such systems accounts for some 20 per cent of the MBT's cost. They can store data on ammunition type, making adjustment accordingly, and are fed by sensors which determine wind speed and direction, air temperature and pressure, barrel wear and temperature, and even whether rain is falling on one side of the barrel, all factors which affect ballistic performance. This means that the all-important first-round hit probability can be as much as 80 per cent when engaging a static target at a range of 3000 m (3,280 yards) or a moving target at 2000 m (2,185 yards).

Ammunition is an equally important factor, and the technological developments since 1945 have been no less dramatic. When the shaped-charge warhead first appeared in 1942 (originally applied to man-portable anti-tank weapons) spaced armour and anti-bazooka plates presented a simple solution if at some expense in mobility. Then post-war as projectile and warhead technology developed through kinetic-energy APDs (Armour-Piercing Discarding Sabot) rounds and che-mical-energy HEAT (High Explosive Anti-Tank) rounds, breakthroughs in armour technology have kept the MBT in the front line. APDS shot was developed by the British at the end of World War II: a round consists of a hard penetrator surrounded by a segmented sleeve or 'sabot' of lighter metal. As the round is lighter than a full-calibre steel shot, muzzle velocity is increased while the full calibre absorbs maximum propellant energy. In flight the sabot falls away while the penetrator (made of a dense material such as tungsten or depleted uranium) flies on at very high velocity.

Further increases in muzzle velocity were made possible by the adoption of smoothbore guns firing fin-stabilized rather than spin-stabilized projectiles. Fin stabilization also allowed length to weight ratios to be increased, thus producing the current 'long rod'

generation of penetrators. The Soviets were first with smoothbore technology, introduced on the T-62 in the early 1960s. Almost two decades later the US Army adopted the 120-mm smoothbore gun developed for the West German Leopard 2 and fitted to later developments of the US Army's M1 Abrams.

Above: The French manufacturer GIAT has developed a modern main battle tank incorporating the latest in AFV technology including laminated armour, significantly improved power-to-weight ratio and a 120-mm smoothbore gun firing combustible cartridges. Curiously, the French army is unlikely to acquire such equipment until the 1990s, with GIAT's AMX-40 design going for export.

The Brazilian armaments industry has become a considerable force in the world armaments market, producing weapons suited to many of the Third World nations unable to operate the sophisticated systems produced by the industrialized world. ENGESA, the major AFV manufacturer, has gone further producing an MBT which can compete with many European models. Here an Osorio MBT fires its main armament, in this case the ROF L7A1 105-mm rifled gun (although the French GIAT 120-mm smoothbore can also be fitted).

Developed from the Chieftain via an order from the ill-fated Shah of Iran, the Challenger is one of the most powerful tanks in service in the world. The 120-mm rifled gun and sloped, laminated Chobham armour provides formidable firepower and protection, gained to a certain extent by less than superlative mobility. The tank is also one of the heaviest in the world.

Supertanks with advanced armour and highly sophisticated fire control systems are not for everybody. Indeed, one of the mainstays of the smaller nations of the Western world is the American M48 MBT, suitably uparmed and upgraded. These Norwegian army M48A5s have been rearmed with M68 105-mm gun (the American version of the noted British L7 gun).

For several years the 120-mm rifled gun fitted to Britain's Chieftain made it the most powerful tank in NATO, although the advent of the Leopard 2 and the M1A1 Abrams with the 120-mm Rheinmetall smoothbore have changed matters somewhat. It remains a powerful fighting vehicle, however, and the photo shows the excellent ballistic shape of the turret.

Left: Bofors of Sweden took a radical route to lowering the silhouette of their tank for the Swedish army; they simply eliminated the turret. By setting the gun in the hull, the designers calculated that the lack of flexibility would be more than offset by decreasing the vulnerability of the whole vehicle.

Right: The Vickers MBT has been produced for India (where it was in licence production for many years until the introduction of the Soviet-designed T-72), Kuwait, Kenya, and Nigeria. Variants proposed have included armoured bridgelayers, armoured recovery vehicles, and various self-propelled artillery pieces using the Vickers chassis.

Main Battle Tanks

Left: Israel's unique success in armoured warfare over a period of decades has led to the impressment of former enemy equipment into Israeli service. Sometimes, equipment is captured in such numbers that it is worth while setting up facilities to service it. More often, as in the case of these captured T-54/55s, the Israelis re-engine them for the sake of commonality, and re-gun them with the battle proven L7 105-mm gun (or its M68 derivative).

Right: The US Army's gas turbine-powered M1 Abrams is the ultimate expression of high-tech weaponry on the land battlefield (at least for the moment!), where it is probably the most agile of the current generation of main battle tanks.

Below: In direct contrast to the Americans and the Germans, whose requirement for high mobility has produced the M1 Abrams and the Leopard 2, Israel's army (who have more experience of modern armoured warfare than anybody else) have in the Merkava a tank whose main attributes are protection and reliable firepower. Mobility is all very well, but Israeli experience has emphasized survivability and the capacity to hit the enemy hard.

Reconnaissance Vehicles

The 'armoured car' is almost as old as the internal combustion engine. It was realized early in the 20th century that by applying armour plate to a motor vehicle and adding a machine-gun there would result a device that (if it could be made reliable enough) would supplant the horsed cavalryman in his traditional role of moving ahead of an armed force and gathering information about the enemy. At the same time armoured cars would be a rival intelligence-gatherer to aircraft, those other offspring of the first decade of the century.

Whereas reconnaissance aircraft now fly at three times the speed of sound and in some roles have been themselves supplanted by all-seeing satellites in space, the terrestrial reconnaissance vehicle in many ways has not really progressed that far from the first generation of armoured cars, and certainly not much at all from the generation of World War II when the modern pattern was set: typically a four-wheel-drive chassis, armoured hull, rotating turret armed with a heavy machine-gun or a quick-firing weapon of up to 75-mm (2.95-in) calibre.

The World War II sub-species of 'scout car' (with less armour protection, an open roof and rifle-calibre armament) has meanwhile dwindled in numbers or drawn closer to the kind of 'internal security vehicle' discussed more fully in the section on armoured personnel carriers. This is significant in itself because armoured cars are also of great value in low-intensity operations, for convoy protection, and an in all-out war for rear-area security. Indeed, in many armies of less than first rank such are their primary if not their only roles. Today's reconnaissance vehicles are sophisticated variations on an old established theme, however, with some interesting side branches from the norm: six- and eight-wheel-drive vehicles, and tracked vehicles such as the British Scorpion light tank, the Soviet PT-76 amphibious reconnaissance tank and the US Bradley M3 Cavalry Fighting Vehicle.

The number of information-gathering systems available to a field commander today is very wide, including satellites and aircraft as already stated, but also electronic and signals intelligence. But for all the sophistication of such systems, the emphasis on deception and anti-deception measures means that much is accessible only to the eyes of a well-trained soldier on the ground.

The Soviet army, for example, puts emphasis on ground-based reconnaissance units or long-range reconnaissance patrols specially trained to operate 50 to 350 km (31 to 217 miles) forward of the main body. The farthest-ranging units are composed of elite paratroops or special forces inserted by helicopter, but there are also motorized patrols of company strength in BRDMs, designed to drive deep using infiltration tactics. Their primary targets are enemy nuclear installations and wherever possible they seek to avoid combat other than a direct attack on a high-priority target. Troop reconnaissance ahead of the main body is again to be conducted with BRDMs up to 50 km or a day's march in front of the division: each reconnaissance battalion sends out six to eight patrols of two to four scout cars supported by one or two BMPs or PT-76 light tanks.

The BRDM-2 amphibious scout car has largely supplanted the late 1950s vintage BRDM-1 in Soviet service, while many examples of the earlier front-engined vehicle continue in Soviet bloc service worldwide. The later vehicle has a more powerful rear-mounted engine, better water performance and fully enclosed armament, either a rotating turret for a 14.5-mm (0.57-in) machine-gun or ATGWs. On each side of the vehicle between the front and rear wheels are two retractable belly wheels giving improved ditch-crossing capability. There is also a central tyre pressure-regulation system, allowing the driver to alter pressure to suit the

Alvis Saladin Armoured Car

The Saladin is armed with a 76-mm gun, a lightened version of the same weapon being fitted to the Scorpion and firing the same range of fixed ammunition.

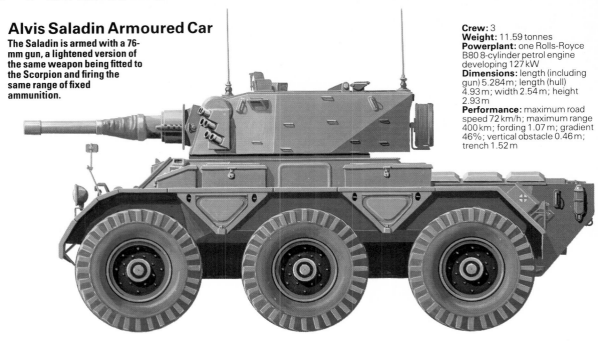

Crew: 3
Weight: 11.59 tonnes
Powerplant: one Rolls-Royce B80 8-cylinder petrol engine developing 127 kW
Dimensions: length (including gun) 5.284 m; length (hull) 4.93 m; width 2.54 m; height 2.93 m
Performance: maximum road speed 72 km/h; maximum range 400 km; fording 1.07 m; gradient 46%; vertical obstacle 0.46 m; trench 1.52 m

Spähpanzer 2 Luchs Reconnaissance Vehicle

The Spähpanzer Luchs continues the German tradition of 8×8 reconnaissance vehicles established during World War II. It carries a four-man crew and is fully amphibious.

Crew: 4
Weight: 19.5 tonnes
Powerplant: one 10-cylinder diesel developing 291 kW
Dimensions: length 7.743 m; width 2.98 m; height (including AA MG) 2.905 m
Performance: maximum road speed 90 km/h; maximum range 800 km; fording amphibious; gradient 60%; vertical obstacle 0.60 m; trench 1.90 m

PT-76 Amphibious Light Tank

Designed to provide firepower and mobility in the reconnaissance role plus armour support during river crossings and amphibious landings, the PT-76 equips the Soviet Naval Infantry as well as the reconnaissance units of the motor rifle divisions.

Crew: 3
Weight: 14 tonnes
Powerplant: one V-6 6-cylinder diesel developing 179 kW
Dimensions: length (with armament) 7.625 m; length (hull) 6.91 m; width 3.14 m; height 2.255 m
Performance: maximum road speed 44 km/h; maximum range 260 km; fording amphibious; gradient 60%; vertical obstacle 1.10 m; trench 2.80 m

AMX-13 Light Tank

This French light tank has an oscillating turret in which the gun is fixed in the upper part, which in turn pivots on the lower part. It has 12 75-mm shells which it can fire off very quickly, although its magazines must be reloaded from outside the vehicle.

Crew: 3
Weight: 15 tonnes
Powerplant: one SOFAM 8Gxb 8-cylinder petrol engine developing 186 kW
Dimensions: length (including gun) 6.36 m; length (hull) 4.88 m; width 2.50 m; height 2.30 m
Performance: maximum road speed 60 km/h; maximum range 350-400 km; fording 0.60 m; gradient 60%; vertical obstacle 0.65 m; trench 1.60 m

Seen here deployed to Norway as part of the NATO ACE mobile force, Scimitar light tanks have the same chassis as the Scorpion but carry a 30-mm Rarden cannon instead of a 76-mm gun. One such vehicle shot down an Argentine aircraft during the Falklands campaign.

type of ground being crossed. Variants include an air-defence vehicle armed with SA-9 'Gaskin' SAMs, and the BRDM-2-rkh specially equipped for radiological and chemical reconnaissance and safe-lane marking.

NATO reconnaissance units by contrast tend to follow late World War II practice, and have the added function of providing a screening force that can come to battle if necessary. They are designed as strong combined arms forces able to fight on their own for information. Hence NATO reconnaissance vehicles tend to be heavier and more powerfully armed than Soviet 'scout cars'. The West German Bundeswehr's Spähpanzer Luchs was introduced in 1975, weighs 19500 kg (42,990 lb) and is a big eight-wheeler owing something in outline at least to the German army's 8×8 heavy armoured cars of 30 years earlier. The long boat-shaped amphibious hull is all-welded steel, providing protection from small arms and shell splinters, and the amidships turret mounts a Rheinmetall Mk 20 Rh 202 cannon as installed in the Marder MICV. The 350-bhp (261-kW) turbocharged Daimler-Benz V10 multi-fuel engine is situated to the right and rear of the turret, and makes possible a top road speed of 90 km/h (56 mph). The Luchs has the same speed forward or reverse, with an auxiliary driving position at the rear of the vehicle.

Above: The Fox is a Jaguar-powered development of the late-production Ferret family, and is capable of over 100 km/h. Armed with a Rarden 30-mm cannon, its aluminium armour gives protection against machine-gun fire and shell splinters.

Crew: 2 or 3
Weights: empty 2850 kg; loaded 3550 kg
Powerplant: one Peugeot XD 3T 4-cylinder turbocharged diesel developing 78 kW
Dimensions: length 3.82 m; width 2.02 m; height without weapons 1.70 m
Performance: maximum road speed 100 km/h; fording amphibious; gradient 50%; side slope 30%

Panhard VBL Scout Car

The fully amphibious VBL light armoured vehicle carries Euromissile Milan anti-tank guided missiles when fitted for the anti-tank role and several machine-guns when used purely as a scout car. The French army plans to buy a total of 3,000.

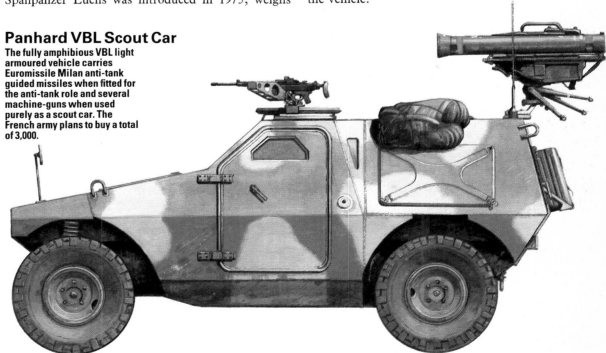

Reconnaissance Vehicles

The British army decided in the mid-1960s that it would need two distinct kinds of reconnaissance vehicles, tracked and wheeled. The combat Vehicle Reconnaissance Tracked requirement resulted in the CVR(T) Scorpion light tank, which was used operationally in the Falklands campaign. Here its low ground pressure and good power to weight ratio (courtesy of a derated Jaguar XK engine delivering 90 hp/67 kW) offered useful performance over peaty ground. The all-aluminium armour hull provides protection against 14.5-mm projectiles frontally and 7.62-mm (0.3-in) overall. The Scorpion is armed with a 76-mm (3-in) gun, while its stablemate the Scimitar is armed with a 30-mm Rarden cannon. In the British army of the Rhine the Scorpions are organizationally centred in divisional reconnaissance regiments for medium reconnaissance. Each armoured reconnaissance regiment has 32 Scorpions, 40 Scimitars, 12 Spartan APCs (five of them carrying ground surveillance radars), seven Sultan command vehicles, four Samson recovery vehicles and three Samaritan armoured ambulances, all these vehicles being based on the original FV101 Scorpion chassis.

Developed in parallel with the Scorpion series and powered by the same engine was the CVR(W) FV201 Fox armoured car, a traditionally configured 4×4 vehicle with a central turret mounting a 30-mm Rarden cannon. The Fox is well equipped with such devices as passive night sights, IR headlights, and such details as external cooking vessel electric sockets and inter-vehicle starting sockets. It was intended to develop in parallel with the Fox a scout car/liaison vehicle called the Vixen, but this was cancelled as a cost-saving measure in 1974. Meanwhile the British army will continue to use the 1950s vintage Ferret in this role until the 1990s.

Foreign success

Armoured cars, often using standard automotive components, are not so technically demanding as main battle tanks for a national arms industry to develop, and some interesting vehicles have come from less than traditional manufacturing countries. For example, the Brazilian ENGESA EE-9 Cascavel, in production since 1975, has been widely exported and shows some interesting technical innovations. The all-welded hull has 'dual hardness armour' developed in Brazil: an outer hardened layer and an inner layer of softer steel, rollbonded and heat treated to give the best ballistic protection. The Cascavel has a six-wheel chassis and originally a French-designed turret. Current production vehicles have a Brazilian-designed turret mounting a locally developed EC90-III 90-mm (3.54-in) smoothbore gun. Power is provided by a Mercedes-Benz or General Motors diesel. ENGESA also manufactures the EE-3 Jararaca light scout car, which has also been widely exported.

France is also a significant manufacturer of reconnaissance vehicles. The AMX-10RC six-wheel heavy armoured car is an important vehicle equipping reconnaissance regiments of armoured divisions and the cavalry regiments of infantry divisions, supplanting the old Panhard EBR. The six-wheel Renault VBC 90 is designed for export but on order for the Gendarmerie

Above: Seen while under test at the US Marine Corps Combat Center at Twenty-Nine Palms, California, the GM Canada Piranha was the winner of the US Light Armored Vehicle competition. This 8×8 version of the Swiss MOWAG Piranha is now in US MC service.

Right: An ENGESA EE-9 Cascavel of the Brazilian Marines comes ashore during an exercise. Armed with a 90-mm gun and fitted with a variety of optional extras, the Cascavel has been widely exported and has been used by Iraqi forces in the Gulf War.

Nationale, while another six-wheeler, the Panhard ERC Sagaie, is another export hopeful with Argentina an important customer; several were engaged in the Falklands campaign. The Panhard AML 4×4 armoured car in production since 1961 has been progressively developed and very widely exported, particularly to Francophone African countries.

Other significant reconnaissance vehicles in production or service worldwide include the Belgian FN 4RM/62 built on a truck chassis for Gendarmerie use, the Hungarian FUG amphibious scout car, the Israeli RBY light armoured reconnaissance vehicle, the Italian Fiat OTO-Melara Tipo 6616, the South African Eland, the British Alvis Saladin, and the US M113 Lynx used by the Canadian and Dutch armies. Numbers of World War II British Daimler and US M3A1 and M8 armoured cars linger on in service with armed forces in Africa and South/Central America.

This Panhard 4×4 VCR APC is armed with the Euromissile Mephisto launcher system for the HOT long-range ATGW. The UTM800 HOT turret variant of the 6×6 Panhard VCR/TT has also seen action with the Iraqi army in the Gulf War.

BRDM-2 Amphibious Scout Car

In service with over 40 different armies, the Soviet BRDM-2 is seen here carrying AT-5 'Spandrel anti-tank missiles. Egyptian BRDMs armed with the AT-3 'Sagger' proved very successful in the 1973 Yom Kippur war.

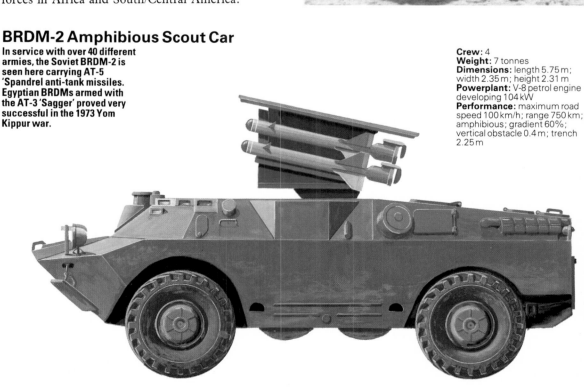

Crew: 4
Weight: 7 tonnes
Dimensions: length 5.75 m; width 2.35 m; height 2.31 m
Powerplant: V-8 petrol engine developing 104 kW
Performance: maximum road speed 100 km/h; range 750 km; amphibious; gradient 60%; vertical obstacle 0.4 m; trench 2.25 m

The US Marines will use the LAV for a variety of roles including reconnaissance, breakthrough and pursuit operations. This model carries a 25-mm Chain Gun, as carried by the M2. The LAV has a three-man crew (commander, gunner and driver) and can carry six Marines.

The latest production ENGESA EE-9 Cascavel carries a laser rangefinder mounted above its 90-mm gun and a 7.62-mm machine-gun above the commander's station. All models have a central tyre pressure-regulation system so that ground pressure can be modified according to the terrain.

Infantry Fighting Vehicles and Armoured Person

Main battle tanks, however heavily armoured and electronically sophisticated, cannot fight on their own: they need thorough reconnaissance before they can advance; they need fire support from artillery, anti-aircraft and anti-tank weapons, as well as a multitude of back-up vehicles and logistic resources; and they also need infantry support during an advance to deal with the tank's second greatest enemy, not rival main battle tanks but enemy infantry armed with anti-tank missiles operating effectively in broken country.

But armoured warfare is mobile warfare. Infantry are not expected to plod behind heavy tanks, making set-piece assaults at walking pace, but must keep up with fast moving armoured spearheads and be able to survive and fight at the heart of the high-intensity battlefield. There is thus no virtue in transporting infantry around in a lightly armoured bus: they need to move around the battlefield in their own specialized infantry fighting vehicle. An infantry squad should be able to fight effectively from within as well as outside its transport, and should be armed sufficiently to take on enemy main battle tanks as well as rival infantry fighting vehicles.

The vehicle operating alongside the tanks in the front line of attack or defence is thus the MICV (Mechanized Infantry Combat Vehicle). This is a much more formidable vehicle than the old Armoured Personnel Carrier (APC), from which it is distinguished by the fact that it carries its own tactical weapons system rather than just a defensive machine-gun or two, and allows troops to fight from inside if necessary. Many older-generation APCs, however, have been reworked to carry turret-mounted weapons or anti-tank missiles.

The Soviet army was a pioneer in the development of the MICV with the deployment of the BMP-1 (*Bronevaya Maschina Piekhota* or armoured vehicle, infantry) in the early 1960s to equip motor rifle divisions and the motor rifle regiments of tank divisions for the demands of high-speed offensive warfare on a potentially nuclear battlefield. The prototype BMP was designed to be fast rather than heavily armoured, was amphibious and had extensive NBC (Nuclear, Biological and Chemical) protection. The original model was armed with six AT-3 'Sagger' wire-guided anti-tank missiles with a single launcher above the main armament, a 73-mm (2.87-in) smoothbore low-pressure gun firing fin-stabilized rocket-assisted projectiles with a shaped-charge HEAT (High Explosive Anti-Tank) warhead capable of taking on NATO armour at 1000-m (1,095-yard) range. Updates include installation of laser-homing 'Spandrel' ATGWs and a new turret mounting a 30-mm cannon rather than the 73-mm low-pressure gun.

The BMP-1's crew are protected by armour plate, although this is considerably lighter than that of a main battle tank, with aluminium alloys replacing steel for the structural shell, and by an NBC air-conditioning system with an automatic shutdown system in the

event of a nearby nuclear explosion. When the shock wave has passed, the driver activates a system which provides for the delivery to the crew compartment of scrubbed decontaminated air at a pressure above the ambient external pressure.

Combat debut

In spite of its advanced design and battleworthy features, the BMP-1's combat debut on the Golan Heights with the Syrian army in 1973 was a disaster, large numbers of burned out hulls littering the Valley of Tears after hurling themselves at the Israeli defences, but clumsy handling and tactical inflexibility were largely to blame. The inadequate armour protection of the BMP-1 has also been highlighted since that time in Afghanistan, where additional armour has had to be installed to protect the occupants from 12.7-mm (0.5-in) machine-gun fire. However, in Soviet hands and working with tanks, the BMP-1 is still judged to be a formidable instrument of mobile armoured warfare, exploitation and pursuit even some 20 years after its introduction.

The first Western equivalent of the BMP-1 was the West German Marder, which was introduced in 1969. The Marder carries six infantrymen in an all-welded armoured hull and, in its original version, was armed with a 20-mm cannon in a two-man turret. The West German army's sizeable inventory is being reworked to mount a harder-hitting 25-mm cannon and to carry Milan anti-tank guided missiles.

The French AMX-10P, which entered service with the French army in 1973, was another step forward in western MICV development with an all-welded alloy hull, NBC protection, a 20-mm dual-feed cannon and accommodation for a nine-man infantry squad, whose men cannot fire their individual weapons from within the vehicle. Later variants have been equipped with HOT and Milan ATGWs.

GKN Sankey AT 105
Crew: 2+10
Combat weight: 10.6 tonnes
Performance: maximum road speed 96 km/h; maximum range 510 km

Few armies can afford to equip all their infantry with MICVs; the British army has ordered 1,000 Saxon APCs for use by regular and Territorial regiments.

Above: APCs are not just used to carry infantry about the battlefield, but also serve as weapons platforms and command vehicles. This Verne Dragoon carries long-range video optical surveillance equipment and serves as a high-mobility observation vehicle.

A British MCV-80 kicks up the mud as its 24-tonne bulk speeds across a field. Doubting the possibility of firing accurately from a moving vehicle, the British designers omitted the firing ports fitted to the German Marder and US Bradley.

M113 APC
Crew: 2+11
Weight: 11.3 tonnes
Performance: maximum road speed 68 km/h; maximum range 483 km
Armament: one 12.7-mm M2HB with 2,000 rounds of ammunition

The standard US APC for over 20 years, the M113 has been sold to over 50 different countries and has seen combat in Africa, the Middle East and South East Asia.

The Commando V-100, V-150 and V-200 range of 4×4 APCs have been widely exported, being suited to the kind of low-intensity, counter-insurgency battles encountered in the Third World. This V-150 is seen in the hands of Marcos loyalists in the Philippines before the President was ousted.

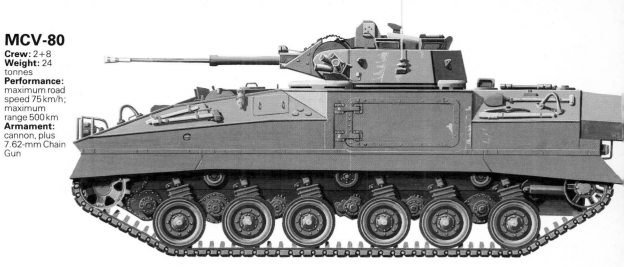

MCV-80
Crew: 2+8
Weight: 24 tonnes
Performance: maximum road speed 75 km/h; maximum range 500 km
Armament: cannon, plus 7.62-mm Chain Gun

The GKN-Sankey MCV-80 will shortly enter production for the British Army, but is unlikely to completely replace the fleet of FV 432 APCs.

In contrast with German, US and Soviet practice, the British MCV-80 Mechanized Infantry Combat Vehicle will not carry anti-tank missiles, as the British Army believes that it is not really the role of APCs to engage enemy armour.

The US Army took a long time to get an MICV into service, the original requirement being drafted in the early 1960s. After a very protracted development the first prototype XM2 Infantry Fighting Vehicle and XM3 Cavalry Fighting Vehicles were accepted by the US Army in 1978, and in spite of Congressional reservations about the vehicles' ability to keep up and fight with M1 main battle tanks, large-scale orders followed.

The M2, now named the Bradley, has an all-welded aluminium-armour hull with spaced laminated armour fitted to the sides, front and hull rear. The driver at left front sits alongside the turbocharged 550-hp (410-kW) 8-cylinder diesel which makes possible a top speed of 66 km/h (41 mph) on roads. The two-man turret, containing commander and gunner, mounts a Hughes M242 25-mm Chain Gun with a co-axial 7.62-mm (0.3-in) machine-gun. The Chain Gun is a formidable weapon, also fitted on the Hughes AH-64A Apache attack helicopter, and the gunner can select single shots, or 100 or 200 rpm rates of fire. The General Electric turret drive and stabilization system allow the armament to be laid and fired while the Bradley moves across rough country. The six-man infantry squad accommodated in the vehicle rear can fire their weapons through individual firing ports.

Firepower advantage
This kind of firepower means the M2 has a considerable advantage over the BMP-1. While the Soviet vehicle's 73-mm HEAT round has tank-killing capacity, its low rate of fire and individual inaccuracy offset this advantage. A 25-mm weapon will be on target before the single-shot BMP-1 can fire, and rapid fire from a Chain Gun will knock out a lightly armoured BMP-1 as surely as a 73-mm shell.

While the Chain Gun is designed to tackle MICVs and APCs, the M2 Bradley can engage heavy tanks with its TOW wire-guided missiles. The twin TOW launcher is carried retracted alongside the left hand side of the turret and in operation can engage enemy armour at ranges up to a maximum of 3750 m (4,100 yards). The M2 carries seven TOWs, the M3 12 mis-

AMX-10P
Crew: 3+8
Weight: 14.2 tonnes
Performance: maximum road speed 65 km/h; range 600 km
Armament: 20-mm cannon and co-axial 7.62-mm machine-gun

The French AMX-10P MICV chassis forms the basis of a whole family of vehicles, ranging from weapons carriers, command vehicles and ambulances.

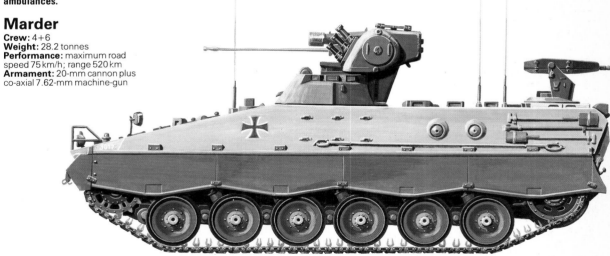

Marder
Crew: 4+6
Weight: 28.2 tonnes
Performance: maximum road speed 75 km/h; range 520 km
Armament: 20-mm cannon plus co-axial 7.62-mm machine-gun

The West Germans were the first NATO army to introduce an MICV. The Marder is well armoured and highly mobile, enabling it to work with the Leopard MBTs as a combined arms team.

Renault has developed a 6×6 model of the 4×4 VAB in service with the French army. Available for export, it is typical of modern APCs in their ability to be fitted with a variety of weapon systems. This is the 20-mm model.

Right: US infantry de-bus from an M2 Bradley MICV, which has six firing ports in the troop compartment. The Bradley plays a key role in the US Army's combined arms team concept, but has been criticized as being far too expensive.

Infantry Fighting Vehicles and Armoured Personnel Carriers

siles but with a total crew of five.

The latest MICV to enter service, the British MCV-80, was designed with a basic requirement to accommodate eight fully-equipped infantry and to sustain them for 48 hours on the battlefield. During development, mobility and protection were judged equal second in importance, and firepower last, with missile armament rejected as a distraction from the vehicle's primary role.

The personnel compartment in the rear holds seven infantry and their equipment. Access is via rear double doors and, with equipment stowed along the inside of the walls, there are no firing ports though there are periscopes to allow surveillance. The commander (who operationally is expected to dismount with the infantry) and the gunner for the 30-mm Rarden cannon are accommodated in the turret, and the driver in the left front of the hull. The turret is offset to the left of the vehicle to balance the weight of the 550-hp (410-kW) Rolls-Royce 8-cylinder diesel engine and automatic transmission in the right hull front. Maximum road speed is 75 km/h (47 mph) forward and 48 km/h (30 mph) in reverse.

Specialized versions

MICVs also form the basis for specialized vehicles. Here the BMP-1, the oldest and most numerous MICV, has spawned the greatest number. Normally one of the MICVs in a platoon will have extra radio equipment for the platoon commander, while in the case of BMP-1 there are also company and battalion command variants, reconnaissance versions, some with radar for use by divisional reconnaissance battalions or to carry out surveillance and targeting for artillery battalions, and small numbers adapted to carry mortars and to act as light recovery vehicles. The West German Marder is being developed to mount anti-tank and anti-aircraft missile armament. The M3 Cavalry Fighting Vehicle variant of the M2 carries only two people in addition to the operating crew of three, and acts more as a light tank, with extra ammunition compared with the infantry model.

While most first-division armies are busily developing or acquiring MICVs, they represent a formidable investment (£1,000 million to equip the British Army

Right: The French company ACMAT has widely exported its range of military trucks, and has now developed this TPK 4.20 VSC APC on the same chassis. Offered in several configurations, this model has a Creusot-Loire one-man turret with a single machine-gun.

Above: Malaysia has bought 186 of the Belgian SIBMAS APC. Most of the vehicles have been the AFSV-90 Armoured Fire Support Vehicle armed with a Cockerill Mk III 90-mm gun, another example of an APC serving as a light tank.

Right: An M113 of the US Army is headed by an M577 armoured command post while on the move during exercises in West Germany. US interest in the MICV concept stems partly from the Vietnam War, when some units fought from their M113s, mounting extra guns and improvised turrets.

of the Rhine with MCV-80s for example). One solution to keeping costs down is to adapt and upgrade the existing generation of APCs and to deploy simpler and cheaper wheeled vehicles for operations in rear, wooded or urban areas.

Large numbers of 1950s-generation tracked APCs serve with armies around the world. Among the most prolific is the American M113 series, of which 70,000 were built between 1960 and 1980 to serve with the armies of over 50 nations. The number of variants and modifications in the M113 'family' is enormous, while the US Army has an extensive product improvement

Armscor Ratel Infantry Fighting Vehicle, 12.7-mm Command Variant

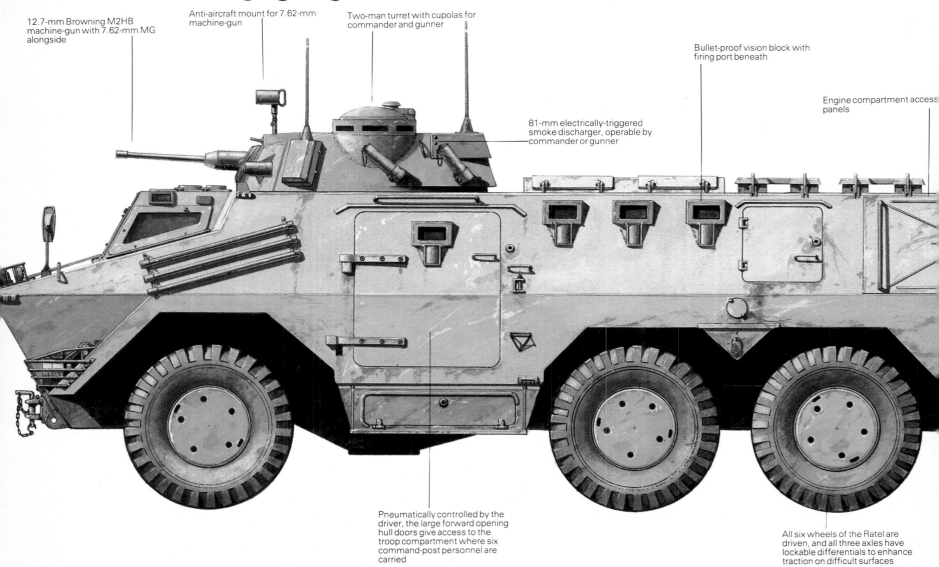

12.7-mm Browning M2HB machine-gun with 7.62-mm MG alongside

Anti-aircraft mount for 7.62-mm machine-gun

Two-man turret with cupolas for commander and gunner

Bullet-proof vision block with firing port beneath

Engine compartment access panels

81-mm electrically-triggered smoke discharger, operable by commander or gunner

Pneumatically controlled by the driver, the large forward opening hull doors give access to the troop compartment where six command-post personnel are carried

All six wheels of the Ratel are driven, and all three axles have lockable differentials to enhance traction on difficult surfaces

programme for its M113 inventory. The standard M113 suffers from the APC drawback that it has no tactical fighting ability of its own. Hence various modifications have been made by armies around the world: for example, the Israelis have fitted TOW launchers, the Australians have installed Scorpion light tank turrets, the Norwegians have added the 20-mm cannon from the Marder, and so on. A significant development for the US Army is the fitting of a self-contained TOW-launching system on the M113 chassis to create the M901 Improved TOW Vehicle (ITV), for which the US Army has a 2,500-plus requirement.

M113 equivalent

Broad equivalents of the M113 tracked APC are the Austrian Steyr 4K, the Chinese K-63 (Model 531), the Czech OT-62, the French AMX-VCI, the West German Schützenpanzer 12-3, the Japanese Type 73, the Swedish Pansarbandvagn 302, the Soviet BTR-50P, the British FV432 and Yugoslav M-60. All should remain in service, with various upgrades and modifications, for some time to come. An unusual special-purpose APC is the US LVTP7 (Landing Vehicle Tracked, Personnel), an amphibious assault vehicle which can carry up to 25 fully equipped marines, propelling itself through the water with twin waterjets.

Wheeled armoured personnel carriers are cheaper and less technically demanding than their tracked counterparts. They remain in production and service for less demanding defined battlefield roles such as operations in rear or urban areas. They also overlap with the internal security type of vehicle used in lower-intensity guerrilla warfare or police operations.

Major wheeled APCs in worldwide production and service include the Brazilian ENGESA EE-11 Urutu, the Chinese Types 55 and 56, the Czech OT-64, the French VAB, VXB-70 and Panhard M3, the British Saracen, the Italian Fiat 6614, the West German Transportpanzer 1, the Dutch DAF YP-408, the Soviet BTR-60P, BTR-152 and BTR-40, the Swiss MOWAG Piranha and the US V-100 Commando.

In the past two decades specialized internal security vehicles, based largely on standardized commercial vehicle components, have proliferated along with opportunities for their use in guerrilla conflict around the world from Ulster to Zimbabwe. The West German Rheinstahl UR-416, for example, is basically a standard Mercedes-Benz Unimog truck fitted with an armoured body proof against small arms fire. It can carry eight men, who can fire their weapons from inside the vehicle. Equivalent vehicles are the British GKN AT104 and 105, the Short SB 401, the Humber FV1611 'Pig', the Swiss MOWAG Roland used extensively in South America, the MOWAG SW-1 used by the West German border police, and the South African Rhino.

BTR-60PB Armoured Personnel Carrier

Early BTR-60s were open-topped vehicles with one or two machine-guns on pivot mounts at the front but this later model, the BTR-60PB, carries the same turret as the BRDM-2 scout car.

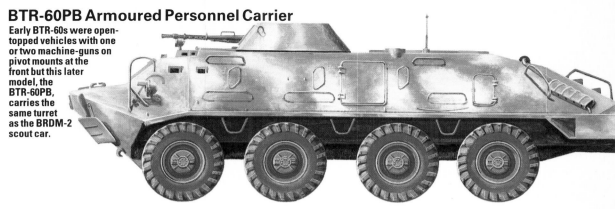

Crew: 2+14
Weight: 10.3 tonnes

Performance: maximum road speed 80 km/h; range 500 km

Armament: 1×14.5-mm and 1×7.62-mm machine-guns

MT-LB Multi-Purpose Tracked Vehicle

Originally introduced to tow artillery, the MT-LB is also used as an APC, especially in snowy or swampy areas where its wide tracks give greater mobility than the BMP series MICVs.

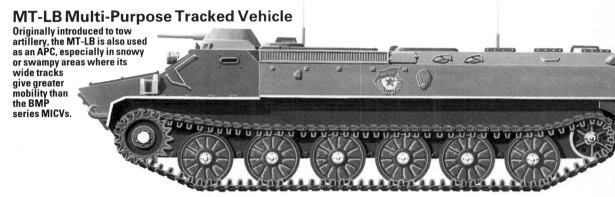

Crew: 2+11
Weight: 11.9 tonnes

Performance: maximum road speed 61 km/h; range 500 km

Armament: 1×7.62-mm machine-gun

BMD Airborne Combat Vehicle

The BMD airborne combat vehicle is used only by the Soviet air assault divisions, and has seen extensive action in Afghanistan. Its turret is similar to that of the BMP, but some BMDs now carry AT-4 'Spigot' ATGWs instead of AT-3 'Sagger'.

Crew: 7
Weight: 6.7 tonnes

Performance: maximum road speed 70 km/h; range 320 km

Armament: 73-mm gun and either AT-3 or AT-4 ATGW

oof hatch, which can be fitted
ith a second anti-aircraft mount

Right: The South African Ratel APC was developed with impressive speed, and has proved a great success in combat since it was first used operationally in 1978. Several models have been produced, carrying a wide variety of weapon fits.

R 27104

Combat Engineer Vehicles and Equipment

The disastrous Anglo-Canadian raid on the German-occupied French port of Dieppe in August 1942 underlined the need for specialized assault armour if a seaborne invasion of 'Fortress Europe' was to have a chance of success. The British learned the lesson well and the so called 'funnies' (the mine-clearers, carpet-layers, swimming tanks and bridgelayers etc.) of the 79th Armoured Division were one of the great successes of D-Day, cracking open beach obstacles and demolishing concrete pillboxes while the Americans, who had not developed sophisticated engineer assault armour, suffered much higher casualties in their beach landings. One of the most useful of the 79th Division's vehicles was the specially developed assault tank called the AVRE (Armoured Vehicle Royal Engineers), a Churchill Mk IV tank with its main armament replaced by a spigot mortar firing a demolition bomb to a range of about 82 m (90 yards). Brackets were fitted for the fitment of various devices including anti-mine rollers, mechanical charge placers, carpet bobbins etc., and for towing fascines, explosives and other stores a simple steel runner sledge was provided. Three regiments each with 60 AVREs were formed as the 1st Assault Brigade Royal Engineers, and their contribution to the liberation of Europe from D-Day to the Rhine crossing was invaluable.

Today's combat engineer equipment ranges from specialized armoured engineer assault vehicles (lineal descendants in fact of the pioneering wartime AVRE) via armoured bulldozers and earthmovers, to bridge-laying equipment, soft-skin construction equipment and importantly mine warfare equipment which is considered in more detail elsewhere. There is also specialized armoured equipment for the battlefield recovery of disabled vehicles.

Assault engineers are expected to fight at the heart of a battle both in attack and defence, and this is the reason that so wide and sophisticated a range of fighting vehicles has been developed to match their needs. As the US Army's 1982 field manual defines their role: 'The engineer system has three basic purposes: It preserves the freedom of maneuver of friendly forces; it obstructs the maneuver of enemy in areas where fire and maneuver can be used to destroy him; it enhances the survivability of friendly forces with protective construction.'

In the Soviet army great emphasis is put on maintaining the speed and momentum of any advance, and this gives great importance to the activities of combat engineers equipped to clear obstacles and minefields, to bridge water obstacles, to build and repair roads and to do much else besides. They are judged to be a highly effective force with equipment that is rugged and simple yet technically excellent. The PMP pontoon bridge, for example, is judged to be the best in the world while engineer equipment is widely distributed throughout the army as a whole, with 'strap-on' equipment such as mine-rollers and dozer blades available for ordinary combat vehicles. Engineer units are pro-

vided at all levels from regiment up to front, usually being attached downwards to the units that most need their support. Command of engineers is centralized, while all units of regimental strength and above have a chief of engineers to control activities in his formation.

FV180 Combat Engineer Vehicle

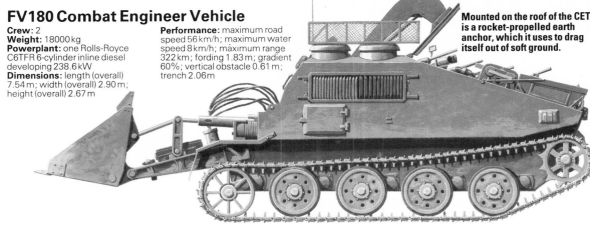

Crew: 2
Weight: 18000 kg
Powerplant: one Rolls-Royce C6TFR 6-cylinder inline diesel developing 238.6 kW
Dimensions: length (overall) 7.54 m; width (overall) 2.90 m; height (overall) 2.67 m
Performance: maximum road speed 56 km/h; maximum water speed 8 km/h; maximum range 322 km; fording 1.83 m; gradient 60%; vertical obstacle 0.61 m; trench 2.06 m

Mounted on the roof of the CET is a rocket-propelled earth anchor, which it uses to drag itself out of soft ground.

AMX-30 Engin Blindé du Génie

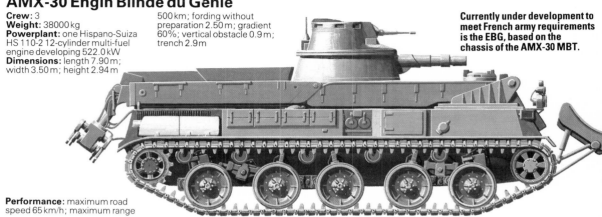

Crew: 3
Weight: 38000 kg
Powerplant: one Hispano-Suiza HS 110-2 12-cylinder multi-fuel engine developing 522.0 kW
Dimensions: length 7.90 m; width 3.50 m; height 2.94 m
500 km; fording without preparation 2.50 m; gradient 60%; vertical obstacle 0.9 m; trench 2.9 m

Currently under development to meet French army requirements is the EBG, based on the chassis of the AMX-30 MBT.

Performance: maximum road speed 65 km/h; maximum range

M728 Combat Engineer Vehicle

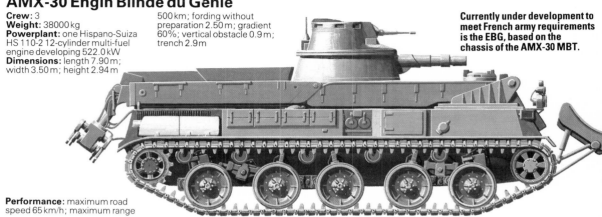

Crew: 4
Weight: 53200 kg
Powerplant: one Teledyne Continental AVDS-1790-2A 12-cylinder diesel developing 559.3 kW
Dimensions: length (travelling) 8.92 m; width (overall) 3.71 m; height (travelling) 3.20 m
Performance: maximum road speed 48.3 km/h; maximum range 451 km; fording 1.22 m; gradient 60%; vertical obstacle 0.76 m; trench 2.51 m

The standard combat engineer vehicle of the US Army, the M728 is an M60 MBT with its 105-mm gun replaced by a 165-mm demolition gun, an A-frame for lifting and a hydraulically operated dozer blade.

The Leopard Armoured Engineer Vehicle is based on the chassis of the Leopard 1 MBT and has been designed to carry out a wide variety of missions on the battlefield, including ripping up road surfaces to make them impassable for wheeled vehicles.

Leopard AEV

Crew: 4
Weight: loaded 40800 kg
Powerplant: one MTU MB 838 Ca.M500 10-cylinder diesel developing 618.9 kW
Dimensions: length (overall) 7.98 m; width (overall) 3.75 m; height (with MG) 2.69 m
Performance: maximum road speed 65 km/h; maximum road range 850 km; gradient 60%; fording 2.10 m; vertical obstacle 1.15 m; trench 3 m

Leopard Armoured Engineer Vehicle

Winch
The Leopard AEV can pull a load of up to 70 tonnes with its winch, which pulls 90 m of 33 mm cable

Bow machine-gun
This has an elevation and depression of 15° and a traverse of 15°

Commander's machine-gun
This is fired from the commander's hatch and is mainly intended for anti-aircraft defence

Dozer
The blade has a capacity of 200 m³ of soil per hour and also serves to stabilize the vehicle when using the crane

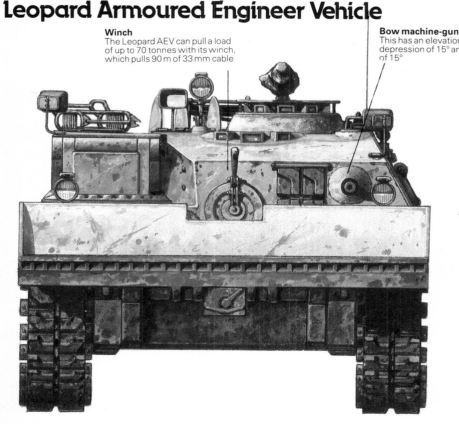

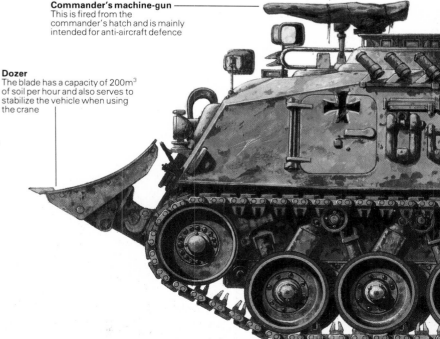

Above: A Combat Engineer Tractor uses its hydraulically-operated bucket to move soil. This can also be used as an earth anchor when the winch is being deployed.

Right: This M60A3 of the US Army is fitted with a mine-clearing roller device to detonate mines before the tank runs over them.

Left: This is one of the prototypes of the GPM armoured engineer vehicles (a Leopard derivative), which was developed specifically to prepare and clear river crossing points for tanks.

Armoured Combat Engineer Vehicles

Like the wartime Churchill AVRE, most armoured combat engineer vehicles are based on redundant main battle tank chassis reworked to suit a particular role. The Soviet IMR (Inzhenernaia Maschina Ragrazhdeniia, or engineer obstacle-clearing machine) is a typical example: it is based on a T-54/55 tank chassis, is armoured against small arms fire and shell splinters, and has NBC protection and IR searchlights. It lacks a demolition gun, but can clear obstacles or dig emplacements under fire using its front-mounted dozer blade or the hydraulic crane and grab which replaces the turret. The crane operator is provided with an armoured cupola equipped with observation devices.

The French VCG (Véhicule de Combat du Génie, or engineer combat vehicle) is based on the AMX VCI infantry combat vehicle, which in turn was based on the AMX-13 light tank. It has a substantial dozer blade at the front and a collapsible A-frame with a lift when erected of 4000 kg (8,818 lb). Its successor is the EBG (Engin Blindé du Genie, or armoured engineer vehicle) using automotive components from the AMX-30 main battle tank. The vehicle has a large dozer blade with teeth at its bottom edge for ripping up road surfaces when the vehicle is driven in reverse. There is a hydraulically operated lifting arm equipped with a pincer-type grab similar to that of the Soviet IMR. Mounted in the centre of the hull is a turret containing a 7.62-mm (0.3-in) machine-gun and a 142-mm (5.6-in) demolition charge projector capable of throwing a 17-kg (37.5-lb) fin-stabilized demolition bomb to a range of 30 to 300 m (33 to 330 yards).

The German Leopard armoured engineer vehicle uses the Leopard 1 main battle tank suspension, engine and transmission under a purpose-designed hull equipped with dozer blade and substantial crane with a lift of 20000 kg (44,092 lb) when the dozer blade is used as a stabilizer. A hydraulic earth auger can be fitted, and thus be able to drill 0.7-m (2.3-ft) diameter holes up to 2 m (6.6 ft) deep. For demolition work the Leopard AEV carries 117 kg (258 lb) of explosive demolition blocks plus igniters and fuses.

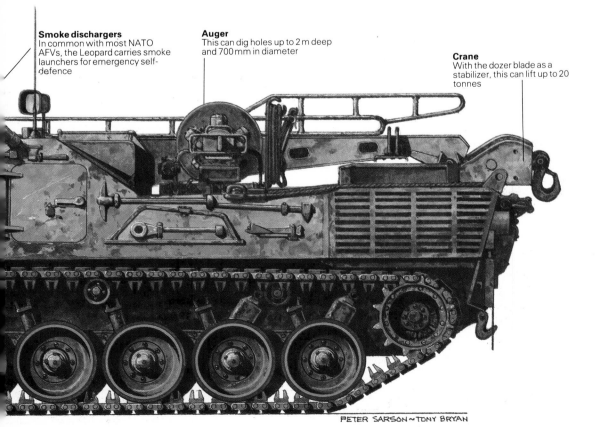

Smoke dischargers
In common with most NATO AFVs, the Leopard carries smoke launchers for emergency self-defence

Auger
This can dig holes up to 2 m deep and 700 mm in diameter

Crane
With the dozer blade as a stabilizer, this can lift up to 20 tonnes

PETER SARSON ~ TONY BRYAN

Combat Engineer Vehicles and Equipment

The US Army used the M728 Combat Engineer Vehicle based closely on the M60A1 main battle tank, and this retains the configuration of a turreted tank. Main armament is a 165-mm (6.5-in) demolition gun in a turret with 360° traverse. A substantial A-frame fits over the turret and has a lifting capacity of 11340 kg (25,000 lb). The dozer blade is hydraulically operated and is mounted at the hull front. The M728 has IR night-driving equipment and a powerful Xenon IR searchlight mounted over the main armament for night operations.

In the British army the successor to the wartime AVRE is a vehicle based on the Centurion tank chassis which first entered service in 1962. Main armament is a 165-mm demolition gun firing a HESH projectile to a maximum range of 2400 m (2,625 yards). At the hull front is a hydraulically-operated dozer blade plus a fitting for a lifting jib if required. A 1.8-m (6-ft) diameter fascine (bundle of wooden staves used for filling ditches) can also be carried in a cradle above the dozer blade. The British army also deploys the purpose-designed FV180 Combat Engineer Tractor, the result of an abortive co-operative venture with France and West Germany which ended with the UK going it alone and building only 141 of this specialized vehicle. The CET is tracked, and has an aluminium armour hull fitted with a hydraulically-operated dozer blade and bucket excavator. The CET has a self-recovery earth anchor mounted on top of the hull: this device is rocket propelled and can be thrown with its line to a maximum of 90 m (100 yards). Once emplaced the CET can haul itself along towards it by pulling in on the line with its winch.

Bridgelayers

The range of devices deployed by armies round the world for crossing rivers and anti-tank ditches is very wide, ranging from assault bridges of the 'scissors' type carried on tank chassis via floating pontoon bridges (such as the Soviet PMP used successfully by the Egyptians during the 1973 crossing of the Suez Canal) to prefabricated lines of communication bridges which can be built into very large semi-permanent structures. The scissors-type assault bridge has been developed by

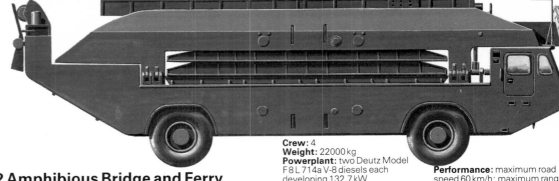

M2 Amphibious Bridge and Ferry
The M2 amphibious bridging and ferry system was introduced by West Germany and was also adopted by the British Army of the Rhine. Bridges capable of carrying MBTs can be formed by lining up M2 units side by side.

Crew: 4
Weight: 22000 kg
Powerplant: two Deutz Model F8L 714a V-8 diesels each developing 132.7 kW
Dimensions: length (travelling) 11.315 m; width (travelling) 3.579 m; height (travelling) 3.579 m
Performance: maximum road speed 60 km/h; maximum range 1000 km; endurance (water) 6 hours; fording amphibious; gradient 60%; trench no capability

TMM Truck-Mounted Treadway Bridge
The Soviet TMM truck-mounted treadway bridge system in the travelling mode is mounted on the back of the older KrAZ-214 6×6 truck. More recent models are mounted on the more powerful KrAZ-255B 6×6 truck chassis, which is also used to launch the PMP bridge system.

Crew: 3
Weight: 19500 kg
Powerplant: one YaMZ M206B 6-cylinder water-cooled diesel developing 152.9 kW
Dimensions: length (with bridge) 9.30 m; width (with bridge) 3.20 m; height (with bridge) 3.15 m
Performance: maximum road speed 55 km/h; maximum road range 530 km; fording 1.0 m; gradient 60%; vertical obstacle 0.4 m; trench no capability

AMX-30 CPP
The bridge laid by the AMX-30 armoured vehicle launched bridge is 22 m long and 3.1 m wide, and to lay it it must be swung through 180°, which tends to advertise the vehicle's position. The West German Biber and Soviet MTU-20 lay their bridges horizontally to avoid this problem.

Crew: 3
Weight: 42500 kg
Powerplant: one Hispano-Suiza HS-110 12-cylinder multi-fuel diesel developing 522.0 kW
Dimensions: length (with bridge) 11.40 m; width (with bridge) 3.95 m; height (with bridge) 4.29 m
Performance: maximum road speed 50 km/h; maximum range 600 km; fording 1.0 m; gradient 60%; vertical obstacle 0.93 m; trench 2.9 m

Above: Like the French AMX-30 bridgelayer, the Centurion Mk 5 AVLB used by the British Army must swing its bridge up nd over in a 180° arc when being deployed.

The rapid laying of pontoon bridges can be of critical importance in modern warfare: here Israeli M113 APCs and a Centurion tank cross the Suez canal in 1973 just north of the Great Bitter Lakes. This assault led to the triumphant advance on Ismailia which ended the war.

several countries including Brazil (a vehicle based on the wartime M3A1 Stuart light tank), Czechoslovakia, East Germany, Poland and the USSR (vehicles based on the T-54/T-55), France (AMX-13 and AMX-30 bridgelayers), West Germany (the Biber based on the Leopard 1), Japan (the Type 67 based on the Type 61 main battle tank), Switzerland (Brückenlegepanzer 68), the UK (Chieftain and Centurion bridgelayers) and the USA (vehicles based on M48 and M60 tanks.

Construction equipment

Armoured bulldozers are employed by several armies for operations where the hazards are not great enough to need a full-blown assault engineer vehicle. The US M9 High Speed Combat Earth Mover is for example an unarmed lightly armoured bulldozer with a wide range of applications and a high road speed so that it can be placed up with the lead tanks in a convoy. The Japanese Type 78 is another high-speed dozer with a fully armoured cab. There is a very wide range of militarized civilian equipment in use by combat engineers in the world's armies, these items including graders, scrapers, dump trucks, bucket excavators, forklifts, mobile cranes, ditch diggers, drills, loaders and so on.

Above: A Soviet-supplied MTU-20 armoured bridgelayer of the Finnish army approaches its launch position on a recent exercise. When fully open, the bridge is 20 m long and can span a gap of up to 18 m.

Left: One of the many roles performed by the ubiquitous Combat Engineer Tractor is the preparation of river banks for bridging by pontoons. Here the CET, having done its job, waits as the pontoon bridge is placed in position.

Below: An M60A1 of the US Army clears a road of anti-tank mines with its front-mounted roller system. The Soviets have been using similar systems for many years, but the US Army has only recently bought them in significant numbers.

Self-Propelled Artillery

Looking at the history of the development of armoured fighting vehicles, the point where the 'self-propelled gun' proper branched off the evolutionary tree from the 'tank' is hard to determine. A tank proper can be said to be designed to go into the heart of the battle and fight it out under armour at the front line. The original tanks of World War I were designed to do just this, with quick-firing guns or machine-guns fitted in embrasures on caterpillar-tracked vehicles able to move over broken or shelled ground, and by the end of that war the classic tank with a high-velocity gun mounted in a rotating turret had made its appearance.

Further experiments of the interwar years in the UK and USA produced a series of artillery pieces mounted on tracked chassis and designed not for the direct battle but for mobile fire support. These early purpose designed self-propelled (SP) guns did not need to be heavily armoured as tanks proper because they need not go into the heart of the fighting: that is what their shells were for, but they were much more tactically mobile than horse-drawn or tractor-towed artillery.

The German army achieved its Blitzkrieg victories of 1939-41 equipped not just with turreted tanks but with purpose-built 'assault guns' (*Sturmgeschütze*) able to add their firepower to a tank or infantry attack and with enough armour protection to go where tanks might go. Without rotating turrets they were cheaper and simpler to manufacture, and furthermore, by scrapping the turret a given chassis could carry a larger-calibre weapon and, if employed correctly, could be just as useful. Through World War II the Germans fielded a very sophisticated array of self-propelled weapons, assault guns and tank hunters ranging in size from the diminutive 75-mm (2.95-in) Hetzer tank-hunter based on a Czech Pz 38(t) chassis to the mighty Sturmtiger with a 280-mm (11.02-in) assault mortar installed in a Tiger tank chassis.

The wartime Allies soon caught up with vehicles such as the US M7 Priest with a 105-mm (4.13-in) howitzer mounted in a Sherman tank chassis, the 76-mm (3-in) M18 Hellcat tank destroyer and the British Sexton with a 25-pdr mounted again in a Sherman. The Soviet SU-75 tank destroyer, the SU-85 and SU-100 SP guns based on T-34 tank chassis, and the big ISU-122 and ISU-152 based on the heavy Josef Stalin tank series were particularly effective fighting vehicles and lingered on in Soviet and Soviet bloc service for many years after World War II.

One of the most widely used of today's self-propelled artillery systems, the M109 155-mm howitzer has been in production since the early 1960s and since that time has seen considerable upgrading. These are M109A2s of one of the artillery batteries of the 1st Independent Mixed Brigade of the Portuguese army, assigned to NATO.

In postwar years the design accent of SP guns gradually changed: survival on a potentially nuclear battlefield, rather than the ability to keep up with tanks, became the dominant rationale. Vehicles thus became heavier, with thicker hides to protect their crews against blast, flash and radiation effects. Then in the late 1950s came emphasis on airmobility and lightness, SP artillery of the period consisting of little more than a gun on a set of tracks with crew and ammunition carried on a second vehicle. Then through the 1960s and 1970s new-generation equipment began to appear (both in the West and in the USSR) which was almost as sophisticated in levels of equipment (computerized fire control, automated ammunition handling and purpose-built chassis design) as main battle tanks themselves.

The Soviet army has, for example, made an enormous effort in replacing its towed divisional artillery with SP versions. According to Soviet doctrine SP howitzers have the mobility and survivability needed in modern warfare. They allow combined arms integration at a progressively lower level, batteries or even battalions being attached to first-line manoeuvre battalions, moving close behind the tanks and BMPs and firing from the short halt. In this direct-fire role SP howitzers firing high explosive are aimed particularly at suppressing forward observation posts and defenders armed with anti-tank guided missiles. Instead of relying on US style complex command and control systems for bringing down 'on-call' fire support, the Soviet army aims to apply firepower where it is needed by a much lower level of integration. In fast-moving mobile warfare each battalion or regimental commander thus has his artillery when and where he needs it.

The two weapons developed for this purpose are the SU-122 and the larger SU-152, both of which entered service in the early 1970s. The 23000-kg (50,705-lb) SU-152 first appeared in 1973, and has been issued on the scale of 18 per artillery division replacing towed 152-mm (6-in) artillery pieces. The chassis is based on that used for the SA-4 'Ganef' SAM, but the road wheels are staggered to bear the weight of the turret and main armament mounted at the rear. The SU-152 is not amphibious, but has an NBC filtration and overpressure system. The large all-welded turret has a sloped front and well sloped sides with a vision block in each. The commander is seated on the left (with the gunner forward and below him and the loader to his right) and his traversable cupola is equipped with multiple vision devices, an IR searchlight, and a remote-controlled machine-gun. The driver sits at front left with the engine to his right.

Artillery was used to a great extent by the Americans in Vietnam. These are men of the 2nd Battalion, 32nd Artillery preparing to fire their long-ranged M107 175-mm Gun at Viet Cong positions during Operation 'Junction City' early in 1967.

Known in the west as the M1974, the SU-122 Gvozdika (Carnation), which has the Soviet designation 2S1, is fully amphibious, unlike the SU-152 or 2S3. The chassis is also used for the TT-LB, a mine-clearing vehicle, and for a new chemical warfare reconnaissance vehicle.

155-mm Bandkanon 1A Self-Propelled Gun

Although it was the first fully automatic self-propelled gun, the Bandkanon 1A was only produced in small quantities for the Swedish army because of its size and lack of mobility. Its unique 14-round armoured magazine is at the rear of the hull.

Crew: 5
Weight: 53000 kg
Dimensions: length (gun forward) 11.00 m; length (hull) 6.55 m; width 3.37 m; height (including AA MG) 3.85 m
Powerplant: one Rolls-Royce

diesel developing 179 kW and Boeing gas turbine developing 224 kW
Performance: maximum road speed 28 km/h; maximum range 230 km; gradient 60%; vertical obstacle 0.95 m; trench 2.00 m

155-mm Self-Propelled Gun Mk F3

Based on a modified AMX-13 light tank chassis, the Mk F3 replaced World War II vintage artillery used by the French army until the 1960s. It has been widely exported to the Middle East and Latin America but is being replaced in French service by the GCT.

Crew: 2
Weight: 17400 kg
Dimensions: length (gun forward) 6.22 m; width 2.72 m; height 2.085 m
Powerplant: one SOFAM 8Gxb 8-cylinder petrol engine developing 186 kW
Performance: maximum road speed 60 km/h; maximum range 300 km; gradient 40%; vertical obstacle 0.60 m; trench 1.50 m

155-mm GCT Self-Propelled Gun

First adopted by Saudi Arabia, the French GCT has also been sold to Iraq, where it has seen combat in the Gulf war. The GCT's automatic loading system enables it to fire up to eight rounds a minute, and the magazine can be reloaded while the weapon is being fired.

Crew: 4
Weight: 42000 kg
Dimensions: length (gun forward) 10.25 m; length (hull) 6.70 m; width 3.15 m; height 3.25 m
Powerplant: one Hispano-Suiza

HS 110 12-cylinder water-cooled multi-fuel engine developing 537 kW
Performance: maximum road speed 60 km/h; maximum range 450 km; gradient 60%; vertical obstacle 0.93 m; trench 1.90 m

OTO-Melara Palmaria 155-mm Self-Propelled Howitzer

Specifically developed for export by the Italian firm of OTO-Melara, the Palmaria has been bought by Libya, Nigeria and Oman. An additional 25 turrets have been supplied to Argentina for fitting on the TAM chassis.

Crew: 5
Weight: 46000 kg
Dimensions: length (gun forward) 11.474 m; length (hull) 7.40 m; width 2.35 m; height (without MG) 2.874 m
Powerplant: 8-cylinder diesel developing 559 kW
Performance: maximum road speed 60 km/h; maximum range 400 km; gradient 60%; vertical obstacle 1.00 m; trench 3.00 m

Self-Propelled Artillery

The main armament is a 152-mm weapon based on the D-20 towed gun/howitzer. The barrel has a double-baffle muzzle brake, fume extractor and barrel travelling lock. The barrel can fire HE, HEAT and RAP projectiles, the last to a reported range of 37000 m (40,465 yards). The barrel can also fire chemical and tactical nuclear ammunition.

Its slightly downsized 16000-kg (35,275-lb) stablemate is the 122-mm (4.8-in) gunned amphibious SU-122 which entered service at the same time. The chassis' ground clearance is variable, facilitating air mobility and lessening battlefield exposure. The SU-122 is issued on the scale of 36 per artillery division, 18 per motor rifle division and six per tank division. The level of NBC protection is similar to that of the BMP, although armour is comparatively light.

The Soviet emphasis on direct fire and close contact with advancing tanks contrasts strongly with NATO doctrines, which envisage direct fire only as an emergency self-defence measure. Nevertheless the US Army's and NATO's most significant SP, the 155-mm (6.1-in) M109, bears a distinct resemblance to the SU-152 which entered service over a decade later. The M109 has an almost identical layout (front offset engine and a big rear-mounted, slab-sided turret) and both hull and turret are all-welded aluminium. Each US Army armoured and mechanized division has three battalions of M109A1/A2s, each battalion being equipped with three six-gun batteries for a total of 54 vehicles per division. The vehicle has been in continuous production since 1961, and more than 4,000 examples have been delivered. The M109A1 has a lengthened barrel capable of firing a RAP to 24000 m (26,245 yards). The M109A2 entered service in 1979 showing various detail improvements over the A1 including a new recoil mechanism and extra ammunition stowage. In service with a wide range of armies including those of the UK and Israel, the M109 can fire a wide range of ammunition including HE, submunition carrier shells, illuminating, smoke, chemical and tactical nuclear.

The other significant SP gun in the US arsenal is the M110 203-mm (8-in) howitzer. Original production was completed in the late 1960s, but in 1979 there began renewed production, this time of the improved M110A2 variant distinguished by longer barrel and muzzle brake. The M110 is a highly significant weapon as it is an important delivery system for tactical artillery weapons (see the section on heavy artillery) and is very much configured for long-range fire support with the gun and crew exposed on top of the chassis. Of the total crew of 13 five are carried on the gun itself, (only the driver under armour) the rest riding on the M548 tracked cargo carrier which also carries the ammunition.

Self-propelled guns and howitzers have been developed by several nations and, as their complexity increases, by international consortia. They remain less technologically demanding than tanks, however, and countries like Czechoslovakia have been able to field their own indigenous designs. The Czech 152-mm equipment is unusual in being mounted on a wheeled 8×8 truck chassis fitted with swing-out stabilizer/jack units. The engine is rear-mounted in an armoured box, while the driver and gun crew sit in an armoured cab at the front. In the middle is an open-topped turret with a hydraulic crane for ammunition handling. The Tatra SP is obviously an indirect fire weapon, not designed to 'keep up with tanks', but for this role a wheeled chassis is no great disadvantage.

A survey of significant front-line SP guns in service round the world would include the British 105-mm (4.13-in) Abbot, the French GCT with its massive turret mounted on chassis derived from the AMX-30 tank and a 155-mm gun capable of firing a RAP to 30500 m (33,355 yards), the various Israeli Soltan 155-mm weapons mounted on old Sherman and Centurion chassis, the Italian OTO-Melara 155-mm type, the Japanese Type 75 155-mm system, and the Swedish 155-mm Bandkanon 1A of early 1960s vintage with its sophisticated automatic ammunition loading system. The Bandkanon has a high rate of fire but also a number of disadvantages: its size and weight reduce its mobility, and once a palletized ammunition clip (HE for example) has been loaded a fire support request for smoke cannot be met until a new clip has been loaded.

In 1973 West Germany, Britain and Italy began joint development of a new 155-mm SP weapon to replace the Abbot and M109 in service with their artillery arms. The resulting SP-70 prototype, for which West Germany had the project design lead, appeared in 1976. SP-70 can fire all NATO standard 155-mm ammunition including RAPs and the Copperhead laser-homing projectile.

Above: The gun and turret of a self-propelled gun can be married to a wide choice of chassis, making for easier maintenance and spare parts organization. This particular vehicle is a combination of the French GCT turret and a Leopard 1 MBT hull.

Below: The first M109s were delivered in 1963 but the system continues to be updated. This is the latest configuration of one of the Howitzer Extended Life Program (HELP) test vehicles, being evaluated as part of the US Army's Divisional Support Weapons Program.

Muzzle brake
M110A2s are easily distinguished from the original M110 model by this large muzzle brake

M110A2 Self-Propelled Gun

Designed to fire a wide range of nuclear, chemical, HE and improved conventional munitions, the versatile M110A2 has now replaced the M107 in US service. Because such guns can engage targets beyond the range even of forward observers, the Israelis have pioneered the use of RPVs which provide real-time target data.

Firing the heaviest HE (High Explosive) shells, and providing nuclear artillery support, the British Army uses the American M110 203-mm self-propelled gun in its heavy batteries.

The French Mk F3 is shown in the firing position with the recoil spade down. Note that the crew have no protection from hostile fire and only two can ride on the vehicle when it moves.

Crew: 5+8
Weight: 26536 kg
Dimensions: length (gun forward) 7.467 m; length (hull) 5.72 m; width 3.149 m; height 2.93 m
Powerplant: one Detroit Diesel Model 8V-71T diesel developing 302 kW
Performance: maximum road speed 56 km/h; maximum range 725 km; gradient 60%; vertical obstacle 1.016 m; trench 2.362 m

Left: The 2S3 152-mm gun howitzer has been supplied to a number of nations, including the German Democratic Republic. In the absence of an official Soviet designation, the system became known in the west as the M1973, after the year it was first seen.

Above left: A pair of British Army M109s are seen deployed in woods during a field exercise in West Germany. The M109 is one of the most widely used SP guns in the world, and has been used in action in the Middle East and South East Asia.

Above: Czechoslovakia is unique in using a wheeled 152-mm self-propelled gun instead of the tracked vehicles being currently introduced to the Warsaw Pact. The DANA is based on the chassis of the Tatra 815 8×8 truck.

Above: Well wrapped up against the bitter cold of South Korea, a US gunner stands in front of his M110A2 203-mm self-propelled gun 'Belligerent'. The US Army plans eventually to provide all M110s with a crew shelter and an NBC system.

Hydraulic rams
These elevate the gun to a maximum of +65° and −2°

Gunner's seat
The M110 has a full crew of 13, but only five can travel on the vehicle.

Ammunition hoist
This lifts the 203-mm shell into the loading mechanism

Driver's position
The driver sits to the left of the engine and is provided with infra-red driving lights

Recoil spade
This is dug into the ground to absorb the recoil produced on firing

Field Artillery

As world armies have turned over their stocks of World War II artillery for a new generation of ordnance, the general adoption of larger calibres has blurred old distinctions of field, medium and heavy artillery. In the US Army, for example, 105-mm (4.13-in) weapons, the standard calibre for field artillery in World War II, are now reserved only for airborne use and the British airportable 105-mm L118 which proved such a success in the Falklands campaign, is classified as a light gun. While the developing technology of artillery has meant larger calibres, greater projectile weight and much higher muzzle velocities for no increase in weight, ammunition technology has progressed in tandem extending the range and lethality, while electronics and computerization have revolutionized target acquisition and fire control, allowing devastating firepower to be brought down with great accuracy at ranges up to 30000 m (32,810 yards). Ammunition technology (including rocket assistance and terminal guidance) is considered in more detail in the section dealing with heavy artillery.

Almost all artillery is organized into battalions, usually of 18 guns split into three batteries with a co-ordinating headquarters battery. Western armies average around 500 artillerymen per battalion, while the Soviets and Warsaw Pact Armies average about 300, but with more under the control of divisional artillery headquarters. Artillery battalions are further grouped into divisional and non-divisional artillery.

Non-divisional artillery is under the control of higher command and incorporates a greater proportion of heavier weapons allocated according to need in the corps fire-support plan. Divisional artillery is simply all the guns assigned to the division, which can include heavy weapons, US divisional artillery, for example, usually accounts for three battalions of 155-mm (6.1-mm) and one of 203-mm (8-in) howitzers and a battalion of Lance missiles, all nuclear capable. In the Soviet model there are two battalions of 122-mm (4.8-in), one of 152-mm (6-in) weapons, one of MRLs and one of longer-range tactical missiles.

The standardization on 155 mm has resulted in a new generation of artillery pieces entering service with world armies in the 1970s and 1980s. The UK, Italy and West Germany for example jointly developed the 155-mm Field Howitzer 70 (FH-70) built round the tactical requirements of high rate of fire, high mobility and increased range and lethality with a new family of ammunition. Loading is semi-automatic, powered by the gun's own recoil, and with rocket-assisted projectiles the FH-70 can attain ranges of over 30000 m. The weapon incorporates an auxiliary power unit (APU) in the form of an 1800 cc Volkswagen engine mounted on

the forward part of the carriage. The APU makes the FH-70 self mobile at low speeds (allowing 'shoot and scoot' tactics) and provides hydraulic power for raising and lowering the main and trailer wheels and lowering the trails when going into action. The availability of an APU means that the FH-70 can be unhooked, manoeuvred into position and brought into action in under two minutes.

The US Army's standard 155-mm towed weapon, the M198, does not incorporate an APU but is significantly lighter than the FH-70 (7076 kg/15,600 lb in travelling order compared with 9300 kg/20,503 lb for the European weapon). The M198 can fire all standard 155-mm NATO ammunition including binary chemical and nuclear. Other significant 155-mm weapons in production and service include the Argentine Citefa Model 77, the Belgian SRC GC 45, the Finnish Tampella M-74, the French TR and Modèle 50, the Israel Soltam M-68 and M-71, the South African G5 and the Swedish Bofors FH-77, while large numbers of the US

During the US Marine involvement in the Lebanese tragedy, their positions around Beirut airport were supported by Marine artillery. This 155-mm M198 howitzer is of 'C' Battery, 24th Marine Amphibious Unit.

wartime vintage M59 gun and M114 155-mm howitzer remain in service with many armies around the world.

The Soviet military is reluctant to scrap older weapons, so large numbers of venerable artillery pieces serve with Warsaw Pact and Soviet client states, and with China. The standard 122-mm D-20 gun/howitzer first introduced in 1955 goes back to a wartime design, and numbers of the Model 1943 and Model 1937 152-mm weapons remain in Soviet, Warsaw Pact and Middle East armies. The same is true of weapons in 130-mm and 122-mm calibres, the 122-mm D-20 howitzer supplanting the M1938 M-30 in Soviet army service from the early 1960s onwards, while the wartime weapon remains in Warsaw Pact, Middle East and third world armies. The Israelis use captured stocks for training.

Iraq has been supplied with large quantities of military equipment by the Soviet Union, not least of which have been the M46 130-mm field guns seen here in action. The long range of the weapon has led to Iraq using them to soften up Iranian rear positions, or in providing radar directed counter-battery fire against Iranian attacks.

The French Modèle 50 155-mm howitzer has been in service for over 30 years, and typifies the post-war generation of towed artillery. Both the howitzer and the Berliet GBU 15 truck are being replaced in French service by more modern equipment, but the Modèle 50 remains in service with Switzerland, Morocco, Lebanon and in some numbers with Israel. It was also licence-built by Bofors in Sweden.

M-46 130-mm Field Gun

Evolved from a naval gun design, the Soviet M-46 130-mm field gun has proved one of the most successful designs of the post-war years. Used by the North Vietnamese Army in Vietnam, it outranged every other artillery piece in the conflict except for the very much larger M-107 self-propelled piece deployed by the US Army.

Calibre: 130 mm
Weight: travelling 8450 kg and firing 7700 kg
Dimensions: length, travelling 11.73 m; width, travelling 2.45 m; height, travelling 2.55 m
Elevation: +45°/−2.5°
Traverse: total 50°
Maximum range: 27150 m

D-30 122-mm Howitzer

Although replaced in Soviet front line service by the self-propelled 2S1 122-mm howitzer (which actually uses a derivative of the D-30 as its armament), the D-30 howitzer is in service in more than 30 countries as well as with lower readiness divisions of the Soviet army.

Calibre: 121.92 mm
Weight: travelling 3210 kg and firing 3150 kg
Dimensions: length, travelling 5.40 m; width, travelling 1.95 m; height, travelling 1.66 m
Elevation: +70°/−7°
Traverse: 370°
Maximum range: with HE projectile 15400 m and with HE rocket-assisted projectile 21000 m

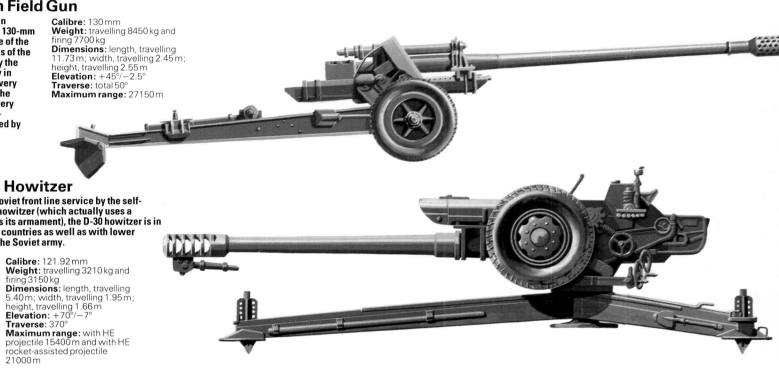

Royal Ordnance Factory 105-mm Light Gun

The Royal Ordnance Factory's 105-mm Light Gun has replaced the OTO-Melara 105-mm pack howitzer in the light regiments of the Royal Artillery, and saw distinguished service during the campaign to retake the Falkland Islands. The US Army has type-classified the weapon as the M119, and intend to order some 500 models, with the first batch of 64 being acquired in Fiscal Year 87.

Calibre: 105 mm
Weight: firing and travelling 1858 kg
Dimensions: length, travelling (gun over trail) 4.876 m; width, travelling 1.778 m; height, travelling (gun over trail) 1.371 m
Elevation: +70°/−5.5°
Traverse: total 11° or on turntable 360°
Maximum range: 17200 m

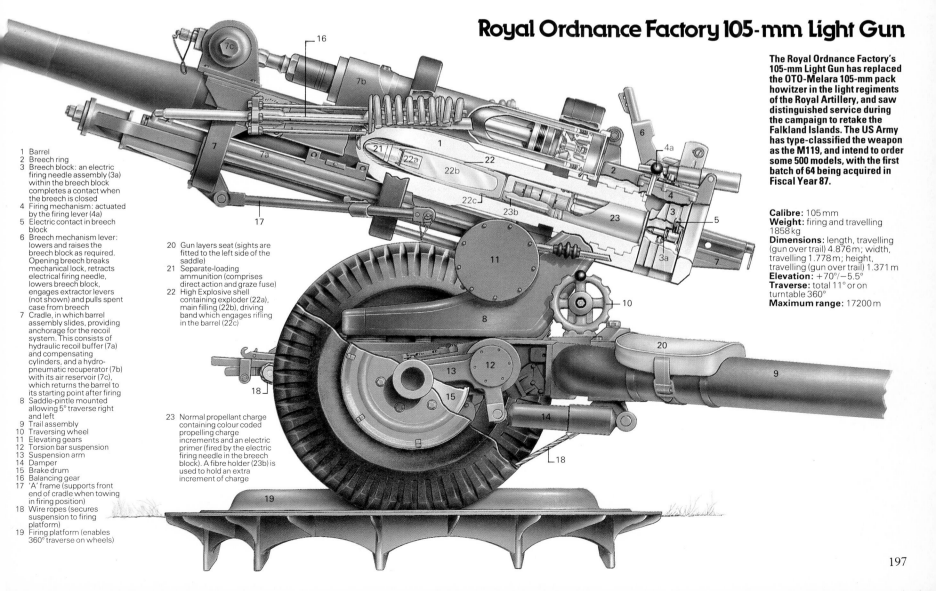

1 Barrel
2 Breech ring
3 Breech block: an electric firing needle assembly (3a) within the breech block completes a contact when the breech is closed
4 Firing mechanism: actuated by the firing lever (4a)
5 Electric contact in breech block
6 Breech mechanism lever: lowers and raises the breech block as required. Opening breech breaks mechanical lock, retracts electrical firing needle, lowers breech block, engages extractor levers (not shown) and pulls spent case from breech
7 Cradle, in which barrel assembly slides, providing anchorage for the recoil system. This consists of hydraulic recoil buffer (7a) and compensating cylinders, and a hydro-pneumatic recuperator (7b) with its air reservoir (7c), which returns the barrel to its starting point after firing
8 Saddle-pintle mounted allowing 5° traverse right and left
9 Trail assembly
10 Traversing wheel
11 Elevating gears
12 Torsion bar suspension
13 Suspension arm
14 Damper
15 Brake drum
16 Balancing gear
17 'A' frame (supports front end of cradle when towing in firing position)
18 Wire ropes (secures suspension to firing platform)
19 Firing platform (enables 360° traverse on wheels)

20 Gun layers seat (sights are fitted to the left side of the saddle)
21 Separate-loading ammunition (comprises direct action and graze fuse)
22 High Explosive shell containing exploder (22a), main filling (22b), driving band which engages rifling in the barrel (22c)

23 Normal propellant charge containing colour coded propelling charge increments and an electric primer (fired by the electric firing needle in the breech block). A fibre holder (23b) is used to hold an extra increment of charge

Field Artillery

In the West 105-mm weapons are classed as light artillery. The British 105-mm in service from 1974 with a range of 17000 m (18,590 yards) replaced the 10000-m (10,935-yard) range Italian OTO-Melara pack howitzer in service with the light regiments of the Royal Artillery. The Light Gun can be towed by a 1-tonne 4×4 Land Rover or carried slung under an Aérospatiale Puma helicopter, while the elevating mass can be removed from the carriage to make two light helicopter (such as Westland Wessex) loads. The gun can be reassembled in under 30 minutes. The OTO-Melara pack howitzer of 1957 vintage breaks into 11 sections, the heaviest of which weighs 122 kg (269 lb), and can be reassembled in four minutes; this is the standard light artillery weapon of more than 25 armies. The Soviet army deploys a 76-mm (3-in) mountain gun similar in layout to the Italian weapon with split box trail, short barrel, split shield and horizontal sliding-wedge breech block. This weapon, designated M1969 by NATO, is believed to fire both HE and HEAT projectiles with a maximum range of 11000 m (12,030 yards). It has a six man crew and is estimated to weigh about 815 kg (1,797 lb).

US airborne and airmobile units use the 105-mm M102 howitzer weighing 1497 kg (3,300 lb) and capable of being lifted by a Sikorsky UH-60 Black Hawk helicopter. Extensive use of aluminium in the carriage construction kept the weight down, so the M102 is 760 kg (1,675 lb) lighter than the weapon it replaced, the wartime vintage M101, yet has higher muzzle velocity and longer range. The weapon can fire HE, chemical, submunition-carrying, and rocket-assisted projectiles, but is not nuclear capable.

Heavy Artillery

From its earliest days, artillery has always implied warfare by numbers, by calculations of range and trajectory and by carefully co-ordinated fire support plans. Not surprisingly, computers have transformed the speed and accuracy of ballistic computation, while parallel advances in target-acquisiton capability and ammunition have allowed 'tube artillery' to hold its own with rockets and missiles for precision fire support out to ranges of 30 km (18.6 miles) at least, as well as giving direct fire support at the front line.

This is the classic role of heavy artillery, arrayed in all its might to bring down sustained firepower at long ranges to pulverize the most determined of defences. Then in the mid-1950s US heavy artillery became a vitally important delivery system for so-called 'tactical nuclear weapons', that is atomic weapons brought down in size to such a degree that they could be packed inside a 203-mm (8-in) or 155-mm (6.1-in) artillery shell, designed not for strategic use but for battlefield employment against enemy field formations and in particular against concentrations of armour. The first nuclear tube artillery system was the US Army's freakish and unwieldy 280-mm (11.02-in) 'Atomic Cannon' firing the first AFAP (Artillery-Fired Atomic Projectile), the Mk 9.

This combination was used in a live firing test ('Shot Grapple') on 25 May 1953 at the Nevada test site with a 15-kiloton explosion as the result. Thenceforward nuclear artillery shells were developed in progressively smaller calibres, 203-mm howitzers from 1956 and 155-mm howitzers from 1963, with ranges of up to 15 km (9.3 miles). While US artillery acquired nuclear capability from the late 1950s, early Soviet nuclear systems were outsize, short-ranged and unreliable enough to endanger their own crews. Self-propelled 310-mm (12.20-in) and 420-mm (16.54-in) guns firing a winged rocket-powered nuclear projectile were built as an answer to the Atomic Cannon and duly paraded through Red Square every year in the late 1950s, but they were in fact only for show, being kept in storage between parades.

Since then the technology of tube artillery firing conventional shells has developed broadly along four lines: firstly, improving the range by advances in ordnance and ammunition; secondly, increasing lethality by applying precision terminal guidance to artillery shells, which may incorporate submunitions; thirdly, bettering co-ordinated firepower by computerized fire-control and communications; and fourthly, adding to tactical flexibility by emphasizing self-propelled mountings for both heavy and medium artillery. Meanwhile larger-calibre weapons, such as the 155-mm type, have become increasingly the norm, supplanting the World War II generation in calibres between 75 and 105 mm (2.95 and 4.13 in), and in the process blurring the distinction between 'field' and 'heavy' artillery.

Longer range

The US Army has made strenuous efforts in pursuit of ever greater range for its heavy artillery, characterized by the provision of longer barrels for 203- and 155-mm weapons, new high-energy propellants, rocket-assisted projectiles and ballistically exotic ammunition, while a programme called AFIS (Advanced Indirect Fire System) undertaken in the late

Three G5 155-mm gun/howitzers of the South African Army are seen deployed for firing. The G5 is normally towed by a SAMIL 100 6×6 10-tonne truck, which also carries the gun crew and ammunition. The G5 has an exceptionally long range.

1970s investigated ramjet-assisted projectiles with ranges of 70 km (43.5 miles) and more, and equipped with 'fire-and-forget' terminal guidance.

The M549 155-mm high explosive RAP (Rocket-Assisted Projectile) round currently in service is less ambitious with a range of 30 km (18.6 miles), while the M650 203-mm round has a solid-propellant rocket motor which burns for four seconds (igniting seven seconds after firing) to provide range greater than that of the standard round (24.3 km/15.1 miles). RAPs must be designed to withstand the stress of their own firing, and to be tolerant of enormous accelerations (up to 40,000 g for the next generation), pressures up to

Below: Unprotected and unable to 'shoot and scoot', towed artillery has been largely supplanted by self-propelled guns in major armies, but survives as it is cheaper and more easily air-portable.

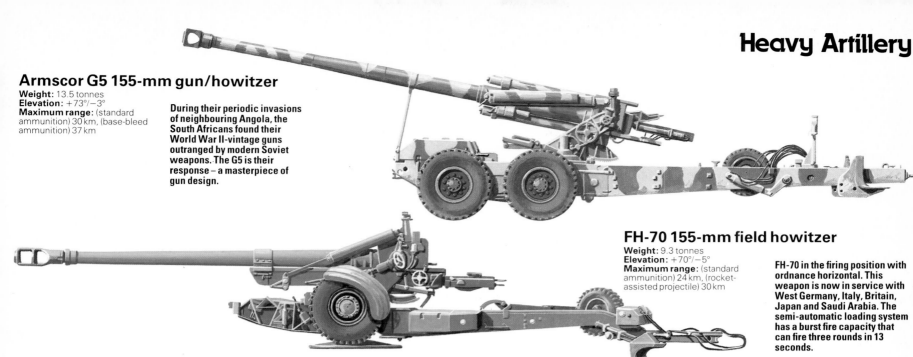

Armscor G5 155-mm gun/howitzer

Weight: 13.5 tonnes
Elevation: +73°/−3°
Maximum range: (standard ammunition) 30 km, (base-bleed ammunition) 37 km

During their periodic invasions of neighbouring Angola, the South Africans found their World War II-vintage guns outranged by modern Soviet weapons. The G5 is their response – a masterpiece of gun design.

FH-70 155-mm field howitzer

Weight: 9.3 tonnes
Elevation: +70°/−5°
Maximum range: (standard ammunition) 24 km, (rocket-assisted projectile) 30 km

FH-70 in the firing position with ordnance horizontal. This weapon is now in service with West Germany, Italy, Britain, Japan and Saudi Arabia. The semi-automatic loading system has a burst fire capacity that can fire three rounds in 13 seconds.

CITEFA (Argentina) Model 77 155-mm howitzer

Weight: 8 tonnes
Elevation: +67°/−0°
Maximum range: (standard ammunition) 22 km, (rocket-assisted projectile) 25.3 km

The Model 77 howitzer is seen in travelling configuration with trails together. The small rubber tyre road wheels under the rear part of the trail assist the crew in bringing the weapon into action.

3000 kg/cm² (42,860 lb/sq in) and rotation rates up to 17,000 rpm. There are penalties in the quest for extreme range such as the effects of hot-burning and high-pressure charges on barrel life and of the blast overpressure effects on the crew, and as ranges increase accuracy suffers as absolute dispersion increases. Precision guidance therefore (for example by laser designation) becomes attractive, but the problem remains of how to effect this 30 km from the front line.

Improved munitions

The second technological thrust therefore has been towards ICMs (Improved Conventional Munitions) in a long-term high-priority US Army programme to develop terminally-guided and cargo-carrying projectiles and thus increase lethality either by being certain of striking the target or spreading destructive effects over a wide area. Copperhead is one result, a CLGP (Cannon-Launched Guided Projectile) destined, after a few bumpy years of mixed results in field trials (when, for example, it was found it would not work in quite average northern European winter weather) and resulting political suspicion, to be procured in large numbers for the US and some NATO armies. (For more detail on 'smart' and submunition-carrying artillery, see the section on anti-tank weapons.)

While improved ammunition has been a fertile avenue of research and advances in fire control have progressed at the pace of computer technology (see the section on battlefield electronics), the technology of the launch systems (the guns themselves) has not stood still entirely although it can be said to be technically mature. The primary towed heavy artillery piece in the Soviet army, for example, is the 180-mm (7.09-in) S-23 gun, which was introduced in 1955 and based on a pre-war naval gun. It weighs just under 21.5 tonnes and features a screw-type breech block typical of Soviet heavy artillery and a pepper-pot perforated muzzle brake. Conventional ammunition is bag type (separate loading and variable charge) and projectiles include HE and bunker-busting 'concrete-piercing' types. A RAP round was introduced during the 1970s and the S-23 can also fire a 0.2-kiloton nuclear round matching US weapons in efficiency. Indeed, with RAPs affording a range of over 43 km (26.7 miles), it is already estimated that Soviet conventional artillery can outrange its US nuclear-capable counterpart, making the latter in effect tactically useless.

The big US M115 203-mm towed howitzer, first introduced in 1939, is still in service with many armies around the world although has been replaced by the self-propelled M110 in the US and most NATO armies. Maximum range is 16.8 km (10.44 miles), and the weapon can fire conventional HE, cargo-carrying, chemical or nuclear munitions including the M422 with a yield of up to 2 kilotons.

The Bofors FH-77A 155-mm field howitzer is seen in firing position, with charges being loaded. The first three shells can be fired in 6-8 seconds; the loading tray on the right of the carriage holds three projectiles.

Left: A 155-mm FH-70 fires at high angle during trials in Sardinia some years ago. The UK is project leader for the FH-70, while West Germany is project leader for the SP model.

Above: The French TR 155-mm gun has an auxiliary power unit on the front of the carriage, which provides power to propel the gun around as well as to operate it.

Below: This was the first picture published of the Soviet S-23 180-mm gun being used by the Iraqis. It fires an 84-kg shell to a maximum range of 43 km, using a rocket-assisted round.

Multiple Rocket-Launchers

The idea of Multiple Rocket-Launchers (MRLs) goes back almost as far as the invention of gunpowder itself. The Chinese used rocket arrows against the Mongols in the 13th century, but it was the gun which then came to dominate five centuries of warfare. In spite of the bold experiments by the Englishman Sir William Congreve with rockets in the Napoleonic wars and in the Anglo-American war of 1812, it was not until the middle of the 20th century that the traditional artillery piece was effectively challenged as the ultimate arbiter of firepower on the land battlefield.

In a traditional artillery piece the propellant charge is burned within the gun barrel, energizing the projectile in a near-instantaneous controlled explosion. The projectile is punched out to fly a ballistic trajectory according to its energy state and how it was aimed at launch, gravity doing the rest. By contrast a free rocket carries its propellant with it, burning it as it flies. It does not need a complex (and very expensive) launching device, but its accuracy in free flight is far more difficult to determine. Hence for short and medium ranges the use of multiple rockets becomes attractive, these weapons making up in blast and area coverage what they lack in individual pinpoint accuracy.

The mass destructive power of 'tube' artillery effectively ruled the land battlefield until 1918, but in the 1930s developments in rocket technology opened up the prospect once again of using the relatively simple unguided rocket, which did not need an expensive, heavy and inflexible gun to launch it, as the means to bring down firepower at ranges equivalent to tube artillery and with comparable accuracy. In the early years of World War II the German army deployed a wide range of light spin-stabilized artillery rockets fired from so-called *Nebelwerfer*, or smoke projectors. When these weapons were first used on the Eastern Front in 1941 and a year later in North Africa, the nerve shattering sound such rockets made in flight combined with their blast effects to produce a devastating effect on the morale of the troops against whom they were used, but they remained comparatively inaccurate. Another application of these German artillery rockets was a half-track vehicle adapted to fire six 32-cm (12.6-in) rockets from crate launchers on their sides. In service this arrangement proved very successful and was known as the *Stuka zu Fuss* or 'ground Stuka'. These rockets were spin-stabilized and engineered to a comparatively high standard.

The Soviet army, in contrast, had chosen to develop much simpler fin-stabilized artillery rockets nicknamed 'Katyusha' which, mounted in and fired from launchers on the backs of trucks, could bring down a devastating concentration of firepower within a very

An Iraqi rocket battery fires a salvo from a truck-mounted Soviet BM-21 122-mm multiple rocket launcher. Pre-registered fire by such batteries has inflicted horrendous losses on the attacking Iranian infantry in the Gulf war.

BM-21 122-mm MRL

Above: Soviet divisional artillery regiments include an 18-strong battalion of BM-21s, and some first-line motor rifle regiments have six launchers attached.

Crew: 6
Combat weight: 11.5 tonnes
No. of tubes: 40
Rocket weight: 77 kg
Range: 21 km

Below: The SS-60 fires a 300-mm calibre missile up to 60 km and is the largest of the Avibras modular MRLs which Brazil is exporting. All based on the same Tectran 10-tonne truck chassis, options available include 32×127 mm, 16×180 mm or 4×300 mm rockets.

short time and which were very tactically flexible. Truck-mounted multiple rocket batteries could be driven into position, fired and driven out again far more quickly than an artillery battery could be brought into action. So effective did Soviet Katyusha batteries prove on the Eastern Front that the Waffen-SS began production of their own direct copies of the weapon which they had nicknamed 'Stalin's Organ' and which the German infantry had learned to fear.

During and after World War II the Soviet army became the world leader in multiple rocket-launchers, and has kept MRLs in constant development since 1941. The USSR has supplied these weapons to all its client states. MRLs fit Soviet tactics and weapons design philosophy well: they are cheap and easy to mass produce, are light and highly mobile, and can bring down a mass of firepower with high shock value in an opening salvo, although the rate of fire is slow (10 minutes for a full reload). Although the Soviets see MRLs primarily as offensive weapons because of their reload time, they can be used in pre-planned defensive operations as well as for counterbattery attacks on rival systems and for the disruption of enemy offensive operations. They are thought to be of particular importance in plans for chemical warfare, being capable of bringing down with great rapidity a deadly concentration of blood agents, for example.

Avibras have developed a series of light single-stage, solid propellant missiles fired from multiple mounts either on their own two-wheel trailer or from the back of a truck. The SBAT-70 fires 36 70-mm rockets; the SBAT-127 fires 12 modified air-to-surface missiles. The earlier FGT-108 has been used in action by Iraq in the Gulf war.

LARS II 110-mm MRL

Left: The West German LARS system has recently been upgraded, with new fire control systems. All 36 rockets can be fired in 17.5 seconds.

Crew: 3
Combat weight: 17.5 tonnes
Chassis: MAN 7-tonne truck
No. of tubes: 36
Maximum range: 14 km

Type 70 130-mm MRL

Crew: 6
Combat weight: 13.4 tonnes
No. of tubes: 19
Rocket weight: 33 kg
Warhead weight: 14.7 kg
Range: 10 km

Right: China is replacing copies of Soviet rocket launchers with her own models, armoured divisions receiving the Type 70 mounted on the YW531 tracked APC chassis.

D-3000 80-mm smoke rocket launcher

Left: The 1.5 m long smoke rocket fitted to Walid APCs in a 12-round box has also been mounted in quadruple launchers on the side of the turrets of T-62 tanks.

No. of tubes: 12
Chassis: Walid 4×4 wheeled APC
Duration of 12-round smokescreen: 15 minutes
Length of smokescreen: 1000 m

BM-27 220-mm MRL

Crew: 6
Combat weight: 22.75 tonnes
No. of tubes: 16
Rocket weight: 360 kg
Warhead weight: unknown
Range: 40 km

Right: The latest Soviet MRL, the BM-27, has been exported to Syria for combat tests against the Israelis, and is as capable a weapon as the US MLRS but much cheaper.

Multiple Rocket-Launchers

From the Soviet BM-13 wartime MRL, several generations have been developed, the most significant of which are the BM-24 and the currently operational BM-21. The Israelis captured large numbers of BM-24s from the Egyptians in the 1967 fighting and keep the launchers operational, but now firing an indigenously-developed rocket. BM-21s were used in Angola, in the fighting in the Horn of Africa, in the Tanzania-Uganda war and in Chad. In all those cases the MRL's morale-shaking sound and fury contributed to its effectiveness. US troops in Vietnam became used to the sound of incoming BM-21s adapted by the Viet Cong for single-round launches and stood their ground, but the same ear-bruising sound has sent hastily trained troops scurrying in the various African conflicts in which MRLs have been used.

The relative cheapness and simplicity of MRLs, the factors which have made them effective in low-intensity warfare, also mean that many countries have been able to develop their own home-grown systems or adapt Soviet models. Countries which have developed their own MRLs include Argentina, Brazil, the People's Republic of China, Czechoslovakia, Egypt, France, Italy, Japan, Poland, Spain, Switzerland, West Germany and Yugoslavia.

The Argentines have deployed a 105-mm (4.13-in) MRL called SLAM-Pampero and are reported to be working on 40-tube 127-mm (5-in) system carried by a tracked armoured vehicle. Brazil has developed five different MRL systems including the 300-mm (11.8-in) SS-60 rocket carried on an ASTROS (Artillery Saturation Rocket System) quadruple launcher fitted to a tracked vehicle, and the 300-mm X-40 carried on a triple launcher and having a range of 68 km (42.25 miles). The 19-tube 140-mm (5.51-in) truck-mounted MRL used by the Chinese People's Liberation Army is very close to Soviet prototypes. The Czech RM-70 system consists of a Soviet 40-round BM-21 installation mounted on an eight-wheel Tatra truck, while the Egyptians have developed 80- and 120-mm (3.15- and 4.72-in) truck-mounted MRLs again derived from Soviet prototypes.

It is interesting that the Chinese have followed Western practice and mounted their 130-mm MRL on tracks, whereas the Soviets still use 6×6 lorries, as they have done since introducing the weapon in 1941.

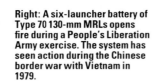

Right: A six-launcher battery of Type 70 130-mm MRLs opens fire during a People's Liberation Army exercise. The system has seen action during the Chinese border war with Vietnam in 1979.

Below: The South African Valkiri MRL is mounted on the highly mobile Samil truck chassis. Entering service in 1981, it has been used in Namibia against SWAPO and in Angola during South African cross-border operations.

The French 30-tube Rafale system, mounted on a Berliet truck, carries anti-armour and anti-personnel submunitions with a range up to 30 km (18.6 miles), while the West German LARS (Light Artillery Rocket System) is also truck-mounted, firing 36 110-mm (4.33-in) rockets up to 14 km (8.7 miles).

The Italian manufacturer SNIA BPD has developed two rocket systems for application on a range of light vehicles, trucks and AFVs: these are the 51-mm (2-in)

Above: This Chinese 12-round 107-mm MRL has been used in Afghanistan by the *mujahideen* guerrillas on its wheeled carriage. The Chinese also mount it on a 4×4 truck, which carries the crew and 12 reloads.

FIROS 6 and 122-mm (4.8-in) FIROS 25 field rocket systems, with 48 and 40 tubes respectively. The Japanese Ground Self-Defence Force has used a 30-round 130-mm (11.8-in) MRL mounted on a light tank chassis since 1975. The Spanish Teruel MRL system is mounted on a 6×6 truck and comprises two 20-round stacks of 140-mm (5.51-in) launch tubes; reload time is five minutes and range more than 18 km (11.2 miles). Israeli Military Industries has developed advanced multiple-launch rocket systems in 160-mm (6.3-in) and 290-mm (11.42-in) calibres. The bigger system has been mounted on Sherman and Centurion tank chassis, and the range of this formidable weapon is estimated to be around 25 km (15.5 miles).

The South African Armscor Company has developed a particularly interesting 127-mm (5-in) artillery multiple rocket system supposedly with Israeli and Taiwanese technical collusion, these countries having deployed very similar systems. Called the Valkiri, the system has been designed for maximum simplicity, lightness and mobility. It consists of a self-contained pack that can be mounted on the back of a four-wheel-drive light truck to fire 24 rockets. The rockets are maximized for anti-personnel operations with 3,500 steel balls cast in epoxy resin surrounding the burster charge, which is activated by a proximity fuse. Lethal area is quoted at 1500 m^2 (1,795 sq yards), and reload time as 10 minutes.

The US Army developed MRLs on a small scale during World War II largely for use in clearing minefields. A device called 'Calliope', in which 90 114-mm (4.5-in) rockets were mounted in a multi-barrel launcher on the turret of a Sherman tank, saw limited service in Europe after D-Day. Some British tank crews also improvised launch rails welded onto tank turrets to fire unguided aircraft rockets. After the war the US Army concentrated on developing longer-range artillery rockets such as the unguided but nuclear-capable Honest John and the later Lance guided missile, and on progressive upgrades and development of its nuclear-capable field artillery. But, by the early 1970s the lack of an effective MRL was felt to be an ever more glaring omission and development of a General Support Rocket System was begun. In 1979 the UK, France and West Germany signed a memorandum of understanding to adopt the system (now renamed the Multiple Launch Rocket System or MLRS) as NATO standard, and Italy joined in 1982. The

Yugoslavia is breaking away from its reliance on Soviet designs and is producing some excellent military equipment, ranging from precision weapons like sniper rifles to this 128-mm MRL.

Vought company was selected as the prime contractor against Boeing in 1980. The MLRS represents a key component of NATO's modernization programme and will be a highly significant system well into the next century. As such it deserves a close-up look.

Mounted on a tracked Self-Propelled Launcher Loader (SPLL) derived from the chassis of the M2 Bradley infantry fighting vehicle, the MLRS can fire up to 12 227-mm (8.94-in) rockets to ranges beyond 30 km (18.64 miles). The use of a tracked high-mobility chassis means that the MLRS can keep up with and support fast-moving armoured spearheads.

Precision guidance

The 4-m (13.12-ft) rockets are unguided, but that does not mean the system is not in the forefront of battlefield technology. Precision guidance begins with the launch platform itself: the launcher box trains and elevates on the bed of the SPLL under the control of the gunner who has a computerized fire-control system which can communicate with the Battery Computer System (BCS) or Tacfire battlefield fire-control systems and perform all the necessary ballistic computations, the re-aiming of rockets during ripple fire and loading and unloading operations. Two remote fire-control units allow operations to be carried out with the crew outside the vehicle, while a new position-determining system gives the battery its own inertial guidance, telling it exactly where it is at any position without the need for surveying. The master fire-control panel has a 256-character alphanumeric display which communicates with the operator in plain language rather than code, or indeed in foreign languages, giving simple next-move prompts.

The free-flight rockets are thus highly accurate but equally are designed to spread their destructive effects over a wide area. The first operational systems are designed to carry M77 submunitions, each of which has destructive power greater than a hand grenade with a shaped charge enabling it to penetrate light armour. A full load of 12 rockets could deliver no less than 8,000 M77s, chewing up anything inside an area of about 25000 m^2 (30,000 sq yards) in a storm of metal and high explosive.

This formidable destructive power is considered sufficient to destroy an enemy artillery battery. It could

also be used to neutralize air-defence sites and to provide a so-called 'surge' capability to supplement conventional artillery presented with too many targets. The development of guided anti-tank submunitions will enable MLRS units to engage heavy armour in follow-on formations, while West Germany is engineering its MLRS batteries to dispense scatterable anti-tank mines.

Above: A 227-mm rocket is fired from the Vought MLRS, which is being bought by the US Army, France, Italy, West Germany, and Britain. Anti-tank submunitions and anti-tank mines are under development. The US Army model will have a binary nerve-gas round.

Below: The political muscle of Western industry seems to prevent the development of a cheap but effective system in the Soviet style. The MRLS is little better than the BM-27 yet far costlier, so it will not appear in the numbers needed to realize its potential.

Anti-Tank Weapons

The lessons of the 1973 Arab-Israeli war, when wire-guided anti-tank missiles in the hands of relatively untrained Egyptian infantry handled Israeli tanks most roughly, were keenly analysed within Western and the Soviet armies. The Soviets were particularly concerned as armoured fighting vehicles (especially tanks) lay then as they do now at the very heart of their operational doctrine, and anything that threatened their predominance had to be understood and rapidly countered. Massing more tanks was judged not to be the answer, for on a breakthrough front any increased number would just present a better target for area weapons (including nuclear weapons). Developing Soviet doctrine, therefore, further emphasized the bypassing of defences (rather than frontal assault), plus speed and surprise. It was also appreciated that technical innovations such as compound armour provided a short-term answer to the threat of existing frontal-attack weapons. As a consequence of the 1973 war, therefore, Soviet artillery and anti-aircraft support were strengthened, while motor rifle battalions were integrated into tank regiments to give infantry support. Thus although for a time it looked as if the tank had been toppled from its pedestal as arbiter of offensive warfare, technological fixes have allowed the tank to remain at the heart of the Soviet army's combat power and NATO's primary front-line target.

The West once took comfort in the 'new lethality' of guided anti-tank weapons of the sort that gave the Israelis such a jolt in 1973, but now that confidence has evaporated with the fielding of 'fourth-generation' Soviet tanks such as the T-72 and T-80 with composite armour. The renewed technological thrust is aimed again at defeating the tank at the front line and, by developing so-called 'deep-strike' weapons, at engaging Soviet follow-on forces long before they reach the forward edge of the battle area.

The problem of sheer numbers is daunting. On any one breakthrough front the Soviet army could be expected to mass over 500 MBTs (Main Battle Tanks) in an operational manoeuvre group, together with as many infantry fighting vehicles plus self-propelled artillery and self-mobile SAMs and anti-aircraft artillery in support. Staged some tens of kilometres behind them would be a second and perhaps a third echelon of follow-on forces ready to drive through the burned-out first wave and maintain the momentum of the advance. These are the sort of figures which make the prospect of abandoning first use of tactical nuclear weapons so hard for NATO to embrace.

As far as NATO is concerned the answer lies in applying precision guidance to traditional and not so traditional weapon systems to increase dramatically their chances of striking and destroying their targets. As the technology-proving programmes stand today, a degree of 'smartness' is being engineered into just about everything from 20-mm cannon shells that can manoeuvre in flight, to mortar bombs, infantry-portable anti-tank missiles, tube artillery, multiple rocket-launchers, mines, and air-to-surface weapons launched by fixed-wing aircraft and helicopters.

Front-line anti-tank weapons

Infantry-operated ATGWs (Anti-Tank Guided Weapons) have come a long way since the first (and relatively crude) generation of the mid-1950s, which required outstanding soldierly skills to be effective. Now they have been evolved through two generations and have all but completely replaced 'traditional' anti-

ASU-57 Airborne Tank Destroyer

Before the development of anti-tank guided missiles, providing mobile anti-tank capability to airborne troops was difficult. The ASU-57 light tank destroyer can be dropped by parachute.

Weight: 3.35 tonnes
Performance: maximum road speed 45 km/h
Maximum range: (HVAP) 1250 m
Penetration: 140 mm at 500 m
Armament: 1×57-mm L73

Right: TOW missiles are fired from M151 jeeps. Vehicle- and helicopter-mounted TOW first saw action in 1972 when North Vietnam invaded the South. TOW scored 73 hits out of the first 89 missiles fired.

Below: Britain developed the Swingfire long-range command-guided anti-tank missile during the 1960s, putting it into service in 1969. Being wire-guided, it is immune to ECM and it is large enough to carry a heavy shaped-charge warhead to a distance of some 4000 m to stop any current tank.

tank guns firing solid shot and the recoilless weapons such as the British 120-mm (4.72-in) Wombat and US M40 106-mm (4.17-in) RCLs firing HEAT (High Explosive Anti-Tank) rounds.

The efficiency of a guided anti-tank missile is a factor of its manoeuvrability, rate of fire, guidance system and penetrating power. This last is almost always based on a shaped charge or HEAT warhead, which replaces the kinetic energy of the high-velocity, solid-shot anti-tank projectile with a jet of hot gas burning through armour plate into an AFV's interior with fatal results. The shaped-charge principle realized as weapons during World War II meant that combatants could field a new type of anti-armour weapon that did not need

(indeed, functioned better without) high impact velocity. Moreover, such weapons could be made small enough and light enough for infantry to carry short-range devices such as the British PIAT, US Bazooka and German Panzerfaust, and descendants of these light unguided LAWs (Light Anti-armour Weapons) are in widespread service throughout the world (see the section on grenades and launchers). The Germans developed a larger but experimental medium-range weapon during World War II and, significantly, this X-7 Rotkäppchen (Red Riding Hood) used wire guidance, but it was not used operationally and the idea was virtually forgotten post-war until the French Nord SS.10 appeared in 1955 as the first modern ATGW.

The first-generation missiles of the mid-1950s flew comparatively slowly and needed sizeable wings to remain airborne. They were MCLOS (Manual Command to Line Of Sight) systems requiring the operator both to track the target continuously and to guide the weapon directly through trailing wires. The second-generation SACLOS (Semi-Automatic Command to Line Of Sight) systems require the operator merely to keep the target in the launcher's cross hairs while electronics do the rest, gathering the missile into the control system's line of sight and generating automatic guidance signals (sent in the form of varying voltages down two very fine wires unspooling from the missile) to bring it in line with the target.

Below: Caught dramatically by high-speed flash photography, the heavy metal penetrator of an APFSDS (Armour-Piercing Fin-Stabilized Discarding-Sabot) round races towards its target.

Right: A TOW ATGW is launched from an M2 Bradley, which carries two missiles ready to fire, plus five re-loads in the hull. TOW 2 can destroy any MBT in service, and has a maximum range of 3750 m.

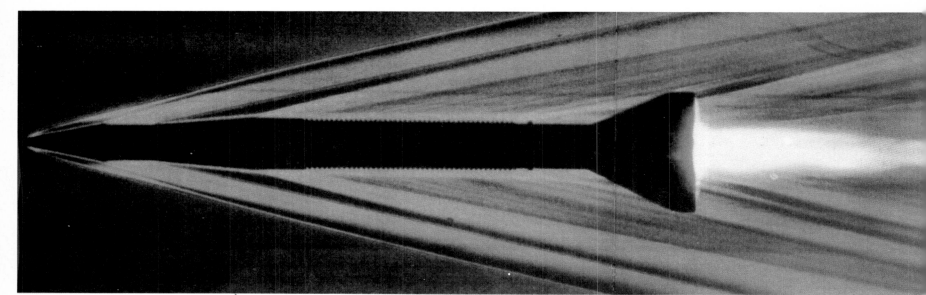

Anti-Tank Weapons

Anti-tank missiles do offer substantial advantages to the defence and have longer range than tank guns, but they have considerable drawbacks. The type has a comparatively long flight time, which can endanger the operator who must keep the target within his sights throughout the engagement; it has a much slower rate of fire than tanks or anti-tank guns and also much bulkier 'ammunition' (a missile-launching vehicle, for example, carries one-sixth the ammunition load of a tank); and, perhaps most important, the current generation will not penetrate composite armour. Thus the latest developmental thrust is towards true 'fire-and-forget' weapons by employing millimetre-wave radar and imaging IR (Infra-Red) seeker head technology and designing such weapons with the ability to make so-called 'top attacks' on enemy armoured fighting vehicles where the armour is thinnest.

The Swedish wire-guided Bofors Bill, for example, is designed to fly 1 m (3.3 ft) above the operator's line of sight so as to pass over the top of the tank, where a proximity fuse senses the target and fires a shaped-charge warhead angled downward at 30° to penetrate the top of the tank, or to reduce the effective thickness of the armour if it hits the angled front.

Both the TOW and Dragon missiles, which represent the US Army's standard current heavy and medium-range anti-tank missiles, employ SACLOS guidance, as do other important missiles in the NATO inventory such as the British Swingfire and the Franco-German HOT and Milan. Dragon in particular has not been an unqualified success in service. Training devices have not been able to convey the sense of actually firing the missile, which has been described as a 'bruising experience'. The operator is instructed to hold his breath during the missile's 12-second flight time and not to blink when the motor fires. The launcher must also be held down tightly on the shoulder lest the instinct to raise the shoulder on launch send the missile into the ground.

The original Dragon replacement programme called for fire-and-forget capability from the beginning. Several development contracts were issued in 1980 around a 'mission element needs statement' for a shoulder-fired weapon weighing under 25 kg (55 lb), operable day and night, with a 2000-m (2,185-yard) range and a warhead capable of defeating new-generation Soviet tanks with compound armour. Meanwhile a separate technology demonstration programme was launched under the guidance of the US Defense Advanced Research Projects Agency (DARPA) to prove less risky technology. While the US Army very soon cancelled the original Dragon replacement programmes because of the bulk and weight of the weapons proposed, the DARPA programme, called Tank Breaker, offered the prospect of putting a lightweight and highly effective weapon in the hands of infantry platoons by incorporating a quantum jump in technology.

The key to Tank Breaker is the seeker head, which uses a 'staring' focal-plane IR array to detect and track hot targets, rather than a mechanically-scanning IR

Above: The Dragon is a tube-launched, optically-tracked, wire-guided missile operated by one man. In service, it has not been an unqualified success: its fierce recoil and conspicuous back blast do not endear it to the troops.

Right: Soviet BMP-1 MICVs carry an AT-3 'Sagger' missile above their 73-mm gun. 'Sagger' briefly enjoyed the reputation of a 'wonder weapon' after Egyptian infantry inflicted heavy losses on clumsy Israeli tank attacks in the first days of the Yom Kippur war in 1973.

seeker. It is thus much lighter and less unwieldy than the generation of ATGWs it might replace. The focal-plane seeker allows the operator to acquire and lock onto a target in daylight, darkness or the fog of battle. Once sighted and fired, the missile's own onboard computer steers it towards the target and the operator can himself disengage immediately. Following launch for a long-range mission the missile's autopilot steers it up to a cruise height of 150 m (500 ft). When the change in line of sight to the target as viewed by the seeker becomes ever more rapid, indicating that it is getting increasingly close, the missile will dive onto the upper surface of the target.

One of the candidate systems for the original Dragon replacement was to be a laser beam-rider in which the missile followed a laser beam pointed at the target by the gunner via a rear mounted sensor, and the Israelis have in fact developed a laser-guided version of the TOW missile called MAPATS. 'Laser designation' is something else, now a mature technology based on original operational experience that came out of the air war over Vietnam. Laser designation works by directing a pencil-thin beam of laser energy from a designator, which may be installed in an aircraft, a remotely-piloted vehicle, a ground vehicle or in the hands of infantry. A target thus 'sparkled' reflects laser energy on a pulsed and coded frequency, radiating like a beacon for any weapon system which has a laser seeker in its nose. In the beginning that meant free-fall bombs of the 'Paveway' variety, allowing infantry in close contact with the enemy to call up close air support which could be delivered with precision accuracy. Today, however, the number of laser-guided weapons has grown to include powered air-to-surface munitions such as the US Maverick, helicopter-launched anti-tank missiles such as the US Hellfire and Soviet AT-6 'Spiral', and artillery shells such as the M712 Copperhead.

Deep-strike anti-armour weapons

One of the Copperhead's shortcomings in early tests was the laser seeker's inability to operate below the kind of cloud base levels obtaining for much of the time in northern Europe. However, a technique known as trajectory shaping allows the round to fly a semi-ballistic flight path under the specified 915 m (3,000 ft). A 'fly under, fly out' trajectory controlled by the projectile's own onboard computer allows for the engagement of targets beyond 8-km (5-mile) range and in bad weather where the Copperhead travels at lower altitude to provide a longer time beneath cloud ceilings. This kind of development effort shows the importance of anti-armour weapons being developed to engage tanks well behind the front line, before they have a chance to make an impact on the battle.

Cargo-carrying artillery shells have been developed in tandem, able to engage enemy forces directly by dispensing 'smart' terminally-guided submunitions, and by creating mine or area denial barriers. They can also be used to disperse autonomous reconnaissance sensors. The basic carrier shell of the US Army, ballistically compatible with other 155-mm improved conventional munitions, is the M438A1 which contains 88 miniaturized dual-purpose submunitions for anti-armour or anti-personnel wide-area attack.

A significant US development of the submunition technique is called SADARM (Sense And Destroy Armour) which allies the cargo-carrying shell concept to terminally-guided submunitions. In the initial concept for SADARM using an M509 203-mm shell as the carrier, submunitions are dispensed over the target area by time fuse, descending by parachute with a

Copperhead is fired from the barrel of a 155-mm gun towards the approximate position of enemy tanks. When the missile approaches the target area, a forward observer designates the chosen target with a laser target marker and Copperhead homes in and destroys it, as seen here in and early trial.

millimetre-wave sensor scanning a 75-mm (245-ft) radius cone beneath them. If a target is located a warhead of the SFF (Self-Forging Fragment) type is detonated attacking the thinner top armour. SFFs are a combination of the kinetic energy and HEAT warheads used in conventional anti-tank munitions: a shaped hollow charge of high explosive is used, faced by a plate of very dense material such as depleted uranium. On detonation the metal forms a ballistically-shaped slug moving at very high velocity, enough to crack open a tank's turret or engine decking from above. The technique is also used in the so-called Enhanced Sensing Munition (ESM) derived from the Avco Skeet anti-tank munition, employed in a system called IRAAM (Improved Remote Anti-Armor Mine), which has opened up the usefulness of tube artillery in being able to lay anti-armour or anti-personnel mine barriers rapidly. By packaging six IRAAMs in an M438A1 carrier shell, a 155-mm SADARM round (designated XM898) is the result. In this role the Skeet can either attack from above or fall to the ground where it waits as a mine for the target to come to it before it springs up and detonates.

While tube artillery provides a very useful delivery system for anti-armour munitions out to ranges of 30 km (18.6 miles), beyond that missiles take over as the means to hold tank formations under threat. In the late 1970s DARPA sponsored a very significant technology-proving programme called Assault Breaker, of which one component was concerned with deep target acquisition and designation, and the other with the means to attack mobile targets far beyond the front line (typically second-echelon armour). The US Air Force in 1975 had begun the WAAM (Wide Area Anti-armour Munitions) programme to improve the prospects for air attack against armour (by a factor of eight in a single pass). It also had a programme for an air-launched missile which could be launched at long range against deep targets without the carrier aircraft having to penetrate hostile airspace (the Conventional Stand-off Weapon, or CSW). The US Army meanwhile had the CSWS (Corps Support Weapon System), a surface-to-surface missile capable of delivering nuclear, anti-personnel, anti-armour, chemical and terminally-guided payloads at greater ranges and with greater accuracy than the existing Lance missile. For Assault Breaker two competing missiles were developed, Martin Marietta's T-16 based on the Patriot SAM and Vought's T-22 based on the Lance but incorporating major improvements including a solid-propellant motor and navigation via ring-laser gyros which conferred a six-fold increase in accuracy. This was demonstrated on the T-22's first flight when it impacted within 25 m (82 ft) of the aiming point after a flight of 64 km (39.8 miles). The T-16's guidance system is no less sophisticated, using stellar inertial navigation which takes a star shot in mid-course to update its computerized guidance. But these were just the delivery systems: it was what they were carrying which made the Assault Breaker programme potentially so important, namely TGSMs (Terminally-Guided SubMunitions).

Guidance systems

Terminal guidance is the system which steers a missile to its target in the last phase of its flight. In an anti-ship or long-range air-to-air missile, for example, the mid-course phase is directed by inertial guidance, a system of gyroscopes and accelerometers which keeps the missile on a preprogrammed heading. In the closing phase, the missile's own onboard system cuts in, typically a short-range radar which picks up the echo of its own emissions from the target aircraft or ship and homes on them. The simplest form of terminal guidance relies on the target's own emissions in the form of heat, and for many years IR seekers have been used in short-range surface-to-air or air-to-air missiles. Tanks on the move equally are emitters of heat, especially from the engine decking which in traditional tank design has been the least protected part of the tank's armoured carapace, the heavy armour being reserved for the frontal area to face other tanks and infantry weapons.

Two types of terminally-guided anti-tank submunitions were tested: the General Dynamics TDSM and the Avco Skeet. General Dynamics' system uses a two-colour IR seeker with special filters to screen out decoys. It is designed to be dispensed in any one of four patterns, two of which are circles of 250- or 350-m (275- or 385-yard) diameter or ellipses of 400- or 800-m (440- or 880-yards) long to attack armour in line of march. The right pattern is determined by the analysis of the target determined by a powerful down-looking air-

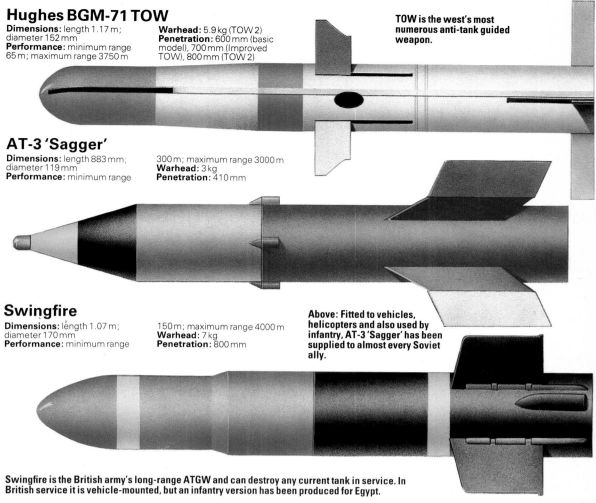

Hughes BGM-71 TOW

Dimensions: length 1.17 m; diameter 152 mm
Performance: minimum range 65 m; maximum range 3750 m

Warhead: 5.9 kg (TOW 2)
Penetration: 600 mm (basic model), 700 mm (Improved TOW), 800 mm (TOW 2)

TOW is the west's most numerous anti-tank guided weapon.

AT-3 'Sagger'

Dimensions: length 883 mm; diameter 119 mm
Performance: minimum range

300 m; maximum range 3000 m
Warhead: 3 kg
Penetration: 410 mm

Swingfire

Dimensions: length 1.07 m; diameter 170 mm
Performance: minimum range

150 m; maximum range 4000 m
Warhead: 7 kg
Penetration: 800 mm

Above: Fitted to vehicles, helicopters and also used by infantry, AT-3 'Sagger' has been supplied to almost every Soviet ally.

Swingfire is the British army's long-range ATGW and can destroy any current tank in service. In British service it is vehicle-mounted, but an infantry version has been produced for Egypt.

Skeet missiles are dropped in groups from ACM cluster bombs.

Skeet's infra-red sensor detects the tank and fires the warhead.

Travelling at 3000 m per second, the warhead strikes the tank.

borne radar designated 'Pave Mover'. As it approaches the target at a height of some 2000 m (6,560 ft), the carrier rocket performs a 'dispense maneuver' in which the outer skin panels are blasted free and the TGSMs are ejected by hydraulic plungers. Four seconds after release, each TGSM deploys its own parachute and folding wings spring out to give it lift for manoeuvring. Six seconds later the seeker activates, beginning its search for hot targets below.

The Skeet system uses a sub-submunition technique. Each Skeet Delivery Vehicle (SDV) fits into the same space as the TGSM but itself contains four 'Skeets' each weighing 2.7 kg (6 lb). The SDVs are dispensed at a height of 3000 m (9,845 ft) and deploy tail fins for stability as they descend. A parachute now deploys at 200 m (655 ft), power is supplied to the individual Skeets and their IR seekers are cooled. At 30 m (100 ft) the parachute is released and a peripheral rocket motor spins the SDV anti-clockwise at 3,000 rpm, forcing the tail fins to close up again and shooting out pairs of spinning Skeets. As the Skeets are ejected a spring-loaded arm pops up causing each Skeet to wobble, enlarging its search pattern. When a target has been detected the Skeet's 6.5-kg (14.3-kg) warhead detonates to produce an SFF, a chunk of heavy metal such as depleted uranium being turned into a streamlined projectile travelling at very high speed, and thus penetrating armour by kinetic energy with deadly effect.

The man-portable Euromissile Milan is seen mounted on the rear of a Bundeswehr Faun Kraka 4×2 light vehicle. The Milan-equipped Kraka carries six re-load missiles.

All this investment in advanced anti-armour systems has a reason. If the deep-strike weapons fail to thin out a Soviet attack to the level that can be successfully held at the front line, then NATO may be compelled to invoke the first use of nuclear weapons, of the tactical battlefield variety described in the section on heavy artillery. It is quite likely that among the first to be used might be ER (Enhanced-Radiation) or so-called neutron weapons, fired from 203-mm and 155-mm howitzers or delivered by Lance missiles and detonated above an armoured formation on the move, to attack not the vehicles but the flesh-and-blood crews inside. Such nuclear use is beset by fearsome dangers and it is a realization of this fact which has spurred the development of deep-strike 'smart' weapons, which perform the function of holding enemy armour 'at risk' and forcing them to thin out just as well as tactical nuclear weapons.

Mobile Anti-Aircraft Systems

The US Army's standard field manual states bluntly that 'No army can expect to win in battle unless its maneuver formations operate under a cohesive, extensive and mobile umbrella of air defence.' The problem is how to develop and deploy systems that are capable of providing such an interlocking umbrella of air defence (long-, short- and medium-range) and themselves be capable of operating on the battlefield, keeping up with or close behind fast-moving armoured units. The result is that many armies have developed specialized mobile air-defence systems mounted on wheeled and tracked vehicles, using SAMs (Surface-to-Air Missiles) for long- and medium-range defence and self-propelled AAA (Anti-Aircraft Artillery) for short-range and point defence.

Missiles and guns have different advantages for different applications, as do the various missile guidance techniques (semi-active radar homing, command to line of sight, heat seeking and so on). The technology of SAM guidance is considered in more detail in the section on fixed-site and man-portable SAMs.

The technology of mobile air defence as a whole has come a long way from a mere truck with an AA gun mounted on its back. Weapon platform and weapon system work together: the launch vehicle is a highly sophisticated target-acquisition system with its radar and fire control (as in the case of the controversial US Sergeant York mobile system) sometimes directly derived from an air-to-air fighter's radar, and just as sophisticated.

The Soviet army recognized long ago that ground-based air defence is an essential component of combined-arms warfare, especially on the offensive, and has built up wide-ranging operational doctrine. Specialized units and equipment give ground troops the chance to hit back or deflect the flail of tactical air power. Soviet air-defence forces are, for example, designed to 'leapfrog' each other, providing a continuously effective shield for an advancing formation, and the large numbers of tracked and high mobility air defence vehicles in service with PVO-Voisk (the air-defence troops of the Soviet army) are designed to keep up with fast-moving armoured spearheads to provide medium-range and point air defence.

In the Soviet army air-defence officers are attached to all headquarters down to regimental level. At Front and Army level there is a separate air-defence commander whose staff works alongside general headquarters

to co-ordinate the efforts of the manned interceptor aircraft of Frontal Aviation and the brigades of long-range area-defence SAMs with the point-defence efforts of manoeuvre units actually in the field.

The efforts of fixed-site and mobile point-defence SAMs and AAA are co-ordinated at divisional level. In fact fighter cover, area SAM defence and divisional mobile short-range point defence are all designed to interlock in their zones of effectiveness. The fighters of Frontal Aviation fly below an altitude of 4000 m (13,125 ft) at their peril, even over friendly airspace, because this is where the ground troops' own defence umbrella begins. In the 1973 Middle East war, for example, Israeli aircraft that got below the medium-range SA-6 missiles launched from a tracked triple launcher were roughly handled by ZSU-23-4 mobile multiple cannon. If they got above the SA-6s they were driven back into the killing zone by long-range area-defence SAMs.

Mobile SAMs

The relatively recent SA-8 'Gecko' mobile medium-range SAM, for example, is designed to fulfil part of the concept of the mobile air-defence 'umbrella', being transported and launched from a high-mobility wheeled amphibious vehicle which has its own integral radar and fire control. The SA-8 has an estimated ceiling of 6000 m (19,685 ft) and a slant range of 12 km (7.46 miles). The radar-command-guided 'Gecko' is usually deployed in batteries of four vehicles (the latest SA-8B version mounting twin triple rather than twin double launchers), each Soviet motor rifle and tank division having five such batteries forming an air-defence regiment.

SA-6 'Gainful'

The SA-6 'Gainful' SAM system, known in the Soviet army as Kub, was used for the first time by Egyptian and Syrian forces during the 1973 Yom Kippur war, and it proved highly effective in preventing the Israeli air force from providing close support during the early stages of the war.

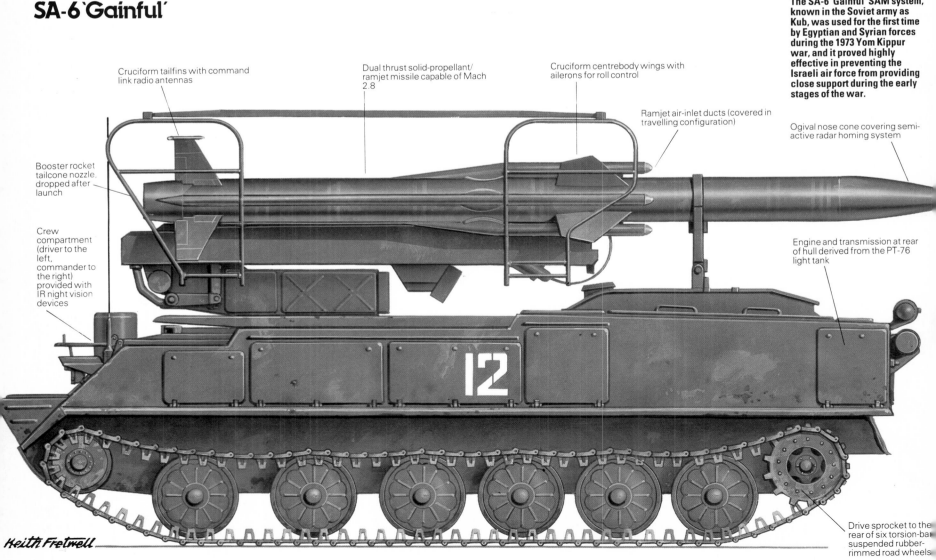

Cruciform tailfins with command link radio antennas

Dual thrust solid-propellant/ramjet missile capable of Mach 2.8

Cruciform centrebody wings with ailerons for roll control

Ramjet air-inlet ducts (covered in travelling configuration)

Ogival nose cone covering semi-active radar homing system

Booster rocket tailcone nozzle, dropped after launch

Crew compartment (driver to the left, commander to the right) provided with IR night vision devices

Engine and transmission at rear of hull derived from the PT-76 light tank

Drive sprocket to the rear of six torsion-bar suspended rubber-rimmed road wheels

Keith Fretwell

SA-8 'Gecko'

First used in combat by Syrian forces in the Lebanon in 1982, SA-8 'Gecko' is a self-contained system incorporating its own tracking and surveillance radars.

Dimensions: length 3.2 m; diameter 210 mm; span 40 mm
Launch weight: 190 kg

Performance: range 12 km; speed Mach 2

M48 Chaparral

The Chaparral SAM system is shown in travelling configuration.

Dimensions: length 2.9 m; diameter 130 mm
Launch weight: 84 kg

Performance: range 6 km; minimum engagement height 350 m; ceiling 3050 m

SA-4 'Ganef'

Known as Krug in the Soviet army, the SA-4 'Ganef' SAM launcher was developed to deal with aircraft at medium and high altitude.

Dimensions: length 8.8 m; diameter 0.9 m
Launch weight: 1800 kg
Performance: range 72 km; speed Mach 2.5; minimum engagement height 1100 m; ceiling 24000 m

Crotale

The French Crotale SAM system has been widely exported and is generally used to defend air bases and other strategic bases. The wheels of the vehicle are raised off the ground by jacks during firing.

Dimensions: length 2.89 m; diameter 150 mm
Launch weight: 850 kg

Performance: maximum range 12 km; speed Mach 2.3; ceiling 3000 m

Development of mobile air-defence systems by the Soviets has been continuous and intensive and a new generation of systems is beginning to appear in the mid-1980s to replace the generation first fielded in the late 1960s. The SA-11, given the reporting name 'Gadfly' by NATO, is reported by US intelligence to be entering service at divisional level in a quadruple mounting on a tracked launcher. Range is estimated at 28 km (17.4 miles) maximum, while targets flying at altitudes between 30 and 14000 m (100 and 45,930 ft) can be engaged. The SA-13 'Gopher' is considered to be replacement for the SA-9 'Gaskin' short-range (about 8 km/5 miles) IR-homing mobile SAM. Whereas the SA-9 is mounted on a 4×4 BRDM wheeled chassis, the SA-13 is mounted on an amphibious tracked vehicle. Range is estimated as 10 km (6.2 miles) and maximum altitude 5000 m (16,405 ft).

The SA-12 'Gladiator' missile under development is thought to be a replacement for the long-range ramjet-powered SA-4 'Ganef' deployed at Front/Army operational level, and is apparently transportable on a high-mobility vehicle with twin vertical launchers. The current SA-4 is carried in pairs on tracked launchers and was designed for high-altitude defence of forward forces although the lead SA-4 battery is never more than 30 km (18.6 km) behind the front line of troops.

Unlike the USSR with its clear-cut doctrinal adherence to air defence and rollover of one generation of systems to the next, the Western alliance has taken much longer to field effective mobile SAM and AAA systems, while at the same time the desire to protect national industries has produced a plethora of different and sometimes competing weapon systems. The Euromissile Roland medium-range SAM, for example, was developed jointly by France and West Germany, first entered operational service in 1981, and seemed set to become an important standardized weapon within NATO as the result of a big US commitment. However, after much political infighting 'US Roland' dwindled to a single light battalion of 27 fire units to operate with the Central Command (née Rapid Deployment Force). Roland serves with the French and West German armies and was used operationally by the Argentines in the Falklands fighting. The Roland employs radar command guidance to line of sight, and is designed to afford protection against medium- and low-altitude air threats including helicopters in all weathers, and its integrated fire unit and radar can be incorporated into a wide range of tactical vehicles, wheeled or tracked. The West German navy and air force deploy an eight-wheel truck launcher designated FlaRakRad Roland, the Bundeswehr uses modified

A West German army Roland SAM system is seen on a Thyssen Henschel Marder chassis with two missiles in the ready-to-launch position and eight missiles in reserve.

A Bofors RBS 70 SAM is launched from a Land Rover, just one of the many launch platforms for this versatile system. The missile is an optical beam rider.

Mobile Anti-Aircraft Systems

Marder IFV chassis, and the French army version is mounted on an AMX-30 tank chassis. The current US production configuration is mounted in a 6×6 M812A truck.

The US Army's standard forward-area short-range low-level mobile SAM system is the Chaparral, a tracked vehicle carrying a quad launcher for the Chaparral missile based on the IR homing Sidewinder AAM. The system had been continuously developed since first introduced in 1966 and now features autonomous IFF (Identification Friend or Foe) and all-weather capability by means of radar tracking and command guidance.

The British army began to receive the first of 70 production examples of the Tracked Rapier system in 1983, consisting of the British Aerospace Rapier missile mounted in two quadruple launchers on an M548 armoured load carrier which also incorporates a surveillance radar and optical tracker. A system known as TOTE (Tracked Optical Thermally Enhanced) is being introduced which gives Tracked Rapier the ability to engage targets in the dark or in bad weather with the incorporation of a thermal imager into the optical tracking system.

Other tactical mobile SAMs in current service include the Swedish RBS 70 which has been mounted in a Land Rover as well as larger tracked vehicles. The French Crotale low-altitude weapon system consists of a separate surveillance radar vehicle controlling up to three combined launch and command guidance vehicles. A typical battery takes five minutes to set up, however, and the missiles cannot be fired on the move. Improved versions of this system have been sold to Saudi Arabia as the Shahine and South Africa as the Cactus. Israel is reported to be developing an advanced self-propelled SAM system under the named ADAMS (Air Defence Advanced Missile System) with 10 vertical launch tubes on an 8×8 vehicle which also carries target-detection and tracking radars.

Self-propelled AA Guns

Multiple cannon have the advantage of sustained mass firepower for short-range use, radar-directed guns mounted in fast-slewing turrets being able to put up a wall of steel in the face of ground-attack aircraft which manage to get through the longer-range SAMs. Such SP (Self-Propelled) guns are also capable of engaging ground targets.

The Soviet ZSU-23-4 mobile multiple cannon, which first appeared in 1965, is still rated after 20 years as a formidable opponent to close air support forces. The ZSU-23-4 (known as the 'Zoo' in US Air Force pilot's slang) is a tracked vehicle with quadruple 23-

Above: One of the prototypes of the Tracked Rapier launches a missile during trials. The Royal Artillery will deploy a mix of Towed and Tracked Rapiers in the British Army of the Rhine. The first system was delivered in 1982.

Right: A Matra R.440 Crotale missile is fired from its launcher vehicle. Each battery consists of one acquisition and two or three firing units, each with four missiles ready to fire. Unusually, the vehicle itself has a diesel electric propulsion system.

mm cannon in a rotating turret, integral radar-directed fire control and the ability to engage targets at up to 2000-m (2,190-yard) slant range. The radar and guns are stabilized and can fire on the move while pouring out armour-piercing incendiary or high explosive incendiary shells at 200 rounds per barrel per minute, normally firing in bursts of 50 rounds per barrel.

Advanced optical sights, a fire-control computer and a moving target indicator make the ZSU-23-4 very accurate and able to engage fast-crossing aircraft while itself moving at speeds up to 25 km/h (15.5 mph). There are drawbacks, however: the guns have a tendency to fire inadvertently when the turret is traversing, the guns overheat, and the radar cannot cope with targets below 60 m (200 ft). Nevertheless, NATO tactical close air support doctrines have afforded the ZSU-23-4 top priority: any such vehicles should be attacked and neutralized before other armoured vehicles, either by missile-firing helicopters or by direct ground fire.

At the time the ZSU-23-4 first appeared there was no direct equivalent in Western armouries. The USA acquired the Vulcan air-defence system in 1967 with a 20-mm 'Gatling' rotary cannon on a tracked vehicle, but the original radar as fitted did not have the ZSU's search and track capabilities. The armies of Western Europe in the meantime have developed a wide range of wheeled and tracked mobile air-defence systems

mounting both radar-guided guns and SAMs, while the US Army is only now beginning to catch up after several false starts.

Sergeant York

The Sergeant York DIVADS (Divisional Air-Defense System) gun was perhaps the falsest start of all. This ambitious project to replace the Vulcan system began in the early 1970s but was finally killed off in August 1985 after problems of escalating costs and disappointing performance proved insoluble. The Sergeant York prototypes had a computerized fire-control system linked to a search and tracking radar derived from the APG-66 used in the General Dynamics F-16 fighter. Armament, mounted in a rotating turret on an M48A5 tank chassis, was twin Bofors 40-mm L/70 guns firing prefragmented proximity-fused rounds each containing 640 tungsten alloy pellets. In theory the Sergeant York's fire-control system should have been able to detect, classify and assign threat priority to multiple targets. The tracking radar automatically locked on and tracked the target while the fire-control system selected the ammunition and opened fire when the target was within range. However, in one spectacularly embarrassing test, the Sergeant York's target-acquisition radar picked up low-speed rotor blades, typical of a hostile helicopter, and opened fire; what it hit, however, was the ventilator fan on a US

Left: On the alert for intruders, the six barrels of the US M163 Vulcan cannon point menacingly skyward. Capable of firing 3,000 rounds per minute, Vulcan has been in service since the late 1960s.

Right: The competition – a column of Soviet ZSU-23-4 SP AA guns. Their radar-directed cannon are rated as significantly more effective than the Vulcan, and pose a major threat to NATO ground attack aircraft.

Left: Sergeant York was to have replaced Vulcan, but after the expenditure of vast sums of money it transpired that the tests had been rigged and the weapon was quite useless. It has since been cancelled.

Right: The M3 VDA is the AA version of the Panhard M3 APC, fitted with Oerlikon 20-mm cannon. Four stabilizers are lowered before firing, although the guns can be fired at low rate without them.

Army mobile field lavatory, which was duly blasted to pieces. The Sergeant York was also intended to provide point defence for field formations against Soviet attack helicopters. Apart from its technical failings, the system was also compromised by intelligence estimates that the latest Mil Mi-24 'Hind-E', armed with laser-guided AT-5 'Spandrel' missiles, could engage targets at ranges of 6 km (3.73 miles), well outside the Sergeant York's own effective range.

Less ambitious high-mobility AA guns now in service include the French AMX-30SA (two 30-mm cannon) and the West German Gepard Flakpanzer, which has twin 35-mm radar-controlled gun and serves with the armed forces of West Germany, Belgium, Switzerland and the Netherlands. Other systems under development or in service include the French TA20/RA20S (two 20-mm cannon), M3-VDA (two 20-mm cannon) and Sabre (two 30-mm cannon), the West German Wildcat (two 30-mm cannon), the Franco-German Dragon (two 30-mm cannon), the Israeli RAM 4×4 vehicle with twin 25-mm guns, the Italian Otomatic mounting a single radar-guided 76-mm (3-in) gun with a range of more than 6 km (3.73 miles), the Japanese AW-X (two 35-mm cannon), the Swedish Bofors Trinity (one 40-mm gun) the Swiss Oerlikon GDF-DO3 (two 35-mm cannon), and the British Marconi Marksman twin 35-mm Oerlikon turret designed for fitting as a direct replacement for the gun turret on a wide range of main battle tank chassis.

Pursuing a line of development from the original DCA turret, Thomson-CSF have developed the Sabre. This twin 30-mm system has been mounted onto various chassis including the Steyr APC, the Chieftain MBT and the Marder.

The Gepard Flakpanzer consists of a twin 35-mm Contraves turret mounted on a modified West German Leopard 1 MBT chassis. It has both tracking and surveillance radars, plus computerized fire control.

M163 Vulcan

Crew: 4
Weight: 12.3 tonnes
Performance: maximum road speed 67 km/h; maximum range 483 km
Armament: 1×20-mm six-barrel Gatling gun

Above: The M163 consists of a 20-mm cannon mounted on an M113 APC chassis. The gunner can select rates of fire of 1,000 or 3,000 rounds per minute in 10, 30, 60, or 100 round bursts.

Wildcat

Crew: 3
Weight: 18.5 tonnes
Performance: maximum speed 80 km/h; maximum range 600 km
Armament: 2×Mauser 30-mm Mk 30-F cannon

Above: Wildcat is built by Krauss-Maffei of Munich as an alternative to expensive systems like Gepard. It is available with a variety of fire-control systems.

Below: Seeing extensive use in Vietnam and the Middle East, the ZSU-23-4 was one of the most effective air defence systems of the 1970s.

ZSU-23-4

Crew: 4
Weight: 19 tonnes
Performance: maximum road speed 44 km/h; maximum range 260 km
Armament: 4×AZP-23 23-mm cannon

Surface-to-Air Missiles

The modern warplane is a formidable combat machine, but consider how much of that multi-million dollar engineering is designed to defeat a single foe: the SAM (Surface-to-Air Missile). The Panavia Tornado GR.Mk 1, entering service with the Royal Air Force for the interdictor/strike role, has variable-geometry wings and highly sophisticated terrain-following radar precisely so that it can penetrate hostile airspace by flying fast and low where hostile air-defence radars controlling SAM batteries will be unable to pick it up.

Where it might carry offensive weapons the modern warplane must now carry electronic warfare pods to jam missile guidance radar, countermeasures pods to dump flares and chaff in the face of an oncoming missile, and direct attack systems such as the radar homing ALARM missile for the self-defence 'SAM-suppression' role. The manned aircraft which must penetrate hostile airspace is now purpose-built not to battle it out with defending fighters like a World War II bomber bristling with gun turrets, but to evade hostile air-defence radars and SAMs. It must be built with this need in mind if it is to have a chance of survival because the technology of SAMs has kept pace with that of the manned aircraft; indeed some experts would say that the SAM has now outstripped the manned aircraft.

This section looks in particular at the SAMs developed for long-range application and for area defence. By their very nature such SAMs tend to be bigger, static or semi-mobile weapons integrated with fixed-site air-defence radars. These tend to be 'strategic' systems designed for the protection of national airspace. Then there are medium-range weapons such as the British Rapier system used in the Falklands fighting, the US Patriot and the Soviet SA-6 'Gainful' all of which are far more tactically mobile. Self-propelled SAMs for the protection of field forces on the move and man-portable SAMs are considered in detail in subsequent sections, although the guidance principles and basic technology of most SAM types is outlined here.

Strategic air defence

In the early days of the period after World War II, with the long-range bomber as the only delivery system for at first atomic then thermonuclear weapons, long-range high-altitude SAMs were understandably given top development priority in both the West and the USSR. Often they were designed, like the 140-km (87-mile) range US Nike Hercules and 300-km (186-mile) range Soviet SA-5 'Gammon', as nuclear-tipped weapons literally to blast formations of attacking aircraft out of the sky. The advent of ICBMs seemed to make such systems less and less relevant, and in the 1960s the UK and USA began to abandon the idea of area missile defence of the homeland. The last US Army missile defence of an American city was deactivated in 1974. The Anti-Ballistic Missile (ABM) Treaty of 1972 meanwhile drastically slowed research on very-fast-accelerating nuclear-armed missiles (such as the US Sprint) designed to intercept incoming ICBM-launched warheads as they re-entered the atmosphere. The USSR maintains a first-generation ABM system round Moscow based on the mid-1960s vintage ABM-1B 'Galosh' missile.

The USSR has also continued to emphasize the strategic defence of the homeland against 'air-breathing threats' (bombers and cruise missiles that fly with wings through the atmosphere) by missile and interceptor aircraft, however, and since 1948 a separate branch of the armed services has been entrusted with carrying it out. This force deploys no less than 12,400 missile launchers at some 1,400 launch sites with an overlapping network of 6,000 air-defence radars and four very long-range OTH-B (Over The Horizon Backscatter) radars.

The first Soviet SAM, the SA-1 'Guild', became operational in 1955 and is now found only in reserve, having been supplanted by the SA-2 'Guideline' with a slant range of 50 km (31 miles) and a ceiling of 18000 m (59,055 ft). The 'Guideline' uses radio command guidance: the target is tracked by a ground radar (named 'Fan Song' by NATO) which feeds information to a computerized fire-control system which in turn transmits guidance commands to the missile in flight. Eight strip antennae are mounted (four forward and four aft of the missile's wings) to receive these signals. The shorter-range (25 km/15.5 miles) SA-3 'Goa' was introduced in 1961 and also uses command guidance. So, like all such command-guidance missiles, it can be considered vulnerable to relatively simple electronic countermeasures designed to break or to 'spoof' the command guidance link.

Subsequent missiles such as the 70-km (43.5-mile) range SA-4 'Ganef' and the 30-km (18.6-mile) range SA-6 'Gainful' introduced in the mid-1960s incorporated terminal guidance in the shape of semi-active radar homing. This means that the missile itself carries

Mobile air defence weapons must be highly portable and tough. The BAe Dynamics Rapier system has proved itself in operation from the searing heat of Oman to the bitter cold of the Falklands.

a small radar receiver in its nose. Directed to the area of the target by ground radar and command guidance, the missile's own system takes over in the terminal phase, homing on the energy reflected by a target 'illuminated' by ground radar. The latest long-range missile for the air defence of the homeland has been allocated the reporting designation SA-10 'Grumble' in the NATO system, and possesses a reported range of 100 km (62 miles). A follow-on system, the SA-12 'Gladiator', has been identified: this has an advanced type of guidance and control system plus the ability to intercept not just supersonic aircraft, but much faster-flying intermediate-range ballistic missiles such as the US Army's Pershing II IRBM (Intermediate-Range Ballistic Missile).

Medium-range SAMs

The most important SAM in the non-Soviet arsenal is the Raytheon Hawk, first operational in 1960, licence-built around the world since then in large numbers, and providing the backbone of NATO short- and medium-range air defence. Hawk uses semi-active homing (in which a ground illuminating radar tracks the target and 'paints' it with sufficient energy to pro-

Left: The Soviet SA-2 missile has had a profound effect on air tactics since it shot down an American U-2 over the USSR in 1960. It is simple and 'soldier proof', with thick switches and large plugs.

Right: An SA-2 is launched from an Egyptian position in the Canal Zone against Israeli aircraft during the war of attrition in 1970. SA-2 has seen more combat than most other SAMs and is credited with shooting down 150 US aircraft over Vietnam.

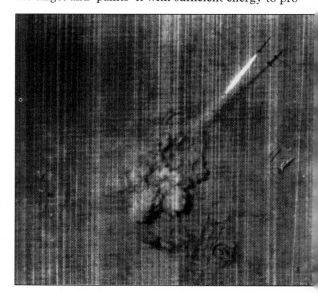

duce reflections which the radar receiver in the SAM's nose can pick up and so use as a homing source). The whole system may be overlarge, cumbersome and manpower-intensive by today's technological standards, but the Improved Hawk (operational since 1972) is still judged to be a highly effective air-defence missile. Nevertheless the new US Patriot SAM has been developed to replace the Hawk and longer-range Nike Hercules in NATO-wide applications. The Patriot reduces the Hawk's multiplicity of ground radars into one single phased-array system which provides target early warning, lock-on, missile tracking, command guidance and semi-active radar homing illumination. Flight speed is just short of Mach 4 and the missile can outmanoeuvre any aerial target.

In 1979, several NATO nations currently operational with Hawk signed a memorandum of understanding to study the most practical and economic ways in which European countries could procure Patriot. The protracted development of a system capable of handling targets at all practicable altitude and the extremely sophisticated electronics have unfortunately led to an extremely high unit cost, so many of the nations currently using Hawk are unlikely to be able to replace it with Patriot.

Britain developed two medium-to-long range SAMs in the 1950s, very similar in appearance. The Army's Thunderbird has been out of service some years now, but the Bloodhound Mk II is still operational with the RAF as Britain's only high-level unmanned air-defence system.

The only other air defence apart from manned fighters (as ever, in short supply) is the British Aerospace Dynamics Rapier. Deployed in tracked and towed form by the British Army, it also provides low-level missile cover to RAF stations. First used operationally by Iran in the Gulf war, Rapier was most thoroughly tested in the South Atlantic campaign, where it was credited with the destruction of a number of attacking aircraft. Since then it has been exported widely, and produced with a number of different guidance systems.

SA-4 'Ganef'
The SA-4 'Ganef' SAM system is used by Bulgaria, Czechoslovakia, East Germany, Poland and the USSR. It was sent to Egypt but withdrawn before the Yom Kippur war.

SA-6 'Gainful': length 6.2 m; diameter 335 mm; launch weight 550 kg; speed Mach 2.8; range 22-30 km

MIM-23B Improved Hawk: length 5.12 m; diameter 356 mm; launch weight 626 kg; range 40 km

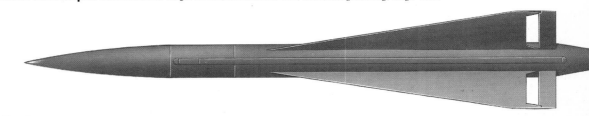

Rapier: length 2.24 m; diameter 133 mm; launch weight 42.6 kg; maximum range 6.5 km

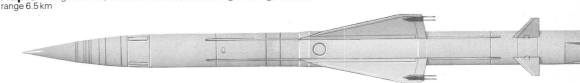

Left: This BAe Dynamics Rapier SAM system was deployed at Port Stanley during the Falklands war. The surveillance radar is under the dome marked 21C.

Above: A Patriot SAM is launched from its canister during early trials. In the US Army, this missile will replace the Hawk and has already replaced Nike Hercules.

Above: A QF-102 target drone is destroyed by a SAM. The introduction of SAM systems has profoundly altered aircraft tactics; even so, most countries except Britain back up their missiles with AA guns.

Right: Raytheon Hawk is the most widely used SAM in the west and is also built under licence in Europe. Since its introduction in 1960 it has been constantly updated to maintain its effectiveness.

Man-Portable Surface-to-Air Missiles

The infantryman crouching in his foxhole hates the ground-attack aircraft with a particular venom. However, the development in the mid-1960s of SAMs which can be fired from a simple tube launcher that a single soldier can carry into action and fire from the shoulder has given the infantryman the chance to hit back. The key technological breakthrough was the development of simple and robust IR (Infra-Red) seeker heads which gave the first generation missile a true 'fire-and-forget' capability: the target's own heat emissions (from a hot engine exhaust, for example) draw the SAM upon it and seal its own fate. If not always lethal (in the 1973 Middle East war, of some 5,000 SA-7 man-portable SAMs launched only two brought down Israeli aircraft, with four more 'possibles'), at least such weapons serve to deflect air attacks which might be made with greater precision. Moreover, the possession of such weapons boosts the morale of the ground forces under attack. For example, during the North Vietnamese conquest of South Vietnam in 1975 the presence of man-portable SAMs such as the SA-7 forced South Vietnamese pilots to abandon the low and slow attacks in which the Americans had trained them and to fly medium-altitude missions that proved ineffective. The number of aircraft shot down did not matter: the deterrent role of air defence was in the circumstances enough.

One of the most famous weapons of the modern era indeed is the Soviet SA-7 man-portable SAM, known as *Strela* (arrow) in Soviet service and given the reporting name 'Grail' in the NATO system. The SA-7 was one of the first generation of man-portable SAMs, appearing during the Vietnam war and rendering obsolete at a stroke the whole category of COIN (COunter-INsurgency) propeller-driven, low-technology aircraft designed to assist in the containment of guerrilla conflicts. Anything which acted as a heat source was vulnerable, and the IR-homing SA-7 proved particularly effective against slow propeller-driven aircraft and against most helicopters, engendering a massive development effort to produce countermeasures against this terrifyingly simple threat.

The biggest heat source on an aircraft is its exhaust, so the relatively crude SA-7 is only effective in a stern chase. This means the target must be flying away from the gunner and the missile must fly fast enough to overtake it. Only aircraft moving at speeds less than 800 km/h (497 mph) were vulnerable to the early SA-7, and it was most effective against targets moving at less than 400 km/h (249 mph), as shown in Vietnam where the type's success rate against gunship and transport helicopters was as high as 33 per cent before countermeasures were adopted.

The early SA-7's simple lead sulphide seeker head had no cryogenic cooling, meaning that it was effective only within a narrow cone of fire, and that if fired with 20° of the sun it would fly towards the greater heat source. Reportedly if the missile was fired at an elevation lower than 30° it picked up the heat of the ground and flew towards that, meaning that it could not engage very-low-flying aircraft, or even helicopters flying 'nap

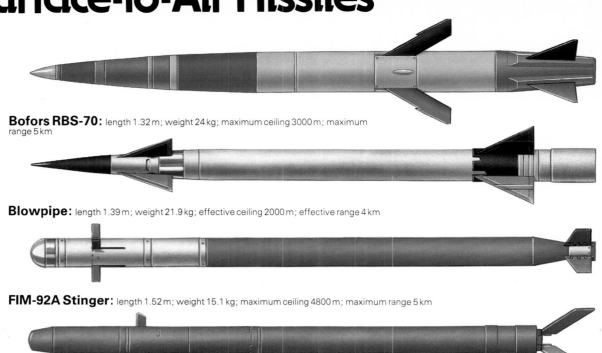

Bofors RBS-70: length 1.32 m; weight 24 kg; maximum ceiling 3000 m; maximum range 5 km

Blowpipe: length 1.39 m; weight 21.9 kg; effective ceiling 2000 m; effective range 4 km

FIM-92A Stinger: length 1.52 m; weight 15.1 kg; maximum ceiling 4800 m; maximum range 5 km

SA-7 'Grail': length 1.3 m; weight 9.2 kg; effective ceiling 1500 m; effective range 3.2 km

Below: A Stinger SAM is fired. Much more effective than Redeye or SA-7, it can hit an aircraft from any angle. Used by the SAS in the Falklands, it accounted for one Pucará ground-attack aircraft.

Right: A Royal Marine shoulders a Blowpipe SAM at San Carlos in the Falklands. Both sides used this missile during the war, several claims being made against targets such as helicopters.

of the earth' manoeuvres. The simplicity of the seeker head also made it vulnerable to simple countermeasures such as artificially modulated heat sources and decoy flares while pilots learned to fly towards the sun before breaking away, leaving a pursuing SA-7 to fly on aimlessly towards the greater heat source. The SA-7 has no IFF (Identification Friend or Foe) facility, but interestingly British and French electronics manufacturers offer add-on IFF kits for the several nonaligned armed forces that field this widely distributed weapon.

The direct equivalent of the SA-7, the US FIM-43 Redeye man-portable SAM entered service slightly earlier than its Soviet counterpart and its mode of operating is very similar: optical aiming and IR-homing, lack of automatic IFF, and limitation to stern-chase engagements against subsonic aircraft. Redeye has a range of around 3 km (1.86 miles) and serves not only with the US Army and Marine Corps but with the armies of Australia, Denmark, Sweden and West Germany. Development of an improvement over Redeye began in the mid-1960s, but the resulting Stinger missile (like the Redeye developed by General Dynamics Pomona Divisision) did not enter US Army troop service until 1981. The FIM-92A Stinger is also a passive IR homer, but its sophisticated homing head gives it a much wider aspect of engagement than Redeye (not just stern chase), filtering out of countermeasures and distracting heat sources, and inbuilt IFF.

A number of Stingers were in the hands of the British SAS during the Falklands fighting, but their performance was judged to be disappointing. One claimed an FMA 1A-58 Pucará ground-attack aircraft, but others went off in search of the largest heat source, in one case

a warship's funnel and an Argentine field kitchen in another. The standard British infantry SAM in the Falklands was the Blowpipe, unusual in a man-portable SAM in being command-guided: once the missile has been fired, the gunner directs the missile to its target by means of a thumb-operated controller and a radio link. The missile has a burning flare in its tail, and a sensor in the aiming unit finds the missile with the aid of this flare and generates commands to gather the missile to the gunner's line of sight: from then on the gunner guides the missile to its target using the controller with up/down, left/right movements. In contrast with heat seekers, therefore, Blowpipe works best in a head-on engagement. In the Falklands, however, most actions were in fact of the tail-chasing variety. The Blowpipe worked well in the hands of trained men but it required skill and determination to gain its full effect. The missile was not as robust as the soldiers thought it should have been, but it claimed eight aircraft, primarily propeller-driven and relatively slow Pucará ground-attack aircraft. In Argentine hands Blowpipe is reported to have downed several British helicopters.

A follow-on from Blowpipe has been developed under the designation Javelin, which dispenses with the thumb controller in favour of a control system which, once the missile is gathered to the tracker's line of sight, is kept on target by keeping the tracker pointing in the right direction. The Javelin has a higher-impulse rocket motor than the Blowpipe and a new blast fragmentation warhead with a proximity fuse.

Other man-portable SAMs in development or in service include the Egyptian Sakr Eye (in essence a locally-produced SA-7), the French Matra Mistral/SATCP IR-homer, the Swedish laser beam-riding RBS 70 and the US Saber laser beam-rider, a private-venture development by Ford Aerospace.

And the SA-7 is remarkably simple. One man can sight and fire the missile from the launch tube supported by his shoulder. The operator sights and tracks the target visually, pulling a trigger to switch on the missile's seeker head. When the seeker head is energized a red light comes on and the gunner points the missile towards the target, the IR detector cells in the seeker head then acquiring the target as a heat source, whereupon a green indicator light and buzzer tell the operator to fire. The first stage fires in the launch tube punching out the second stage, whose tail fins and canard control surfaces unfold as the missile moves out of blast range of the gunner, where the second-stage motor ignites to accelerate the SAM to nearly twice the speed of sound. The guidance system now tries to resolve the difference between the direction of the target heat source (as reported by the homing head) and the missile's direction of flight by activating the SAM's control surfaces. If the missile has not hit the target within 15 seconds it self-destructs.

An improved SA-7B has been developed with a more sophisticated seeker head to overcome some of these shortcomings, together with a bigger propellant charge to boost range and speed. A vehicle-mounted version of the missile has been reported as the SA-9 'Gaskin' by NATO.

Towed Anti-Aircraft Guns

In spite of the development of the surface to air missile, AAA (Anti-Aircraft Artillery) still has an important place on the battlefield. Just as there are many self-mobile AAA systems in world armies, so towed variants also exist for point defence. While in first division armies heavy AAA has all but been replaced by SAMs for long-range area defence, the rapid-firing anti-aircraft gun with radar guidance is still a formidable opponent for the pilot of a strike aircraft or attack helicopter at low altitude. And as British forces found in the Falklands, towed anti-aircraft guns can be very dangerous in the ground role. SAMs in contrast are tactically much more cumbersome and have only one purpose. It is also much easier to run out of very expensive SAMs than artillery shells.

Soviet heavy anti-aircraft guns were phased out of front-line service in the 1960s to be replaced by SAMs, but the 57-mm S-60 anti-aircraft gun is still a standard divisional weapon. S-60s are designed for point defence, deployed to protect HQs and assembly area plus vulnerable points on lines of communication. The S-60 is relatively large and vulnerable and as it is towed by trucks it is seldom employed closer than 10 km (6.2 miles) to the forward edge of the battle area, emplaced in six-gun batteries 4 or 5 km (2.5 or 3.1 miles) apart to provide interlocking coverage.

Unlike most AAA, the S-60 can come into action on the move from its wheeled carriage within five seconds of warning. Within 20 seconds it can be deployed on the ground in action. For a full battery to be in action with its generator, ranger predictor and 'Fire Can' fire-control radar all hooked up takes 25-30 minutes. Operation is automatic when the complete radar-directed fire-control system is used, the guns being trained and fired from a central control while the crews merely load ammunition.

A modern Western equivalent is the Swiss Oerlikon 35-mm GDF-002 automatic AA gun used by the Argentines in the Falklands fighting. The twin 35-mm guns are served by an automatic ammunition feed, a fully loaded container holding 56 rounds. A typical deployment is a two-gun battery (each gun having its own power supply and fire-control unit) and a Contraves Skyguard system providing radar-guided fire control. Cyclic rate of fire per barrel is 550 rounds per minute, and vertical range 4000 m (13,125 ft).

Short-range systems of 20-mm and smaller calibres are also in common use. Oerlikon 20-mm weapons are in service with many countries, while the Soviet ZPU 14.5-mm (0.57-in) series introduced in the immediate post-war period have turned up in numerous conflicts since then in quadruple, twin and single mountings. Similarly the US quadruple 12.7-mm (0.5-in) M55 'meatchopper' AA gun of World War II vintage remains in widespread service with many armies. The M55 was replaced in US Army service by the M167 20-mm Vulcan towed AA gun deployed with airborne

M167 20-mm Vulcan light AA gun

The Vulcan air defence system is used in two forms, the M163 self-propelled version and the M167 towed model, developed by General Electric from the 20-mm Gatling-type gun which was designed for the Lockheed F-104 Starfighter. Essentially a clear-weather system, the M167 is fitted with a ranging radar only.

Calibre: 20 mm
Weights: travelling 1588 kg; firing 1565 kg
Dimensions: length 4.906 m; width 1.98 m; height 2.038 m
Elevation: +80°/−5°
Traverse: 360°
Ranges: effective horizontal 2200 m; effective vertical 1200 m
Crew: 4-5 (1 on mount)

and airmobile divisions on a light wheeled carriage. The six-barrelled M167 has two rates of fire; 1,000 rounds per minute (normally used against ground targets) and 3,000 rounds per minute (for use against aircraft). The effective range in the AA role of 1200 m (3,935 ft).

Above: For many years a standard Soviet air defence weapon, until recently issued on the scale of 24 guns per division, the 57-mm S-60 is still in front-line service with 30 or more countries. This is one of the many guns which the Vietnamese deployed around Hanoi during the Vietnam War (to such effect that attacking American pilots weaving through dense columns of flak nicknamed the place 'Dodge City').

Modern experience has shown that a complementary defence of guns and missiles provides by far the most effective defence against hostile aircraft. The Swiss Skyguard system provides fire control for both ground-launched Sparrow missiles and twin 35-mm Oerlikon guns, selecting the weapon most appropriate to the specific threat.

Towed Anti-Aircraft Guns

Above: Oerlikon's 35-mm GDF system is used by over 20 countries. Recent operators include the RAF Regiment, who acquired a number of systems as a result of the Falklands conflict. In Argentine hands the Oerlikon was the most successful of the defence systems around Port Stanley, shooting down four British Harriers and Sea Harriers (in addition to two of their own aircraft).

Left: The Israeli TCM-20 light AA gun is essentially the old American M55 with its four machine-guns replaced by twin Hispano 20-mm cannon. First used during the War of Attrition of the early 1970s, the TCM-20 is produced in both towed and self-propelled versions (the latter being mounted on the back of an M3 half-tracked vehicle).

Above: The German Rheinmetall 20-mm anti-aircraft gun is fitted with the Italian Galileo P56 computing sight. The gunner uses a joystick to elevate and traverse the guns, and an analogue computer calculates the lead angles necessary to hit the target aircraft. The international industrial co-operation evident here is typical of many of the weapon systems in this field.

Below: Currently being developed by General Electric, the GEMAG25+ Air Defence System combines a 25-mm GAU-12/U gun with four or more Stinger surface-to-air missiles. The gun can fire proximity-fused anti-aircraft ammunition and armour piercing for use against ground targets. A dual feed allows immediate switching from one type of target to another.

Above: The Bofors 40-mm L/70 is one of the most widely used anti-aircraft guns in the world today. Constant development, especially in ammunition design and in fire control techniques, have enabled it to remain effective in spite of a basic design dating back some 40 years. The latest radar-directed BOFI system gives all-weather capacity even against missiles.

Above: Breda of Italy has been involved in the manufacture of light AA systems on land and at sea for many years. The 40-mm 40L70 mount is fitted with two of the famous Bofors L/70 barrels, with 444 rounds of ready ammunition. No crew is required in immediate attendance, as the guns are remotely controlled by the Dutch 'Flycatcher' fire control system.

Air Defence Radars

Most sovereign nations have some kind of ground-based radar monitoring system for watching their national airspace, often integrating civilian air traffic control with military air defence. The means to police such an operation may range from nothing at all to a huge array of interceptor aircraft and SAM sites, but nevertheless such a fixed-site 'ground environment' is not the main concern of this chapter, which looks rather at the tactical, mobile systems designed to accompany armed forces in the field and give them a degree of integrated air warning and missile fire control.

Just as land warfare comes more and more to resemble sea warfare with men travelling and fighting from within machines, just like warships, field formations on the move must take with them long-range air warning and the appropriate anti-aircraft gun and missile cover. Hence the development of tactically mobile air-defence radars which are either mounted complete on a wheeled or tracked chassis, or are light and small enough to be quickly emplaced on an unprepared site. The Soviet army, for example, has a long established and extremely effective army air-defence command and thus a highly developed range of tactically mobile air-defence radars, each one normally associated with a particular SAM system. 'Long Track' is the NATO reporting name for a tactical surveillance radar used as early warning for SAMs, usually the long-range SA-4 'Ganef', though the tracked chassis-mounted 'Long Track' has also been identified with the SA-6 'Gainful' and SA-8 'Gecko'. After making a long-range interception, 'Long Track' might feed the target data to a type of shorter-range radar, one in this case reporting name 'Pat Hand' also mounted on a tracked chassis. 'Pat Hand' then acquires and tracks the target, so providing command signals to guide the SA-4 SAM to an intercept. Other mobile Soviet radars with their NATO reporting names (and associated SAM systems) are the 'Fan Song' series (SA-2 'Guideline'), 'Fire Can' anti-aircraft gun fire-control radar, 'Flat Face' (SA-3 'Goa' and SA-8 'Gecko'), 'Low Blow' (SA-3 'Goa'), 'Spoon Rest' (SA-2 'Guideline'), 'Straight Flush' (SA-6 and SA-11 fire control) and 'Two Spot' aircraft recovery radar.

There are many equivalent systems in NATO. The US Army's TSQ-73 air-defence missile control and co-ordination system is a truck-mounted command and control system for Nike Hercules, HAWK and improved HAWK SAMs: it provides long-range air warning and individual battery control, and the system is in service with the many countries that operate the HAWK system. The new-generation Patriot SAM is serviced by the Raytheon-developed MPQ-53 guidance radar. The antenna is a phased-array planar type carried on a semi-trailer chassis with separate arrays for target detection, missile guidance and IFF (Identification Friend or Foe) functions.

Another important lightweight tactical air-defence radar in service with the US and 20 other armed forces is the Westinghouse-developed TPS-43E. This is palletized for ease of air or road shipment on two M35 trucks and when erected consists of an equipment shelter and rotating antenna assembly. In action it can provide three-dimensional air cover out to 300 km (186 miles), and it was a radar of this type in Argentine service that was the target of raids by RAF Vulcan bombers on Port

Stanley airfield during the Falklands campaign. On one mission on the night of 2 June 1982 a Vulcan armed with Shrike radar-homing missiles tried to entice the radar operators to switch on. Only a partial lock-on was achieved and the missile was reported as missing the target by 30 m (100 ft): it knocked over the antenna array but the radar was operational again in under an hour. The Stanley radar was later captured intact by British troops and brought back to the UK.

There are many air-defence radars manufactured in Europe. Significant self-mobile or palletized systems include the French truck-mounted RAMSA low-altitude system, the Picador mobile 3D radar, the West German Siemens DR 172 and the Telefunken TRMS which is mounted on an eight wheel MAN truck, the Italian Alerter low-altitude surveillance radar mounted

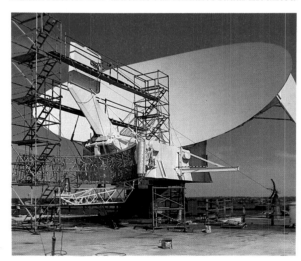

A Soviet built SA-2 'Guideline' is launched near Cairo during a live fire air defence exercise. The 'Fan Song' track-while-scan radar can detect targets out to a range of 150 km (93 miles). Command guidance is transmitted via the dish antenna at the right.

on a tracked chassis, the Swedish Giraffe search radar, and the British Marconi Martello and Plessey AR-3D air-defence radars. Several of these systems (including the Giraffe, Alerter and TRMS) are designed for the detection of low-altitude threats such as attack helicopters. They are thus mounted on folding or telescopic arms which raise the antenna above treetop height as required.

Below left: Marconi Type 85 high powered static radars are typical of the kind of radars that form part of a national defence network. Characteristics of these systems have never been released, even though the UK Air Defence Ground Environment (UKADGE) is undergoing a wide ranging improvement.

Below: The Swedish Ericsson Giraffe search radar was developed for use with the RBS-70 guided missile system, but can also be used in conjunction with light AA guns. From the control cabin, operators can transmit target information to batteries up to 5 km away.

Close range air defence has always been of importance on the modern battlefield. The Franco-German Roland missile system utilizes a French pulse-Doppler scanning radar rotating once per second, and on the German Marder chassis a separate tracking radar between the missile tubes directs the missiles onto target.

Above: The Elta EL/M-2106 point defence alert radar is designed to give the Israeli armed forces early warning capability at temporary airfields, anti-aircraft sites and in forward battlefield locations.

Right: The nerve-centre of the United States Aerospace Defense Command (NORAD) is the massive underground complex deep within Cheyenne Mountain in Wyoming.

Pistols

The idea of a hand-held firearm which could fire several shots without reloading goes back to the 17th century, but it was the development of percussion ammunition with self-contained cartridges from the 1830s that really set the designers free of the clumsy multi-barrel and 'pepper box' designs that had previously been the only solution to the problem. In 1835 Samuel Colt took out an English patent for a revolving cylinder handgun with six chambers. A ratchet with six teeth was cut into the head of the cylinder. As the firer pulled back the hammer a pawl pushed the cylinder round a sixth of a revolution, bringing the next chamber into line to fire. This was a 'single-action' design, requiring the firer to cock the hammer by hand between shots, a pull on the trigger then releasing the hammer to swing forward by its compressed spring.

The double-action pistol developed soon afterwards enables the firer to cock the hammer and rotate the cylinder and then to release the hammer as a result of a single action (a long trigger pull). The revolver was developed further through the 19th century to attain total technical maturity long before World War I. Such pistols were simple, rugged and reliable, and large numbers were used in both world wars. Many wartime revolvers remain in service and US arms manufacturers such as Colt and Smith & Wesson still make them though police forces are now the main customers.

In military service the self-loading pistol has all but completely supplanted the revolver. A self-loading weapon effects its operating cycle using energy derived from the powder charge as a cartridge is discharged. That cycle involves moving the support (locking) from the discharged case in the chamber, extracting that case and ejecting it, storing energy by compressing a return spring, feeding a new round into the chamber and supporting it there. The actual firing is carried out by the operator squeezing the trigger. The trigger must be released then pulled again for each round fired, making such weapons in effect 'semi-automatic' although there are some machine pistol designs such as the Soviet Stechkin which will fire continuously on one sustained trigger pull.

Like revolvers in the 1830s, the semi-automatic pistol became technically possible in the 1890s because of developments in ammunition. These were the jacketed bullet firmly crimped into a brass cartridge case (a case strong enought to stand powder pressure and the stress of extraction) and propellants that would burn rapidly and completely on firing. The Steyr company produced a pioneering self-loader for Austrian cavalry use in 1890 which was charger loaded from the top like a magazine rifle. The Borchardt of 1893, which established the principle of putting the magazine inside the handgrip, was developed by Georg Luger into the famous Luger toggle action weapon so closely identified with the German armed forces and still in production (largely for collectors) by Mauser 80 years later.

Right: The Browning High-Power is one of the world's most widely used pistols, in service with more than 50 countries. Its 13-round magazine capacity gives it a bulky butt grip which does not detract from the overall handiness of the gun.

Above: Automatic pistols have been used by the military for nearly 100 years, and despite the vast number of designs certain classics remain in service. The Browning High-Power seen here was introduced over 50 years ago and is still a first-class weapon.

The Browning High-Power is the chosen hand gun of the SAS, and was carried as a side-arm by the team which stormed the Iranian Embassy in 1980. Close combat demands a gun which is utterly reliable, as a single malfunction can be fatal.

Colt Model 1911

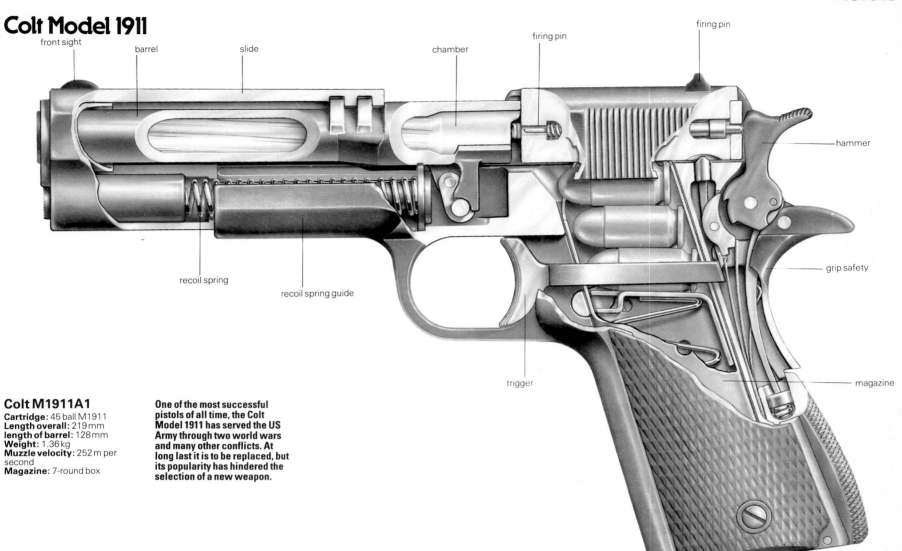

front sight
barrel
slide
chamber
firing pin
firing pin
hammer
recoil spring
recoil spring guide
grip safety
trigger
magazine

Colt M1911A1

Cartridge: 45 ball M1911
Length overall: 219mm
length of barrel: 128mm
Weight: 1.36 kg
Muzzle velocity: 252m per second
Magazine: 7-round box

One of the most successful pistols of all time, the Colt Model 1911 has served the US Army through two world wars and many other conflicts. At long last it is to be replaced, but its popularity has hindered the selection of a new weapon.

Beretta Model 92

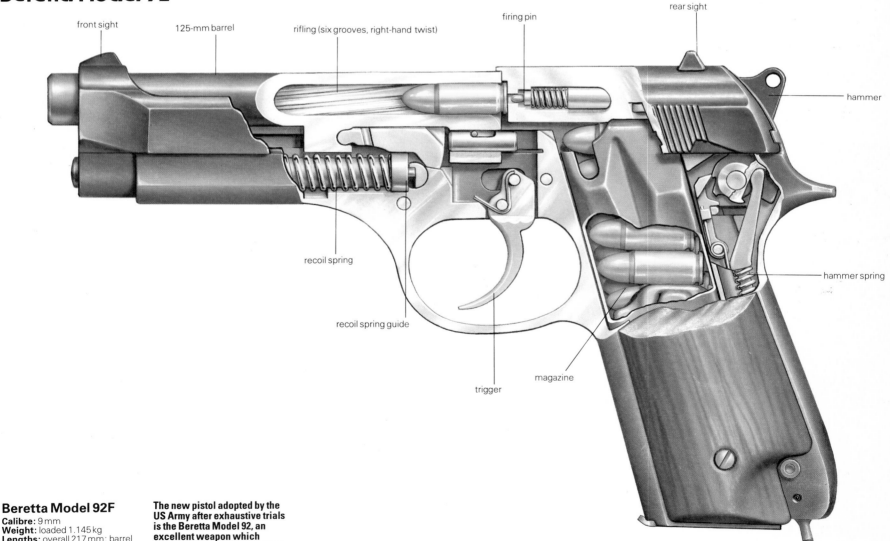

front sight
125-mm barrel
rifling (six grooves, right-hand twist)
firing pin
rear sight
hammer
recoil spring
recoil spring guide
hammer spring
trigger
magazine

Beretta Model 92F

Calibre: 9 mm
Weight: loaded 1.145 kg
Lengths: overall 217mm; barrel 125mm
Muzzle velocity: about 390m per second
Magazine capacity: 15 rounds

The new pistol adopted by the US Army after exhaustive trials is the Beretta Model 92, an excellent weapon which managed to overcome the 'Not Invented Here' syndrome to win a contract worth over $50 million.

Pistols

The first semi-automatic to the design of John Moses Browning was made by the Belgian Fabrique Nationale (FN) in 1899, the sire of a long line of Browning pistols including the standard US Army sidearm the M1911A1 and the Model 1935 or Browning Hi-Power used in large numbers by both sides in World War II and one of the most successful of all automatic pistols. The 0.45-in calibre Browning-designed M1911 (and its M1911A1 variant) manufactured by Colt has been in continuous service for 75 years and is one of the most widespread pistols in the world. The pistol weighs 1.36 kg (3 lb) with a full seven-round magazine, has a muzzle velocity of 253 m (830 ft) per second and an effective range of 50 m (55 yards). In 1984 the Italian Beretta 92F was selected to replace the long-serving M1911A1 as the US Army's standard sidearm.

A survey of automatic pistols in contemporary military service (if not production) would include the Argentine 0.45-in Balester Molina; the Belgian FN Browning designs including the M1910 and the Hi-Power, which is in production and used by over 50 armed forces; the Chinese 7.62-mm Type 54; the Czech Brno vz 52; the French 9-mm MAS and MAB, and the Manurhin-built Walther designs; the German Walther PP, PPK and P5, and the Heckler und Koch HK4 and P9; the Italian Beretta Models 81, 84 and 92; the Polish P-64; the Spanish 9-mm Super Star; the Swiss SIG and SIG-Sauer Pistole 75 and Combat Pistol P225, which arms the Swiss police and West German border police; the Soviet 7.62-mm Tokarev TT-33 and the 9-mm Makarov PM; the US Colt M1911A1; and the Yugoslav ZCZ M57 and M70.

The self-loading pistol is more complex than the revolver (any misfire requiring hand operation to clear) and the trigger action is less smooth. The revolver is bulky, it takes time to reload the chambers generally limited to six, and produces a lower muzzle velocity and volume of fire than an automatic. But the revolver needs no applied safety, it has no misfire problems, and its single-action firing produces a smooth trigger action which enhances accuracy. It is easier to train personnel effectively on revolvers than on automatics. For all these reasons the revolver tends to be very much a police weapon and the automatic a military or para-military one. In the USA, for example, a wide range of both sorts of weapon is available, the military using the M1911A1 self-loader and over 99 per cent of police forces using revolvers.

Above left: The German service pistol of World War II, the Walther P 38 is still in production, military models now being designated P1. The only real change from the original design has been the substitution of a lighter frame for the all-steel one of the pre-war version. It is used today by the West German army as well as by Chile and Portugal.

Above right: Of rugged and simple construction, the Heckler & Koch P7 (PSP) self-loading pistol has been adopted as standard by the West German army, although it was originally designed as a police pistol. The prominent grip safety prevents accidental firing if the gun is dropped, and also functions as a cocking handle for one-handed operation.

Above: A small and notably slim pistol, the 5.45-mm PSM is currently being introduced to the internal security forces of the Soviet Union and other Warsaw Pact nations.

Right: Weapons fitted with a suppressor are in high demand for clandestine operations. This Walther P4 was among a batch intercepted by British Customs on its way to Libya.

Above: This dramatic photograph records a successful hostage rescue mounted by a police SWAT team in California. This squad attacked under cover of tear gas, some officers dealing with the kidnapper while others rushed the captives to safety. Revolvers are often preferred by police departments because of their greater safety and reliability.

Right: The weapon made famous by Clint Eastwood in the 'Dirty Harry' movies, the Smith and Wesson .44 Magnum. At the beginning of this century many armies were equipped with exceptionally powerful, man-stopping hand guns, but whether today's renewed civilian interest will lead to their re-adoption remains open to doubt.

Sub-Machine Guns

The SMG (sub-machine gun) appeared during World War I, devised as a means of restoring to attacking infantry the portable offensive firepower they had lost in the mire of trench warfare. The Bergmann MP18 with its characteristic drum magazine was issued in small numbers to the assault troops that spearheaded the last great German offensive on the Western Front in 1918. Italian troops used the Fiat Revelli in the last months of fighting, but this twin-barrel weapon had such a high rate of fire that it exhausted its magazines within two seconds.

In the USA during 1916 General John Thompson began developing a hand-held automatic weapon to be a 'trench broom' to sweep Allied armies to victory, but it never reached the front line and after several prototypes, it eventually appeared as the Thompson Model 1921, precursor of perhaps the most famous sub-machine gun series of all time. While the weapon's murderous reputation was made by Prohibition gang warfare, the US government bought a small number of Thompsons for the US Marine Corps in 1928 and for the US Cavalry. While the US Army otherwise ignored the weapon, in 1940 the British army ordered large quantities of the M1928. This weapon was complex and expensive to manufacture and from 1941 a simplified version, the M1, was mass produced and widely employed by the Allied armies. Many Thompsons survived the war but their numbers have declined due to lack of spares. Most survivors are the M1 model which used a vertical box magazine rather than the 50-round drum.

Famous designer

The Bergmann MP18 *Maschinenpistole* was designed by Hugo Schmeisser, whose name became much more famous 20 years later when German armies equipped with the 9-mm MP38 burst upon Europe. Attributed to Schmeisser, but actually built by Erma-Werke, the MP38 was a great improvement on any previous SMG with its all metal construction and folding buttstock, but was still costly to manufacture. In 1940 the design was revised and standardized as the MP40.

Rivals to the 'Schmeisser' as the most famous SMGs of World War II are the British Sten, the Soviet PPSh-41 and US M3 'Grease Gun'. Four million Stens were manufactured in several marks but all with the common features of simplicity, a 32-round box magazine, sights fixed for 100 m (109 yards) and a simple selector button for single shot or automatic fire. The simplicity and ruggedness of the Sten was matched by that of the Soviet 7.62-mm PPSh-41 designed by Georgii Shpagin and later PPS-43 SMGs manufactured in enormous quantities up to 1945 and still turning up in conflicts all over the world. The US M3 and M3A1 in 1943-5 were not made in such large quantities and were withdrawn from US Army service in 1957, never having really won the affection of the US infantryman. Nevertheless the M3 was a straightforward gun to shoot and handled as well as any other wartime gun of the same type. It was unusual in having a very slow rate of fire which allowed the firer to control and aim the gun during bursts and it had a muzzle velocity low enough to allow a single shot to be squeezed off without drastically disturbing the aim.

These wartime weapons represented the high tide of the sub-machine gun, over 20 million were manufac-

Left: Seen here being fired by one of South Africa's many black soldiers, the Israeli UZI is one of the most widely-used SMGs in service. With stock extended it will shoot with reasonable accuracy at up to 200 m although it won its reputation at much closer ranges.

Above: Members of the SAS regiment armed with Heckler & Koch MP5 sub-machine guns storm the Iranian Embassy in London during 1980. In a matter of seconds, four terrorists were shot dead, one captured and the hostages freed.

Right: The Swedish Carl Gustav sub-machine gun has been in production for over 40 years, and has seen action in the Middle East with the Egyptian army and in Vietnam, where it was used by US Special Forces.

Above: Spent brass tumbles from an Israeli UZI sub-machine gun, one of the most successful post-war SMGs. First used in combat during the 1956 Arab-Israeli war, the UZI soon won an enviable reputation for reliability even in the worst conditions. Uziel Gal's original design was wooden-stocked, with an action based upon pre-war Czech models. It has since been produced in a smaller form, the Mini-UZI being suitable for commando and security purposes, and is now used by the secret service bodyguards of the President of the United States.

Below: The Ingram SMGs – (top) the Model 11 chambered for 9-mm Parabellum; (bottom) the Model 12, which fires .45 ACP. With its incredible rate of fire and small size, the Ingram is carried by Special Forces like the Special Boat Squadron and the US Navy SEALs.

Right: The excellent Beretta Model 12S combines the elegance of Italian gun design with the performance of a top-class SMG. It is a remarkably steady weapon, even when firing on full automatic, and is designed to cope with tough conditions.

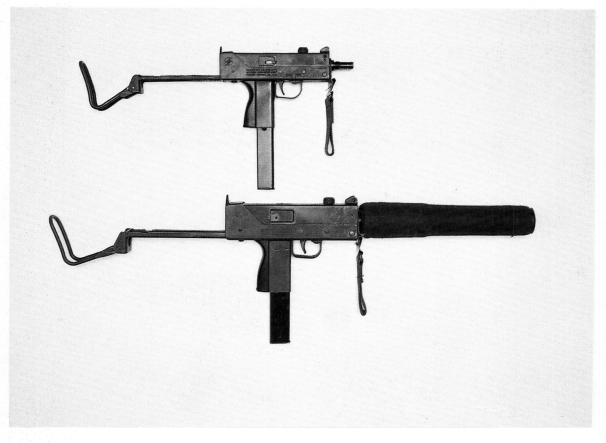

Sub-Machine Guns

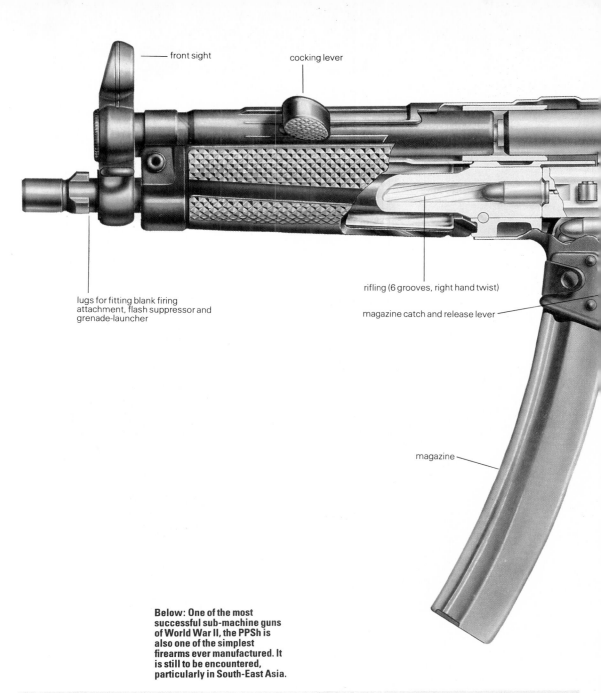

front sight

cocking lever

rifling (6 grooves, right hand twist)

magazine catch and release lever

magazine

lugs for fitting blank firing
attachment, flash suppressor and
grenade-launcher

tured during the period. Sub-machine guns of the post-war generation concentrated on lowering the cost of manufacture and reducing the size and weight but, because of the limitations of their ammunition characteristics, there has been little improvement in performance since 1940. Thus as a front-line instrument the SMG is in decline, replaced in the infantryman's hands by the lightweight high-velocity assault rifle which affords greatly improved performance and battlefield effectiveness for much the same weight.

However, the short range of the SMG means that the type will continue in manufacture and service for police operations if not on the battlefield itself. And for many guerrilla and low-technology armies the sub-machine gun remains attractive for its low initial cost and ease of maintenance. Ease of manufacture means that many undeveloped countries can build their own SMGs: in addition to the traditional arms manufacturing industrialized countries, Brazil, Burma, Egypt, Indonesia, Mexico, Portugal, Taiwan, Vietnam and Zimbabwe build weapons of near indigenous design.

Significant contemporary SMGs include the Argentine PA3-DM firing the 9-mm Parabellum round, the Austrian 9-mm Steyr-Daimler-Puch MPi 69, the British 9-mm Sterling L2A3 which has been in service since the early 1950s and exported to over 90 countries, the West German 9-mm Walther MPk/MPL used by the federal police and by various South Americna armed forces, and the West German 9-mm Heckler und Koch MP5 also widely used by police forces and border guards. A special shortened version of this last weapon, known as the MP5k (*kurz*) has been produced for special police and anti-terrorist squads. The weapon is 325 mm (12.8 in) long, and designed for carriage in a coat pocket or the glove box of a car. The Israeli UZI designed by Major Uziel Gal is another popular police weapon measuring, with the metal stock folded, 470 mm (18.5 in). The US Ingram is an even more compact weapon, 267 mm (10.5 in) long without a stock, not much bigger in fact than a Luger pistol. The various Ingram models fire cyclic at over 1,000 rounds per minute from 16- or 32-round magazines, and are in service with the police and special forces of several countries including the UK, Israel and the USA.

Below: One of the most successful sub-machine guns of World War II, the PPSh is also one of the simplest firearms ever manufactured. It is still to be encountered, particularly in South-East Asia.

Left: The men of the Italian parachute brigade are mainly equipped with the Beretta BM 59 rifle, but the Beretta Model 12S is better suited to close-range work. The 12S is designed to operate in harsh environments, having grooves along the sides of the receiver which catch debris entering the gun.

Right: The Heckler & Koch MP5 is now produced in six versions; the MP5A2 is fitted with a fixed plastic stock. After 1978 the MP5 was fitted with a curved magazine to improve cartridge feed.

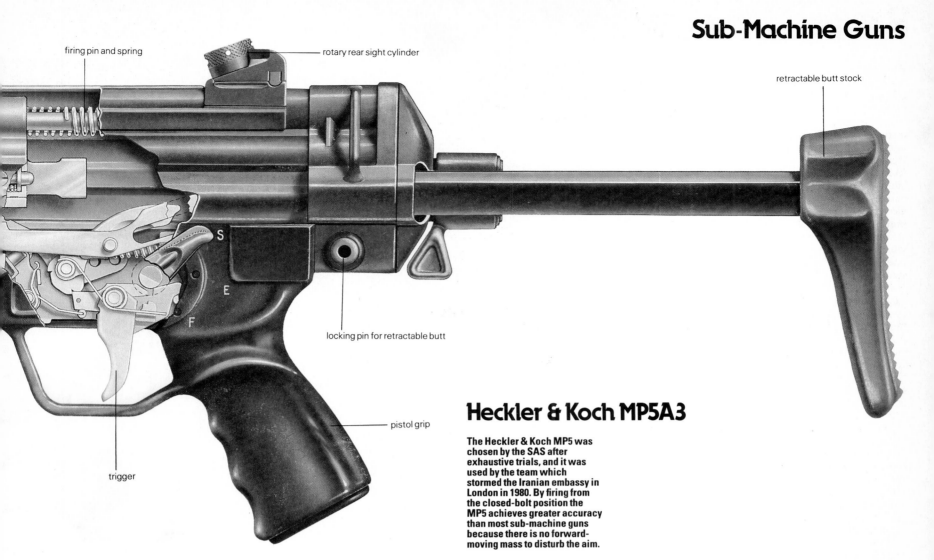

firing pin and spring

rotary rear sight cylinder

retractable butt stock

locking pin for retractable butt

pistol grip

trigger

Heckler & Koch MP5A3

The Heckler & Koch MP5 was chosen by the SAS after exhaustive trials, and it was used by the team which stormed the Iranian embassy in London in 1980. By firing from the closed-bolt position the MP5 achieves greater accuracy than most sub-machine guns because there is no forward-moving mass to disturb the aim.

Sub-machine guns have a rival in military service in the shape of the automatic carbine. This is the AKSU, a cut-down AK-74, the Soviet equivalent to the American CAR 15.

The Polish wz 63 (PM 63) is a handy machine pistol with a flip-down forward pistol grip and an extending stock, and carrying either a 25- or 40-round magazine. It fits nicely into a diplomatic bag.

Replacing the Owen sub-machine gun, the F1 retains the uniquely Australian feature of a vertical top-loading magazine. It is otherwise very similar to the Sterling.

Seen here fitted with a suppressor and with its stock fully extended, the Czech Skorpion is a tiny gun, easy to conceal and a favourite terrorist murder weapon.

Rifles

Through the first half of the 20th century, with its great all consuming wars and massive leaps in military technology, one key weapon system remained virtually unchanged, its technology static and mature. This was the infantryman's rifle, which after sweeping changes between 1870 and 1900 settled down world-wide to be the characteristic bolt-action magazine weapon firing a powerful round of roughly 7.92-mm (0.315-in) calibre. This remained so until the end of World War II when the self-loading rifle (SLAR) began to supplant the vast number of bolt-action weapons already churned out in the two wars. The US Army was holding trials of SLRs as early as 1929 and eventually 10 years later adopted a design by John C. Garand which used propellant gases bled off from the barrel to operate the reloading cycle in place of the manual sequence of the bolt-action rifle. Standardized as the M1, the 0.3-in (7.62-mm) Garand was highly successful, over five million being manufactured between 1939 and 1959, its only drawback compared with later SLRs being the fact that the magazine holds only eight rounds and has to be reloaded with a full clip each time.

By 1960 the new pattern had been established, with first-division armies equipped with self-loading supplied from magazines holding at least 20 rounds. The rounds fired were less powerful than those of the bolt-action rifles, but still effective out to a range of 800 m (880 yards). Both NATO and Warsaw Pact armed forces managed largely to standardize equipment, Western armies largely on the Belgian FN FAL (manufactured in many other countries and in service with over 90), the West German Heckler und Koch G3 and the US M14, this last weapon being the first rifle in the US Army to use the standard NATO round.

Other significant SLRs developed in the post-war period were the Czech 7.62-mm vz 58, the French 7.5-mm (0.295-in) modèle 49/56, the Italian Beretta 70, the Spanish CETME Modelo 58 and the most famous of all, the Soviet 'Kalashnikov'. The assault rifle designed by Mikhail Kalashnikov in 1947, has become one of the most successful and widespread of weapons in history, and was also standardized to 7.62-mm calibre. Warsaw Pact ammunition tended to be shorter in length (firing a heavier and slower bullet in comparison with Western weapons) so the AK-47's bolt and its movement were more compact, in turn leading to more easily handled weapons.

While the old bolt-action rifles were virtually indestructible, the precision-engineered SLRs, with their greater number of moving parts and high rates of fire wear out faster, and after over a quarter of a century's service in some cases were approaching block obsolescence. Something else was happening meantime to force a quickening of the technological pace: the infantryman of the 1960s and 1970s was no longer marching to war on foot but riding to battle in helicopters and mechanized infantry combat vehicles, where space and weight were at a premium. Studies showed that action was rarely joined at ranges beyond 300 m (330 yards) where the high-powered, long-ranged (and by implication heavy) weapon was an unnecessary luxury. The infantryman was becoming personally loaded down wih other equipment such as radios and night-vision devices, and in the jungles of Vietnam in particular, the US infantryman was undergoing a test of fire.

While the 7.62-mm M14 was standardized in the US

The old and the new in action in Manila as rebel troops storm a TV station during the last days of the Marcos regime; the man in the foreground has a CAR-15 with an M203 grenade launcher attached, and the man behind him is firing an M14. Note the spent shell case ejecting.

Army in 1957 as the successor to the M1 Garand, the Infantry Board was already investigating the possibilities of the revolutionary weapon designed by Eugene Stoner of Armalite Inc. in the mid-1950s. The army was looking for a weapon to lighten the infantryman's load and set a specification for a weapon with the lethality and penetrating power of the M1 but weighing no more than 2.7 kg (6 lb). Armalite's experimental AR-15 used a completely new 5.56-mm (0.219-in) cartridge firing a bullet at very high velocity (1000 m/ 3,208 ft per second) but at an impulse low enough to

make a sustained automatic fire controllable, which it was not in the M1. The smaller cartridge and bullet also had the advantage of allowing a box magazine to hold 45 rounds.

After trials at the Aberdeen Proving Ground in 1959, the M16 was adopted by the US Army and Air Force, and volume production began in 1961. To meet the needs of the Vietnam War production was increased and manufacturing licences given to General Motors and Harrington & Richardson. The weapon has also been licence-built in South Korea, the Philippines and Singapore.

A US soldier in Vietnam armed with an M16. This rifle gained a bad reputation at first because an unannounced change in the propellant fouled the mechanism and caused jams.

Below: Spanish soldiers are seen equipped with the last production model of the CETME rifle, designed by part of the Mauser team which fled to Spain after 1945.

Above: The British army is still equipped with its version of the FN FAL, the L1A1, which is modified to prevent fully automatic fire. It has been a popular weapon in service and will not be fully replaced for many years.

Below: The M16A1 can be distinguished from the original M16 by the prominent bolt-closure device above the pistol grip. This was added after combat experience in Vietnam revealed the difficulty of closing the bolt after debris had entered the weapon.

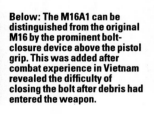

Above: (from top to bottom) A British L1A1 rifle, a Belgian FN FAL with shortened barrel and an Argentine FN FAL Para (with folding stock), captured in the Falklands.

Left: Iraqi infantry are seen armed with a mixture of folding- and wooden-stock AK-47s begin a counter attack against the Iranians in the Gulf War. This interminable war is a proving ground for the weapons of many different countries.

Rifles

Troops in Vietnam were originally told that the M16 was self-cleaning. After many instances of cartridges failing to eject and bolts proving unlockable, a high-level enquiry found that an unannounced change in propellant was producing excessive carbonization and fouling the mechanism after sustained fire on automatic (as was common practice in Vietnam). Chromium plating of the chamber, modifying the buffer to cut down the rate of fire and issuing a cleaning kit solved the problem and the rifle (standardized as the M16A1 by the US Army) subsequently proved as reliable as any counterpart. From 1982 a modified version with new rearsight, heavier barrel, one in thirty-two rifling and revised flash suppressor was standardized on the M16A2. A shortened version of the M16 with cut down barrel and telescopic butt was produced for US Special Forces as the Colt Commando.

The German Heckler und Koch company also produced a weapon in 5.56-mm calibre, the HK 33 with selective single-shot or automatic fire and a 20- or 40-round box magazine. The high-velocity rifle was a scaled-down version of the Heckler und Koch G3, the 7.62-mm SLR adopted by the West German army as its standard weapon in 1959 and subsequently by armed and police forces in over 50 countries. Both weapons use the delayed-blowback principle to power the operating cycle, recoil rather than propellant gases being used to unlock the bolt, eject the spent cartridge, load a fresh round and lock the bolt in an automated sequence.

Home-grown winner

After the 1967 Middle Eastern war the Israeli army was looking for a new rifle and tested the HK 33 against various others including the M16 and AK-47. The winner was a home-grown product, the 5.56-mm Galil designed as a complete weapon system filling the roles of assault rifle, sub-machine gun and light machine-gun. The Galil can also project rifle and anti-personnel grenades from the shoulder, and to launch illuminating and signal grenades when held vertically with the butt on the ground. There is also a version with a shortened barrel and folding stock without bipod and carrying handle called the Galil SAR (Short Assault Rifle). The weapon owes much to the Soviet AK-47 and is considered to be its equal in ruggedness and reliability.

The AK-47 is without doubt the most successful rifle of the post-war era and over 10 million have been produced. It has been the standard rifle of the Soviet army since 1957, the weapon of all Eastern bloc countries and the favourite of communist-inspired nationalists and insurgents worldwide. The AK-47 is compact, sturdy and reliable (dirt, sand and 'soldier' proof), and remarkably accurate for such a short-barrelled weapon. Fed from a 30-round box magazine, fired by average shots in short bursts on automatic fire, it produces tighter target groupings than NATO 7.62-mm counterparts but not the 5.56-mm M16. Muzzle velocity is 710 m (2,329 ft) per second and effective range 300 m (330 yards). It has been manufactured in all the Warsaw Pact countries, North Korea and Yugoslavia, while the Chinese Type 56 is a copy of the AK-47 and the Finnish Valmet M62 and M76 are variants of it. There are numerous variations including plastic, wood and metal butts, folding stocks and folding bayonets but the easiest way to establish country of origin is to inspect the markings and determine the language of the marks on the 'single shot' and 'auto' selector on the receiver.

AK-47 assault rifle

The most successful rifle produced since World War II, the AK-47 is a tough and thoroughly reliable weapon, easy to maintain and 'soldier proof'. The AK-47 family is now produced in the Warsaw Pact countries, China, Yugoslavia, Finland and the Middle East, as well as in the USSR.

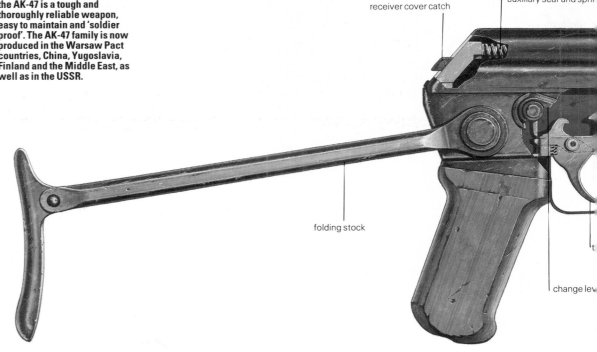

receiver cover catch

auxiliary sear and spring

folding stock

change lev

Below left: The French FA MAS 5.56-mm rifle is one of the smallest and most compact of modern assault rifles. Note the folded bipod attached.

Below: The m/62 is the Finnish development of the Soviet AK-47 and uses no wood in its construction. Its tubular butt holds the cleaning kit.

Above: A Soviet AK-74 captured by the mujahideen guerrillas in Afghanistan. It is basically an AKM modified to fire a smaller-calibre round, which has a hollow tip and its centre of gravity well to the rear. This makes it lethal but it is outlawed by international convention.

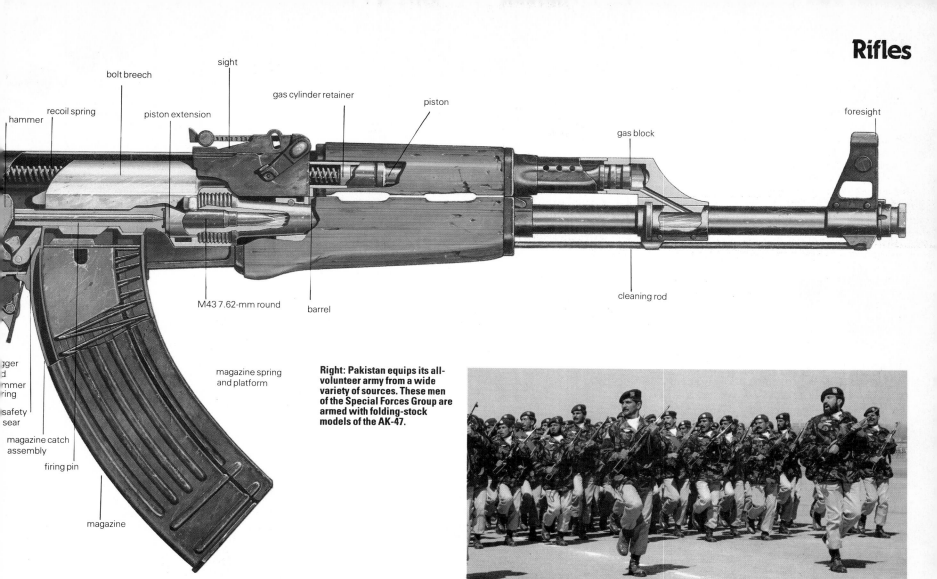

hammer
recoil spring
bolt breech
piston extension
sight
gas cylinder retainer
piston
gas block
foresight

M43 7.62-mm round
barrel
cleaning rod

trigger
hammer
spring
safety
sear
magazine catch
assembly
firing pin
magazine spring
and platform
magazine

Right: Pakistan equips its all-volunteer army from a wide variety of sources. These men of the Special Forces Group are armed with folding-stock models of the AK-47.

Above: Pictured in Ho Chi Minh City (formerly Saigon), this young Vietnamese soldier carries a folding stock AK-47. This can be distinguished from the AKM by the straight-sided muzzle and the long indentation above the magazine. (Compare it with the AKM in the centre of the right-hand photograph.)

Above (from top to bottom): The original AK-47 with folding stock; an AKM (note muzzle attachment); and a Chinese copy, the Type 56 rifle (this particular weapon having been captured from guerrillas during the Rhodesian war).

Left: Developed from the CETME rifle produced in Spain after World War II, the G3 is the service rifle of the modern West German army and has been widely exported.

Rifles

In 1959 a modernized version of the AK-47 appeared as the AKM with more pressed and fewer machined parts. The only mechanical difference is the incorporation of a rate of fire reducer. Again the AKM has travelled very widely, particularly to the Middle East, and been manufactured in the Warsaw Pact countries. A new 5.45-mm (0.215-in) calibre weapon clearly derived from the AKM appeared in 1974, another Kalashnikov design typenamed AK-74. The new weapon has been identified in use with all sorts of Soviet troops and will probably eventually replace the earlier weapons throughout the Warsaw Pact armies.

One of the results of the switch to SLRs in smaller calibres has been revival of interest in sniping (not just on a potential battlefield but in police and anti-terrorist actions) using modern versions of the old bolt-action rifles with their inherent greater range and accuracy than SLRs, but equipped with sophisticated telescopic sights and night-vision devices. Such weapons in current use include the Australian Sportco 44, the Belgian FN sniping rifle, the French FR-F1 based on the action of the old 7.5-mm Modèle 1936, the West German Mauser Model SP66 and Heckler und Koch G3 SG/1, the Swiss SIG 510-4, the Soviet Dragunov SVD, the British Enfield L42A1 and Parker Hale Model 82, and the US M21.

Just as SLRs replaced bolt-action rifles post-war, so in the 1980s a new generation of rifles is entering production based on new ammunition technology and a rethink of the basic layout. The switch to 5.56-mm calibre and the development potential of caseless ammunition has led to the adoption of the so-called 'bull-pup' configuration in several new-generation prototype weapons such as the Austrian Steyr AUG, the French FA MAS, the West German Mauser 911 and the British L85. 'Bullpup' means a rifle in which the mechanism is set back in the stock so that the receiver is in fact against the firer's shoulder making possible a weapon with a full length barrel much shorter than a conventionally-stocked weapon. The in-line design also possesses great advantages in accuracy of aim.

Below: The Yugoslavian M76 semi-automatic sniper rifle is derived from the AK-47/AKM series, and is similar to the Soviet SVD Dragunov. It is seen here fitted with a passive night sight.

Right: The new look for the British army; troops are shown on exercise with the new Enfield Individual Weapon (right) and the squad support variant (left).

Heckler & Koch G3 SG/1 sniping rifle

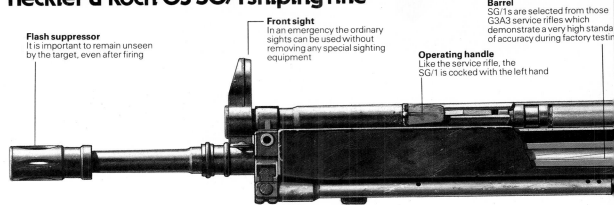

Flash suppressor
It is important to remain unseen by the target, even after firing

Front sight
In an emergency the ordinary sights can be used without removing any special sighting equipment

Barrel
SG/1s are selected from those G3A3 service rifles which demonstrate a very high standard of accuracy during factory testing

Operating handle
Like the service rifle, the SG/1 is cocked with the left hand

7.62-mm round
Like most sniper rifles, the SG/1 uses specially-selected batches of ammunition

Telescopic sight
This SG/1 is seen fitted with a Zeiss 1.5×6 sight

The G3 SG/1 is a special model of the G3 service rifle and is not a purpose-built precision weapon; these often prove too delicate for combat use.

...azine
...contains 20 rounds of ...munition

Special trigger unit
For sniping purposes, the trigger pull can be reduced to effectively give the gun a 'hair trigger'

FN Model 30-11 sniper rifle

The Belgian FN Model 30-11 rifle was originally produced for police and paramilitary use, but many are now in service with armies around the world. The odd butt shape is due to the degree of individual adjustment that can be incorporated.

Calibre: 7.62 mm
Lengths: overall 1117 mm; barrel 502 mm
Weight: rifle only 4.85 kg
Muzzle velocity: 850 m per second
Magazine capacity: 5 rounds

Enfield L42A1 sniper rifle

The L42 is a sniper version of the trusty Enfield rifle, converted to 7.62-mm calibre. It has a new heavy barrel, a 10-round box magazine and many modifications to the original model. It was used to good effect during the Falklands war.

Calibre: 7.62 mm
Lengths: overall 1181 mm; barrel 699 mm
Weight: 4.43 kg
Muzzle velocity: 838 m per second
Magazine capacity: 10 rounds

Soviet SVD sniper rifle

The Soviets have always given snipers a great deal of prominence in the field, and have always provided them with sound weapons. The Dragunov is not the equal of the most advanced Western rifles such as the Enfield L42, but is a well-balanced and soldierly weapon.

Calibre: 7.62 mm
Lengths: overall less bayonet 1225 mm; barrel 547 mm
Weight: complete, unloaded 4.385 kg
Muzzle velocity: 830 m per second
Magazine capacity: 10 rounds

Machine-Guns

The trench warfare of 1914-8 and its terrible slaughter were a direct result of the killing power of the machine-gun. Hiram Maxim's invention of 30 years earlier, a self-actuating automatic gun of rifle calibre which used the power of the propellant to effect the loading and firing sequence (fed with ammunition from a continuous belt and water cooled to be capable of sustained continuous fire) was found to be murderously effective when emplaced behind wire and protected against artillery bombardment in a deeply dug position. World War I also saw the advent of the air-cooled light machine-gun such as the Lewis, but such portable offensive firepower failed to break the trench deadlock. The tripod-mounted, water-cooled belt-fed Maxim ruled the battlefield. In World War II it was different: tanks and aircraft broke down the stalemate while the light, air-cooled generation of medium machine-guns such as the German MG 34 and MG 42 had as much hitting power in attack as defence. Today the machine-gun remains an important weapon with all world armies both as an infantry weapon and as tactical weapons mounted in wheeled and tracked vehicles. In the Falklands fighting, for example, Argentine heavy machine-guns emplaced in carefully prepared positions proved very dangerous in the defence while British 'Gimpies' (L7 series GPMGs, or General Purpose Machine Guns) were used effectively to bring down fire support at long range and to deter air attack.

The modern machine-gun owes its design basis to breakthroughs made 50 years ago to produce such effective weapons as the MG 34 and MG 42. The success and flexibility of the wartime German weapons was eagerly studied after the war, the conclusion being that such weapons were effective in defence when tripod-mounted, yet light enough to be fired from the hip in attack. Post-war NATO planners seized on the idea of 'general-purpose' machine-guns for such multi-role applications. There has been criticism of the GPMG concept in that the weapon performs neither task well, basically because it is too light for sustained support fire. Because GPMGs are air cooled they require frequent barrel changes, yet are still too heavy and too cumbersome with belt feed for use as a light gun accompanying infantry in an assault.

Examples of general-purpose machine-guns in current service with world armed forces include the Czech vz 59, the French 7.5-mm (0.295-in) Arme Automatique 52 and 7.62-mm (0.3-in) AA NF-1, the West German Heckler und Koch HK 21A1, the West German Rheinmetall MG3 closely based on the wartime MG 42, the Swiss SIG 710-3, the Soviet 7.62-mm PK series, the British L7A2 and the US M60.

Above: In the Gulf war, Iraqi machine-gun nests with interlocking fields of fire have wiped out wave after wave of fanatical Iranians in a manner horribly reminiscent of the Great War. This Iraqi is armed with a Soviet supplied RPK 7.62-mm machine-gun.

Below: The development of air-mobile warfare in Vietnam gave machine-guns a new role: here the door gunner of a UH-1B 'Huey' delivers suppressive fire while 'Razorback' overflies a Viet Cong position.

Left: One of the finest light machine-guns of all time, the Bren gun, is still in active use. The latest model is the L4, which is chambered for standard NATO 7.62-mm ammunition and is seen here mounted on a tripod by South African soldiers.

Below left: The light support weapon being adopted by the British Army shares many components with the Individual Weapon, and fires the same ammunition.

Below: Australian infantry in action in Vietnam dismount from an M113 APC. The first man out carries an Owen SMG and the second an M60 GPMG.

Below: FN have responded to the change to 5.56-mm calibre by producing the Minimi light machine-gun. This has been adopted by the US Army and is entering service.

Right: General Purpose Machine Guns are being replaced by heavy-barrel versions of small-calibre rifles. Steyr now offer this LMG version of their AUG rifle.

Machine-Guns

Left: South East Asia was inundated with American equipment following the US withdrawal from Vietnam. This North Vietnamese soldier has charge of a captured M60 machine-gun.

Above: A surprise in the cabbage patch – a paratrooper of the 82nd Airborne Division with an M60 GPMG (General Purpose Machine Gun) seen on a field exercise.

The M60 is a typical modern GPMG, designed in the late 1950s and largely based on German wartime principles. Criticism of earlier models for frequent stoppages, a clumsy barrel change procedure and poor handling were overcome by detail improvements, and the M60 is now judged to be a classic of weapon design. The M60 is gas operated: small vents inside the barrel bleed off enough gas pressure once a round is fired to force a piston backwards driving an operating rod with a sharp impulsive blow, this providing enough energy to carry out the complete cycle of unlocking the bolt, ejecting the spent round, loading the succesive round, and locking the bolt. The weapon is designed to fire at full automatic only at a cyclic rate of 550 rounds per minute, slow enough for a skilled operator to fire single shots if required.

Light machine-guns still abound in world armies, fed either from belts or from magazines charged with ammunition compatible with other squad weapons. LMGs are virtually always tended by a two-man team, the gunner and a number two who handles the ammunition, loads the gun, observes the fall of shot and protects the position with his rifle. Most LMGs weigh roughly double what a rifle of the same calibre would weigh, but with bipod mount and magazine feed are tactically more flexible than GPMGs or the older medium machine-gun. Examples still in service include the Belgian FN MAG, the Chinese drum-fed Type 53, the Czech vz 52, the Finnish Valmet M62, the German Heckler und Koch HK 11A1, the Soviet Degtyarev DP and DPM, the RP series of company machine-guns and the Kalashnikov weapon designated TPK. This last is basically an AKM assault rifle with a longer and heavier barrel plus a 40-round box or 75-round drum magazine. The weapon can also take the standard rifle magazine. With no barrel change facility its rate of fire is limited to some 80 rounds per minute. The British Bren gun, either in the original 0.303-in (7.7-mm) calibre or converted to the NATO standard 7.62-mm calibre, has been out of production for many years but is a light machine-gun still in widespread service with many armies.

M60 7.62-mm General Purpose Machine Gun

The M60's design was heavily influenced by German machine-guns encountered by US troops in World War II, but it was initially not as successful as the original German weapons, being a bulky, temperamental and unpopular gun.

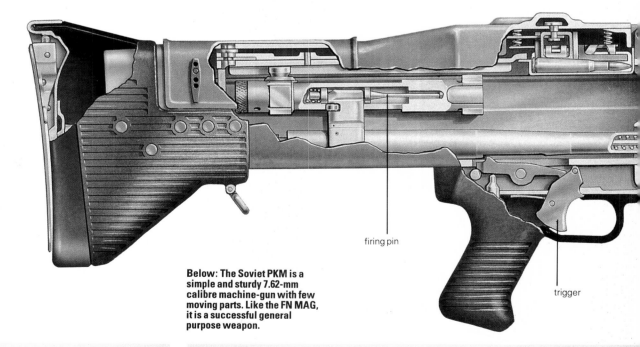

firing pin

trigger

Below: A series of modifications have made the M60 a usable machine-gun, but it remains a heavy weapon to be used as a squad support firearm.

Below: The Soviet PKM is a simple and sturdy 7.62-mm calibre machine-gun with few moving parts. Like the FN MAG, it is a successful general purpose weapon.

Right: GIs in Vietnam dubbed the M60 the 'Pig', as it was heavy and trouble-prone. A tin can was sometimes fitted underneath the ammunition feed to prevent a twisted ammunition belt misfeeding a round and jamming the gun at a critical moment.

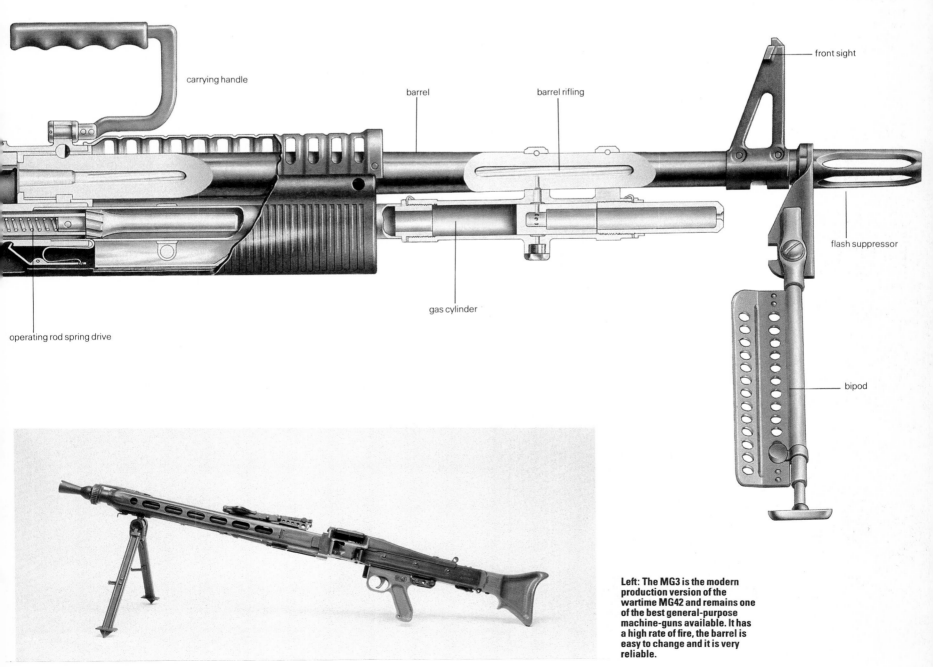

carrying handle

front sight

barrel

barrel rifling

gas cylinder

operating rod spring drive

flash suppressor

bipod

Left: The MG3 is the modern production version of the wartime MG42 and remains one of the best general-purpose machine-guns available. It has a high rate of fire, the barrel is easy to change and it is very reliable.

Machine-Guns

The M60 pumps out rounds at a rate of nearly 10 a second, providing the bulk of a rifle squad's fire power. The US Army is now replacing it with the FN Minimi so that the infantry will all be using the same ammunition.

Below: Browning machine-guns have been in service since 1917 and are no less effective today. Seen here on an M75 APC of the Belgian army, the Browning 0.50-cal machine-gun is a common and extremely potent vehicle-mounted weapon.

Heavy machine-guns are generally categorized as firing ammunition larger than standard rifle size but below 20 mm, where they become cannon. The most widespread calibre is 12.7 mm (0.5 in), and most weapons of this size are to be found mounted on tactical vehicles or on specialized anti-aircraft mounts, although the famous air-cooled 0.5-in Browning (designed in 1918) is tripod-mounted and, as the M2, is still in production and service with US forces and at least 20 other countries. The equivalent Soviet 12.7-mm Degtyarev heavy machine-gun (designed in 1938) is also in very wide service with Communist bloc forces and still turns up on the uniquely Russian 'Solokov' mount, with its characteristic spoked twin wheels.

Veteran machine-guns from World War II and even I still turn up in arms caches and guerrilla conflicts around the world, while such famous weapons as the British 0.303-in Vickers Mk 1 (declared obsolete in the British Army in 1968) are still used by some Third World armed forces. Other such veterans include the Russian and British manufactured 0.303-in Maxim known to be held in reserve by China and Finland, the Danish Madsen, the German MG 34 and MG 42, and the US 0.3-in water-cooled Browning Model 1917 and air-cooled Model 1919, this last having been adapted for vehicle mounting by many armed forces around the world.

Left: The British Army has been using Belgian-designed rifles and machine-guns for many years. The GPMG, derived from the FN MAG, is designated L7A1 and is seen here on its buffered tripod for the sustained fire role.

Above: Soviet tanks carry 12.7-mm machine-guns for anti-aircraft defence. This Soviet-built T-55 has just been captured from the Iranians by the Iraqis in the Dezful area.

Above: During the Falklands campaign the anti-aircraft defence of the British Task Force was augmented by large numbers of GPMGs on improvised AA mounts.

Below: 0.30 cal Browning M1919s are still in service with several armies, these belonging to machine-gun teams of the Mexican army, seen here deployed outside a grocery store.

Right: An M60 in sustained fire role, fitted to a tripod with its bipod legs folded up under the barrel. In the US Army an M60 is operated by a three-man gun crew.

Infantry Support Weapons

Left: US Recondos in distinctive 'Tiger Stripe' fatigues shoot M79 grenade launchers on a firing range in Vietnam where the M79 was known as the 'blooper' after a children's toy.

Right: The French MAS 49/56 rifle has a combined muzzle brake/grenade launcher which enables it to launch grenades by firing a special cartridge.

Below: Festooned with grenades and machine-gun ammunition, men of the 25th Infantry Division advance on Duc Pho, Quang Ngai province, Vietnam, in June 1967.

Grenades

The hand grenade is an ancient military invention, at least as old as gunpowder, being an explosive charge surrounded by a frangible casing (whose flying fragments do the damage) with a short fuse to give the grenadier time to light, throw and wait for the bang. Hand grenades were used in siege warfare from the 15th century onwards. They were generally spherical and likened to the pomegranate or *granada* in Spanish, hence the derivation of the word. By the 18th century grenades and companies of grenadiers were an important part of field warfare. 'Grenadiers' were selected for their size and strength necessary to hurl a 2-kg (4.4-lb) bomb 30 m (33 yards) or so into the enemy ranks and they functioned as a military elite, distinguished by their tall, rimless mitre caps.

With improvements in musketry and the demise of siege warfare grenades fell from use in the 19th century, but the first years of the 20th century saw the type's revival. The Russo-Japanese War of 1904-5 saw the emergence of trench warfare, and both sides improvised primitive weapons. But it was in the great trench siege of World War I that the hand grenade became a key weapon of modern war and weapons such as the British No. 36 'Mills Bomb' and German Stielgranat or 'potato masher' stick grenade first became familiar. Trench lines were so close that a hand-hurled grenade could get near enough to the enemy to do damage, while many improvised devices were conjured out of springs and rubber to achieve more than human muscle could manage in the way of range.

In trench raids and assaults the hand grenade could winkle out defenders with its area effect and blast where bullet or bayonet could not reach. This was also the grenade's role in World War II, dealing with troops in concrete fortifications and (particularly) in house to house fighting. Under these conditions two types of grenade evolved. The defensive type has a thick frangible casing which will explode in many deadly fragments on detonation and be effective over a wide area; the grenadier must stay under cover having thrown it. The offensive type has a thin casing designed to subdue defending troops by its blast effects while not endangering the thrower who can follow up quickly to make his attack. Further forms of specialized grenade have evolved for the smoke screen, smoke signal, anti armour and riot-control roles.

Lethal radius

Early grenades of the defensive type relied on their cast iron casing breaking up on detonation and travelling outwards at very high velocity (about 1500 m/4,921 ft per second) to create a lethal radius up to 15 m (50 ft) from the point of burst. Individual fragments might fly much farther (up to 200 m/220 yards), but their chances of hitting a target were too small to make them effective. The size of fragment was also unpredictable, but modern grenades are made of graphitic cast iron with the metallurgy carefully controlled to ensure that the casing breaks into regular-sized particles. Another technique is to use square-section notched wire wrapped round the explosive core within a thin outer case to give a preset number of fragments flying in a predictable pattern. The notched coil grenade can function both as offensive and defensive type: it guves a dense pattern of fragments at close range in defence, while the lethal area dies away quickly in attack, so that beyond 20 m (66 ft) the thrower will not be harmed by his own weapon.

The hand grenade is in essence a simple weapon but its fuse must be effective and the time delay reliable.

There are two types of fuse, time and impact. The time fuse is the most familiar: the thrower pulls a pin holding down a spring-loaded arm, holding the arm down with hand pressure. On release the arm flies up, a striker ignites a percussion cap which ignites a delay fuse taking four or five seconds to reach the main high explosive burster charge. Impact fuses are more complex to manufacture and need to strike a hard object falling in the correct trajectory to be effective.

The German Diehl M-DN 11 is a typical modern defensive type grenade. Looking like a traditional 'pineapple' grenade, the case of the M-DN 11 is in fact made of plastic, ribbed for hand grip and with 3,800 steel balls embedded in it. The delay fuse consists of a spring-activated hammer held back from hitting the primer cap by a long safety lever. When the ring is pulled the hammer springs over to hit the primer, which in turn ignites the delay pellet, the booster, then the main charge in a sequence taking 6.5 seconds. Diehl also make a dual-purpose offensive/defensive grenade, the DM 51. This consists of a high explosive hand grenade body and fuse mechanism and a separate fragmentation jacket into which it can be inserted to form a defensive grenade. The high explosive body alone will produce concussive blast, and the body plus jacket a lethal storm of 6,500 tiny steel balls. Several grenade bodies can be joined to make a cluster charge or connected end to end to form a Bangalore torpedo for obstacle demolition.

Rifle grenades and grenade-launchers

Hand throwing at best can lob a grenade 30 m (33 yards) and also limits the weight of the weapon. From the age of the smoothbore musket onwards, grenades were projected farther by using an adapting cup positioned over the musket's (and later the breech-loading rifle's) muzzle. The muzzle cup was in use until the end of the World War II, the usual technique being to aim the grenade for a high plunging trajectory like that of a mortar bomb rather than to follow the line of sight. The muzzle cup technique was replaced post-war by a new generation of weapons incorporating a hollow boom in the tail of the grenade which fitted directly over the muzzle of the rifle. Most modern assault rifles are designed for this very purpose. The propellant is usually a special cartridge filled with a powerful charge but no bullet, loaded into the same breech as a standard round and fired by the same trigger. Some grenades can be launched by standard ball cartridges, but they have to incorporate a special bullet trap and are not as effective. These modern rifle-launched grenades are specialized rather than dual-purpose weapons, though there are a few designs in which hand or rifle launching is possible.

Left: The Mk 19 automatic grenade-launcher, seen here loaded with armour-piercing grenades, can shoot at a maximum rate of 375 rpm.

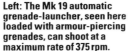

Below: Firing 30-mm HE, incendiary and flechette rounds, the AGS-17 has a high elevation, making it especially valuable in mountain warfare.

Above: A Tamil separatist guerrilla in Sri Lanka sports a US M203 grenade launcher attached to an M16 rifle. This single-shot pump action grenade-launcher is a great improvement over the M79, and in no way impedes the conventional use of the rifle. The launcher sights can be clearly seen behind the rifle foresight.

Below: The AGS-17 *Plamya* (flame) gives Soviet infantry a powerful long range area fire capability. It has proved very effective in Afghanistan.

Infantry Support Weapons

The French Luchaire company has developed a range of typical rifle grenades which can be fired using special cartridges or standard ball ammunition. Looking broadly similar externally (a cylindrical tapering body, an extended tail boom and multiple radial tail fins) the grenades come as anti-tank, anti-personnel, smoke, illuminating or practice. The anti-tank variant has a combat range of 100 m (110 yards) and can penetrate 350 mm (13.78 in) or armour plate. The anti-personnel weapon is effective over 300 m (330 yards) with a lethal radius of 15 m (50 ft), and the illuminating round produces 150,000 candlepower.

There are also weapons which can launch grenades through rifled barrels. The US has pioneered this type of weapon with the 40-mm M79 grenade-launcher, which looks like a single-barrel combat shotgun. The M79 fires grenades that are in effect small shells, the rifling giving the grenades considerable accuracy. Some practice is required to judge the range correctly as the trajectory is high, although a trained soldier can put grenades through the windows of a house at about 150 m (165 yards), but the lethal area of the comparatively small grenades is itself restricted. The bulk of the M79 means that the gunner can carry no other weapon so the US army is replacing it with the M203 40-mm grenade-launcher which fits under the barrel of an M16A1 assault rifle with its own trigger and sighting mechanism, allowing the grenadier to take part in a high-velocity firefight as well as firing grenades. The 400-m (440-yard) range M203 built by Colt first entered service in 1969, fires at the same velocity as the M79 (79 m/260 ft per second) and uses the same range of munitions, including high explosive, airbursts, anti-armour, anti-personnel and a wide range of smoke, illuminating and riot-control ammunition.

Soviet motor rifle companies are equipped with an automatic tripod-mounted grenade-launcher known as the AGS-17, firing grenades from a belt or drum. Effective range is 800 m (880 yards) firing 30-mm anti-tank or anti-personnel rounds.

Mortars

Like grenades, the mortar as a weapon goes back to the introduction of gunpowder. By definition a mortar is a simplified artillery piece, a high-trajectory weapon in which the recoil force is passed directly to the ground via a baseplate. The conventional mortar, its basic design perfected and standardized in World War I, is a smoothbore muzzle-loading weapon firing a fin-stabilized low-velocity bomb. Range is established by variation of the amount of charge and in the elevation of the barrel.

The essence of mortars is their simplicity, which tends to make them long lasting. The tiny ML 2-in (51-mm) mortar has, for example, been in continuous service with the British army from 1938 to the early 1980s, and the standard Soviet army 82-mm (3.2-in) mortar is in essence a weapon introduced in 1936.

The operational cycle is very simple: the bomb with its propellant charge in the tail is simply dropped down the tube by hand to strike a firing pin. The propellant charge detonates and the bomb is projected. The simple bomb and its ease of loading make a very high rate of fire possible and the steep angle of descent creates a nearly circular lethal area. Light and simple mortars are very mobile and flexible, can be switched very quickly from target to target, and are deadly against personnel in the open. They cannot as yet effectively engage armour or highly mobile targets, or troops under cover (although using a time airburst fuse doubles the effectiveness against dug-in troops).

A new generation of mortars may be set to change this, however. The British Merlin system under development is a 'smart' 81-mm (3.2-in) mortar bomb with an active millimetric seeker in the nose, a guidance computer and control surfaces which deploy in flight, and a top-attack anti-armour warhead. The US Army has a development requirement for a similar system called GAMP (Guided Anti-Armor Mortar Projectile) for deployment by the end of the 1980s. Range will be about 8 km (5 miles) and guidance of the IR type, with a top-attack self-forging doing the damage to enemy armoured formations. The French have followed another route in the production of a 120-mm round effective against lightly armoured vehicles within a radius of 14 m.

Large mortars have long been in use in the Soviet army, with calibres of 160 mm and 240 mm taking them into the realms of artillery.

Breech loading is a feature of several rifled mortars, in an attempt to improve accuracy (lack of precision being the mortar's major inadequacy).

M203 40-mm grenade-launcher

The M203 can be used to engage point targets up to 150 m away and against area targets at up to 350 m. Men equipped with the old M79 could only carry a pistol for self-defence, but a rifle fitted with M203 can still be fired normally.

Calibre: 40 mm
Length: 394 m
Weights: 1.36 kg (unloaded), 1.63 kg (loaded)
Trigger pull: 2.2 kg
Maximum range: 400 m
Minimum range: 30 m

Soviet M1953 160-mm mortar

The Red Army made extensive use of mortars during World War II; simple and reliable weapons, they provided front-line infantry with their own fire support. After the war the Soviets introduced two very large breech-loading mortars, this 160-mm weapon and a 240-mm mortar, although their standard service mortar remains the M1943 120-mm muzzle loader.

Calibre: 160 mm
Length: 4.56 m
Weight in action: 1300 kg
Maximum range: 8000 m

Brandt 120-mm mortar

The Brandt 120-mm mortar has a rifled barrel and is shown with a standard High Explosive bomb with a full array of propelling charges forward of the tail. The number of charges attached is proportional to the range of the target, some rounds are rocket assisted to give extra range.

Calibre: 120 mm
Length: barrel 2.08 m
Weights: mortar 582 kg; bomb (HE) 18.7 kg
Maximum range: (rocket assist) 13000 m

Above: Seen here in the capable hands of the French Foreign Legion parachutists, the Brandt 120-mm light mortar combines the firepower of a large-calibre mortar with the mobility of a light weapon.

Above right: The Finnish army relies heavily on its excellent Tampella mortars, as the terrain is mostly unsuitable for conventional artillery.

Right: Paratroopers from the 82nd Airborne Division fire a 4.2-in mortar. This weapon is usually carried in an M106 carrier, together with the crew and 88 bombs. A terminally guided 4.2-in mortar is under development, its bombs will home in on enemy tanks and attack their thin top armour.

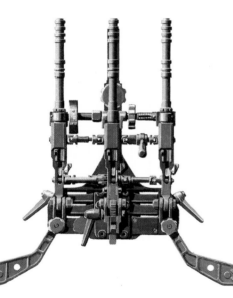

AP/AV 700 multiple grenade-launcher
The Italian AP/AV 700, shown here on its ground mounting, is an unusual weapon which fires three rifle grenades to a range of up to 700 m. It can fire either anti-personnel or armoured-piercing grenades, and can be fitted to vehicles.

Length: spigots 0.3 m
Weights: launcher 11 kg; grenade 0.93 kg; grenade warhead 0.46 kg
Maximum range: 700 m

Soltam 120-mm heavy mortar
The Soltam standard heavy 120-mm mortar is seen here in travelling position with its towing eye secured to the muzzle. The bomb illustrated is the IMI illuminating round, fitted with six propelling charges.

Calibre: 120 mm
Length: barrel 2.154 m
Weights: in action 245 kg; bomb 12.9 kg
Maximum range: 8500 m

IMI
MORTAR SHELL
120 mm
ILLUMINATING

Infantry Support Weapons

Above: A Swedish soldier carries a Lyran illuminating mortar into action. The container in his right hand holds the barrel and two illuminating bombs; the other container holds four bombs. Lyran is a simple system designed solely to fire parachute flare bombs and has been widely exported.

Above: A soldier of the US 9th Infantry Division loads a smoke round into the turntable-mounted 81-mm mortar carried in an M125. The mortar is firing smoke rounds which are being spotted by a forward observer; when he sees the smoke bursting in the target area the crew will begin firing high explosive.

The Brandt 120-mm rifled mortar in action. Note that this model rests on its baseplate and travelling wheels for firing, which not only provides extra stability but also allows the weapon to be deployed very rapidly. Despite its size, it is still muzzle-loaded by hand with bombs weighing nearly 19 kg.

Assault Weapons

The American SMAW (Shoulder-launched Multi-purpose Assault Weapon) is a derivative of the Israeli B-300 anti-tank weapon. The US Marines use SMAW as a 'bunker buster' and can be aimed using a spotter rifle under the launching tube.

The infantryman of the future will probably carry more of his support weapons with him. Rifle grenades carry only a small amount of explosive and have a limited fragmentation radius, but Brunswick Defense in the USA have produced a rocket projectile designed to fit under a service rifle such as the M16 in exactly the same fashion as the M203. The Rifleman's Assault Weapon (RAW) is a sphere, 140 mm in diameter, which produces a 'squash head' effect enabling it to demolish walls and penetrate fieldworks or even armour plate. It is launched by firing a bullet in the normal manner; some of the cartridge gas leaving the muzzle is diverted to ignite the RAW's rocket motor via an ignition cap, and the flat trajectory of the projectile gives it an effective range of about 200 m, although maximum range is well over 1000 m.

During the Falklands war it was revealed that Milan wire-guided anti-tank missiles made excellent weapons for destroying machine-gun or sniper positions. Both sides in the Vietnam War had also used their anti-tank weapons as 'bunker busters', and the potentially disastrous consequences of using up anti-tank weapons in this way had already been discovered. The US Marines have recently adopted the Shoulder-launched Multi-purpose Assault Weapon (SMAW); this is based on an Israeli 'bazooka' style anti-tank weapon, the B-300, which has too small a warhead to engage the latest generation of Main Battle Tanks with any chance of success. The shaped charge warhead of SMAW will be used to attack pillboxes and field works from a range of up to 250 m, which makes much more sense than expending guided anti-tank munitions or having to get close enough to put a grenade through a loophole.

B-300 light support weapon

The Israeli B-300 anti-armour projectile is connected to the launcher while still inside a sealed, pre-packed container. Only the part of the launcher in front of the support leg is re-usable.

Calibre: 82 mm
Lengths: loaded 1.35 m; launcher only 0.755 m
Weights: launcher unloaded 3.5 kg and loaded 8 kg; rocket container 4.5 kg; rocket 3 kg
Range: 400 m
Armour penetration: 400 mm

Rifleman's Assault Weapon (RAW)

The Brunswick RAW is mounted under the muzzle of a normal rifle, in this case an M16A1, and is launched by firing a bullet, the flash from the round igniting the RAW's rocket motor.

Projectile diameter: 140 mm
Length: overall 0.305 m
Weights: overall 2.72 kg; projectile 1.36 kg
Range: maximum 2000 m; operational 200 m

Mines

Mines are a classic weapon of defence. If they do not actually physically damage the enemy, then anti-tank and anti-personnel devices deny him ground and channel his movements to fit defensive plans. While the weapons themselves have become ever more sophisticated and deadly, the means for delivery have come a long way from squads of sappers with shovels. Minefields can now be created very rapidly by specialized vehicles or by such means as strewing from helicopters and delivery by long-range cargo-carrying artillery shells or cluster bombs.

In broad terms mines are of two types: anti-personnel and anti-tank. In addition there are signal and illuminating mines to give warning of an attack. The anti-personnel 'bounding' mine is a particularly deadly device developed during World War II. It is triggered by tripwires, a pull on which initiates the firing sequence. A propelling charge projects the mine (which may be buried just below the surface of the earth) to a height determined by a tethering cable, but generally around the heads of the unfortunate troops who triggered it. It then bursts in the air producing a spherical fragmentation pattern of metal pellets scything down anything in its lethal volume.

Another type of anti-personnel mine is the directional type. The US M18A1 Claymore, for example, is used for defence or ambush and consists of a curved moulded case of plastic with 700 steel spheres embeded in one face in front of a sheet of plastic explosive. The fragmentation face is shaped to produce a pre-set blast pattern, a fan shaped area in a 60° horizontal arc covering 50 m (55 yards) and a height of 1 m (3.3 ft). There is a danger area of 16 m (17.5 yards) behind the mine, and triggering can be via a remote electrical firing cable or by a tripwire.

Anti-tank mines are usually simple explosive devices with enough power to blow the track off an AFV, and usually activated by the direct pressure of a vehicle on top of them or by magnetic influence. Such mines are often made of plastic or other non-metallic substances to avoid detection by magnetic anomaly metal detec-

Mines have been an invaluable adjunct to the defence for hundreds of years; even if the enemy detect a minefield and do not suffer casualties from it, their movement will be channelled in a direction of the defender's choice. Towed systems like the Royal Ordnance Bar Minelayer enable mines to be planted very rapidly.

tors. For example, wooden-cased and tar-impregnated cardboard anti-tank mines of World War II vintage are still in the Soviet inventory and were widely encountered in the Vietnam war. In addition to a simple pressure plate or magnetic fusing system, many modern mines incorporate anti-handling and anti-sweeping devices to make removal that much more difficult.

There are various devices for the rapid creation of minefields. The Swedish FFV minelayer is typical of the devices mounted behind trucks or AFVs for the

simultaneous ploughing of a furrow in the ground and the sowing of anti-tank mines into it. The device can be towed behind a truck or fighting vehicle: it ploughs a trench up to 0.25 m (10 in) deep, dispensing mines

The Royal Ordnance Bar Minelayer is seen here fitted to a Centaur half-track. Bar mines are placed on the chute of the minelayer which arms the mine, buries it and replaces the soil. Six hundred mines can be laid per hour. The bar mine is made almost entirely of plastic, making it difficult to locate with a mine-detector.

Sporting the famous 'Death's Head' badge of the 17th Lancers on the door, this Centaur is fitted with the Thorn-EMI Ranger Mine system which is designed to lay small anti-personnel mines in great numbers by firing them like a multiple rocket-launcher. The 72 tubes each fire 18 mines and another 1,296 mines can be re-loaded in just six minutes.

between 3.5 and 13 m (11.5 and 42.7 ft) apart, laying up to 20 mines per minute at a speed of 7 km/h (4.3 mph). Similar systems have been developed in France (ARE, Matentin and Creusot Loire), the USSR (PMR-2 and PMZ-4 towed minelayer types), the UK (Bar Minelayer) and the USA (the M128 Ground Emplaced Mine Scattering System or GEMSS popularly known as the 'Frisbee Flinger').

Anti-personnel minefields can be created very rapidly by rapid dispersal techniques. The British Ranger system is typical: it ejects light plastic anti-personnel mines from a battery of tubes looking very much like a multiple rocket system. Mounted on a fighting vehicle, the Ranger system can 'fire' a complete minefield very rapidly in a selected pattern, the 72 tubes each holding 18 mines. Two men can reload the full 1,296 mines in under six minutes. Similar anti-personnel or anti-tank minefields can be rapidly created by helicopter laying, using systems such as the US M56 scatterable mine system or the Italian Valsella scatter dropping mine system.

The Soviets are known to practise a technique for sowing anti-tank mines down a simple chute from the rear of a low-flying Mil Mi-8 helicopter. Although the system is somewhat clumsy and vulnerable it means that a field commander can effectively protect the flanks of a mobile armoured spearhead with a rolling minefield.

The above techniques are for the rapid creation of minefields within defended territory. But for some years the USA has been developing techniques by which minefields can be created within enemy territory for purposes such as impeding the enemy's movement to the front line or interdicting the progress of follow-on forces. FASCAM is the name of a development programme for a 'family of scatterable mines' which can be delivered by aircraft bomb (known as the Gator mine), or by 155 mm artillery shells (known as the Area-Denial Artillery Munition). A battery of six 155-mm (6.1-in) guns can lay a minefield 300 by 250 m (330 by 275 yards) at a range of 17 km (10.6 miles) in just two salvoes, each shell containing nine circular M75

anti-tank mines dispersing in the terminal stages of flight.

And while all sorts of munitions are having 'smartness' (computerized precision guidance) engineered into them, mines are no exception. ERAM is a development programme for what is in effect an intelligent mine or an 'Extended-Range Anti-armour Munition'. Dispensed from aircraft, ERAM is strewn by parachute over a wide area. On impact with the ground, three probes are automatically extended and the two Avco Skeet warheads armed. When a target is detected by the probes, the computer classifies it and assesses its position, generating commands to rotate the top half of the mine to aim a warhead. This is launched at an angle of 45° away from the ground on a trajectory which will intercept the target. The Skeet's own seeker then detects the target and the Skeet is detonated above it, sending a self-forging fragment of high-velocity depleted uranium into the AFV's thin top armour. The ERAM launcher then rotates 180° preparing to launch the second Skeet at a new target.

Extended Range Anti-Armour Munition (ERAM)

Dropped by aircraft, the ERAM launcher (far right) deploys three acoustic and infra-red sensors to detect the presence of hostile armour. It launches Skeet submunitions to a point above the target vehicle where it explodes, directing a very high velocity projectile against the thin top armour of the tank. The projectile is what is known as a Self-Forging Fragment – in effect a disc of copper which the shaped charge explosion forces into a molten penetrator, effective over 15 m above the target.

Battlefield Electronics

Information technology, the alliance of computer power with telecommunications, has not only transformed warfare on land, sea and in the air, it has made the electromagnetic spectrfum itself an arena for a titanic struggle. Electronic warfare (EW) is one of the most complex and fast-changing aspects of military science, right at the cutting edge of technology.

What distinguishes modern weapon systems from the generation of World War II is the inclusion of some degree of 'smartness', of artificial intelligence or automation, in their target acquisition and guidance sequence. A modern main battle tank, for example, drips with laser designators, rangefinders, sensors and fire-control systems which all but cut out the human crew from the business of fighting, while even 20-mm cannon shells can be equipped with terminal guidance to steer them unerringly towards their target. All this smartness is designed to concentrate destructive force with the maximum efficiency in time and space while armed forces that deploy these weapons depend themselves upon a web of electronic systems to carry out the vital tasks of command, control and communications (C^3) which stitch the electronic battlefield together. Huge research and development efforts are going into systems for the computerized handling of the tactical data which all the sensors and systems generate, the sheer volume of which would swamp human operators.

Armed forces in the field use radios to transmit and receive orders and data at all levels of command. They use a mass of sensor systems (radar, IR, electro-optical and laser) to find their targets, co-ordinate firepower and guide weapons to them. Thus in battle the side which can deny the enemy the full use of the electromagnetic spectrum while defending its own electronic systems from jamming has gained a potentially decisive advantage.

Electronic warfare on the land battlefield show a different emphasis to air and sea applications where, as a rule, the main thrust is protection for warships and aircraft against radar-directed or heat-seeking threats such as surface-to-air or sea-skimming missiles. Finding targets against that most radar-baffling surface, the Earth, is much more difficult although great research efforts are being made to create autonomous deep-strike systems with terminal guidance able, for example, to find and attack tank formations far behind a recognizable front line. This branch of battlefield EW seems set to hot up dramatically with all sorts of electronic countermeasures (ECM) and electronic counter-countermeasures (ECCM) being developed for land forces just as they have been for sea and air forces.

Electronics have penetrated to the heart of the modern battlefield, with a typical surface-to-air weapon system being controlled automatically by a gunner keeping a target within his sights, computers homing the weapon via a radio or a wire guidance link.

Airborne down-looking radars, for example, are under development with moving target indicators able to distinguish troops and vehicles against a background of the Earth. But such systems could be spoofed and the system overloaded, typically by having suitably spaced soldiers with corner reflectors on their headgear running around to show up as innumerable vehicles moving from hide to hide. Terminally-guided sub-munitions could be spoofed in similar ways, by trucks masquerading as tanks, by decoys and chaff long used in air and naval warfare, by extending exhaust pipes to distance heat sources, and even by buildings and trees. In 1984 a Swedish manufacturer demonstrated a giant can of foam which would quickly turn a tank into a shapeless blob and mask its heat signature as a countermeasure against heat-seeking top-attack warheads.

For the time being, land-based EW tends to be offensive in nature, with enemy tactical communications as the prime target. The land battle commander, faced with equal or superior forces, has to get a local advantage where he can use his reserves and firepower to throw the enemy off balance. Attacking the enemy's C^3 nervous system is an essential part of gaining such a local advantage, and the Soviet army knows this as well as any other.

The Soviet army has made a speciality of ground-based EW systems aimed at compromising the West's much more technology-intensive forces. The Soviets have built 'radioelectronic combat' power throughout their armed forces and not just in specialist units, and it is judged by outside observers to be formidably effective. The EW capability allows them to intercept and analyse hostile radio and radar transmissions, to find and identify targets by radio direction-finding and electronic support measures and to jam hostile C^3 networks. Personnel are also trained how to break into enemy communications networks and spread falsified orders.

It follows that protecting communications networks is the first priority, and modern tactical radio systems have such countermeasure techniques as frequency agility (in which the frequency hops around at

Above: RITA is an automated integrated transmission network in service with France and Belgium and on order for the US Army. The system is capable of handling speech, data, telegraph and picture transmission across the whole battlefield.

Right: The AN/MLQ-T6 is a mobile, general-purpose ground-based communications and data-link jammer which is being used to test and evaluate potential future communication systems for the United States Air Force.

UPPER – UNAIDED EYE   LOWER – TAS VIEW

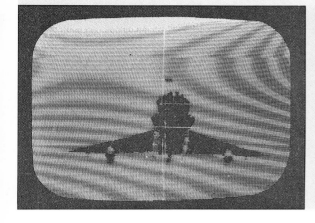  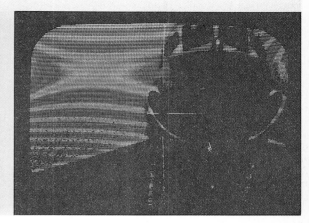

thousands of times a second) built into them. The US Joint Tactical Information Distribution System uses such frequency agility, which makes it highly jam-resistant, and computerized encryption for security against unwelcome eavesdropping.

While this kind of high-technology secure communications system makes for tactical flexibility as long as the enemy has not developed a countermeasure, in a way the more electronics-based land forces become, the more vulnerable they are to EW. A US tank company, for example, operates on four internal radio nets plus a fifth battalion net. A Soviet tank company's

commander by contrast is netted only into other company commanders, the vehicles under his control and higher command. Requests for support or target information have to be relayed up the chain of command and back again to be acted upon, although there are some shortcuts. Individual tank radios are set to receive only and much use is made of hand signals, flares and runners, crude but of course immune to EW.

While tactical communications and the struggle to disrupt and protect them make up the core struggle of EW on the land battle, the application of electronics is far wider. Artillery fire control is a prime example, with

Electronics can be used for more than communications and guidance. Modern television systems can enhance normal vision to a great extent – especially valuable to an AA system observer in a high ECM environment.

highly sophisticated target-acquisition sensors (which may be mounted on aircraft or remotely piloted vehicles) feeding data into fire-control systems which can whip up a storm of highly accurate fire in seconds, while the ancient artilleryman's art of counterbattery fire has been revolutionized by battlefield radars that can instantaneously read the trajectory of an incoming shell or mortar to back plot its launch point.

The AN/PRC-70 HF/UHF transceiver is operational with the US Special Forces and is in production for the US Army. It is capable of a variety of transmission modes, including FM (frequency modulation), AM (amplitude modulation), FSK (frequency shift keying), CW (continuous wave) and SSB (single side band). Maximum range in SSB mode is about 4000 km.

Index

Page numbers in **bold** denote an illustration. Page numbers followed by an asterisk * denote a specification.

252

Index

Glossary

AA Anti-Aircraft
AAA Anti-Aircraft Artillery
AABNCP Advanced AirBorNe Command Post
AAM Air-to-Air Missile
AAR Air-to-Air Refuelling
AAW Anti-Air Warfare
ABM Anti-Ballistic Missile
ACM Advanced Cruise Missile
ACV Air Cushion Vehicle
ADAM Area-Denial Artillery Munition
ADAMS Air Defence Advanced Missile System
ADCAP ADvanced CAPabilities
ADV Air-Defence Variant
AEV Armoured Engineer Vehicle
AEW Airborne Early Warning
AEW & C Airborne Early Warning and Control
AFAP Artillery-Fired Atomic Projectile
AFIS Advanced Indirect Fire System
AFV Armoured Fighting Vehicle
AIRS Advanced Inertial Reference Sphere
ALARM Air-Launched Anti-Radiation Missile
ALCM Air-Launched Cruise Missile
AMAC Aircraft Monitoring And Control
AMRAAM Advanced Medium-Range Air-to-Air Missile
APC Armoured Personnel Carrier
APDS Armour-Piercing Discarding-Sabot
APU Auxiliary Power Unit
ARM Anti-Radiation Missile
ARMAT Anti-Radar MATra
ASAT Anti-SATellite
ASM Air-to-Surface Missile
ASMP Air-Sol Moyenne Portée (medium-range air-to-surface)
ASROC Anti-Submarine ROCket
ASTROS Artillery SaTuration ROcket System
ASV Anti-Surface Vessel
ASW Anti-Submarine Warfare
ASW-SOW Anti-Submarine Warfare – Stand-Off Weapon
ATB Advanced-Technology Bomber
ATGW Anti-Tank Guided Weapon
ATM Anti-Tank Missile
AVRE Armoured Vehicle Royal Engineers
AWACS Airborne Warning And Control System
BCS Battery Computer System
BTH Beyond-The-Horizon
C³ Command, Control and Communications
CAPTOR enCAPsulated TORpedo
CAS Close Air Support
CEP Circular Error Probable
CET Combat Engineer Tractor
CGI Cruise Guide Indicator
CIA Central Intelligence Agency
CIWS Close-In Weapons System
CLGP Cannon-Launched Guided Projectile
CLOS Command to Line Of Sight
CMB Coastal Motor Boat
COD Carrier Onboard Delivery
COIN COunter-INsurgency
Comint Communications intelligence
CSW Conventional Stand-off Weapon
CSWS Corps Support Weapon System
CTOL Conventional Take-Off and Landing
CV Carrier, conventionally-powered
CVN Carrier, Nuclear-powered
CVR(T) Combat Vehicle Reconnaissance (Tracked)
CVR(W) Combat Vehicle Reconnaissance (Wheeled)
CW Chemical Warfare
CWS Container Weapon System
DARPA Defense Advanced Research Projects Agency
DE Destroyer Escort
DIVADS DIVisional Air-Defense System
DLGN Frigate, Guided-missile, Nuclear-powered
DoD Department of Defense
ECCM Electronic Counter-CounterMeasures
ECM Electronic CounterMeasures
EDSA European Distribution System Aircraft
Elint Electronic intelligence
ELF Extremely Low Frequency
ER Enhanced Radiation
ERAM Extended-Range Anti-armor Munition
ESM (i) Electronic Support Measures
(ii) Enhanced Sensing Munition

EUCOM EUropean COMmand
EW Electronic Warfare
FAC (i) Fast Attack Craft
(ii) Forward Air Controller
FAC(M) Fast Attack Craft (Missile)
FASCAM FAmily of SCAtterable Mines
FBW Fly-By-Wire
FF Frigate
FFG Frigate, Guided missile
FIROS FIeld ROcket System
FLIR Forward-Looking Infra-Red
FOBS Fractional Orbital Bombardment System
FOST Force Océaniqe STratégique
FRAM Fleet Rehabilitation And Modernization
GAMP Guided Anti-armor Mortar Projectile
GLCM Ground-Launched Cruise Missile
GP General Purpose
GSRS General Support Rocket System
GUPPY Greater Underwater Propulsive Power
HARM High-speed Anti-Radiation Missile
HAWK Homing All-the-Way Killer
HEAT High Explosive Anti-Tank
HEP High Explosive Plastic
HESH High Explosive Squash-Head
HLH Heavy-Lift Helicopter
HOT Haute subsonique Optiquement téléguidé tiré d'un Tube (high-subsonic, optically-guided, tube-launched)
HUD Head-Up Display
ICBM InterContinental Ballistic Missile
ICM Improved Conventional Munitions
IDS InterDictor/Strike
IFF Identification Friend or Foe
INF Intermediate Nuclear Force
INS Inertial Navigation System
IR Infra-Red
IRAAM Improved Remote Anti-Armor Mine
IRBM Intermediate-Range Ballistic Missile
ITV Improved TOW Vehicle
LAMPS Light Aircraft Multi-Purpose System
LANTCOM ATLANTic COMmand
LANTIRN Low-Altitude Navigation and Targeting Infra-Red for Night
LAPES Low-Altitude Parachute Extraction System
LARS Light Artillery Rocket System
LAW Light Anti-armour Weapon
LCAC Landing Craft Air Cushion
LCC command and control ship
LCM Landing Craft, Mechanized
LCT Landing Craft, Tank
LCVP Landing Craft, Vehicle/Personnel
LD/SD Look-Down/Shoot-Down
LERX Leading-Edge Root eXtension
LGB Laser-Guided Bomb
LHA amphibious assault ship
LKA amphibious cargo ship
LLLTV Low-Light-Level TeleVision
LPD Landing Platform, Dock
LPH Landing Platform, Helicopter
LRMTS Laser Ranger and Marked Target Seeker
LSD Landing Ship, Dock
LSM Landing Ship, Medium
LVTP Landing Vehicle Tracked, Personnel
MAD (i) Magnetic Anomaly Detector
(ii) Mutually Assured Destruction
MAF Marine Amphibious Force
MBT Main Battle Tank
MCLOS Manual Command to Line Of Sight
MCM Mine CounterMeasures
MGB Motor Gun Boat
MICV Mechanized Infantry Combat Vehicle
MILAN Missile d'Infanterie Leger ANtichar (light infantry anti-tank missile)
MIRV Multiple Independently-targetable Re-entry Vehicle
MLH Medium-Lift Helicopter
MLRS Multiple Launch Rocket System
MMS Mast-Mounted Sight
MP Maritime Patrol
MR Maritime Reconnaissance
MRAAM Medium-Range Air-to-Air Missile
MRL Multiple Rocket-Launcher
MSC Military Sealift COMmand
MTB Motor Torpedo Boat

MX Missile, eXperimental
NASA National Aeronautics and Space Administration
NBC Nuclear, Biological and Chemical
NEARTIP NEAR-Term Improvement Program
NVG Night Vision Goggles
OTH-B Over The Horizon – Backscatter
PACOM PAcific COMmand
PAL Permissive Action Link
PBV Post-Boost Vehicle
PD Pulse-Doppler
PDES Pulse-Doppler Elevation Scan
PDNES Pulse-Doppler Non-Elevation Scan
PHM Patrol Hydrofoil, Missile
PIAT Projector Infantry Anti-Tank
PNVS Pilot Night Vision Sensor
QRA Quick Reaction Alert
R&D Research and Development
RADAG RADar Area Guidance
RAP Rocket-Assisted Projectile
RBOC Rapid Bloom Offboard Countermeasures
RCL ReCoilless Launcher
RFA Royal Fleet Auxiliary
Rint Radiation intelligence
RPV Remotely-Piloted Vehicle
RV Re-entry Vehicle
RWR Radar Warning Receiver
SAC Strategic Air Command
SACLOS Semi-Automatic Command to Line Of Sight
SADARM Sense And Destroy ARMour
SALT Strategic Arms Limitation Talks
SAM Surface-to-Air Missile
SAR Search And Rescue
SARH Semi-Active Radar Homing
SATCP Sol-Air Tres Courte Portée (very short-range surface-to-air)
SDI Strategic Defense Initiative
SDV Skeet Delivery Vehicle
SFF Self-Forging Fragment
Sigint Signals Intelligence
SINS Ship's Inertial Navigation System
SLAR Side-Looking Airborne Radar
SLBM Submarine-Launched Ballistic Missile
SLCM Sea-Launched Cruise Missile
SLEP Service Life Extension Program
SLR Self-Loading Rifle
SMG Sub-Machine Gun
SNLE Sousmarin Nucléaire Lance Engins (missile-firing nuclear submarine)
SONAR SOund Navigation And Ranging
SOSUS SOund SUrveillance System
SP Self-Propelled
SPLL Self-Propelled Launcher Loader
SRAM Short-Range Attack Missile
SSBN Submarine, Ballistic-missile, Nuclear-powered
SSGN Submarine, Guided-missile, Nuclear-powered
SSM Surface-to-Surface Missile
SSN Submarine, attack, Nuclear-powered
STOL Short Take-Off and Landing
STOVL Short Take-Off and Vertical Landing
STUFT Ship Taken Up From Trade
SUBACS SUBmarine Advanced Combat System
SUBROC SUBmarine-launched ROCket
SURTASS SURveillance Towed-Array Sensor System
TACAMO TAke Charge And Move Out
TADS Target Acquisition Designation Sight
TASM Tactical Anti-Ship Missile
Telint Telemetry intelligence
TERCOM TERrain COntour Matching
TGSM Terminally-Guided SubMunition
TLAM-C Tactical Land-Attack Missile – Conventional
TLAM-N Tactical Land-Attack Missile – Nuclear
TNF Theatre Nuclear Force
TOTE Tracked Optical Thermally Enhanced
TOW Tube-launched Optically-tracked Wire-guided
TFR Terrain-Following Radar
Unrep Underway replenishment
VDS Variable-Depth Sonar
Vertrep Vertical replenishment
VIP Very Important Person
VLF Very Low Frequency
VLS Vertical Launch System
V/STOL Vertical/Short Take-Off and Landing
WAAM Wide Area Anti-armor Munition